The
Defining
Moment

Simon & Schuster

FDR's
Hundred Days
and the Triumph
of Hope

Jonathan Alter

NEW YORK   LONDON   TORONTO   SYDNEY

SIMON & SCHUSTER
Rockefeller Center
1230 Avenue of the Americas
New York, NY 10020

Designed by Paul Dippolito

Manufactured in the United States of America

3 5 7 9 10 8 6 4 2

Library of Congress Cataloging-in-Publication Data
Alter, Jonathan.
The defining moment : FDR's hundred days and the triumph of hope / Jonathan Alter.
p. cm.
Includes bibliographical references (p.) and index.
1. Roosevelt, Franklin D. (Franklin Delano), 1882–1945. 2. Presidents—United
States—Biography. 3. United States—Politics and government—1933–1945.
4. United States—Economic policy—1933–1945. 5. United States—Social
conditions—1933–1945. 6. New Deal, 1933–1939. 7. Presidents—United
States—Election—1932. I. Title.
E807.A784 2006
973.917092—dc22   2006042262
[B]

ISBN-13: 978-0-7432-4600-2
ISBN-10: 0-7432-4600-4

For information regarding special discounts for bulk purchases,
please contact Simon & Schuster Special Sales at 1-800-456-6798
or business@simonandschuster.com.

PHOTO CREDITS

Franklin D. Roosevelt Presidential Library and Museum: 1, 2, 3, 4, 5, 6, 8, 12, 13, 14, 17,
20, 21, 24, 26, 27, 31, 33, 35, 36, 38, 39; © CORBIS: 7, 11; © Bettmann/CORBIS: 9, 10,
15, 16, 18, 19, 23, 28, 29, 30, 34, 37; GABRIEL OVER THE WHITE HOUSE © Turner
Entertainment Co. A Warner Bros. Entertainment Company. All Rights Reserved: 22;
Peter Arno. Courtesy of *The New Yorker*. Reprinted by Permission. All Rights Reserved:
25; "Hoarding Is About Over" by Edmin Marcus from *The New York Times*,
March 12, 1933, used courtesy of the Marcus family: 32

To my parents

Here in America we are waging a great and successful war. It is not alone a war against want and destitution and economic demoralization. It is more than that; it is a war for the survival of democracy.

—President Franklin D. Roosevelt, June 27, 1936

~ CONTENTS ~

~ AUTHOR'S NOTE ~

I N MORE THAN TWO DECADES covering politics, I've had a good look at many of the leaders who shape our world. Sometimes I interview them one-on-one; more frequently, I watch from the crowd, where the vantage is often superior. Once in a while, I'm lucky enough to witness what since the early 1980s has been known as a "defining moment," when the character or perception of a political figure is crystallized. I was in the theater in Prague in 1989 as Václav Havel announced that the Czech Communist Party had fallen from power; I rode around in a small bus with Bill Clinton in 1992 and with John McCain in 2000 as each defined himself for a national audience in just a few weeks in New Hampshire; I stood five feet from George W. Bush at a smoldering Ground Zero as he vowed through a bullhorn to retaliate for the attacks of September 11, 2001.

But whenever I think about defining moments, I keep going back to the one that took place a quarter century before my birth—the desperate winter of 1933 when Franklin D. Roosevelt narrowly escaped assassination, then restored hope with his "fear itself" Inaugural Address, his first "Fireside Chat," and the thrilling legislative experimentation of what came to be known as the Hundred Days.

This book is not a full account of Roosevelt's life or of the early New Deal. Instead, it's the story of how at one of the darkest moments in American history, a political and communicative genius saved American democracy. FDR's intelligence was hardly at genius levels; he was lampooned right up until 1933 as a lightweight. So I've included a biographical opening that examines where he acquired the sense of security that he later conveyed to the world. This section takes him from mama's boy through Washington operator through the trauma of polio. Then I focus much more closely on one pivotal year: from June 1932, when he was nominated for president in Chicago on the fourth ballot, until June 1933, which marked the end of the Hundred Days. The culmination of that momentous period is covered in a final chapter on Social Security and in the Epilogue.

This is a thematic narrative—a slice of history—that details how Franklin Roosevelt became president of the United States and revived the spirits of a stricken nation. I try to trace both his manipulative streak and his famously first-class temperament, which helped lift Americans out of their mental depression without curing their economic one. FDR's stunning debut in office was the flowering not just of versatile thinking but of brilliant instincts for leadership. Who influenced him? How did he grow himself into a surpassingly inspirational figure? What grand mixture of timing, cunning, and character gave him and his generation what he later called a "rendezvous with destiny"?

Roosevelt died in office in 1945 before he could write any memoirs, and his letters in this period are mostly dutiful and unrevealing. He was the first president who did most of his domestic business on the telephone, where, with a few exceptions after 1940, his conversations went unrecorded. So another angle of vision is required. Sometimes my lens is journalistic, as I scan for the revealing anecdote; sometimes it is more historical, a search for deeper connections with the help of archival material from the 1932–33 period or for the leadership secrets behind FDR's swift "turnaround" of a failing enterprise. Taking a cue from FDR, who referred to himself at Warm Springs, Georgia, as "Old Doc Roosevelt," I also see my role almost as a doctor examining a patient, in this case a man who became the most important president since Abraham Lincoln, and the most underestimated.

FDR was, by many accounts, the most consequential man of the 20th century. Yet it is now nearly 125 years since his birth and more than sixty years since his death. With that in mind, I've included footnotes with bits of historical context and a few comparisons to recent presidents to help illuminate the main roads of the story. The Notes section identifies sources and provides amplification.

Although the Roosevelt literature is vast, no previous book about FDR has concentrated so closely on his role in the 1932–33 period. In recent decades, most authors have focused on the later years of his presidency. FDR may be commonly remembered for bringing victory in World War II, but it's worth recalling that he did so only with the help of the Allies. The first time he saved democracy, in 1933, he accomplished it more on his own, by convincing the American people that they should not give up on their system of government. Before he confronted fascism abroad, he blunted the potential of both fascism and communism at home.

Instead of viewing the Hundred Days as the opening act of the Roosevelt presidency—the more traditional historical approach—I depict it as the climax of an exquisite piece of political theater. This performance was only possible because of a supreme self-confidence in his ability to lead the country when it was, as he later put it, "frozen by a fatalistic terror." The story that follows, then, is not just about the early days of the Roosevelt presidency but about where his confidence came from, and how he used it to win power, restore hope, and redefine the bargain—the "Deal"—the country struck with its own people.

The result was a new notion of social obligation, especially in a crisis. In his second Inaugural, in 1937, FDR took stock of what had changed: "We refused to leave the problems of our common welfare to be solved by the winds of chance and the hurricanes of disaster."

We live in an age when the question raised by any work of history is: Why now? Roosevelt is of lasting interest not just because we, too, must face our fears, real and imagined; not just because of a few similarities and many differences between him and another president with a famous name, confronted with big problems. I wrote this book to better understand a few timeless questions about the nature of crisis leadership and the meaning of the American experiment in self-government. What is government for? How can it be mobilized in an emergency to secure safety and ease suffering? Where do hope and inspiration come from, and what might they accomplish?

Nations, like politicians, occasionally experience defining moments, where their course is fixed for generations in the historical blink of an eye. "His most dazzling successes were domestic and psychological," wrote the novelist Saul Bellow, who grew up worshiping Roosevelt in Chicago. "It is not too much to say that another America was formed under his influence." My goal is to explain and re-create that psychological success, the one that brought us this new America—a country of commitment to one another, with a set of governing values we are debating anew today.

Sunday, March 5, 1933

O N THIS, HIS FIRST FULL DAY in the presidency, Franklin Delano Roosevelt awoke in a creaky narrow bed in the small bedroom of the White House family quarters he had chosen for himself.
After his valet, Irvin McDuffie, helped him with the laborious task of
putting on his iron leg braces and trousers, McDuffie lifted him into his
armless wooden wheelchair for the elevator ride downstairs. The new
president's schedule called for him to attend morning services at St.
Thomas's Church with his family, host a luncheon for twenty at the
White House, and then chair an emergency Cabinet meeting, where
he would outline his plans to call Congress into emergency session.

None of the staff or reporters who saw him that Sunday noticed that
FDR was anything other than his usual convivial self. He had stayed up
past one o'clock the previous night talking with Louis Howe, his longtime chief aide and campaign strategist, while Eleanor and their five
children attended the Inaugural Ball without him. The crippled president, now fifty-one years old, hadn't wanted to sit passively while
everyone else danced; passive was not his style. Besides, he and Howe
had important things to discuss, beginning with how to extricate the
United States from its gravest crisis since the Civil War.

The American economic system had gone into a state of shock, its
vital organs shutting down as the weekend began. On Friday, the New

York Stock Exchange suspended trading indefinitely and the Chicago Board of Trade bolted its doors for the first time since its founding in 1848. The terrifying "runs" that began the year before on more than five thousand failing banks had stripped rural areas of capital and now threatened to overwhelm American cities. At dawn on Saturday, only a few hours before FDR's swearing in, the governors of New York, Illinois, and Pennsylvania signed orders closing the banks in those states indefinitely, which meant that thirty-four out of forty-eight American states, including the largest ones, now had no economic pulse. Each state's closure had its own financial logic, but collectively they proved merciful. Without them, Saturday morning would have brought even more ruinous bank runs, with legions of depositors descending on their banks in desperation at the very moment the new president took the oath of office.

The outgoing president, Herbert Hoover, was on his way back to California, a study in failure. As late as 1:00 a.m. on Inauguration Day, he was still haggling with FDR on the telephone about the banking crisis. In late morning, they rode in uncomfortable silence to the Capitol. Hoover's brilliant understanding of complex issues had brought him and the country nothing. For more than three years, since the aftermath of the stock market crash, he had been sullen and defensive as disease spread through the American economy.

As frightening as life had become since the Great Depression began, this was the bottom, though no one knew that at the time. The official national unemployment rate stood at 25 percent, but that figure was widely considered to be low. Among non-farm workers, unemployment was more than 37 percent, and in some areas, like Toledo, Ohio, it reached 80 percent. Business investment was down 90 percent from 1929. Per capita real income was lower than three decades earlier, at the turn of the century. If you were unfortunate enough to have put your money in a bank that went bust, you were wiped out. With no idea whether any banks would reopen, millions of people hid their few remaining assets under their mattresses, where no one could steal them at night without a fight. The savings that many Americans had spent a lifetime accumulating were severely depleted or gone, along with 16 million of their jobs. When would they come back? Maybe never. The great British economist John Maynard Keynes was asked by a reporter the previous summer if there were any precedent for what had happened to the world's economy. He replied yes, it lasted four hundred years and was called the Dark Ages.

Late in 1933, the journalist Earle Looker peered backwards several months to assess the Hobbesian stakes as FDR assumed office: "Capitalism itself was at the point of dissolution. Would men continue to work for profit as our forefathers understood it and as our people now understand it? This was a real question, for money was now useless. Would it be necessary soon to organize our families against the world, to fight, physically, for food, to keep shelter, to hold possessions?"

Even two generations later, the terror remained indelible for those who experienced it. "It was just as traumatic as Pearl Harbor or the destruction of the Twin Towers," the scholar Richard E. Neustadt, who was a teenager at the time, recalled. "It wasn't on television, but the banks were failing everywhere, so you didn't need television to see what was going on."

Roosevelt's Inaugural Address had begun the process of restoring hope, but not everyone caught the new mood right away. The press coverage that morning largely downplayed or ignored FDR's line: "the only thing we have to fear is fear itself." *The New York Times* and most other newspapers relegated the line to their inside pages, while focusing instead on the vivid wartime allusions he employed five times during his speech—martial metaphors that suggested that there was, in fact, plenty to fear after all. The greatest applause from the large crowd on the east side of the Capitol came when Roosevelt said that if his rescue program was not quickly approved: "I shall ask Congress for the one remaining instrument to meet the crisis: broad executive power to wage war against the emergency, as great as the power that would be given to me if we were in fact invaded by a foreign foe."

The United States had not been "invaded by a foreign foe" since 1812, but this felt like it. Arthur Krock of the *Times* compared the mood in Washington on Inauguration Day to "a beleaguered capital in wartime." For the first time since the Civil War, armed men patrolled the entrances to federal buildings, while machine gunners perched on rooftops. Editors knew that the world war, just thirteen years in the past, had concentrated great power in the hands of Woodrow Wilson's government. To them it looked as if FDR were proposing the same thing. And so the approving headline FOR DICTATORSHIP IF NECESSARY ran in the *New York Herald-Tribune* on March 5, with similar notes stuck in the Inauguration coverage of other major papers.

Exactly what was "necessary"? No one knew, including Roosevelt. Even before being sworn in, he had decided on a federal bank "holiday" (a festive term he preferred to Herbert Hoover's "moratorium") to give the people who now ran the country a few days to figure out what to do. Then what? Should he assume wartime authority on a temporary basis? Call out the Army to protect banks and maintain order? Mobilize veterans? Unrest was already growing in the farm belt, where mobs had broken up bankruptcy auctions. Four thousand men had occupied the Nebraska statehouse and five thousand stormed Seattle's county building. The governor of North Carolina predicted a violent revolution, and police in Chicago clubbed teachers who had not been paid all school year. Everywhere, bank runs threatened to turn violent. By the Inaugural weekend, police in nearly every American city were preparing for an onslaught of angry depositors. At least some were certain to be armed.

With so many banks involved, the U.S. Army—including National Guard and Reserve units—might not be large enough to respond. This raised the question of whether the new president should establish a makeshift force of veterans to enforce some kind of martial law. The temptation must have been strong. It hardly seems a coincidence that FDR decided that the first radio speech of his presidency would be specially addressed to a convention of the American Legion, the million-member veterans' organization co-founded after World War I by his fifth cousin, Theodore Roosevelt, Jr.

The short speech was scheduled for that Sunday evening at 11:30 p.m. EST, with all radio networks carrying it live across the country. In preparing for the broadcast, someone in the small Roosevelt inner circle offered the new president a typewritten draft of suggested additions that contained this eye-popping sentence:

As new commander-in-chief under the oath to which you are still bound I reserve to myself the right to command you in any phase of the situation which now confronts us.

This was dictator talk—an explicit power grab. The new president was contemplating his "right" to command World War I veterans—mostly men in their late thirties—who had long since reentered civilian life. It was true that they had sworn an oath to the United States on entering military service and that the 1919 founding document of the American Legion pledged members to help "maintain law and order" and show "devotion to mutual helpfulness." But the commander in chief had no power over them. Here Roosevelt would be poised to mobilize hundreds of thousands of unemployed and desperate men by decree, apparently to guard banks or put down rebellions or do anything else he wished during "any phase" of the crisis, with the insistence that they were dutybound to obey his concocted "command."

That word—"dictator"—had been in the air for weeks, endorsed vaguely as a remedy for the Depression by establishment figures ranging from the owners of the *New York Daily News*, the nation's largest circulation newspaper, to Walter Lippmann, the eminent columnist who spoke for the American political elite. "The situation is critical, Franklin. You may have no alternative but to assume dictatorial powers," Lippmann had told FDR during a visit to Warm Springs on February 1, before the crisis escalated. Alfred E. Smith, the Democratic nominee for president in 1928, recalled with some exaggeration that "during the World War we wrapped the Constitution in a piece of paper, put it on the shelf and left it there until the war was over." The Depression, Smith concluded, was a similar "state of war." Even Eleanor Roosevelt, more liberal than her husband, privately suggested that a "benevolent dictator" might be what the country needed. The vague idea was not a police state but deference to a strong leader unfettered by Congress or the other inconveniences of democracy. Amid the crisis, the specifics didn't go beyond more faith in government by fiat.

Within a few years, "dictator" would carry sinister tones, but—hard as it is to believe now—the word had a reassuring ring that season. So did "storm troopers," used by one admiring author to describe foot soldiers of the early New Deal, and "concentration camps," a generic term routinely applied to the work camps of the Civilian Conservation Corps that would be established by summer across the country. After all, the Italian Fascist Benito Mussolini, in power for a decade, had ginned up the Italian economy and was popular with everyone from Winston Churchill to Will Rogers to Lowell Thomas, America's most influential broadcaster. "If ever this country needed a Mussolini, it needs one now," said Senator David Reed of Pennsylvania, outgoing President Hoover's closest friend on Capitol Hill. The speech draft prepared for FDR brought to mind Mussolini addressing his black-shirt followers, many of whom were demobilized veterans who joined Il Duce's private army.

Roosevelt came to office just as the appetite for strong leadership seemed to be surging worldwide. For Americans, German chancellor Adolf Hitler was worrying but new, his leadership to be ratified in a legal election held across Germany that very day, March 5. While Hitler was already seen in the United States as a reckless buffoon, almost no one in the country yet focused on the threat posed by fascism.

The most powerful American publisher, William Randolph Hearst, seemed to favor dictatorship. The Hearst empire extended to Hollywood, where Hearst that winter had personally supervised the filming of an upcoming hit movie called *Gabriel Over the White House* that was meant to instruct FDR and prepare the public for a dictatorship. The movie's hero is a president played by Walter Huston who dissolves Congress, creates an army of the unemployed, and lines up his enemies before a firing squad. FDR not only saw an advance screening of the film, he offered ideas for script rewrites and wrote Hearst from the White House that he thought it would help the country.

"There was a thunder in the air as when the Fascisti marched upon Rome," wrote one journalist close to the Roosevelt camp, of the fevered climate that chilly March weekend. "It was the same tension that quivered about the Kremlin at the beginning of the Five Year Plan. Insiders thought there was to be a peaceful revolution involving a dictatorship."

FDR knew the consequences of failing to seize the day. A visitor—unidentified in the press—came to him not long after the Inauguration and told him, "Mr. President, if your program succeeds, you'll be the greatest president in American history. If it fails, you will be the worst one." "If it fails," the new president replied, "I'll be the *last* one."

This sounds melodramatic to Americans in the 21st century, when freedom is flourishing in so many parts of the world. But during the

1930s, democracy was on the run, discredited even by subtle minds as a hopelessly cumbersome way to meet the challenges of the modern age. At the time, history offered little precedent for a leader taking power amidst a severe military or economic crisis without seizing more authority for himself. The few republics ever established—from ancient times to modern Europe—had eventually bent before such demands. So did the American system. During the Civil War, Abraham Lincoln suspended habeas corpus and twisted the Constitution in order to save the nation.

But on March 5, 1933, an astonishing thing happened—or more precisely, did not happen. The draft of that American Legion radio address was destined not for the ears of millions of veterans and other Americans, but for nothing more than the speech files of the Roosevelt Library, where it lay unexamined for more than seventy years.* The five-minute speech that FDR delivered that night built on the military tone of the Inaugural. He argued for the "sacrifice and devotion" of wartime and noted that it was "a mistake to assume that the virtues of war differ essentially from the virtues of peace." But there was no hint of the need for a private army.

No one knows who wrote the unused draft or why FDR discarded the suggested additions, but something inside the man kept him from moving in an extraconstitutional direction. Some combination of personal and democratic conviction set him on a different course, at once more traditional and bold. This most pragmatic of modern American presidents sensed the unworkable nature of untrammeled power, even in the hands of the only person he completely trusted—himself.

In the days ahead, FDR moved in the opposite direction, passing the word on Capitol Hill that he did not believe in a constitutional dictatorship and asking his friend Felix Frankfurter to tell Lippmann to stop hawking dictatorship and disrespect of Congress in his columns. It was not as if Roosevelt was letting the cup pass; for the next twelve years, he would fully exploit the authority of the presidency, sometimes overreaching to the point where his enemies accused him of becoming a dictator. He would flirt with fascistic (or at least corporatist) ideas like

---

*To the author's knowledge and that of the FDR Library, this draft of the American Legion speech has never been referred to or quoted by historians before.

the National Recovery Administration and in 1937 try to pack the Supreme Court. But even then, he would do so in the context of democracy, without private armies or government-by-decree. Even at his worst, he would eventually submit his schemes for the approval of Congress. Instead of coercion, he chose persuasion; instead of drawing the sword, he would draw on his own character and political instincts. He would draw, too, on the subconscious metaphor of his own physical condition. Although it was only rarely mentioned in the press, the American people knew at the time that he had polio (though not the extent of his disability) and it bound them to him in ways that were no less powerful for being unspoken: If he could rise from his paralysis, then so could they.

The deeper questions would take time to plumb. If character was to be FDR's weapon for confronting the crisis, how was it forged and then deployed? Which complex combination of temperament, background, and experience allowed Roosevelt to bring off his act in his famous Hundred Days? Whatever the verdict of history on his expansion of government and particular policy prescriptions, this much is clear: Rather than succumbing to dictatorship or chaos, the United States underwent a "laughing revolution," as a reporter covering FDR put it, the projection of one man's faith in his own performance and in the capacity of democratic institutions to confront the terror of the unknown.

That March of 1933, the new president did not have to mobilize aging members of the American Legion under martial law. Franklin Roosevelt mobilized himself and his latent talent for leadership. He found his voice, and his voice defined America.

PART ONE

Lightweight Steel

BEFORE MAN MET MOMENT in 1933, there was little on the public record to recommend Franklin Roosevelt as a world-class leader. He had thought about being president at least since Harvard at the turn of the century, when his distant cousin Theodore moved into the White House. Young Franklin consciously imitated TR's idiosyncrasies by wearing a pince-nez and pronouncing himself "dee-lighted!" But this hardly made him seem closer to his extraordinary relative or a plausible future president; if anything, it caused his sophisticated classmates to laugh at him. And with good reason. Beyond possessing a Roosevelt gene for exuberance, FDR did not seem a compelling and formidable figure until much later.

Yet in the half century from his birth in 1882 until 1933, certain legacies, experiences, and relationships shaped his political character in ways that would prove decisive in a crisis. His family background offered enormous security and a sense of ease and confidence that he learned to convey to others. The manipulative skills he developed to handle his father's illness and his mother's meddling were essential emotional equipment. His marriage to a strong-willed woman, Eleanor, and his political marriage to a talented handler, Louis Howe, showed self-knowledge, even wisdom. In Woodrow Wilson's sub-Cabinet from 1913 to 1921, he became an effective operator with an understanding of the levers of power. Although effete and seemingly out of touch, he stood up to the streetwise and widely respected governor of New York, Al Smith, which provided him a critical psychological lift. Most of all, the polio he contracted at age thirty-nine in 1921 changed the way he related to other people; the iron braces on his legs helped to forge his iron will. He learned to reject received opinion and respect "the common man" who had previously escaped his attention. His establishment of a rehabilitative clinic at Warm Springs, Georgia, offered Franklin matchless experience in lifting the spirits of afflicted people even if he could not greatly change their medical condition—the perfect preparation for the Hundred Days, when he restored hope without changing the material condition of the country.

This unusual combination of being underestimated yet well seasoned, calculating yet intuitive, would help FDR's grand debut in 1933. It was as if he had been preparing for a life in the theater: the theater of the modern presidency, with its emphasis on dramatic entrances, perfect timing, and an instinct for performance.

Chapter One

Security

FDR COULD CONVINCINGLY EMBODY a sense of security for millions of Americans in part because he possessed so much of it himself. Even when he felt a trifle insecure among his dismissive peers at school, he could always fall back on his proud heritage and storied name as a source of strength. Character development is always a mystery, but in Franklins case the combination of the entrepreneurial success of his mother's family, the Delanos, and the old-money stability and impeccable social standing of the Roosevelts seemed to protect him behind a double-bolted door of invulnerability, reinforced by the unusually strong love and attention of his parents.

Security for his family was Warren Delano's aspiration when he first sailed for China in 1833, a hundred years before his grandson was sworn in as president. Delano could trace his roots back to a Huguenot, Philippe de la Noye (eventually shortened and conjoined), who arrived in Plymouth Colony just months after the *Mayflower*. But lineage has never been a convertible currency in the United States; even the most aristocratic American families must replenish the family fortunes every few generations, as Warren Delano did by trading opium and other commodities in China. Delano was an autocrat and what later came to be known as a rock-ribbed Republican. He liked to say that

while not all Democrats were horse thieves, it was his experience that
all horse thieves were Democrats.

Delano's daughter Sara accompanied her father to China as a girl
and would pass on her family's sense of adventure to her son. As a
young woman, she had fallen for the famous architect Stanford White,
but her father disapproved and it seemed for a time as if she might not
marry. Sara was twenty-six, with impeccable posture and a strong will,
when she met a country squire named James Roosevelt, whose mutton
chops made him look less like the British lord he aspired to be, sniped
one relative, and more like the lord's coachman. "Mr. James" was twice
her age—fifty-two—a widower and father (his first son, James "Rosy"
Roosevelt, was FDR's little-remembered and much older half brother)
who had found success in business and become a reliable Democrat,
thanks in part to a post–Civil War friendship with General George B.
McClellan, the 1864 Democratic presidential candidate.

James was descended from the Dutchman Claes Van Rosenvelt, who
arrived in the New World about 1650. The family fortune was founded
when James's great-grandfather, Isaac, imported sugar from the West
Indies to make rum, then used the profits to invest heavily in New York
real estate. FDR would boast that Isaac led George Washington's horse
in the first Inaugural Parade, though this was likely one of his embell-
ishments.

James's father (Franklin's paternal grandfather, whom he never
knew) was a medical doctor afraid of the sight of blood, insecure to the
point of being a shut-in. James learned not to say anything that might
upset the old man, a sense of discretion passed on to Franklin. Perhaps
rebelling against his father's nervous disposition, James also developed
an easy equanimity. This, too, would be bequeathed.

To opium dealing in the Delano line, add draft avoidance among the
Roosevelts. James had been thirty-two when the Civil War began, still
young enough to take part. Like many gentlemen of his day, he paid a
substitute to serve for him in the Union Army. FDR's Hudson River
Valley branch of the Roosevelt family felt none of the embarrassment
experienced by cousin Theodore over his father having shirked service
in Lincoln's war. In fact, after two decades of ambitious ventures in the
business world—including an abortive effort to finance a canal through
Nicaragua and the presidency of the largest railway in the South—

James developed a sense of ease about his position in the world. Recriminations, his son later learned, were for others.

Buffeted by the Panic of 1873 and forced to resign as president of the coal company he founded, James Roosevelt's fortune slipped below that of other prominent families in the Hudson Valley. But he appeared unflappable amid this personal setback, perhaps because he still held enough assets to assure that his branch of the family would remain relatively wealthy for at least another generation. Outside the business world, James was perhaps best known for breeding horses at "Springwood," as he called the estate he built near the tiny village of Hyde Park, New York, ninety miles north of New York City. With sweeping views of the Hudson River, the house at Hyde Park would become the anchor of this branch of the Roosevelt family for the next two generations. By the 1880s, he had also bought a fifteen-room Victorian summer "cottage" on Canada's Campobello Island, just off the coast of Maine.

The circumstances of FDR's birth may have contributed to his sense of security because the trauma made him all the more precious to his parents. Sara was in labor for twenty-five hours and nearly died. To save her, chloroform was administered, with the assumption that the baby would be stillborn. When the boy was born on January 30, 1882, he was blue and not breathing; the nurse was sure he was gone. But the doctor began mouth-to-mouth resuscitation and he came around. He was named after Sara's childless uncle, Franklin Delano.

Chapter Two

"My Boy Franklin"

T HE INTENSITY OF SARA'S LOVE for her son was destined to make him either a basket case or the most self-possessed of men. It proved to be the latter. Sara was a walking advertisement for the benefits of ceaseless, even suffocating devotion—the only source of consistent affection in her son's life, a rock not just of financial security but of the deep maternal love so central to instilling genuine self-confidence. Although a self-satisfied and often imperious woman of the 19th century, she nonetheless possessed a warmth and generosity that held her family together.

Roosevelt was Sara's only child,* so the bond went far. She breast-fed Franklin for nearly a year, bathed and dressed him, and took him everywhere, holding and carrying him with a constancy highly unusual for women of her station, who normally left such duties to wet nurses. She couldn't bear to leave her baby behind, in part because he seemed to have been born with such a nice disposition. Baby Franklin "crows

---

* Many American presidents have been the products of exceptionally strong mothers. Lincoln's frontier stepmother, Sarah, was a critical influence. The same goes for Rebekah Johnson, Hannah Nixon, Lillian Carter, Nelle Reagan, and Virginia Kelley, mother of Bill Clinton. George W. Bush is often described as inheriting more from his mother, Barbara, than his father, the former president. But none beside FDR were only children.

and laughs all the time," Sara wrote. He is "always bright and happy" and "never cries," which, if true, suggests that some of his famous temperament may have been present from birth.

When he was two and a half, the age when first memories are often formed, Franklin experienced his greatest childhood shock. It occurred during a visit he made with his mother to the Delano estate at Algonac, New York. As the Delanos dressed one morning, they heard an explosion, then Sara's younger sister, Laura, screaming. She had been heating curling irons over an alcohol lamp, a common household task more often performed by servants. When the lamp was somehow knocked over, burning alcohol spilled all over her robe. Her father Warren later wrote: "Laura flashed down the stairway a cloud of fiery flame." Outside on the grass, others in the household, including Sara, tried to smother the flames with a carpet, too late.

There is no record of Roosevelt ever writing or even speaking of his aunt's death, but he almost certainly heard her shrieking and may have witnessed the gruesome scene on the lawn. After contracting polio, he admitted that the possibility of fire haunted him; he sometimes practiced crawling out of his bedroom to safety. As he told his son James on the night of his 1932 election as president, fire was the only thing he ever truly feared in life.

A few months after Laura's death came another moment of trauma, though this one ended differently. James, Sara, and Franklin were on the way home from England on the ocean liner *Germania*, when the ship plunged sharply beneath a huge freak wave. As passengers shrieked in terror, Mr. James said calmly, "We seem to be going down." Franklin called out for his toy jumping jack as it floated past their berth.

"I never get frightened," Sara later recalled. "And I was not then." According to family lore, she took her fur and wrapped it around three-year-old Franklin, who had awakened as water began to fill their compartment. "Poor little boy. If he must go down, he's going down warm." The captain was knocked unconscious by the force of the wave, but he was revived and eventually righted the ship, which made it back to Liverpool. This scene—and his parents' calm fatalism—left enough of an impression on Franklin that he recalled it often to friends.* Whether the "shipwreck story" helped shape Roosevelt (it did nothing to dampen his love of the sea), his associates over the years would consistently remark on his calmness in a crisis.

But if Franklin was surrounded by family love, he grew up with few playmates and little company beyond parents and tutors. The Roosevelts were snobs. They reminded the historian Richard Hofstadter of "secondary characters in Edith Wharton novels who provide the climate of respectable and unfriendly opinion in which her characters live." (Wharton, a resident of the Hudson River Valley, was an acquaintance of the Roosevelts.) Although they lived practically next door, Mr. James and Sara declined an invitation from the far wealthier Vanderbilts to dine, for fear of having to invite the *arrivistes* back.

However, unlike many aristocrats, the Roosevelts never wrote off politicians as socially inferior. When Franklin was older, Sara told her son it was a "fallacy" that anyone could be too refined or well-bred for the White House. If Roosevelt was not bred to be president, he was raised to believe that the presidency was entirely within reach, should he be interested. In the winter of 1887, the Roosevelts lived in Washington, D.C., for a few months, where they socialized with James's old friend from upstate New York Democratic politics, President Grover Cleveland. Just before leaving town, James dropped by the White House to say good-bye to the president with his five-year-old son. "My little man, I am making a strange wish for you," the president, besieged by political problems, told Franklin, patting him on the head. "It is that you may never be president of the United States." Fifty years later, FDR enjoyed telling that story when children visited him in the White House.

Another family story told by Sara (who, unlike her son, usually resisted embellishment) reflects Franklin's almost supernatural confidence that fortune would always smile on him. One day, Franklin came in the house looking for his gun. He had spotted a winter wren in a tree by the

---

* It may have left a deeper mark. In her studies on war and children, Anna Freud examined the London Blitz during World War II and found no difference in the trauma experienced by the children who dodged bombs in London versus that of children removed to the safety of the countryside. The only variable was the mood of the mothers. "A child will shake and tremble with the anxiety of its mother," but if the mother was calm, the child stayed calm.

river and wanted to shoot it for his taxidermy collection. His mother laughed at the idea of the wren waiting patiently for him to return. "He looked surprised but quite unperturbed. 'Oh, yes,' he said confidently. 'He'll wait.' " And the bird did.

Sara was clearly obsessed with her son but took pains to assert that she was not overprotective. In *My Boy Franklin*, an odd little memoir she wrote with a ghostwriter (and with plenty of help from FDR) just before the 1933 Inauguration, Sara couldn't quite decide how Franklin had developed his sense of social command. The same child who ordered playmates around was "self conscious when he talked to anyone other than members of the immediate family."

These are the classic signs of a "mama's boy." Here was a solitary, bossy child who developed perfect pitch in telling his parents what they wanted to hear. He played instinctively on the knowledge that his mother would do anything for him, even sacrificing much of the socializing of others in her set. Despite chafing occasionally under Sara's rigorous schedule for him and the schooling of private tutors, he doesn't seem to have been lonely, and he developed none of the brooding quality of the lonely affluent child.

Most of the time, he preferred the company of adults, particularly his father. Mr. James took "Master Franklin" skating, horseback riding, and on his rounds of civic activities in Hyde Park and Poughkeepsie, where his quiet authority and Episcopalian reverence left an impression on the townspeople and on his son. Even so, FDR's burgeoning sense of *noblesse oblige* may have come less from his father directly than from the image of his father that was built within his family.

At the other extreme, FDR's much older half brother, Rosy, became an object lesson, playing an underappreciated role in Franklin's later development. Rosy married an Astor and led a life of conspicuous languor, punctuated by outbursts of embarrassingly crude anti-Semitism (he complained endlessly about having to see Jews in New York and on vacation). Sara, who took a second wife's view of her grown stepson, often used Rosy as a prod to make FDR aspire to something more useful and noble in life and to sound less vulgar in his opinions. Whatever the explanation, FDR's early correspondence, unlike Eleanor's, contains little of the casual anti-Semitism that characterized their social class.

There's also no record in their correspondence of any grief or other unpleasantness. The Roosevelts wrote scores of letters each year throughout FDR's youth, and several mention a boy named Archie Rogers, a Hyde Park neighbor who had become Franklin's best friend. But there's no mention of Archie's death from diphtheria when Franklin was nearly eight. This suggests a childhood devoted to keeping up appearances and masking one's true feelings behind a screen of tranquility and good humor. The Roosevelts did so not out of status anxiety but because poise and propriety were so highly valued in their family circle. This couldn't have been much comfort for a child, but it offered exquisite training.

Chapter Three

"Miss Nancy"

T HE VALUES OF THE ROOSEVELT FAMILY were put to the test in 1891, when Mr. James suffered a heart attack and recurring angina. Although he would live another decade, the effect of his illness would bind his wife and nine-year-old son even closer. Just as strong mothers have often bred strong presidents, so the absent or weak father appears again and again in presidential family history, often as pitied by their sons.*

For FDR, his father's decline left a different imprint. From age nine, Franklin saw Mr. James not as his protector but as someone to be protected, an early lesson in the imperative to tend the lame and repay debts of gratitude to once strong figures who have fallen into trouble. FDR's notion of the country as a family with basic responsibility for its most vulnerable members—the animating spirit of the New Deal—could well have begun inside his own small nuclear family.

Franklin and Sara routinely conspired to shield James from anything upsetting. When Franklin found a nanny "perfectly awful," he hid his

---

* Lincoln was estranged from his father, Thomas, while Lyndon Johnson's father, Samuel, and Richard Nixon's father, Frank, were conspicuously depicted by their sons as failures in business. The alcoholism of Jack Reagan and Roger Clinton (Bill Clinton's stepfather) rendered them weak in the eyes of their sons.

feelings because his father had taken the trouble to hire her. When a steel curtain rod fell aboard their private railroad car and cut his forehead deeply while his father was in another compartment eating breakfast, young Franklin made his terrified mother promise not to tell James. He put on a cap to cover the bloody wound and spent the rest of the day on the observation platform, avoiding his father. And when a friend at Campobello Island accidentally knocked out his front tooth with a stick meant to bat pebbles, Franklin wouldn't cry or open his mouth to show his mother the exposed nerve, much less tell his father.

Franklin was showing not just physical courage and a talent for deception but the guts to play the angles on his parents without actively rebelling. His new approach allowed him to maintain freedom of movement and yet be seen as respectful and concerned about his father. At an early age, Franklin was self-reliant and a bit of an operator. In later years, he liked to recount the story of how as a fourteen-year-old he was denied admission to London's Museum of Natural History in South Kensington, which was closed that day to the general public. He pulled out a membership card from the New York Museum of Natural History and somehow convinced the guard that he was a scientist. Even if the story was exaggerated, it reflected his pride in improvising to get his way.

The combination of fortitude and guile would turn up again and again, from Roosevelt's response to polio to his handling of Herbert Hoover to deceiving the public about how far he would go to aid Britain in 1940 to riding through New York City in the rain at the end of the 1944 campaign, drenched to the bone, knowing his health was shot, fortified only by a swig of brandy and his old grit. Like John F. Kennedy and Bill Clinton, Roosevelt was a compartmentalized president, able to put his life into separate sealed boxes. This ability to separate or integrate great warmth and utter detachment—depending on the context—would prove a superbly useful trait.

Though his temperament was largely inborn, some authors have offered tentative Freudian speculations about Franklin and Sara. John Gunther, who became friendly with the family, wrote that "of course Roosevelt had an Oedipus complex as big as a house." But he was spared by his father's age. Had James been younger than fifty-three when Franklin was born, Gunther wrote from the distance of the more psychoanalytic 1950s, "Franklin might have turned into a very neurotic and unstable child." What Franklin most liked about his father, Gunther heard from a family member, was that he controlled his mother, who in turn controlled *him*.

Actually, Sigmund Freud, contrary to reputation, did not focus much on mothers in his case histories. But his conclusions—still persuasive despite the challenge to so many of his theories—were clear. "A man who has been the indisputable favorite of his mother keeps for life the feelings of a conqueror," he wrote. "That confidence of success often induces real success." While Sara was never what Carl Jung calls a "power devil," whose smothering attention incapacitates her son, she drove him to seek refuge within himself. Franklin developed a lifelong habit of not letting his mother or anyone else know much about what he was thinking—a habit that could be maddening but gave him an edge in handling other people. One thing he wasn't thinking about was what might go wrong. He seemed to be missing the normal emotional equipment that produces worry.

For all of his attachment to home and family, Franklin quickly came to think of himself as cosmopolitan, and not just because his extensive stamp collection made him a whiz at geography. The Roosevelts sailed for Europe eight times during his first twelve years, often bound for the baths of Bad Nauheim in Germany to "take the cure" with other wealthy invalids. Franklin grew accustomed to being around sick people all searching for the curative power of water, a foreshadowing of his life in Warm Springs. Where another child might have retreated into surliness, he was compassionate on these trips—a younger English boy confined to a wheelchair remembered his kindness many years later— but he was also clearly ready for at least some measure of independence from his parents.

When he left, it was to Groton, an elite boys' boarding school in Massachusetts that was only a decade old when Franklin entered. He had, in fact, been enrolled at birth before the school even opened. Such was the respect that James and his circle had for the founder and headmaster, the Reverend Endicott Peabody, an ambitious Episcopal clergyman whose preparatory school, based on the British model (minus the flogging), appealed to their anglophilia. Peabody, who later performed the marriage of Eleanor and Franklin, preached a muscular

Christianity in the raising of boys. The rigorous schedule was academically challenging, but the rector was suspicious of intellectuals and he emphasized athletics and spartan living, including open cubicles for sleeping and cold showers, even in winter.

While Peabody would be a lifelong influence, Groton was not an experience Franklin looked back on with much nostalgia. He wasn't popular, in part because he entered at fourteen, two years behind the rest of his classmates, whose parents, unlike James and Sara, were willing to part with their sons when they were twelve. As a result, he had to work hard to win the approval of his schoolmates, which may have intensified the anxiousness to please that is so characteristic of politicians. His summers abroad had left him with an accent the other boys considered "too English." He seemed affected, perhaps a trifle effeminate, and his ingratiating manner annoyed many of his classmates.

More important, skinny "Uncle Frank," * as he was nicknamed, was neither a scholar nor an athlete. He excelled only at Latin and "high kick," a game favoring long-legged students that entailed kicking a tin pan strung from the ceiling and enduring embarrassment after the inevitable and painful falls. The game was emblematic of his desperate attempts to win favor, even if it meant hurting himself. Franklin may have been secure in background but not in his ability to make his way in the world. He was off-key with schoolmates, and even as an adult his gaiety and sociability always had a slightly forced quality to it.

For the next decade, F. D. Roosevelt would be seen as effete even by the standards of the nation's most effete subculture. His own cousins mocked him as "Miss Nancy" or "the man on the handkerchief box," a reference to a drawing of a snooty-looking gentleman on a toiletry they all recognized. To imply something not quite manly about this Roosevelt cousin was a particular slur in the testosterone world of Theodore Roosevelt and his brood. Alice Roosevelt, daughter of TR and an acerbic wit (until her death in 1980 she kept a pillow on her couch with the embroidered line: "If you don't have anything nice to say . . . come sit by me"), was particularly vicious, especially after it be-

---

* The nickname came in part from the presence in an upper form (grade) at Groton of "Taddy" Roosevelt, the ne'er-do-well son of Franklin's half brother, Rosy. Franklin was thus the uncle of an older relative.

came clear that FDR had eclipsed the Oyster Bay branch of the family. "He was the kind of boy whom you invited to the dance, but not the dinner," she recalled, "a good little mother's boy whose friends were dull, who belonged to the minor clubs and who was never at the really gay parties." She and her cousins used the foppish young man's initials to call him "Feather Duster" Roosevelt, a nickname that stuck so long that it was still used to damage him as late as the 1932 Democratic Convention.

But if Franklin seemed light and unsubstantial, he was anchored. "All that is in me goes back to the Hudson," he said in later years. When he traveled and had landed safely, he often wired back one word: "Algonac." The name of the Delano estate was a family code word for "all is well." In the White House, FDR fell asleep imagining himself sledding down the hill behind his Hyde Park home, then dragging his sled back up for another run—a crippled president at a time of crisis drawing sustenance from happy boyhood memories of frolicking in the snow.

In studying the sources of optimism, therapists are increasingly focusing on such "illusive inner islands of strength" that people build in their heads, especially childhood places of comfort in which they can take refuge throughout their lives. These secure mental images help build what is now called emotional intelligence, a trait that can be acquired and nurtured as well as innate. Emotional intelligence entails not simply picking up cues from other people and intuiting their motives but regulating one's own frustrations deftly enough to keep moving forward.

In school, Franklin never seemed hurt by the slights. He began zestfully embracing activities even when he wasn't good at them. His ever-growing list of eclectic interests—stamps, stuffed birds, Navy ships, rare books—later contributed to his reputation as a dilettante, but they reflected the spirit of a happy collector. Eventually, he would collect people and ideas, too.

His mother knew this quality helped define him. "Whether he excelled at what he tackled or whether he met with indifferent success had little or no influence upon his enthusiasm for the project," Sara wrote of his teenage years. Under the same impulse, FDR worked diligently to transform shortcomings into strengths. Like young Theodore

Roosevelt turning himself from a childhood weakling into an icon of manhood, Franklin's lack of popularity as a student made him even more determined to hone his charm into a subtle instrument for advancement.

After the Spanish-American War broke out in 1898, Franklin wanted to lie about his age and run off to volunteer, or so he later claimed. The historian Geoffrey C. Ward suggests this was likely a fib he told to link himself more closely with Theodore Roosevelt and to cover for the fact that he never served in the military. More plausible was his recollection that he hoped to apply to the U.S. Naval Academy, but his father told him a life at sea would be too cruel to his mother. Instead, his path was to be Harvard and the law, per Mr. James's instructions.

When Franklin was a Harvard freshman, James Roosevelt died of a heart attack. It was no surprise and Franklin was not distraught, but it proved hard on Sara. The following two winters, she rented a house in downtown Boston, a few miles away from her son's apartments on Dunster Street in Cambridge. This has often been depicted as an example of her suffocating attention, but it might more accurately be seen as the understandable reaction of a grieving widow with almost no other immediate family. She mostly saw Franklin on weekends, when he would sometimes host parties at her house.*

A middling B student, Franklin's great passion in Cambridge was the student newspaper, the *Harvard Crimson*, where his big scoop was an interview with his distant cousin, Vice President Theodore Roosevelt, soon to become president after the assassination of William McKinley. Fending off his bitter *Crimson* rival, Arthur Ballantine, who would reappear in his life during the banking crisis of 1933, Franklin eventually worked his way up to managing editor and then, in a postgraduate year, to president of the daily. Even then, he provoked radically different reactions in people. One fellow editor recalled him as an effective and easygoing leader of the newspaper; another remembered "a snob—

---

* Might there be some connection between mothers following their sons to college and great success? Douglas MacArthur's mother took a room near West Point and Adlai Stevenson's mother did the same at Princeton.

he did not have the common touch in those days." Over time, the former trait would dominate.

If running the *Crimson* was his major college accomplishment—and one he liked to brag to White House reporters about in the 1930s—Franklin's major setback was his failure to win election to the most prestigious of all Harvard "finals" clubs, the Porcellian, to which his father (who had gone to Harvard Law School, but not to the college), his half brother, his rector, Endicott Peabody, and many other relatives had belonged. His easily lampooned emulation of President Theodore Roosevelt (a Porcellian member) might have generated opposition, or a highly publicized scandal involving his relative, Taddy Roosevelt, who was caught around that time in a sex scandal.*

Regardless of its cause, the Porcellian blackballing would sting. Fifteen years later, Franklin told his cousin, W. Sheffield Cowles, Jr., that it was "the biggest disappointment of my life," a measure, of course, of how easy his life was before polio. Eleanor said the rejection gave her husband "an inferiority complex." This sounds like an exaggeration. Eleanor, whose father was hopelessly alcoholic and whose mother proved so cold and withholding that she called her own daughter "granny," was the one who often felt insecure, and she may have been projecting that onto her husband. Even so, the rejection no doubt contributed to the overeagerness for social acceptance in FDR that irritated so many of his contemporaries.

Here was a young man who had not yet bridled his ebullience. But he was gaining self-confidence, and the ones who laughed at him would be left a step behind.

---

* Taddy dropped out of Harvard and married a Hungarian prostitute he met in New York's Tenderloin district, a disgrace that made headlines while Franklin was a Harvard freshman. He later became an auto mechanic, and left his huge estate to the Salvation Army.

Chapter Four

Eleanor and Sara

Whatever Franklin's social setbacks at Harvard, Anna Eleanor Roosevelt represented at least a partial solution. They had seen each other as toddlers at Hyde Park and at one family party in New Jersey when Franklin was seventeen and Eleanor fourteen. But in the New York social season of 1903, the fifth cousins once removed were thrown together at a Madison Square Garden horse show. While not a beauty, Eleanor at eighteen was willowy, refined by a European education, and—before her teeth bucked—considerably less homely than later photographs reflected. Franklin, age twenty-one and a Harvard senior, fell hard; his letters to his "angel" sound genuinely passionate.

Seemingly shy and docile, Eleanor had more to offer on closer inspection. Like Franklin, she felt slightly awkward in the easy social whirl of their set but could laugh about it when talking with Franklin one-to-one. She felt secure with him, and he appreciated her intelligence—rare for suitors of the time, who were usually satisfied with charm and social position in a woman. Eleanor's commitment to social justice opened new worlds to him and softened some of his self-satisfaction. She worked with poor Jewish immigrants at a settlement house on the Lower East Side, where FDR was shaken after climbing the stairs of a tenement to a cold-water flat. "He kept saying he could not believe human beings really lived that way," Eleanor later recalled.

He may well have been in love, but her relationship to her uncle certainly didn't hurt. Eleanor's proximity to power must have served as an aphrodisiac for Franklin, who treasured an invitation from her to dine at the White House. After all, President Theodore Roosevelt was the most exciting thing to happen in public life in a generation and Eleanor was his favorite niece. The Hyde Park Roosevelts were distant relations, and all through college Franklin had his nose pressed up against the glass. This caused some tension with his mother. "Please don't make any more arrangements for my future happiness," he wrote Sara tartly after she declined an invitation he received for a party at Oyster Bay without telling him—an attitude quite at odds with his "mama's boy" reputation.

When Franklin informed his mother of the engagement on Thanksgiving Day, 1903, she was dumbfounded: Franklin had kept the couple's intention to marry a secret for many months, reflecting an instinct for deception not just on little things but on important matters involving people he loved. This was no small achievement. Sensing how hurt his mother must be, he wrote her: "I am the happiest man just now in the world; likewise the luckiest—And for you, dear Mummy, you know that nothing can ever change what we have always been and always will be to each other." Here Franklin, sensing that Sara and Eleanor would now begin competing for him, indicated that he would allow neither a total victory.

To the extent that marriage is a rational decision, Eleanor was a highly pragmatic choice. Rather than giving up his independence by getting married, Franklin figured he would be gaining it. Whatever Sara's misgivings, he knew she couldn't openly object, couldn't yank back his "freedom" as if he were a five-year-old again. After all, Eleanor was from the right family and solicitous of Sara (whose Delano family offered a "sense of security I had never known before," Eleanor wrote). On paper, anyway, the good feelings were reciprocated. In her letters to Eleanor and Franklin, Sara was loving toward "the children," as she would refer to them for several years thereafter.

But after Franklin's intentions were clear, a subtle battle of wills developed between mother and son. Sara wanted to see Franklin alone at

Hyde Park instead of letting him spend more time with Eleanor. In chatty letters, Franklin mastered the art of seeming good-natured and vaguely agreeable toward "Mama" while doing as he pleased, a trait he would use to great effect in politics.

Sara tried to fight back by arguing that, at twenty-one and eighteen, they were too young. She convinced them to delay the announcement of the engagement for a full year, then began scheming to break it off by winning a job for Franklin in the U.S. Embassy in London. But he was too young for the post. Instead, he enrolled in Columbia Law School, where he proceeded to flunk two courses.

Franklin and Eleanor were married the following St. Patrick's Day, 1905, at a friend's home in Manhattan, with the president of the United States giving away his niece. For one awful moment, the couple recalled, they stood entirely alone, ignored at their own wedding, as the crowd abandoned the bride and groom to hover around the president. TR famously insisted on being "the groom at every wedding and the corpse at every funeral," as one relative put it, and this event was no exception.

Franklin's ego was a bit bruised by the experience. Moreover, he was struck by the fact that everyone congratulated him for winning Eleanor, but not Eleanor for winning him. From then on, he resolved to break the social tradition in his circle against congratulating brides, and he did so, effusively, at every wedding he attended thereafter. Later, he came to dislike other social and political traditions he considered "silly" and delighted in breaking them, too.

Franklin's resolve to "never change" his relationship with his mother was itself a major decision, as any man caught between his wife and mother knows. It meant that Eleanor would never become the most important woman in his life. For all of the indispensable practical help she provided him in politics, Eleanor was not Franklin's emotional rock. There is little evidence that she fueled his ambition or bolstered his self-confidence. That would remain Sara's psychic role, which she conveniently performed from the adjoining town houses (with a doorway connecting the fourth-floor bedrooms) that she built for herself and Franklin and Eleanor on East Sixty-fifth Street in New York.

All told, Franklin and Eleanor had six children between 1906 and 1916. A daughter, Anna, and son, James, came first. In 1909, their third child, Franklin Junior, developed a heart ailment. When he was failing to thrive, his parents left him for a time in the care of his grandmother at Hyde Park, where it was thought the autumn air would help him. It didn't. Franklin Junior died at seven months and this apparently contributed to some of the bitterness between Eleanor and Sara. Eleanor sank into a deep depression. The trauma also caused her to question her own abilities as a mother when a doctor cruelly suggested that perhaps the infant might have lived had he been breast-fed. Eleanor bore three more sons—Elliott, a second Franklin Junior and John—but in the years that followed, she increasingly sacrificed child rearing in favor of fulfilling political and social activities.

On the surface, Eleanor maintained a pleasant correspondence with her mother-in-law, but much later, after Sara's death, she lashed back at her. "She [Sara] determined to bend [our] marriage to the way she wanted it to be. What she wanted was to hold on to Franklin and his children," Eleanor wrote in an article she decided not to publish. "She wanted them to grow as she wished. As it turned out, Franklin's children were more my mother-in-law's children than they were mine."

But Sara was only secondarily at fault for moving in next door or using her money to enforce her family decisions or otherwise making her daughter-in-law feel like a stranger in her own home. That was principally the responsibility of Franklin Roosevelt. It was FDR who let his mother pay his bills until the end of her life; who let her sit at the other head of the table, with Eleanor and the children in the middle; who thought nothing at age fifty-five of allowing his mother to write a thank-you note for a scarf sent to her son the president.

He deferred to his mother again and again, mostly because it was easier for him that way. "He lived in an atmosphere almost totally devoid of conflict," John Gunther later wrote. "Perhaps that gave him his confidence in later life, and perhaps, too, it might have contributed to his touchiness and sensitivity to criticism."

It was Franklin who arranged to keep the atmosphere conflict-free, at least on the surface. That made him, finally, responsible for his own self-confidence and ease. For all of his great advantages in life, he would make his own world. Just as his mother told him.

Chapter Five

Dilettante

W HEN FDR BECAME PRESIDENT, he had no carefully worked
out political philosophy or rigorous approach to governing beyond a penchant for action. This sounds like a shortcoming but proved
a hidden asset. Had he been an intellectual or ideologue, he would
have lacked the flexibility and spirit of experimentation the times required. Instead, he had a short attention span, an eye for the spotlight,
and a fierce ambition—traits that sound unworthy but would prove surprisingly well suited to confronting the Great Depression.

Young Franklin Roosevelt was, by most accounts, a dilettante. After
Columbia Law School, he tried to practice law as he began a family, but
it bored him and ended badly. His boss, Commodore Lewis Ledyard,
one of the name partners in the Wall Street firm of Carter, Ledyard &
Milburn, finally had to tell Sara that "it was no use"—Franklin simply
wasn't focused or hardworking enough to be a good lawyer. About the
only impression he made was that of an ambitious swell. In 1907, he
told fellow law clerks that he wanted to be president of the United
States, and would follow the path of his cousin Theodore. "Once you're
elected governor of New York," he said. "If you do well enough in that
job, you have a good show to be President." He decided to be a Democrat to honor his father and because he figured he could not compete
with the Oyster Bay Roosevelts in Republican politics.

Roosevelt was, by his own description, "a poor little rich boy who wanted to do something constructive." According to one story, he decided to run for the New York State Senate in 1910 after being visited by a delegation of local politicians who needed a sacrificial candidate in the heavily Republican district that included Hyde Park. "I'd like to talk to my mother about it," Roosevelt supposedly said. "Frank," one of the bosses is said to have replied, "there are men in Poughkeepsie waiting. They won't like to hear you asked your mother."* This tale rings false; Franklin by that time had long since begun to make his own decisions in life and put distance between himself and his mother. But that such a story was told widely for decades suggests how far the "mama's boy" impression had spread.

In truth, Sara thought it acceptable to be "in politics," like cousin Theodore, just so long as one wasn't "a politician." Franklin accepted the bosses' challenge, campaigned tirelessly as a reformer, and pulled an upset. He later remembered that first campaign mostly for the surprise he felt over something perfectly obvious—the extent to which ordinary voters coveted the birthright he took for granted. "Every individual wanted security in one form or another," FDR recalled with amazement. "The desire for security was an eye opener for me."

As a Roosevelt, not yet thirty, he was noticed in the State Senate from the start. "With his handsome face and his form of supple strength he could make a fortune on the stage and set the matinee girl's heart throbbing with subtle and happy emotion," wrote the correspondent for *The New York Times*. The family name and good looks that meant little inside his social circle made him stand out in impressive contrast to the grubby Albany politicians with stains on their ties.

More important, he happened to show up in Albany in early 1911 in time for a highly publicized brawl that showed he could seize events to make a strong public impression. Only two years later, an amendment to the U.S. Constitution required the direct election of U.S. senators. But until then, elections in New York and other states to the U.S. Senate were still decided in state legislatures. The choice that year of Tam-

---

* One of these Poughkeepsie men, Tom Lynch, became a close friend and supporter for the next twenty years.

many Hall (the Democratic machine that ran New York City) was "Blue-Eyed Billy" Sheehan, a mediocre lawyer and party hack not qualified to go to Washington. Roosevelt and a group of other lawmakers who met at Franklin and Eleanor's large Albany house decided to fight Tammany's Senate candidate.

FDR made an early name for himself by helping to defeat Sheehan, but he wasn't yet politically smart. He publicly compared his Tammany foes to the "hopelessly stupid" children of "hillbillies," and privately ridiculed their Irish brogues, which quickly opened him up to the charge of anti-Catholic bias.* The clerk of the State Senate remembered him as "bristling with the conceits of a silly prig," and in later years, FDR didn't disagree, admitting that he had been "an awfully mean cuss when I first went into politics."

Among those who found him insufferable and felt snubbed at the Albany mansion FDR and Eleanor rented was the young State Assembly Speaker, Alfred E. Smith. But events were soon to bring the two men into closer contact. On March 25, 1911, only a few days after the Roosevelt forces prevailed in the Sheehan fight, the Triangle Shirtwaist Co., a factory in Greenwich Village, burst into flames, killing 146 young women workers. The Triangle fire marked a major turning point in both social policy and Democratic politics. The next decade brought a revolution in state government, including a shorter workweek, the first workman's compensation legislation, an end to child labor, and dozens of other health and safety reforms, thanks in large part to Al Smith. Many of these initiatives were copied in other states and their spirit eventually animated the New Deal.

Roosevelt later claimed that as a freshman state senator he was instrumental in obtaining the 54-hour maximum workweek for women and children, the first of the big reforms in 1911. In fact, Frances Perkins—the Brahmin head of the New York Consumer League, who had heard the screams from the fire while having tea near Washington Square and was soon appointed chief investigator of the commission investigating the disaster—had been disgusted by how unsupportive of reform Roosevelt was in those years. Later, his contemporaries were un-

---

* FDR's attitude toward Catholics was complicated. Many of his closest aides and companions were Catholic, but he always remained slightly patronizing toward the Irish.

sure how a liberal impulse developed in the callow young man. Perkins, whose dour public persona and Margaret Dumont voice belied her subtle insight into FDR's character, wrote that liberal ideas of social reform "penetrated into his personality by a kind of intellectual and spiritual osmosis" that she considered "a miracle."

It was no miracle. Roosevelt's compassion was there all the time. His family saw it when Mr. James was ill and his son tended to him; Eleanor would not have married him without it. The great political influence of his early years—his cousin Theodore—had stamped him as a progressive reformer, and most of the politicians he associated with in Albany were part of that movement. But these embers of empathy were buried beneath a heedless, know-it-all exterior. If he was going to make it in politics, he would need the guidance of an experienced political professional.

Chapter Six

"The Medieval Gnome"

During the contest with Tammany Hall over Billy Sheehan, FDR met a cantankerous reporter for the *New York Herald* named Louis McHenry Howe. Before long, the reporter was advising the young state senator, eleven years his junior, on Albany tactics. They made an odd couple: the pretty boy and the gnarled scribbler. FDR was naive about politicians but eager to hear gossip about their raffish exploits. Howe was always ready with racy descriptions of the lowlife of the capital, which provided Franklin a welcome relief from the high-minded expectations of his family. From their first meeting, Howe later recalled, he thought of Roosevelt as "presidential timber." Whether Howe was seduced by the Roosevelt name or simply smitten by the golden boy himself, he was alone in that assessment.

In an earlier campaign, Howe explained one of his rules of political success: "If you say a thing often enough, it has a good chance of becoming a fact." Howe, wrote his biographer, "had immense confidence in his ability to trick the ordinary man." Under Howe's tutelage, FDR never became a con artist, but he did develop a talent for manipulating public impressions.

From the start, Howe cultivated his image as a wizened, abrupt, and invariably rude superloyalist. At five foot four and less than 100 pounds, he was a tiny bag of bones; his hollow face, hideously pitted from a serious boyhood bicycle accident, looked as gray as the gravel road he fell on. He described himself as "one of the four ugliest men in New York, if what is left of me can be dignified by the name of man. Children take one look at me on the street and run from 'the man with the wicked kidnapping eyes,' " he said. Later, he said the same of himself in Washington, again without mentioning the other three.

His most common nickname—"the Medieval Gnome"—suited him perfectly, and he sometimes answered the phone, "This is the Medieval Gnome speaking." In time, he convinced authorities in Kentucky to make him an honorary colonel, in part because "Colonel Howe" sounded almost like Colonel Edward House, the legendary presidential adviser, who was not a real colonel either. Eventually, Howe had cards printed up with the name "Colonel Louis Rasputin Voltaire Talleyrand Simon Legree Howe."

By the time he was joking that way, he and FDR had long since bonded. That took for good in 1912, when Roosevelt arranged for Howe to help him promote a dark horse Democratic presidential candidate—New Jersey governor Woodrow Wilson. When Wilson was finally nominated on the forty-sixth ballot, Franklin shouted himself hoarse. Former President Theodore Roosevelt, denied the Republican nomination in favor of incumbent President William Howard Taft, ran for president that year as the Progressive Party "Bull Moose" candidate. But by then Franklin was already committed to Wilson.

Wilson's nomination put FDR in a good position with the national Democratic Party and Howe's congratulatory letter began, only half facetiously: "Beloved and Revered Future President." This was exactly twenty years before Howe helped make FDR the 1932 nominee. Soon, Howe got the chance to show his indispensability. If Wilson won in 1912, FDR wanted a job in Washington. But to get a good one, he had to win reelection to the New York State Senate. After Labor Day, Roosevelt was looking like a loser, sidelined by typhoid fever. FDR had no choice but to ask Howe to come take charge of the campaign and essentially run for the seat himself.

With the candidate in bed, Howe toured the district in an automobile and pulled what he later called his "great farmer's stunt"—a form letter to farmers that was designed to look like a personal note from their fellow Hyde Park agriculturalist. Under FDR's signature, Howe promised to introduce legislation to standardize apple barrels at 16¼ inches instead of 17⅛, which would save farmers money by allowing them to include fewer apples per barrel. This was the key to reelection in 1912. Louis Howe saved Franklin Roosevelt's political career by less than an inch.

"Keep that temperature down so you can get on the job," Howe wrote FDR. "I am having more fun than a goat. Your slave and servant, Louis Howe."

But Howe and Roosevelt were not just slave and master. From that point forward, they were two parts of the same political organism, brilliantly complementing each other. Howe, the skeptic, did the worrying for both of them, concentrating on the mechanics of politics—patronage, press manipulation, and intrigue. Roosevelt loved that game, too, but floated above it, projecting a warm aura of smiles and gauzy inspiration.

Sara gave Franklin the confidence he needed to thrive, and Eleanor changed him, making him more liberal and open to new views. But Howe was the indispensable man in the prosaic business of making him president. Over a twenty-five-year period, he devoted his life to Roosevelt—the longest uninterrupted toil by a handler in the history of presidential politics. Howe was FDR's Theodore Sorensen, Hamilton Jordan, Michael Deaver, and Karl Rove rolled into one, except that he alone among them was older than his boss and thus more influential. His job, he said, was to "provide the toe-weights" that kept FDR's flights of fancy from becoming political problems and his feet on the ground. Later, Howe would be blunter, saying he had been put on earth "to hold Franklin down."

For all his bonhomie, Roosevelt was notorious among his staff for the stinginess of his praise. But he knew at some level how important Howe was to his life. "Dear Old Louis," Franklin wrote him when the presidency was at last in sight. "Just a line to send my love and tell you, if it does any good, to take care of yourself and try not to overdo and worry. All is really coming out so well and you are the main spring!"

The love, of course, went more strongly in the other direction. Howe's wife and son were subordinated to his worship of FDR. The effects on Roosevelt's ego must have been significant. When a subordinate is utterly devoted to you, it can give the recipient of the adulation a powerful feeling of superiority—a sense that everyone else in the world must also adore you, or would if they knew you as well.

Louis Howe once confessed that as a child he wanted to be an artist. Franklin Roosevelt turned out to be his canvas. "At heart," he later told the novelist Fanny Hurst, "I am a minstrel singing outside the window of beauty."

Chapter Seven

The Operator

ONLY WEEKS AFTER ROOSEVELT was reelected to the State Senate in 1912, he went to Washington and won an appointment as Wilson's assistant secretary of the Navy under Josephus Daniels, a deceptively shrewd old North Carolina newspaper editor who knew nothing of the sea. FDR was acutely aware that Theodore Roosevelt had held the same assistant secretary post fifteen years earlier under William McKinley and used it as a stepping stone. In those days, this was a significant job, with oversight of ship procurement and management of 65,000 men.

This training proved highly useful when FDR became president. Had he come to the White House with only state government experience, Roosevelt would have been far more susceptible to conventional Washington thinking. Because he spent the years from 1913 to 1921 working in the trenches—learning the little tricks that middle-level federal officials use to sabotage their superiors—Roosevelt was harder to resist when he wanted something done. The experience gave him the potential for much greater accomplishment than was possible for less bureaucratically sophisticated chief executives. As president, FDR thought big and would not take no for an answer, a skill he learned at the Navy Department.

Franklin at thirty-one was seven years younger and far less accomplished than TR had been when he went to Washington. But he knew the world, having already crossed the Atlantic twenty times, and he approached his task with the same prodigious energy as his fifth cousin. At first, the changes he undertook were almost comically calculated and self-serving. His mother convinced him to convert his official signature to something bolder and less cramped (though for the rest of his life, most of his personal correspondence, even to intimates, was signed simply: "FDR"). He designed a new flag with the insignia of the assistant secretary to be flown on board naval vessels during inspection tours. It was in this period, long before polio made it hard to put on an overcoat from a seated position, that he took to wearing dark and dramatic Navy capes.

He was preening and increasingly practiced in the art of charming Washington. With Howe as his secretary, FDR became one of the dashing young men of the Wilson era, a member of what was known informally as "the Little Cabinet." He seemed always in motion in the capital—impressing congressional committees with his terrific memory for facts and figures about the Navy; pushing his hawkish views on military intervention; exploiting his authority to build a minor patronage operation back in New York; teaming up with his naughty cousin Alice to eavesdrop with a crude spying device on a pair of high society lovers sitting in someone else's parlor.

President Wilson rarely talked to the press, which left room for young Roosevelt to become one of the biggest sources in town. The reporters repaid the favor with a mountain of favorable press clippings, many of which worked in the fact that Theodore Roosevelt had been assistant secretary of the Navy before becoming president.

Members of the Cabinet were struck by FDR's self-confidence. "Young Roosevelt knows nothing about finance," said the Interior Secretary, Franklin K. Lane, "but he doesn't *know* he doesn't know." This utter certainty that he knew as much about the economy as any Cabinet secretary or titan of industry sounds impertinent, but it would serve him well in resisting received wisdom. The foppishness was fading. The man initially described as a sucker for prep school chums seeking Navy favors began spending time with the urban bosses and labor leaders he needed to get things done. Frances Perkins says it was in this period that FDR "unbent, laughed with them, swapped yarns" and became the engaging politician the world later knew. The result was eight years of labor peace at the Navy Yards and a reputation as a man who could talk to anybody.

Even so, the dominant impression of Roosevelt in those years was of an impossible young man in a hurry. In 1914, when he was thirty-two and just constitutionally eligible, he claimed implausibly that a "stern sense of duty" compelled him to enter the race for U.S. Senate, which in those days he was allowed to undertake without resigning his government post. He ran in the New York Democratic primary against the Tammany candidate and was crushed.* Howe had a plan to salvage his career at home. The next year, 1915, he told FDR to give a speech touting Tammany's candidate for sheriff of New York County, Al Smith. From then on, Roosevelt would never fight Tammany Hall directly again, maintaining a respectful distance that kept him from being either tool or enemy.

Because he was wealthy, Franklin could afford to be independent; he didn't need a large political machine for support and was thus less dependent on the sense of loyalty that glued other politicians together. Roosevelt, who once called his boss Daniels "the funniest-looking hillbilly I had ever seen," was so shockingly insubordinate that Interior Secretary Lane had to tell him he should stop flaying his chief at dinner parties. "You should be ashamed of yourself," Lane told him. "Mr. Daniels is your superior and you should show him loyalty or you should resign your office."

But even as he schemed and manipulated, he was learning from Josephus Daniels about power. When two contractors came into the office with suspiciously similar bids, then claimed the apparent bid-rigging was merely coincidence, Daniels told them: "Sharpen your pencils, think it over during the night, and don't have another 'coincidence.'" Roosevelt, who liked to tell that story, picked up Daniels's knack for listening patiently, nodding amiably, then placing an iron fist in the velvet glove. It would be his modus operandi in the years ahead.

The new skills were on full display during World War I when Joseph

---

* FDR had hoped to run as a fusion Democrat-Progressive against William Randolph Hearst, but Hearst declined the race. In a primary campaign that lasted only seventeen days, he lost to James Gerard, who was Wilson's ambassador to Germany.

P. Kennedy, then the assistant manager of a Quincy, Massachusetts, shipyard, visited FDR at the Navy Department. The ambitious Massachusetts businessman thought he could snow the rich kid playing at politics. Kennedy's shipyard had built two battleships for the government of Argentina and he was in Washington to tell Roosevelt he would refuse to deliver them until the Argentines paid for them in full. Roosevelt told Kennedy the money would arrive in due time, but there was a world war on, and Kennedy should deliver the ships. Kennedy and his boss, Charles M. Schwab, president of Bethlehem Steel, were sure the young Navy official was bluffing.

He wasn't. As Kennedy watched in amazement, four tugboats full of armed U.S. Marines landed in his shipyard and seized the new battleships, then turned them over to the Argentine Navy, waiting patiently just off the coast. "I was so disappointed I broke down and cried," Kennedy remembered. Fifteen years later, Kennedy became an early supporter of FDR for president, only to find himself suffering further humiliation at his hands.

On balance, his impatient drive and nose for newspapermen made Roosevelt a memorable and important young second-tier official. This was especially true during wartime, where many of the bold acts of government (particularly its intervention in the American economy) became a template for the early New Deal.

Roosevelt moved aggressively to leave his mark. First, he created a Naval Reserve to match the Army's, then—acting essentially on his own authority—he ordered 100,000 advanced sea mines planted in the North Sea within a few months to block German submarines. When colleagues objected that the mining operation could not possibly be done in so short a time, he used his oceanic knowledge and force of personality to make it happen. The effectiveness of the sea mines was in dispute, but not the determination of the man who implemented the idea.

In 1918, more than five years into the job, Franklin made a trip to the European war zone and fell ill on the return voyage. He was carried by stretcher from the ship amid concern that he might have contracted influenza, which killed millions worldwide that year and the next. Back at the Sixty-fifth Street town house, Eleanor was unpacking Franklin's bags and discovered a bundle of love letters to Franklin from her former social secretary, Lucy Mercer. "The bottom dropped out of my own particular world and I faced myself, my surroundings, my world honestly for the first time," Eleanor later told her friend Joseph Lash.

Although the affair lasted only a few months, Lucy was the love of Franklin Roosevelt's life. Little is known of the details—no letters between them survive—but it's clear that Franklin, in his letters to Eleanor at Campobello, tried to hide Lucy in plain sight by mentioning her presence as the date of various friends during picnics and boating excursions. A friend lent them a house to use on the outskirts of Washington and many in their circle, including Alice Roosevelt Longworth (who had taken to mimicking her first cousin Eleanor behind her back), were in on the secret.

In an often-published but never confirmed story, Eleanor offered Franklin his freedom and he nearly accepted. But Lucy was Catholic, and her religion prohibited her from marrying a divorced man. Moreover, according to the recollections of family members, Sara told her son that she would disinherit him if he left his wife and five children. Louis Howe advised him that divorce would end his political career. While the private family conversations of the time are impossible to reconstruct, this much is known: Franklin and Eleanor never shared a bed again.

Eleanor's wound would be permanent, but so was her determination to continue investing herself in Franklin's future. In the remaining twenty-seven years of their marriage they formed a political partnership in which she became her husband's willing instrument. "He might have been happier with a wife who was completely uncritical. That I was never able to be, and he had to find it in other people," Eleanor recalled. "Nevertheless, I think I acted sometimes as a spur, even though the spurring was not always wanted or welcome." Then she added an icy line that cut to the hard interior of FDR's view of other people, even those closest to him: "I was one of those who served his purposes."

But something deeper still bound them together. At Eleanor's death in 1962, a tattered clipping was discovered atop her bedside table in New York. It contained a poem, "Psyche," by Virginia Moore, with the lines: "The soul that had believed/and was deceived/ends by believing more/than ever before." Scrawled across the top of the clipping was simply: "1918."

The private family drama made FDR grateful he had decided not to run for governor that fall. But by 1919, Franklin was so energetic and visible that he began to be mentioned as a figure of consequence in national politics, especially after Theodore Roosevelt died suddenly at age sixty and was mourned across the nation. At first it seemed that FDR might run for vice president with none other than Herbert Hoover. In early 1920, Hoover came across like Dwight D. Eisenhower in a later era, a national hero with no discernible political affiliation who was avidly sought for president by both parties.

Roosevelt and Hoover had begun as "good friends," as Hoover remembered, two energetic young officials in Wilson's Washington who liked to get things done. FDR was the on-the-make bureaucrat, Hoover the nonpartisan big-time problem solver. After meeting around 1916 at the home of Interior Secretary Lane, the Hoovers and Roosevelts enjoyed each other's company, and their social calendars suggest that the two couples met for dinner at least eight times over the next few years.

An Iowa-born orphan, Hoover worked his way through Stanford University and made his fortune running mining operations all over the world. When war broke out in 1914, he helped thousands of Americans escape to safety in London, then became famous as "the Great Humanitarian" for his astounding feats of relief organization, particularly in Belgium and the Soviet Union, ravaged by famine. Franklin wrote to Hugh Gibson, the U.S. Ambassador to Poland, that "I had some nice talks with Herbert Hoover before he went West for Christmas [1920]. I wish we could make him President of the United States."

During their "nice talks," Roosevelt advised Hoover that all Hoover had to do to become president was to let it be known that he was a Jeffersonian Democrat. Colonel Edward House, only recently the second most powerful man in Washington after his boss, President Wilson, told Attorney General A. Mitchell Palmer that a Hoover-Roosevelt ticket was the Democrats' best chance to hold the White House.*

---

* One evening in 1919, Franklin returned to his house in Georgetown to find blood and body parts on his doorstep and the front windows smashed by an anarchist's bomb that blew up the home of Palmer across the street, one of eight such terrorist bombs planted around the country that day. (No one except the anarchist was harmed.) Roosevelt was fully supportive of Wilson's espionage and sedition laws that criminalized all opposition to the war and the "Palmer Raids" that rounded up dissidents.

After Hoover declined these overtures and joined the GOP, the Democrats nominated Ohio governor James A. Cox on the forty-fourth ballot as their 1920 candidate for president against Senator Warren G. Harding. Following the tradition of picking nonentities for vice president, Cox was convinced that he might win some Progressive Republican votes by selecting as his running mate an energetic young Roosevelt with a golden name and a reputation for independence.* Although he had never met the assistant secretary of the Navy, Cox also thought he would bring youth and geographical balance to the ticket. When he asked the legendary Tammany boss Charlie Murphy about him, Murphy replied: "This young Roosevelt is no good, but if you want him, we'll vote for him."

Once selected for the national ticket, FDR barnstormed the country by train and gave close to a thousand exuberant speeches in four months. He was a natural, effervescent campaigner, who loved nothing more than giving seven or eight speeches a day. But Howe, while covering for FDR at the Navy Department, could not "keep him down" enough for his own good. In August 1920, at a farmer's picnic near Butte, Montana, FDR made one of the first "gaffes" of the modern media age. In explaining why much of the Western Hemisphere would vote with the United States in the League of Nations (support for the League was the Cox-Roosevelt ticket's central issue), Roosevelt went overboard: "You know, I had something to do with running a couple of little Republics. The facts are that I wrote Haiti's constitution myself, and if I do say so, I think it's a pretty good constitution."

This was Roosevelt at his most cocky and least attractive. He had visited Haiti as assistant secretary but did not engage in what would now be called "nation-building." To make matters worse, Roosevelt quickly denied ever having made the remark. When he blamed the Associated Press stringer for fabricating it, thirty-one citizens of Butte signed an affidavit backing up the reporter.

---

* A stunt FDR pulled early in the 1920 convention helped bring him to Cox's attention. Seeing the Tammany men sit stonily in the New York delegation during a raucous floor demonstration honoring the ailing President Wilson, a show-boating Roosevelt grabbed the New York standard (the pole placard identifying each state). After a brief scuffle with Tammany delegates, he leapt over seats and marched triumphantly into the delirious throng. The press loved it.

With the country seeking a postwar "return to normalcy" and Harding on his way to a landslide, the gaffe hardly mattered politically. But it showed that the restlessness and energy that would serve FDR in the White House had not yet been tempered by good judgment. In one sense, the episode was a blessing in disguise. It brought Howe out on the campaign train, where he got to know Eleanor better. They soon became close friends and Eleanor later said that the trip marked the beginning of her political education. Howe also taught Eleanor how to speak publicly (his main advice was to stop a nervous laugh and avoid reading prepared texts in favor of extemporaneous remarks). This, too, would prove of enormous benefit to Roosevelt's political prospects in the years ahead.

As the 1920s began, FDR still often came across as a snobby aristocrat. But coming of age in the Progressive Era, he also believed that the security he assumed as his birthright could be extended to many more Americans, and that it was the duty of government to do so. In the years before he was forty, he took that governing philosophy—increasingly called "liberal"—and wedded it to a distinctive personal style. He was shrewder now, and tougher than he looked. Beneath the sheen of privilege lay not just a talent for manipulation but uncommon determination. His street smarts were learned on the playing fields of Groton, not the Lower East Side, but he compensated by developing extraordinary political antennae. Over time, he would use his wily refinement on behalf of forgotten Americans he did not know when growing up.

Chapter Eight

The "Ghastly Affliction"

F IRST CAME THE GREATEST CHARACTER TEST of his life. A debilitating illness is never easy, but it hit Franklin Roosevelt harder than it would a more sedentary person. When he was a few years out of college, Roosevelt became something of a jock—one of those men who were not successful athletes in school but planned to spend the rest of their lives making up for it. He was a good golfer, an avid swimmer, and an energetic outdoorsman.

One of the ironies of the polio attack is that it probably saved his political career, which was headed downhill fast in the summer of 1921. The problem was what came to be known as "the Newport Scandal." In 1919, while Navy Secretary Daniels was in Europe, FDR apparently signed off on an undercover investigation in which enlisted men were engaged by a secret Navy unit to entrap homosexuals around the Newport, Rhode Island, naval base, where complaints had surfaced of widespread solicitation.

Astonishingly, these enlisted men were actually ordered to perform oral sex on suspected homosexuals in the Navy and others in their circle, including a prominent clergyman. After the *Providence Journal* broke the story of "vicious practices in the U.S. Navy," Roosevelt, claiming memory lapses about the whole thing, said in a May 1921 hearing that he couldn't remember approving the operation, and, more plausibly, that he had not known the graphic details of what would actually be done to crack down on homosexuality in the ranks.

When Republicans consolidated control of the Senate after Harding's victory in the 1920 election, it was payback time after eight years of Woodrow Wilson. Roosevelt "is a well-meaning, nice young fellow but light," Senator Henry Cabot Lodge had written to a friend the previous year, summing up the conventional wisdom in the capital. So now he would be taken down.

A congressional committee found that Roosevelt was either a knave or a fool, a moral reprobate or totally incompetent—he had either known of and approved "the most deplorable, disgraceful and unnatural" activities or "he did not inquire and was not informed," in which case "he was most derelict in the performance of his duty." The report concluded it was the former, that a man of Roosevelt's intelligence "must have known" of the activities of the unit performing the sexual entrapment. The July 20, 1921, *New York Times* carried a front-page story about the former vice-presidential candidate in which the scandal was laid directly at his feet:

> ### LAY NAVY SCANDAL TO F. D. ROOSEVELT
> ### SENATE NAVAL SUBCOMMITTEE
> ### ACCUSES HIM AND DANIELS
> ### IN NEWPORT INQUIRY
> ### DETAILS UNPRINTABLE

The "unprintable" details quickly circulated in Washington, but because reporters were more interested in the new Harding administration than the old Wilson crowd, the story faded. It would be resurrected, FDR feared, once he ran again for office.

Roosevelt was exhausted physically and emotionally from the ordeal and this almost certainly made him more vulnerable to the polio virus, which he apparently caught the following week during an appearance with other politicians at a Boy Scout camp in Bear Mountain, New York. At Campobello, Franklin felt a little achy, but went sailing with Eleanor and raced the children two miles on foot to a freshwater lake. Back at the house, he saw the mail had arrived and sat reading on the porch in his wet bathing suit, too tired even to change. "I'd never felt quite that way before," Franklin later said. He felt a violent chill and went to bed before supper. The next morning, August 11, 1921, he staggered into the bathroom to shave before collapsing on the bed. At age thirty-nine, he would never walk—in the conventional sense of that word—again.

Franklin lay in excruciating pain for the next several days as doctors, believing he might die, tried to figure out what was wrong. The man who would later try to banish fear experienced plenty of it himself. "I know that he had real fear when he was first taken ill," Eleanor reflected. Roosevelt later confessed to a friend that his despair then was absolute. He had always believed in himself as a chosen instrument of God and now felt abandoned.

At first his bowels were affected, and Eleanor, sleeping beside him on a camp bed, administered enemas. Whatever marital problems they had experienced before and would face again, this "trial by fire" would bind them closer. But she could not alleviate the dread. He stared at the ceiling, seeing for the first time the floral pattern of the wallpaper, which reminded him of a tomb.

A doctor prescribed deep massage, which proved to be the worst remedy imaginable. When Eleanor and Louis began dutifully massaging his legs, it caused pain as intense as torture and actually worsened the paralysis. He didn't blame them, but he never forgot how badly his first doctors botched his case. "[It] cured him permanently of any belief in the conventional wisdom of experts," wrote the columnist Max Lerner, who knew him well in later years, "whether in medicine, politics, economics, warfare or diplomacy."

This distrust of experts would prove fundamental to FDR's later success in the presidency. He drove aides to distraction by constantly pitting them against each other. But by gathering so much different advice, he was able to sort through the options and make up his own mind—on everything from polio treatment to fighting the Depression to winning the war.

Roosevelt never liked the diagnosis of infantile paralysis; he thought it made him seem like a child. But he did not challenge it, either. After the initial crisis, he was all good cheer with visitors, never referring to his disease, as did others in his family, as a "ghastly affliction." One doctor reported from Campobello that it was the patient himself who "has been such a comfort to all who tried to help."

The quality that the critic Edmund Wilson later called a "slightly unnatural sunniness" emerged during this period. Like his reaction to his father's illness, FDR made a point of studied cheerfulness amid calamity. Sara, who had been traveling in Europe, rushed to his bedside in early September to find "those beautiful legs quite, quite useless," but she put on a brave front. "I realized that I had to be courageous for Franklin's sake," she wrote her brother. "And since he was pretending to be unworried for mine, the meeting was quite a cheerful one." In the years ahead, she tried to have him spend as much time as possible recuperating at Hyde Park, but contrary to many reports, there is no evidence she demanded he forswear politics.

Louis Howe dropped everything to nurse Franklin. It's easy to attach oneself to a politician on the way up. Howe did so when his patron seemed finished politically. Almost any other faithful retainer would have showed up in Campobello for a few days, then, when appearances allowed, moved on with his life. Howe did the opposite, in part because he had no other prospects. He had invested seven years of his life in his hero and was determined to see some return. So he intensified his commitment, all but abandoning his own family and moving in with the Roosevelts. But Howe refused to indulge Franklin, a departure from the standards of the day. His decision not to treat Roosevelt as a hopeless invalid helped FDR insist that others not treat him that way either— an important component of his psychological recovery.

Howe carefully tended to FDR's public image with a fastidiousness that would be critical to Roosevelt's later success. It was necessary to move Franklin from Campobello to New York without the press realizing his true condition, a delicate maneuver. Howe knew that if the townspeople and press saw Roosevelt on a stretcher, they would think the worst. So Roosevelt was carefully laid out of sight on the floorboards of a boat, which slipped around the dock where the spectators had gathered, and landed on the other, quieter side of the harbor. Away from the gawkers, a few strong men carried him from the boat to the train. A window was removed from the railroad car, and FDR's stretcher lifted through the opening. Then he was propped up just in time for the townspeople and reporters who streamed over from the other side of the port to see him smiling and waving jauntily from the window as the train pulled away, an early pose of what a decade later became an iconic gesture. When friends, including Tom Lynch, met the train in New York, they burst into tears.

The next day's front-page story in the *Times* was quite different in tone than the one less than two months before. The Newport Scandal was forgotten amid concern that the 1920 vice-presidential candidate was seriously ill. In a hopeful tone, the story quoted Dr. George Draper, FDR's principal physician, as saying that while he had lost use of both legs below the knee, "he definitely will not be crippled."

That day, Franklin wrote a witty note to Adolph Ochs, publisher of the *Times*, saying he had not quite believed his doctors when they told him this, but "now that I have seen the same statement officially made in The New York Times, I feel immensely relieved because I know it must be so." His name would appear in *The New York Times* more than a thousand times in the seven years before his Inauguration as governor, but only a half dozen articles made reference to his polio, including one early in 1928 suggesting that "he has almost completely recovered from infantile paralysis." His disease, contrary to later impression, was never a secret, but it was hardly advertised, either.

Today, with barbs directed at the handicapped placed in the same category as racism, it's hard to imagine the severity of the stigma. Family members of victims talked in hushed tones of "shame" and "pity." Vaudeville entertainers could always get a laugh out of a fake limp or a joke about spastics. Contracting a disease such as polio meant being excluded from normal life, if not shunted away in dark back bedrooms or dismal hospitals that looked like prisons and had names like the Home for Incurables and the New York Society for the Relief of the Ruptured and Crippled.

During FDR's six-week hospital stay in New York, Dr. Draper worried about the psychological effect. "When we attempt to sit him up he will be faced with the frightfully depressing knowledge that he could not hold himself erect," he wrote another doctor working on the case. "He has such courage, such ambition, and yet at the same time such an extraordinarily delicate emotional mechanism, that it will take all the skill which we can muster to lead him successfully to a recognition of what he really faces without crushing him."

None of this "delicate emotional mechanism" was shown to the world. That would have run counter to FDR's stiff-upper-lip childhood, conditioned by his ailing father. Moreover, complaining of illness or even a bit of hard luck was simply poor form in that more stoic time and in his social class. But FDR took forbearance further, displaying a natural trait for performance. Even when he fell, as he did in the lobby of an office building after he ventured downtown for the first time, he was all smiles and joshing humor when passing strangers picked him up off the floor.* (One of them, Basil O'Connor, soon became his new law partner.) Eventually, this compensation for his polio would lead to serious misapprehensions about his character. The writer Milton MacKaye much later found Roosevelt "all light and no darkness; all faith and no skepticism; all bright hope and no black despair. One expects shadow and depth in a great man." And one would have found them, had FDR allowed MacKaye or anyone else to look.

After polio, Roosevelt developed an almost professional acting ability. Sensing his audience's discomfort, he perfected a casual verve and ingratiating laugh that left him at once accessible and out of reach. His way around intimacy (and other matters he chose not to confront) was to joke and reminisce, so that friends were amused and distracted from the invalid they were seeing.

"Gotta run!" he would say brightly, when the time came to go.

In later years, FDR would invariably be seated during the entire visit—or moved around by attendants, as one young friend of the family remembered, "totally immobile, like a doll." But early on, friends might arrive at the Sixty-fifth Street house to find him sitting upright on the floor, dragging himself along with his powerful arms, pulling his body across a landing by grabbing balustrades, a book between his teeth. The conversation with guests was lively, easy, about nothing in particular.

For visitors, it wasn't what Roosevelt said, but the simultaneously

---

* FDR was less cheerful when he tripped in the darkness while reaching to shake hands with an elderly poet and fell as he made his way to the podium to accept the 1936 presidential nomination outdoors at Philadelphia's Franklin Field. "Fix the God-damned brace! If it can't be fixed, there won't be any speech," he barked.

shocking and inspiring contrast between the tone of the conversation and the man who could not even stand up, much less walk, without help. For Roosevelt, these encounters provided practice in the politician's art of charming people while also working on an entirely different plane. He was developing a more complex set of instincts that allowed him to impress others and keep them off balance at the same time. Even those close to him were consistently surprised by his store of guts and good cheer. His favorite expression seemed to be an exuberant, "I love it!"

FDR was also developing the trait "polios" call "walking on your tongue." One doctor recalled that "he had to be reminded not to hog all of the conversation." This loquaciousness, which would characterize FDR for the rest of his life (as it does many politicians), was also a function of his condition: Because disabled people sometimes assume that others are only staying out of kindness, they often compensate by trying to entertain them. If you need someone to push you in your wheelchair around a room, it's easier and less uncomfortable if it's all part of a running act.

These early years were especially tough. Josephus Daniels's son, Jonathan, was studying law at Columbia. Eleanor, anxious to get Franklin back in the habit of seeing people, invited Jonathan over to dinner and suggested he bring a few of his law school classmates as well. He thought of his roommates, but they had excuses for why they couldn't make it. "Jonathan, look, I'm on the make here now," one candid roommate finally told Daniels. "And I haven't any time to spend with has-beens."

At first, Roosevelt was determined to resume his old life. After losing for vice president in 1920, FDR had joined a Baltimore-based surety bond business, the Fidelity & Deposit Company, as head of the New York office, a job that mostly meant networking with potential clients. The bank president, Van-Lear Black, was invariably friendly and understanding when FDR's visits to the office dwindled. But some other bank officials were less supportive. Roosevelt responded with anger and hurt when he learned that he was so out of the action that he had not even been invited to the annual brokers' party.

Yet at the same time, he was almost pathetically optimistic, writing to Admiral Richard E. Byrd, the polar explorer, that "by next autumn I will be ready to chase the nimble moose with you." Just as he would later experiment with many Depression remedies, he took a flier on every treatment or quack cure imaginable and corresponded with countless doctors and other "polios" about restoring muscle function. He even agreed to Howe's suggestion that he try burying his shriveled legs in hot sand at the beach.

Nothing worked. In FDR's case, there were hardly any muscles left to "restore." Two years after the onset, Dr. Draper all but gave up. "I am very much disheartened about his ultimate recovery," he wrote to another physician. But for another four years, Roosevelt made recovery his first priority, and for the rest of his life he never admitted that he would not someday walk alone.

In the mid-1920s Roosevelt still followed politics closely and he remained determined to keep his name in play. But he felt awkward and out-of-sorts. Eleanor was on his back to exercise and continue his recovery at her pace. He dreaded going to church in Hyde Park, where he was senior warden, because he felt self-conscious sitting while the congregation rose. Locking and unlocking his heavy metal braces embarrassed him. He was so reluctant to be the focus of attention that when his eldest child, Anna, was married, she was escorted down the aisle by her brother Jimmy. On the surface, FDR was still relentlessly upbeat, laughing heartily at remarks that weren't particularly humorous. But he wasn't happy in New York and finally fled.

Over Eleanor's objections to its cost, he bought a half-interest in a peeling 71-foot wreck of a houseboat he dubbed the *Larooco*. In 1925, he proceeded to run away on it with Marguerite "Missy" LeHand, the blue-eyed, prematurely graying secretary—still in her twenties—who had begun working for him during the vice-presidential campaign in 1920 and would stay at his side through most of the years of his presidency. Between cruising off the coast of Florida on the *Larooco* and visiting Warm Springs, FDR was out of New York more than half the time in the next four years, for a total of 116 weeks. He was with Eleanor for 4 of those weeks (mostly annual Thanksgiving vacations in Warm Springs), Sara for 2 and Missy LeHand for 110 out of the 116.

Eleanor became FDR's surrogate at New York political events, which proved essential in keeping his career alive; they forged a fruitful and enduring political partnership. But he found it hard to relax

around her. So Missy became "the office wife," the charming and enor-
mously efficient gatekeeper who managed Roosevelt's life and served as
his hostess, then stayed for the after-hours banter that helped him ward
off loneliness. By now, Eleanor and Franklin had worked out an
arrangement that suited them both. Because Eleanor didn't like boats
or tropical weather, she was never comfortable aboard the *Larooco*,
where Franklin and Missy were so closely quartered that they shared a
tiny bathroom. Later, in Warm Springs, Missy was the only other person who stayed in Roosevelt's cottage and she had to pass through his
bedroom to get to the bath. It is not uncommon for the bedrooms of invalids to be less than private space (Roosevelt later held staff meetings
in his), but this was strikingly close proximity for a man and woman
who were not married to each other.

Eleanor, now involved in her own circle of friends, didn't seem to
mind; she thought of Missy as an employee from a different social class
and gave no sign of believing an affair was taking place. So began a pattern in which Missy and Franklin entertained a stream of visitors with
plenty of drinking (during Prohibition), joking, and superficial conversation. They shared what Missy's friend and fellow secretary Grace
Tully called Franklin's "sense of nonsense"—a high-spiritedness that
kept FDR relaxed and energetic.

Missy clearly loved him ("Gosh it would be good to get my eyes on
you again," she wrote) and Franklin's cousin, Laura Delano (named for
their deceased aunt), once said: "Missy was the only woman Franklin
ever loved, *everyone* knew that." In fact, everyone did not. Elliott Roosevelt claimed they had a long affair because he saw her sit on his
father's lap in her nightgown on board the *Larooco*. But the older Roosevelt children, Anna and James, while more than willing to discuss
Lucy Mercer, thought there had been no affair with Missy, and the limited Franklin-Missy correspondence contains no evidence of it.

Franklin's condition did not prevent him physically from having
sex. Many polio victims, however, suffer from a psychological barrier
related to fear of performance. Hugh Gallagher, himself a polio victim
and the author of an insightful book about FDR's affliction, never knew
Roosevelt, but was "almost certain" there could not have been an affair.
His supposition is based on his understanding that "polios" are especially vulnerable to sexual "hurt and humiliation."

Perhaps so, but plenty of others afflicted with polio function well sexually. It's also evident that men who become president of the United States tend to have stronger than average libidos. Moreover, rumors of extramarital sexual contact involving presidents have generally turned out to be true, whatever the risks of exposure. Roosevelt—who clearly adored the company of women—exhibited no other performance anxieties, so why in this area?

Either way, Missy later confided how low Franklin himself had sunk in the mid-1920s. For all of the friends impressed by his mental state— "he must have been psychoanalyzed by God," said one—Missy saw another, more melancholy side. "There were days on the *Larooco* when it was noon before he could pull himself out of depression and greet his guests wearing his lighthearted facade," she told Frances Perkins. He would need something in his life to bring him back to the land of the living.

Chapter Nine

Warm Springs Dress Rehearsal

T HE PRESS IS ALWAYS KINDER to the politician who has left the arena, especially if he seems ennobled by suffering. Polio wiped the residue of Harvard snobbery off FDR's public image, just as the Rough Riders' experience had done for his cousin TR. The disease became FDR's mythological log cabin, indispensable to his rise. Without it, he would have been like Theodore Roosevelt, Jr., or his own sons James, Elliott, and Franklin Junior in later years: the bearer of a famous name and a fierce political ambition but nothing else to set him apart.

Without polio, he certainly would not have made such an impression at the 1924 Democratic Convention, which took 103 ballots to nominate its presidential candidate, John W. Davis. As he stood offstage before his entrance, FDR began sweating profusely. He asked a Democratic functionary to "go over and shake the rostrum." He knew he would have to lean on it for balance and didn't want to tumble off. Then, with one arm on his son James and the other on a crutch, he slowly made his way to the podium to nominate his fellow New Yorker, Al Smith, for president. He hadn't wanted to call Smith "the Happy Warrior"; the idea for borrowing the moniker from Wordsworth had been that of a Smith speechwriter. But Roosevelt delivered the line with gusto.

FDR's absence from the New York scene for much of the mid-1920s didn't mean he gave up on getting ahead. But the dilettante lived on. He tried writing a screenplay treatment about the life of the naval hero John Paul Jones—it was sketchy and pedestrian, though he later claimed, like every failed screenwriter, to have been ripped off by Hollywood. Aboard the *Larooco*, he embarked on an ambitious single-volume history of the world, then quit after writing only a few pages.

Like so many others in those years, Roosevelt wanted to get rich quick and took the bait on practically every dubious investment scheme that crossed his desk: variety stores in Haiti; "automats" in New York, with a primitive tape recording that allowed the vending machine to say, "Thank you" (he missed the boom in these restaurants); advertising in taxi cabs; a substitute for coffee called "Yerba Mate"; oil drilling (no luck); dirigible balloons to take passengers between New York and Chicago (no passengers); live lobsters (a business that failed when the price went down instead of up and cost FDR $26,000). He served on the boards of three different companies trying to exploit German hyperinflation and invested in one company, the Sanitary Postage Service Corporation, that was too far ahead of its time in making self-adhesive stamps.

FDR lent his name to so many schemes that the general secretary of the Society for Promoting Financial Knowledge wrote him that he was misleading people into believing these were safe investments: "It seems such a pity that a distinguished and honored name should be commercialized in such a manner." None of these plunges involved huge sums, but they were all indications of his yen to experiment, then move on without a backward glance if the effort fizzled—just as his mother noticed in boarding school. In that sense, FDR's attitudes toward both polio and business were of a piece with the governing philosophy of his presidency: Try something, and if it fails, try something else.

There was, however, one business venture and polio treatment that fell in a different category. Roosevelt's friend George Foster Peabody, the Wall Street banker who later gave his name to famous journalism awards, owned an old beaten-down resort near Bullochville, Georgia, called The Meriwether Inn, soon to be renamed for the mineral springs nearby. When Roosevelt heard that another man with polio had found the 88-degree waters of the pool restorative, he decided to visit. After a youth spent searching for European mineral waters for his ailing father, FDR was predisposed to believe the best.

From the start, Roosevelt found that the buoyancy of the steaming mineral water allowed him to swim for longer and even eventually stand unaided in the pool. It rekindled the risk taker and optimist within. Peabody finally sold the property to Roosevelt in 1926 for $195,000, nearly two thirds of the $300,000 estate (about $5 million in 2005 dollars) he inherited from his father. Eleanor was aghast; they had five children in private school. But Franklin was adamant. Sara would pay for school, he reasoned. She had plenty of money.

It was the riskiest and most pivotal decision of his life so far. He hoped to make some money, but the project was mostly a labor of love—a perfect way to channel his energies and tangled emotions. The experts had coined a term for a certain mental stage during a patient's illness: "polio progress." This was not when the patient walked again, but the moment at which he begins to concern himself with others—a priceless ingredient in any recovery. For FDR and thousands of others, that moment came at Warm Springs.

He hadn't planned on so many other "polios" making the trip, but a profile of him in the *Atlanta Journal* was syndicated in newspapers all over the country and brought six hundred inquiries, well before the resort could handle new patients. "There I was, large as life, living proof that Warm Springs had cured me of 57 ailments," Roosevelt wrote dryly in a column for the *Macon Daily Telegraph* he had begun writing. "Every human being, male or female, between Florida and Alaska who has a stomachache, a cold in the nose or a gouty toe, it would seem writes to old Dr. Roosevelt with a firm belief that I can point out to them, from personal experience, how to get cured."

Many patients simply showed up unannounced at the train station. After a doctor checked to see if they were near death (in which case the resort was not the right place), Roosevelt often administered the muscle strength tests personally. He pioneered not just a makeshift type of hydrotherapy but an early form of mind-body treatment, with great emphasis on helping patients build confidence in muscle recovery and in themselves. Most of them were well-to-do or middle-class polio victims who had been locked away in bedrooms and hospitals and arrived in Georgia suffering great guilt that they were not contributing to their families, the same sense of uselessness and hopelessness later experienced during the Depression by the unemployed.

The place was never fashionable or profitable, despite Roosevelt's efforts to maintain it as a resort for the healthy as well as the sick. No lake was dug, as planned, and the healthy guests all drifted away, even after Roosevelt built them their own pool and dining room. These guests were not the only ones under the mistaken impression that polio was still contagious after the initial fever passed. "You no doubt think me very fussy not to want the boys [FDR's sons] to go into the patients' pool," Sara wrote him in 1928, by which time she should have known better. "But quite aside from any danger to them, if they or anyone were to develop the disease after being at Warm Springs, it would give a 'black eye' to the place."

Her son was unconcerned. He was completely in his element, in ways he may never have been before. He could scoot from his car into cottages on his hands and buttocks without feeling the slightest bit self-conscious and indulge his building plans without the approval of his mother or anyone else. With the help of local workers, many of them black, he built a dance hall, a golf course, a sewage system—immersed in every detail. He led exercises in the pool with a cross section of Americans of different ages, religions, and body types—holding even the fattest or most deformed, exhorting them to do better, evaluating their progress (or more often, lack of it) in careful reports.

"Old Doctor Roosevelt," as he called himself, only half-facetiously, made no secret of his practice of medicine. "I undertook to be a doctor and physiotherapist all rolled into one," he wrote. He tried a long string of experimental medical treatments (the Lovett Method, Golthwaite Method, Hibbs Method, St. Louis Method, Chicago Method), none of which worked conclusively. But, like the alphabet agencies of the New Deal, each carried at least a measure of hope.

After serious exercise, FDR insisted on a cheerful atmosphere, full of horseplay and laughter. The physical therapists wore one-piece bathing suits instead of white uniforms; the menus for the big annual Thanksgiving banquet, which he attended religiously for the rest of his life, included "Potato Crips" and "Tibia Turnovers." He appointed himself "Vice President for Picnics" and took depressed polio victims on a drive to Dowdell's Knob for the spectacular view.

FDR sketched a plan and engaged a mechanic to attach steel rods from the steering column to the foot pedals of a used car. To push in the clutch with one hand and change gears with the other required the paraplegic driver to lean forward and hold the steering wheel steady with his torso. He roared off in his retro-fitted Model T all over Meriwether County, driving fast and recklessly, yelling "hiya neighbor" to everyone he saw.

Forty years later, the farmers he met on these drives still remembered chatting with him. It was the beginning of a lifelong effort to stay in touch with ordinary people, not just once in a while, but any chance he got. The man who had once derided rural folks as "hillbillies" now genuinely wanted to know his southern neighbors. Because he was courting southern white politicians, he did nothing to challenge the Jim Crow segregation of the Deep South (the stark racism was one of the things that made Eleanor uncomfortable at Warm Springs), but living there for so many months each year exposed FDR to rural poverty among blacks and whites much worse than anything he saw up north. His empathy deepened.

In 1926, Roosevelt requested that he be allowed to appear before the American Orthopedic Association's convention in Atlanta to describe his underwater therapy. "You're not an orthopedist. You're not even a physician—you know nothing scientifically," a doctor told him on the phone, or so he related the story. Undeterred by the prospect of being deemed a quack, Roosevelt hung up, was hoisted behind the wheel of his hand-controlled car, and set out for Atlanta, where he buttonholed physicians. They responded coolly at first, but in the months that followed, he wore them down with a steady barrage of information about patients who had come under his supervision. None was cured, but several showed some discernible improvement. Eventually he received a qualified endorsement of hydrotherapy and launched the Warm Springs Foundation.

By the time of the 1928 Democratic Convention in Houston, FDR was determined to reach the podium to nominate Smith once again, but this time without a crutch, which he thought of as the symbol of a cripple. Working with his sons Jimmy and Elliott, he developed a slow, painful way of propelling himself forward that entailed gripping a strong man with his left arm and a small cane or walking stick with his right hand. He would pretend to "walk" by rotating out one heavily braced leg, then the other, in a semicircle in front of him. In truth, he was using his shoulders and hips to shift his weight from his son (or bodyguard) to the cane and back, then hitch himself forward. For months he practiced by straining to get to the end of the long driveway in Hyde Park; it took tremendous effort that left him sweating profusely even in cool weather.

The effect on eyewitnesses was overpowering. After he "walked" this way to the podium to once again nominate Smith in 1928, the historian Will Durant, writing in the *New York World*, called FDR "Beyond comparison, the finest man that has appeared in either convention . . . pale with years of struggle against paralysis . . . a man softened, and cleansed and illumined with pain." His "rare combination of stoicism and chronic buoyancy," as his friend Louis Wehle put it, now launched him into the front rank of his party. By November 1928, he would be elected governor of New York. But throughout, Roosevelt was insistent that no wider audience see him moving painfully from one place to another, so no newsreels of the stirring moment (or the one from the 1924 convention) were ever shown or have surfaced since.*

To compensate for his withered legs, he lifted weights to build his upper body, which became so strong that the skinny young man with the fey affect now appeared barrel-chested and manly in photographs. Even so, it was hard to tell how much of the change in Roosevelt was real. The "spiritual transformation" noticed by Frances Perkins may have been an exaggeration; he was still the clever and often dissembling operator of the Navy Department years. But Perkins was not alone in thinking that he had "purged the slightly arrogant attitude."

Nearly two decades earlier, she had loathed State Senator Franklin Roosevelt as a supercilious prig, always standing in the chamber with

---

* Stephen Early, who had begun working for FDR during the 1920 campaign, was employed during this period by a newsreel company. He and Howe were no doubt influential in preventing such filming.

his small mouth pursed, nostrils distended, insisting in a remote tone: "No, no, I won't hear of it!" Young Roosevelt, Perkins remembered, was "not particularly charming, artificially serious of face, rarely smiling, with an unfortunate habit—so natural that he was unaware of it—of throwing his head up. This, combined with his pince-nez and great height gave him the appearance of looking down his nose at most people."

After polio, that habit of throwing his chin forward and head up—with the trademark cigarette holder clenched jauntily between his teeth—would have the opposite effect on people, conveying a sense of courage and hope. In the early years she knew him, Perkins had noticed that he simply walked away from bores; now, he couldn't walk away, except mentally. He had either to listen to the concerns of other people or do a good job faking it. He even learned to seem as if he enjoyed calling out the moves in a Virginia Reel, a favorite square dance of his before he was crippled and one that could have brought him no pleasure afterward.

The old "streak of vanity and insincerity" would have sunk him, Perkins surmised, because people without some humility eventually get smacked down. He learned equanimity. "If you can't use your legs and they bring you milk when you wanted orange juice, you learn to say, 'That's all right. I'll drink it,' " she recalled.

When asked about the impact of polio, Eleanor's standard answer was that without it "he would certainly have been president, but a president of a different kind"—less sensitive to those handicapped by poverty, disease, or ignorance. But he probably would not have made it to the White House. He would likely have tried too soon—in 1924 or 1928—and even by 1932, he was not particularly popular within the Democratic Party; the consensus was that he was far inferior to Al Smith as a governor—unserious and unprincipled. Had he been just another ambitious New York politician, it's unlikely he would have survived the convention. Any perceived weakness from the polio was more than made up for with what a future generation called an "X Factor"—indefinable but formidable.

"Having handled that, he probably thought there wasn't anything he couldn't deal with," Henry Morgenthau's son, Robert, who saw President Roosevelt often when young Morgenthau was a child, recalled many years later. "Once you've conquered that kind of illness, anything's possible."

That was the view of his best political advisers at the time, as well. Stephen Early, FDR's long-serving press secretary, later said that before the onset of the disease, Roosevelt was a "playboy" who preferred to play cards than do serious work. "You couldn't pin him down. He rode, he swam, he played golf, tennis, he sailed, he collected stamps, he did every damn thing under the sun a man could think of doing," Louis Howe told his secretary, Lela Stiles. "Then suddenly he was flat on his back with nothing to do but think. He began to read, he talked, gathered people around him—his thoughts expanded, his horizons expanded. He began to see the other fellow's point of view. He thought of others who were ill and afflicted or in want. He dwelt on many things which had not bothered him much before. Lying there, he grew bigger by the day."

This is no doubt overstated; a redemptive narrative always sounds impressive. Even after polio, FDR was neither especially well-read on policy issues nor conspicuously concerned about "the other fellow's point of view." And the ennobling effects of illness are more often in the eyes of the beholder.

But the proof of Roosevelt's deepened character can nonetheless be found in Warm Springs. The affliction brought out traits that would prove instrumental to the presidency: his compassion for others dealt a bad hand—for people who needed some vocational retraining or just an outstretched arm to help them back on their feet; his theatricality— the way he tuned his voice and planned his entrances and exits for maximum effect, because he could no longer dominate a room with his physical size and presence; his willingness to deceive himself, when necessary for fortitude, and others, when necessary to advance his interests and for the convenience so coveted by the handicapped; his utter distrust of expert opinion—whether in the world of medicine, economics, or foreign and military policy—which gave his mind a suppleness that brought him so frequently to the right decision; and, most inspiring, his implausible but invigorating hope, where the line between the realistic and the wishful almost didn't matter because he sold it to you either way. He had triumphed over hardship and despair and embodied that most motivating of ideas: "If I can, so can you."

While most of Roosevelt's fellow "polios" never recovered any more use of their muscles than he did, they all remained devoted to him. By bringing hope and leadership to their lives—by lifting them up—he helped these Americans feel better about themselves and their lot, however grim the reality. They rose, without ever walking again. It was a dress rehearsal for a conjuring act FDR would replicate in the years ahead, on a larger stage with a more widespread affliction.

Chapter Ten

"I've Got to Be It Myself"

T O FRANKLIN ROOSEVELT'S ADORING MOTHER, his devoted
aide, Howe, and the crucible of polio, add one more indispensable influence: a complex and ultimately poisonous relationship with
his occasional patron and rival—Al Smith. It's a sign of FDR's complicated feelings toward Smith that a picture of the two men happily shaking hands in the early days of FDR's governorship hung in Roosevelt's
bedroom at Hyde Park the day he died, and hangs there still.

Smith, who in 1932 would do everything he could to destroy Roosevelt's political career, did not feel the same. When a reporter later
asked him why their friendship went sour, he replied: "Frank Roosevelt
just threw me out of a window." That seems unfair to Roosevelt. It was
more like two men of different ages wrestling on the window ledge. The
older lunges with a snarl toward the passive-aggressive upstart, then falls.

For FDR, besting Smith was critical to his self-confidence. A decade
older, Smith represented all of the people throughout Roosevelt's life
who underestimated him, belittled his skills, and thought he was too
weak—both physically and mentally—to be president. To beat someone with such a legendary common touch boosted his faith in his own
connection to voters. It must have been privately exhilarating to move
his wrecked body from the side of the road, then pass Smith at high
speed en route to the presidency.

Frances Perkins once said that the two driving forces in Franklin Roosevelt's life were to outshine Smith and to outshine his cousin Theodore.

These motivations "were so deeply buried in his subconscious that he could hardly have been aware of them, but they were always driving elements, driving him to do things. They were partly what made him so active when there was a great deal of indolence in his nature."

Alfred Emanuel Smith's second-generation multi-ethnic Catholic background was a world away from Franklin Delano Roosevelt's. Fatherless at fourteen, young Al put food on his family's table icing fish at the Fulton Fish Market (he later joked that he had an "FFM" degree). He proved so outgoing and loud that he got a job yelling out the results of boxing matches—including Jim Corbett's famous victory over John L. Sullivan—as they clattered over the wires. He won a patronage job at twenty-one and began making his way up the ladder, a streetwise politician with backslaps and a ready "Noo Yawk" line of banter for every "poissun" who was willing to "woik."

But there was more to Smith than his street personality. Elected to the State Assembly in 1903 at age thirty, the young lawmaker developed his own unusually strong work habits, and with the help of a German immigrant legislator named Robert Wagner became a master of the legislative and administrative process. When he met FDR in Albany in 1911, he resented him immediately as a showy upstart with more money than sense. The best judges of talent in both parties agreed. By contrast, all respected Smith for his wit, force of character, and deep knowledge of politics and government.

Smith was elected governor in 1918, and served for most of the next decade as perhaps the most successful governor in the history of the state. Throughout that time, an enduring fiction developed in the press that "Al" and "Frank" were close personal friends. This was mainly peddled by FDR, who worked successfully (and with Eleanor's help) to create the impression that he was still a force in New York politics. In truth, while Franklin and Eleanor invited the Smiths to Hyde Park a few times for barbecues, the men had little more than an uneasy political partnership.

Smith was clearly the senior partner, and not just because he was governor and FDR—despite his base among upstate Democrats—an ailing political bench warmer. When Smith first ran for president in 1924, he asked Roosevelt to be chairman of his campaign, figuring that a well-known New Yorker who wasn't part of Tammany Hall was an asset. But Smith assumed that the young polio victim was just a figure-head and would let Smith aides handle everything. This set the pattern for how the Smith camp viewed Roosevelt, and FDR came to resent it.

Their relationship first deteriorated in 1924 over a New York State sinecure FDR wanted for Louis Howe. Smith's aide, Robert Moses—who was known to call Roosevelt "a pretty poor excuse for a man" and Howe "lousy Louie"—wrote to FDR that if he "wanted a secretary or valet," he would have to pay for it himself, not out of the funds of the Taconic State Park Commission, which FDR chaired. Smith backed up Moses, a decision Roosevelt never forgot.

In 1927 and 1928, Roosevelt started to complain to Smith about Moses withholding funding for the commission ("I wasn't born yester-day"). This prompted a patronizing response that captured Smith's true feelings toward FDR. First, the governor laid it on thick: "I will not get into a fight with you for anything or anybody." Then he lowered the boom: "But that does not prevent me from giving you a little tip and the tip is: Don't be so sure about things that you have not the personal handling of yourself."

Howe later argued that this condescension actually helped Roosevelt: "Smith considered Franklin a little boy who didn't know anything about politics; that left Franklin free." But if being underestimated by his rival carried advantages for Roosevelt, it must have hurt, too. Smith, with little formal education, was clearly more intelligent and knew more of the policy details of government, a reality that no amount of pride could erase from Roosevelt's mind. And for all of FDR's political skills, he was simply incapable of being one of the boys. Local politics before the era of television entailed a sense of loyalty and obligation, even honor, nurtured by a web of tribal relationships. Franklin Roosevelt didn't belong to this club.

Nor did he want to. Tammany—Smith's base—was still alien terri-tory, as it had been early in his career. Roosevelt, despite his get-rich-quick schemes, was still committed to a genteel world of under-statement at odds with the ethos of the Roaring Twenties; Smith was friends with New York's flashy mayor, Jimmy Walker, and liked to pal around with self-made businessmen. FDR didn't approve of his mother directing little snooty barbs at Smith behind his back. But he sensed that perhaps Smith and his crowd were directing a different kind of barb at him. It was snob versus reverse snob. Both men had their shoulders chipped by the other, but couldn't admit it.

The year 1928 seemed to be the peak of their partnership, but it also marked their breach. After another fine nominating speech by FDR, the Democratic Convention in Houston chose Al Smith as its candidate for president, which meant that the party needed a candidate for governor who could help carry New York for the national ticket. It was always reported that Smith handpicked Roosevelt to succeed him, and FDR believed this himself at the time. Only in the 1990s did details of a private meeting surface showing that Smith didn't want FDR to be his successor; he thought he was too weakened by polio (Smith preferred Herbert Lehman). But as the first Catholic presidential nominee, Smith was worried about losing his home state because of defections to the GOP by Protestant votes in upstate New York, a fear that proved justified. He was finally persuaded by Rockland County chairman Jim Farley and other New York State political operatives that Roosevelt—with his unusual profile as a rural New York Democrat— might help. When Smith called FDR on a scratchy telephone line to Warm Springs with the request that he run, it was Eleanor who helped close the deal.

Smith quickly rationalized the decision. When an associate, Dan Finn, asked him whether he wasn't afraid "you are raising up a rival who will some day cause you trouble?" Smith replied: "No, Dan, he won't live a year." A decade later, when finally told by Finn of Smith's remark, Roosevelt recalled that many people "believed—some honestly and some because they wanted to—that I was headed for a tombstone."

At first, FDR himself did not want to run for governor in 1928. He thought it would interrupt his polio treatment and end any hope of his walking again. Howe, too, was opposed, in part because it looked like a Republican year. "If ever a man was 'drafted' for an office, that man was 'Frank' Roosevelt in 1928," *Time* magazine later reported. The Republican press savaged him as a "cripple" and a "joke." But FDR found that he loved campaigning. "If I could campaign another six months, I could throw away my canes," he wrote Sara.

It was hardly an easy adjustment. When he learned of the absence of a ground-floor stage entrance at one speech venue, Roosevelt insisted that it would inspire too much pity for him to "walk" painstakingly up the long center aisle, with a cane and the arm of his bodyguard. So he climbed the backstage fire escape with his strong arms, moving with great difficulty up the ladder, and entered through a second-floor window. When he arrived just in time for the speech, his shirt was soaked with sweat.

On election night, 1928, Franklin and Eleanor went to bed believing he had lost. The morning newspapers would report the same. Then, just as Howe saved his career in 1912 with the 16½ inch apple barrel gambit, a newer friend, Bronx boss Ed Flynn, unveiled a brilliant bluff that spared Roosevelt's political life. Flynn knew that the longer upstate votes remained uncounted, the greater the chance for ballot-tampering. So at 2:00 a.m. he told the press that a hundred high-powered lawyers and prosecutors would be on the 8:30 a.m. train to upstate cities where Republican vote fraud was suspected. It was a total fiction, but the bluff worked. Returns started flowing in more rapidly, and as dawn neared, Roosevelt was narrowly elected governor. His mother and Frances Perkins (now helping FDR's campaign) were the only ones still at the headquarters to hear the news.

Smith, meanwhile, was crushed by Herbert Hoover. "The time hasn't come when a man can say his [rosary] beads in the White House," he said bitterly. His mood fouled, the outgoing governor apparently didn't think his successor could function in Albany. First Smith and Roosevelt squabbled over the details of the New Year's Day Inauguration, with Smith insisting that the swearing in be held indoors, where the new governor would not have to negotiate steps. The event was held outdoors, as FDR preferred, but that Smith would presume to arrange someone else's Inaugural was indicative of his attitude that he was still in charge. Then he suggested that FDR might want to spend the winter months after he was sworn in resting in Warm Springs while he continued to look after state business back in Albany. Smith went so far as to take a suite at the Hotel DeWitt Clinton nearby and even kept some clothes in the Governor's Mansion after the Roosevelts moved in just in case.*

---

* Roosevelt didn't help matters when he promised Smith he would show him an advance copy of his Budget Message and then neglected to do so.

The breaking point came over Belle Moskowitz, Smith's domineering secretary and link to his old power base. Roosevelt knew and respected Moskowitz but resisted suggestions that he retain her. Smith sent Frances Perkins—soon to be FDR's state industrial commissioner—to find out why Moskowitz had to go. When she arrived, Roosevelt looked out the window, went silent a moment, and then opened himself up to Perkins in ways he seldom would in the years to come with anyone.

> You know, I didn't feel able to make this campaign for governor, but I made it. I didn't feel that I was sufficiently recovered to undertake the duties of Governor of New York, but here I am. After Al said that to me [about appointing Moskowitz], I thought about myself and I realized that I've *got* to be Governor of the state of New York and I've got to be it *myself*. If I weren't, if I didn't want to do it myself, something would be wrong in here.

When she looked back on it, Perkins believed this moment marked a rite of passage for Roosevelt, like a younger sibling coming out from the shadow of his older brother or a protégé surpassing his mentor. The consequences of the rift would eventually be damaging to FDR's ascent to the White House, but indispensable for the independent character he showed once he arrived there.

It's tempting when analyzing a successful leader to work backwards—to assume every event in his background prefigures his performance in office. Life is always messier than such determinism, and Franklin Roosevelt's pre-presidential career is no exception.

Even so, FDR does seem to have carried a critical series of qualities into the 1930s. If he had not been preternaturally secure, he could not have convincingly conveyed such security to others. If he had not been manipulative and theatrical, he could not have won the prize in the first place, or inspired the country as president. And if his character had not been deepened by suffering, the steel within it might never have materialized in public view.

As it was, he continued to be underestimated throughout 1932 and early 1933, which played perfectly into his hands.

PART TWO

The Ascent: 1932

Chapter Eleven

"Brother, Can You Spare a Dime?"

ANYONE WHO WASN'T ALIVE at the depths of the Great Depression is at an empathetic disadvantage when considering it, like a mentally healthy person trying to imagine what it must feel like to be clinically depressed. Americans were flat on their backs, hit with something worse than job loss or poverty. They began to think this convulsive change in their lives was permanent. Fifteen percent fewer children were born in 1933 than in 1929, a reflection of severely diminished expectations. Suicide rates tripled. Almost no one dared start a business or try something new in life, except when forced by circumstance.

The job losses were unfathomable by today's standards. By 1932, unemployment had tripled in three years. More than 16 million Americans—25 percent of the workforce—found themselves without jobs, many with three or more dependents. Of the remaining 75 percent, more than a third were working only part time. That left less than half of the workforce employed full time. Because few women worked in that era (and those who did often gave up their jobs to breadwinning men), only a little more than one quarter of all able-bodied adults were fully employed, and most of them at reduced wages.

Amid our mental images of stock tickers and dust bowls, the true origins of this misery have been obscured. Few Americans owned stocks, so neither the October 1929 Crash, nor the partial recovery at the end of that year, nor the plunge in the months that followed hit most of them directly.

Soon enough, deflation reverberated through the economy and restrictive money supply, the Smoot-Hawley tariff and adherence to the gold standard proved disastrous. But the most direct cause of the problem—the disease that threw millions out of work and paralyzed the country on the eve of FDR's 1933 Inaugural—was the culture of American banking. The simple, critical fact was that the United States in the early 20th century had far too many mom-and-pop banks; an astonishing ten thousand banks eventually failed, almost all of them capitalized at well under $100,000. It was part of the American frontier ethos that every small town must have its own saloon and bank, even if it couldn't afford a general store. In Canada, where nationwide branch banking was the rule, only one bank went under during the entire period, which made that country's economic troubles much less severe.

The small American banks fell into trouble after their biggest customers—farmers—lost their markets. In the early 1920s, well before the Crash, a farm crisis developed when European countries recovered from World War I and no longer needed to import food from the United States to feed their people. By the early 1930s, demand slackened further, stretching farmers to the breaking point and imperiling the banks that lent them the money to plant their crops. With half of the American population dependent on agriculture, credit for other businesses dried up, which led to liquidation and rampant unemployment. Prices plummeted, but purchasing power fell even faster.

Of all the leading members of the American establishment at the time, President Herbert Hoover was, on paper, the best equipped for the job of fighting the Depression. He was a fertile problem solver and master of detail, with a history of calmly coping with World War I adversity. Later, Hoover organized the chaotic aviation and broadcasting industries as a powerhouse secretary of commerce under Presidents Harding and Coolidge. In 1927, Coolidge designated him to oversee relief of the flooding of the Mississippi River, which left 700,000 homeless. Secretary Hoover, "The Great Humanitarian," did such a good job (and put out so many self-congratulatory press releases) that he won the Republican nomination for president in 1928. "I am 100 percent for him," Supreme Court Justice Louis Brandeis announced. So were such hard-headed luminaries as Ida Tarbell, Robert Benchley, and Dorothy Parker.

Economic management was Hoover's specialty. He was known around the world for being unflappable, indefatigable, and extraordinarily bright. Assessing the president's brain, his secretary of state, Henry Stimson, who served every president from Theodore Roosevelt to Franklin Roosevelt, said Hoover had "the most unceasing mental energy with which I have ever come into contact." The financier Bernard Baruch, another adviser to several presidents, said, "Facts [for Hoover] are as water to a sponge . . . absorbed into every tiny interstice."

But facts don't help if they are rendered in such a monotone that nobody wants to hear them. Even Stimson said Cabinet meetings were "like sitting in a bath of ink." Hoover, described by one acquaintance as "clammy," had his greatest trouble with the presentational part of the job, just where Roosevelt would excel. While FDR knew how to say "My friends" in several different languages and appear to mean it in every tongue, Hoover could seem as if he were addressing strangers even in a roomful of friends. He talked endlessly about "confidence" but couldn't seem to exude it. Because most earlier economic collapses in American history had been labeled "panics," Hoover thought it would help to call this one something less inflammatory. In late 1929, he settled on reviving the word "depression," which immediately took on a much graver connotation.

Hoover claimed until his dying day that if he had been reelected, everything would have been fine soon enough. International negotiations and the natural recuperative powers of the economy would have restored prosperity, he wrote. But the business cycle has never been an immutable economic truth and recovery was far from inevitable. His prescription of balanced budgets, tax increases, and strict adherence to the gold standard certainly would not have brought it about.

Breaking through the gloom required an extra dimension that Hoover never possessed. As a mining executive and large-scale relief organizer, he could bark orders without worrying about the give-and-take of politics. But the presidency required supple skills that were beyond him. Years after he left office, he continued confirming the impression that he was hopelessly miscast in the job. One of the most memorable images of the Depression was of apple sellers on the street. Hoover insisted in his memoirs that this was the result of a marketing campaign by Oregon and Washington State apple growers, who shrewdly set up a new kind of distribution network to raise prices and dispose of their surpluses. Perhaps so. But when the ex-president added the falsehood that "many persons left their jobs for the more profitable one of selling apples," he reminded readers of how out of touch he was.

Hoover was not a do-nothing president. When his Treasury secretary, Andrew Mellon, told him to "leave it alone" and "purge the rottenness out of the system" by allowing the liquidation of everything in sight, he didn't go along. Instead, the president returned to what had brought him success in famine relief—people of goodwill voluntarily collaborating to solve a problem. When voluntary efforts failed, he finally responded, launching a fifteen-point plan in late 1931 to combat the Depression. "We didn't admit it at the time," Rexford Tugwell, a top FDR aide, said much later. "But practically the whole New Deal was extrapolated from programs that Hoover started." Public works, agricultural price stabilization, bank restructuring, and even a bit of federally supported relief were begun under Hoover. But the initiatives were mostly small and lightly funded, and Hoover remained largely in the grip of laissez-faire conservatism, which dictated that the federal government had no statutory role in relieving local suffering.

To humanize him, his aides put Hoover in high boots fishing near his Virginia cabin. But he posed standing in a river in a buttoned collar and tie.* Later he took a special train to Philadelphia to throw out the first ball at a baseball game. The photographers clicked away as the president posed in the stands with the ball in his outstretched arm for so long that the game began without him. Reporters later learned that Hoover had dropped the baseball into his pocket, forgotten about it, and never thrown out the first ball at all.

---

* Four decades later, President Richard Nixon would be photographed wearing wing tips on the beach. And President Jimmy Carter, who was often belittled as "Jimmy Hoover," was lampooned on vacation when his fishing boat was attacked by a "killer rabbit."

To strike a positive note, Hoover personally asked the singer Rudy Vallee for a song that would make people feel better, which he hoped might also be used in his campaign. The crooner came up with Yip Harburg and Jay Gorney's "Brother, Can You Spare a Dime?"—a melancholy tune about a panhandler that hardly conveyed what Hoover intended. The sculptor Gutzon Borglum, who carved Mount Rushmore, quipped that "if you put a rose in Hoover's hand, it would wilt."

But as the 1932 campaign began, there was no assumption on the part of the American public that a rose would blossom in the hands of Franklin Roosevelt.

Chapter Twelve

"This Doesn't Go for Above the Neck"

A S A SIGN of how underwhelming FDR looked as he began his presidential campaign, consider the reaction of the brightest and most respected commentators and writers in America.

Walter Lippmann was a few years behind Roosevelt at Harvard but miles ahead of him in influence with Woodrow Wilson during World War I. By the early 1930s, he was the most prestigious syndicated columnist of that or any other era. It was said that the American elite didn't know what to think until it read Lippmann over breakfast.

For years, Roosevelt had tried to charm Lippmann with lunches, dinners, and other invitations. It didn't work. In November 1931, the columnist wrote his friend Newton Baker that Roosevelt's record in Albany showed "that he just doesn't have a very good mind, that he never really comes to grips with a problem which has any large dimensions, and that above all the controlling element in almost every case is political advantage." He was, Lippmann concluded, "a kind of amiable boy scout."

In January 1932, he rendered his assessment in a column: "He is an amiable man with many philanthropic impulses, but he is not the dangerous enemy of anything . . . a pleasant man who, without any impor-

tant qualifications for the office, would very much like to be president."
His fellow mandarins of journalism—Herbert Bayard Swope, Arthur
Krock, and Frank Kent—all were in the "Anybody But Roosevelt"
camp, too.

As governor, FDR was viewed as a poor imitation of Al Smith, who
had set such a strong progressive course that there wasn't much for
Roosevelt to do at first, beyond building on his predecessor's initiatives
and pushing publicly owned hydroelectric power. In the summer of
1931, with the state economy sinking, he sent his industrial commissioner, Frances Perkins, to England to study that country's unemployment insurance system. When she returned, FDR fashioned a
temporary emergency relief program for New York. His gift for publicity
gave the cause of "old-age security" pensions—the forerunner to Social
Security—a boost, though the state legislature balked. In part because
a farm he bought near Warm Springs lost money even before the Crash,
he came early to farm relief. He co-opted the Republicans by forging a
consensus among state farm organizations. Whatever the combined
farm interests wanted was fine with him, an approach he would later repeat in Washington.

This Albany record didn't carry much weight with pundits. Lippmann later said he would maintain "to my dying day" that he had accurately depicted the FDR of 1932. But he never came to grips with his
underestimation of Roosevelt, who was, already, a "dangerous enemy,"
as Lippmann might have gathered from Al Smith that year, and a man
equipped by temperament and personal experience with all the important qualifications for office. His compassion and common sense cut
through the abstractions favored by Lippmann's set. ("People aren't
cattle, you know!" Roosevelt told an economist.) Most of all, Lippmann neglected FDR's political talents, which have always been a
much more central part of leadership than the columnist appreciated.
Lippmann never understood that skillful bobbing and weaving and
maneuvering—in other words, seeking political advantage—is not a li-
ability but a practical asset for success and achievement when found in
a species known, after all, as "politician."

In 1932, Lippmann's only rival in journalistic stature was H. L.
Mencken, "the Sage of Baltimore," who had won renown skewering
the folly of the 1920s. Mencken favored a home state candidate in

1932—Maryland governor Albert Ritchie, whom he respected because Ritchie never equivocated on supporting repeal of Prohibition. Mencken's objection to FDR was largely aesthetic: "Roosevelt is one of the most charming of men, but like many another charming man he leaves on the beholder the impression that he is also somewhat shallow and futile. It is hard to say precisely how that impression is produced; maybe his Christian Science smile is to blame, or the tenor overtones in his voice." He thought FDR a sure loser against Hoover, whose incumbency and reputation for competence were still seen as advantages.

Lippmann and Mencken were not so far from FDR politically; they just weren't impressed by him personally. But for many intellectuals of the period, it wasn't about FDR or any other politician. They simply thought democracy was done. In 1931, Nicholas Murray Butler, long-time president of Columbia University and recipient of that year's Nobel Peace Prize (for promoting the 1928 Kellogg-Briand Pact renouncing war), told students that totalitarian regimes brought forth "men of far greater intelligence, far stronger character and far more courage than the system of elections." Whether the common man agreed was still an open question.

In 1932, fascism was socially acceptable and even a little trendy. Mussolini was still hugely popular well beyond the Italian-American community and some of the same anti-Semitism coming out of the Nazi Party in Germany could be heard in the common rooms of great American universities. The poet T. S. Eliot gave a lecture at the University of Virginia arguing that "reasons of race and religion combine to make any large number of free thinking Jews undesirable."

On the left, 1932 marked the high point of Marxism as a fashionable intellectual movement. The novelist F. Scott Fitzgerald, hardly the picture of a commissar, noted in midsummer that "to bring on the revolution it may be necessary to work inside the Communist Party." Other Communist intellectuals that year (almost all of whom backed away by the end of the decade or became merely "pink") included Upton Sinclair, Edmund Wilson, Sherwood Anderson, Erskine Caldwell, Malcolm Cowley, Lincoln Steffens, Granville Hicks, and Clifton Fadiman. Even Will Rogers and William Allen White expressed admiration for the full-employment policies of the Soviet

Union. The urban historian Lewis Mumford, not exactly a bomb-thrower, noted that "If I vote at all it will be for the Communists, in order to express as emphatically as possible the belief that our present crisis calls for a complete and drastic reorientation."

That year, the whole idea of substantive change from the status quo sounded to many ears like more empty campaign rhetoric. The novelist John Dos Passos, also planning to vote Communist, suggested that *The New Republic* print "This Is All Bullshit" at the bottom of each page of the magazine. He thought that even joining Norman Thomas and the Socialists was a waste of time—like "drinking near beer."

FDR did not enjoy being maligned by his peers, the smart set, and intellectuals. There was no deliberate strategy to diminish his political stature so as to make a bigger splash later on. But the belittling of his abilities did give him an edge in the expectations game,* just one of the arenas of public psychology in which he was proving himself a master. He sensed that the experts—the same know-it-alls who had misdiagnosed his polio—were likely to be wrong.

Roosevelt was not supposed to run for president in 1932. Louis Howe's meticulous game plan had called for him to run for governor in 1932 and president in 1936. The reason for the longer time frame was FDR's polio. Howe developed two cardinal rules for Franklin and politics. First, he must never be carried in public or photographed as a cripple.† Of the 35,000 still images in the Roosevelt Library, only two pictures, taken for private use by his trusted cousin, Daisy Suckley, show him in a wheelchair, though he used it (built by the Hyde Park village black-smith from a simple armless kitchen chair) several times a day. Second, FDR and Howe agreed he could not run for office until he could "walk" without crutches. Propelling himself forward with a cane and the steady arm of his son or bodyguard was barely acceptable, but crutches,

---

* Like Ronald Reagan and George W. Bush, FDR thrived on being, in Bush's words, "misunderestimated."
† In the 1990s, this did not prevent the designers of the FDR Memorial on the Mall in Washington from including, under pressure from groups representing the disabled, a sculpture of Roosevelt in a wheelchair.

they felt, looked weak. Even when FDR met those requirements at the 1928 Democratic Convention, Howe still thought it too early to return to public life.

But when circumstances led to the 1928 gubernatorial campaign, then a record-setting margin in FDR's 1930 reelection (New York gubernatorial terms were two years), Howe and Roosevelt adjusted their planning. The 1930 landslide was due in part to what was dubbed FDR's "waffle iron campaign," in which he went on the radio to compare how much less a woman in Toronto with Canadian public power paid for her irons, toasters, and other appliances than did a woman in the United States, where private companies controlled the distribution of electricity. He was a hit on the "wireless" and suddenly a big national player again. (FDR's 1930 campaign also featured the first moving pictures with sound made on behalf of a politician). "The Democrats nominated their 1932 [presidential] candidate yesterday," Will Rogers reported on the day after the 1930 election, a bit prematurely. But the humorist sensed something in Roosevelt—a kindred showmanship, a winning smile—that was missed by most pundits.

The standard thinking among national reporters and politicians was that for all the grit he showed at the 1924 and 1928 conventions, FDR was unfit physically to be president and still little more than a rich dilettante, far inferior in brains and accomplishment to others in his party. Rather than brushing these objections aside, Roosevelt set about directly refuting them, one by one. In February 1931, a seemingly independent journalist named Earle Looker was engaged by the Roosevelt team to bring up the still taboo subject of his polio. It was a setup: Looker's assignment was to "challenge" FDR to prove through an independent medical examination that he was healthy enough to endure the strains of the presidency. But Roosevelt hoped to inoculate himself politically by venturing even further into the realm of private health issues that had until then been out of bounds in American politics. He expanded the inquiry, telling Looker that his probe should be broadened to his mental capacity because, in FDR's words, "paralysis is sometimes understood to either affect the brain or be caused by a brain condition."

Not surprisingly, the examination by "three of the country's leading diagnosticians" found Roosevelt in fine shape. Jim Farley, promoted from state party official to campaign manager, told the press that FDR's "lameness" was of no more significance than "a glass eye or premature baldness."* To reinforce the point, Farley soon disclosed that in 1930 an insurance company had granted FDR a $500,000 life insurance policy (with Warm Springs as the beneficiary). Eleanor, who was privately nervous about the presidential campaign because of the way it would change her own life, had no concerns about the impact on her husband's health. "If the paralysis didn't kill him," she told Looker in the payoff quote for his piece in *Liberty* magazine, "the presidency won't."

The medical exam was legitimate, but a telling little exchange between the doctors went unreported at the time. One of them, Samuel Lambert, refused at first to sign the statement confirming Roosevelt's fine health beyond the polio. As he sat peering out the window, the other physicians grew impatient.

"Come on, Sam," said one of the doctors. "Sign up and let's get through."

"All right," Lambert replied. "But remember, so far as I'm concerned this doesn't go for above the neck."

Roosevelt was not yet viewed as "a traitor to his class." Lambert had no serious reason to disdain him. He just thought the governor was a lightweight, and he represented the conventional wisdom throughout the educated public.

After his comments to Looker, Roosevelt never again discussed polio at length with the press. He had offered passing reference to it during his 1928 campaign for governor ("Well, here's the helpless, hopeless invalid my opponents have been talking about. I've made 15 speeches today"), but thereafter made a point of not mentioning the disease specifically, even when he had a clear civic obligation to do so.

For instance, in January 1932, after he delivered the big State of the State speech, he wrote to his chief counsel, Sam Rosenman: "I proposed this for the annual message and didn't use it: 'Except for the epidemic of poliomyelitis, the health of the state continued good during 1931.' " Apparently, Roosevelt's determination not to draw attention

---

* Nowadays, a disabled candidate would likely give interviews explaining how much he had struggled and "grown" from the experience.

to his condition was so great that he deleted a reference to a polio epidemic that struck New Yorkers that year. Then, perhaps feeling a bit chagrined, he privately admitted as much to Rosenman.

When *Time* magazine put FDR on the cover of its February 1, 1932, issue, he offered no comments about his affliction, leaving it to the magazine to say, "This sudden calamity he met with supreme courage and cheer. To this day no one has ever heard him admit that he could not walk. . . . Never has [sic] his crippled legs deterred him from going where he would."

Showing that polio would not damage his brain was not enough. He needed to build an organization. So even after FDR became governor, Howe continued an ingenious ritual begun in the mid-1920s. Every day, the New York newspapers would carry the names of all the buyers in various industries who were visiting town and in which Manhattan hotel they were staying. Louis made sure that many of them received by special delivery a letter from Franklin Roosevelt inviting them to come over and share their thoughts on life in their part of the country. If they had any interest in Democratic politics, the businessmen from Chicago or St. Louis or San Francisco would meet for a few minutes with FDR or, more often, Howe and a new supporter for a future presidential campaign was usually born, ready to spread the word back home. Soon Louis and Franklin's card file of supporters around the country grew thick.

Another stratagem involved Jim Farley, whose convivial "joiner" qualities had led him to become an "Exalted Ruler of the Elks." In those days, the Elks Club was a huge fraternal organization, and as an Exalted Ruler Farley had an excuse to visit Elks Lodges across the country en route to the 1931 Elks Convention in Seattle. Farley combined his fraternal duties with discreetly looking for delegates. That summer he talked with the Democratic leaders of nineteen western states in twenty-one days, passing out favors all the way. It proved to be a masterstroke, as he secured scores of commitments for FDR.

Louis Howe was an amateur poet and watercolorist; a subtle thinker and wit. But he had a one-track mind. He told the Roosevelt campaign staff: "Remember this: You're nothing. Your face means nothing. Your name means nothing. . . . I don't want to catch you or anybody else trying to crowd into a photograph. . . . All you have to worry about, night and day, day and night, is this man Roosevelt, and getting him to the White House no matter what."

Only Howe, who declined a job in Albany to work full time in New York City on winning the presidency, had the standing to talk back to FDR. A secretary once heard him say over the phone: "Franklin, you damned, idiotic fool! You can't do it, I tell you!" Then: "All right, all right, *pighead*. Go ahead if you insist. But don't say I didn't warn you." Finally, when he heard Roosevelt was going for a swim, Howe exploded a third time: "Well, go ahead, dammit, and I hope you drown!" before slamming down the phone.*

Al Smith might have felt better if he could have expressed his own frustration with Roosevelt. Instead, he let his anger twist him out of shape. It was galling to contend with someone he considered so patently inferior and underhanded. Even after all he had been through with Roosevelt, he continued to underestimate him. "[Smith] doesn't really think of him as an equal," said Colonel Edward House, Woodrow Wilson's onetime adviser, now advising FDR. It was only a short step from there to patronizing hints about Roosevelt's health.

In 1928, Smith had calmed fears about FDR's polio by noting that he was running for governor, not "acrobat." But by 1932, Smith was taking the opposite view, arguing that a presidential campaign "requires a man of great vigor and bodily strength to stand the physical strain of it." Smith had company. Everyone from his own doctors to the bosses who ran conventions thought Franklin Roosevelt wasn't up to it. For the next nine months, even after his election as president, that assessment didn't change much. They might have looked a bit more closely above the neck.

---

* After Howe's death, the only other associate who could talk so candidly to FDR was Ed Flynn, perhaps the least well-known of Roosevelt's closest advisers. It was Flynn who was responsible for convincing FDR to put Senator Harry S. Truman on the ticket for vice president in 1944.

Chapter Thirteen

"Try Something" for "the Forgotten Man"

B Y THIS TIME, Roosevelt had decided not just to campaign hard for president but to show Hoover no mercy. As the Depression deepened, FDR dictated this memo to Howe:

Here is a subject for a campaign cartoon:
Caption: Are you carrying the Hoover banner?
Below this: Picture of a man holding his trouser pockets turned inside out.
Underneath: The words "nuff said."

This suggests FDR not only had an instinct for the jugular but fancied himself competing with the legendary publicist Charlie Michelson (known as "the Ghost"), the former Hearst reporter and pioneer of yellow journalism hired by the Democratic National Committee (DNC) to castigate Hoover at every opportunity. It's often forgotten that Hoover didn't just sink under the waves of the Depression; he was drowned anew every day by Michelson.

The popularization of the folk epithets "Hoovervilles" to describe encampments of the unemployed on the outskirts of cities and

"Hoovercarts" for cars drawn by mules because the drivers could not afford gas were only two of the successful gambits of Michelson and his DNC research department. Nearly every day, Michelson issued a savage press release. Through repetition he spread the myth that Hoover said "prosperity is just around the corner" (Hoover never actually said it, though he said many similar things) and popularized a joke that the president had asked Treasury Secretary Andrew Mellon for a nickel because he wanted to call a friend. Mellon is said to have replied, "Here's a dime. Telephone both of them."

Hoover's woes helped Roosevelt, but FDR still had to execute some delicate maneuvers within his own party. At the March 1931 meeting of the DNC, Al Smith and his "wet" friends—who controlled the party apparatus—were disturbed to learn that their proposal for an unequivocal stand for repeal of Prohibition was opposed by none other than the governor of New York. He wasn't dry, but he wasn't wet either. A straddling FDR was known as a "damp," a politician favoring a compromise that dumped the issue back in the lap of the states.

This was a pivotal moment in Roosevelt's march to the 1932 nomination. The southern "drys" in the party were turning to FDR not out of any affection but as "the most effective way of killing off Smith," in the words of Tennessee senator Cordell Hull, a dry. They hoped to pull together North and South and "bury the hatchet—in Al Smith's neck."

Smith did harbor hopes of running again, and he saw FDR's temporizing on Prohibition as sleeping with the enemy. To him, it all went back to 1928 and the hate campaign against him when he ran for president. The southern and rural anti-Catholic bigots who wrecked his chances against Hoover that year were also the "drys." Anyone who decried what happened to him in 1928 should also decry Prohibition, he thought. "Why in hell don't he [Roosevelt] speak out?" Smith complained. "This ain't the time for trimming."

But FDR was focused on the relevant issues. For Smith to make legalizing booze his big concern in the Depression year 1932 was like complaining about the absence of a "Happy Hour" on board the *Titanic*. Desperate for money, Smith was throwing in his lot with the high hats, who hoped to profit off the repeal of Prohibition. The millions of newly unemployed did not seem to register with him. After returning from Albany, he had moved from First Avenue to Fifth, and not just physically. As H. L. Mencken put it, "the Al of today is no longer a politician of the first chop. His association with the rich has apparently wobbled him and changed him."*

Eventually, it showed. In April 1932, FDR gave one of his most famous and important speeches, penned by Raymond Moley, the political science professor on whom he increasingly relied. Roosevelt said that sound prosperity depends upon plans "that build from the bottom up and not the top down, that put their faith once more in the forgotten man at the bottom of the economic pyramid."

Moley had bastardized a concept originated by William Graham Sumner, a famous Yale professor in the 1880s. Sumner's original "forgotten man" was not a poor worker, but in the same family as Richard Nixon's "Silent Majority" ninety years later: solid, middle-class men of thrift and hard work who, in Sumner's words, "attend no meetings, pass no resolutions, never go to the lobby, are never mentioned in the newspapers, but just work and save and pay."

Smith, whose close ties to labor had once made him the tribune of such "forgotten" men, fired back fiercely at FDR, anticipating all of the GOP "class warfare" arguments to come: "I will take off my coat and fight to the end any candidate who persists in any demagogic appeal to the masses of the working people of this country to destroy themselves by setting class against class and rich against poor." Thus the gist of the anti–New Deal argument was developed, ironically, by FDR's onetime ally more than two years before it was taken up by Republicans.

At the time, Roosevelt responded with charming indifference. When told by the press that Smith was attacking him, he replied with a grin: "Attacking me? I haven't read the papers, not closely. . . ." After a Hearst reporter said that of course he must have heard it on the radio, FDR joked, "My radio isn't working now."

Roosevelt was showing a national audience how to deflect attacks with a bit of humor; nothing especially witty, just light and dismissive.

---

* Smith had invested heavily in the construction of the Empire State Building. When low occupancy rates nearly wiped him out, he grew dependent on John J. Raskob, the General Motors executive and "wet" conservative who changed parties and took over the chairmanship of the Democratic National Committee.

This natural skill would serve him well in the years ahead (most famously during World War II when Republicans accused him of sending a destroyer to transport his dog and he delivered a hilarious speech defending the wounded pride of "my dog Fala"). The difference between first-rate politicians and ordinary ones is often no more than their capacity to deprive a big story of oxygen, and to disarm an opponent or score on him with a quip.

Most of FDR's governorship had been taken up playing defense against the Depression. By 1932, unemployment in New York State was surging past 30 percent, up fivefold since he arrived in Albany. At first, Roosevelt had been reluctant to act, even when two large New York City banks failed, the biggest bankruptcies in history. He blamed the legislature for not passing a banking protection bill when he hadn't introduced one. Although he remained popular in New York and any governor of the Empire State was then automatically a potential presidential candidate, that tardiness hurt his reputation nationally. "Whaddya mean—'progressive'?" a midwestern editor gibed. "The guy just doesn't have any stuff."

But Roosevelt was slowly building a progressive record he would borrow from in the presidency. He expanded public works projects and workmen's compensation and pioneered unemployment insurance. It was merely a start. Combined, these programs helped fewer than one tenth of the nearly 1.5 million New Yorkers who had lost their jobs.

FDR's main innovation was to begin changing the terms of debate. Government owed a "definite obligation to prevent the starvation or the dire want" of its citizens, he said in 1931. Roosevelt was talking about state government then; he was actually well behind several other governors in calling for large-scale *federal* relief. But by 1932 FDR came around to supporting a federal role in directly helping the unemployed—a watershed in his thinking.

This notion—that Washington had a duty to fight poverty—had been considered a radical idea, until the radicals began moving further left toward overhauling the whole capitalist system. Now it increasingly went by the resurrected label "liberal," which had traditionally been used in Europe and the United States more to describe individual freedom than social obligation to the less fortunate. Those on the other side, who didn't believe government owed any such "obligation," were increasingly called "conservatives." They thought charities could handle the problem, with some coordination from above. The question of what government owed the afflicted had come into sharp relief after the Great Mississippi Flood of 1927 reverberated through the middle and southern part of the country. The failure of the feudal barons who ran Louisiana to respond more forcefully helped pave the way for a young populist firebrand named Huey Long, who was elected governor in 1928 and proclaimed "Every Man a King."

FDR hardly had the pedigree of a populist; he was more in tune with the Progressive movement embodied by Theodore Roosevelt and Woodrow Wilson. But Progressives hadn't focused much on direct government aid to the needy. So, because these issues were new to national politics, Roosevelt stayed vague. Exactly how government should fulfill its obligation to "the forgotten man" was a detail that would be worked out later. For now, FDR just wanted to establish the principle that action to help ordinary people was part of the president's job description.

In May 1932, a month before the Democratic National Convention in Chicago, four of the reporters assigned to cover his presidential campaign didn't think he was getting that message across. At a picnic with the governor and Missy LeHand at Dowdell's Knob near Warm Springs, they told him good-naturedly that his speeches so far were timid and unfocused. Roosevelt had a commencement speech coming up at Oglethorpe University in Atlanta and he threw down a challenge:

"Well, if you fellows think my speeches are so bad, why don't *you* write one for me?"

Ernest K. Lindley, then of the *New York Herald-Tribune* (later a longtime *Newsweek* columnist), replied: "All right, I will!"

The reporter's speech—which today would get him fired for unethical behavior—became what Sam Rosenman called a "watchword for the New Deal." Toward the end, Lindley wrote and Roosevelt said: "The country needs and, unless I mistake its temper, the country demands bold, persistent experimentation." And then, in wise words for every president with a thorny problem, he added, "It is common sense to take a method and try it: If it fails, admit it frankly and try another. But above all, try something."

For a politician with a reputation for being unprincipled, this was a masterstroke: flexibility as a principle! But it was a principle that, in the right hands, might change the world. In the years ahead, Roosevelt could not "admit failure frankly"—no president does. But he did come to embody the long-standing American spirit of innovation and pragmatism. For conservatives, "bold, persistent experimentation" was a generally bad idea; they believed in those days that the government tended to mess things up when it experimented or acted quickly. But the idea of trying one thing, trying another—above all, trying *something*—was central to Roosevelt's success for the rest of his life.

In that era before presidential debates, the only time President Hoover and his presumed challenger saw each other during the entire election year was at a Governors' Conference dinner held at the White House in late April 1932. There's no record of the two men conversing, but the dinner apparently loomed large in each one's impression of the other. It simultaneously fed FDR's resentment of Hoover and increased Hoover's underestimation of Roosevelt. It foreshadowed the confrontation ten months later that would paralyze the country.

When the governors arrived, the president was detained upstairs. So before Hoover came down to receive his guests, they waited and circulated in the East Room. Twice, FDR, awkwardly propped up in his metal braces, was offered a chair and twice he declined; protocol called for remaining standing until making one's way through the receiving line. The day was hot and the New York governor was perspiring heavily and in need of a seat. His legs ached. Finally, at least a half hour behind schedule, Herbert and Lou Hoover appeared.

For Eleanor, this was more than an ungracious oversight; it was a grave and intentional insult directed toward her husband, who could not stand for long in his leg braces without great pain and fatigue. (Eleanor was further annoyed that the musicians, many of great national reputation, were not asked to stay for dinner.) Franklin and Eleanor nursed this grievance for years.

There was certainly bad blood. Since the day after his smashing

1930 reelection, FDR had been the front-runner to challenge Hoover. The president felt that the governor of New York had primary responsibility for supervision of the Stock Exchange, which was located in his state, and he resented that FDR had not been held more responsible for the Crash. In Hoover's moments of self-pity, Roosevelt's social ease no doubt reminded him of all the swells at Stanford who had rejected him.

Even so, it is hard to believe that Hoover would intentionally treat a crippled man in such a cruel way; he later wrote that the very thought of it was absurd and he was probably right. Most likely, he was just careless of the time of the governors or had important business to attend to; the need to prepare for a disabled guest must have escaped everyone's attention, which was hardly unusual in those days.

And yet FDR's handicap clearly left an impression on Hoover that evening. A White House usher, Alonzo Field, vividly recalled the moment Roosevelt entered the White House dining room to sit down at last. "Dragging his legs from his hips," Field remembered, the governor "literally fell in the seat." The scene was witnessed by the Hoovers and all of the dinner guests. "Everybody said, 'That man, what is he thinkin' about?'" Field recalled. "'How is he gonna be president? He's only half man.'"

President Hoover did not appear to be greatly sympathetic. He had certainly seen FDR before he finally sat down and done nothing to ease his apparent discomfort. Hoover later told his friend James MacLafferty (who recorded it in his diary) that he noticed that when Roosevelt arrived at the White House to attend the dinner, his aides shielded him from the cameramen as he was helped from his automobile.

This raises an intriguing question. How did Hoover know this? Did the president witness the maneuver in the driveway from the window of an upstairs room where he was supposedly detained for half an hour by pressing business? Is it possible that Hoover figured that if FDR wanted to deceive the public about his disability, he would make no special effort to accomodate it at the White House?

Whatever the truth that night, it set the stage for an epic confrontation between the two men less than a year later.

Chapter Fourteen

The Brain Trust

To get to the White House, Roosevelt needed more gravitas on national issues. Despite presiding over an economic collapse, Hoover was seen as an expert and Roosevelt was not. And so FDR began the process of boning up on substance. The result was the recruitment of several of the key architects of the first Hundred Days.

The origins of the "Brain Trust" lie, strangely enough, in dime-store detective novels. In 1928, before becoming governor, Roosevelt was appointed to the National Crime Commission. His staff person, the one who did the actual work, was once again Louis Howe. Both men liked to read detective stories (later, as president, Roosevelt even launched a writing contest for a detective magazine) and they were interested in the payroll robberies often featured in such true-crime stories. There's no sign they actually knew anything more than that about such robberies, which meant that as part of FDR's commission work, they had to find someone who did.

Ray Moley was their man. An acerbic Columbia professor with piercing black eyes, Moley was too hard-boiled to be a fuzzy-headed academic—he had horse sense and real political experience to match. In 1920, he had managed a comprehensive study of crime in Cleveland, which was relevant experience for Roosevelt and Howe. He completed his report on payroll robberies for them in 1929 and resumed his teaching.

In March 1932, Moley was suddenly called back into service for his broader perspective. Sam Rosenman, the canny Jewish lawyer who had become FDR's closest adviser in Albany, told Roosevelt that he wanted to bring a few professors to the Governor's Mansion to discuss problems he would face as president. Howe, who was running the presidential campaign from New York City, loathed Rosenman for getting to spend so much time in Albany with the governor and he thought importing professors was a bad idea. FDR's first reaction was also skeptical: "Do you think these professors can be trusted not to talk about it on the outside? If it gets into the papers too soon it might be bad." Rosenman said they would just have to take their chances.

So Moley began riding the train from the city up to Albany for dinner with Roosevelt, Rosenman, and Basil O'Connor, FDR's law partner. Soon, he was recruiting other guest professors, all covering their own expenses, starting with Rexford Tugwell, a handsome Columbia colleague so dapper that he made a point of matching his blue shirt to the color of his eyes. (Later, when a newspaper during the Hundred Days distributed pictures of New Dealers and asked shop girls and female passersby which was their favorite, Tugwell won easily.)

Tugwell's expertise was agriculture, but a trip to the Soviet Union had convinced him that more state planning was in order for the entire economy. His aim was not communism but what he called "a concert of interests"—business, labor, and government playing nicely together. "Rex was like a cocktail: his conversation picked you up and made your brain race along," Moley observed.

Then came Adolf Berle, a brilliant young Columbia Law professor and expert on corporations, who had entered Harvard at fourteen and begun practicing law with Louis Brandeis at twenty-one. Still in his thirties, Berle had been one of the star lecturers at the Harvard Business School and his forthcoming book, *The Modern Corporation and Private Property,* would become so influential that it was used to teach law and business students well into the 1970s. Berle wasn't much of a loyalist—by the time of the convention he was looking for another candidate—but in the early years Roosevelt was usually glad to have Berle's brain around, even when Berle dispensed with the formalities during the Hundred Days and cheekily opened a few letters to the president with the salutation: "Dear Caesar."

FDR found some professors too stuffy or pedantic for his tastes, so after the Chicago convention, a handful of non-PhDs were admitted to the charmed circle. Hugh Johnson was a hot-tempered veteran of 1918 war mobilization efforts and a creative thinker. He often went off on week-long benders, but when he was sober, he added zest. Senators James F. Byrnes of South Carolina (future Supreme Court justice and secretary of state) and Key Pittman of Nevada (another big drinker) were included for their expertise on what was possible in Washington.

Finally, there was one Charles Taussig, president of the American Molasses Company. Other brain trusters could never explain his presence beyond pointing out that he was related to a renowned economist with whom he was often confused. Taussig, who had no college degree, became an amusing hanger-on, whose offers of help were resented by aides who saw him almost as an imposter. But FDR apparently enjoyed having "the Molasses King" around, even if he wasn't the famous economist.*

These men plus Rosenman comprised the group that FDR originally called "my Privy Council." In July 1932, James Kieran of *The New York Times* dubbed it "The Brains Trust," which was later shortened to "The Brain Trust." It wasn't a new idea; Theodore Roosevelt had consulted professors at the turn of the century. But the phrase now caught the fancy of the press.

At their dinners, Roosevelt's curiosity level was high. He undertook an "intellectual ransacking of his visitors," remembered Moley, "at once a student, a cross-examiner and a judge." For all of his charm, "when crossed, he is hard, stubborn, resourceful, relentless." The "hit or miss" skipping and bouncing through intricate subjects made the professor wince—and FDR clearly had no training in economics. But his amiability wore well. Moley wrote his sister Nell: "I used to think [this] was 'lord of the manor'—'good to the peasants'—stuff. It isn't that at all. He seems naturally warm and friendly. The stories about his illness and its effects on him are bunk. Nobody in public life since TR

---

* Taussig was an early advocate of financial transparency, particularly disclosure of stock offerings. His ideas found their way into the Securities Act of 1933.

has been so robust, so buoyantly and blatantly healthy as this fellow." Though he lacked true wit, his exuberant teasing could be fun. Sam Rosenman was "Sammy the Rose" and Morgenthau, Jr., "Henry the Morgue." In one April 1932 letter to his sister, Moley broke down the components of the Roosevelt temperament: "The man's energy and vitality are astonishing. . . . I've been amazed with his interest in things. . . . I believe that his complete freedom from dogmatism is a virtue at this stage of the game."

But what did he believe? Roosevelt understood that with the economy in shambles it wasn't smart to believe too much in anything just yet, beyond experimentation and rejection of economic shibboleths and tired palliatives on restoring confidence. "He was a progressive vessel yet to be filled with content," Tugwell wrote later. The battle for Roosevelt's mind cut about eight different directions. Was he an antitrust, small-is-beautiful, individual rights liberal like Brandeis, or a dreamy Big Government corporatist planner like Tugwell and Johnson? Was he a sound money internationalist or an inflation-happy nationalist? A free trader or a protectionist? Budget balancer or buster? At the beginning, anyway, he positioned himself as a little of each. Not surprisingly, this satisfied no one.

And yet FDR was clearly moving the Democratic Party in a new direction. In a May 19, 1932, memo, Moley explained that Al Smith's party believed that if the favored few were helped, prosperity would "leak through" to the working class (later this became "trickle down"). The Roosevelt view, Moley suggested, should be that "there is no room in this country for two reactionary parties." Whatever the policy specifics, new Democrats would be "a party of liberal thought, of planned action" on behalf of labor, farmers, and small business men. The governor's secretary of state in Albany, Ed Flynn, an educated man who was no longer just the boss of the Bronx, began a series of conversations with FDR about Pope Leo XIII's landmark 1891 encyclical, which shocked the world with its insistence on the natural rights of workers to form labor unions and receive a "just wage." Soon, FDR's speeches began to strike these more liberal notes, quite at odds with the reigning conservative orthodoxy of the Democratic Party.

Some new idea of how to respond to the Depression was slouching toward Washington to be born.

Chapter Fifteen

The Hair-Splitter

S AVING HIS PARTY AND DEMOCRATIC CAPITALISM could wait. First FDR had to save his own political skin. To do so meant exploiting every manipulative advantage, even if he looked like a duplicitous trimmer with an instinct for playing devious word games on everything from Prohibition to the League of Nations to the chairmanship of the Democratic National Convention.

Jim Farley's "Exalted Ruler" Elks trip the previous summer had been a huge success, yielding a list of 140,000 supporters offered by regional politicians with big local organizations. The southern and western delegations were coming in particularly well, reflecting Roosevelt's delegate strength through broad swaths of rural America.

But it wasn't enough. To try to seal the deal with conservative Democrats, FDR made a 180-degree turn on the League of Nations. He had practically run for vice president in 1920 on the single issue of supporting the League, but by 1932 he felt intense pressure to change his mind. When he tried to temporize behind closed doors, his bluff was called. In an open letter in all of his newspapers, William Randolph Hearst wrote: "If Mr. Roosevelt has any statement to make about his not being an internationalist he should make it to the public publicly, and not to me privately." Hearst added that FDR should get in the habit of using the word "AMERICAN" more in speeches.

Roosevelt caved, drawing a labored distinction between *economic* internationalism, which he said he favored, and *political* internationalism, which he said he opposed. The League, he noted accurately, was not the League conceived by Woodrow Wilson but instead had become a "mere meeting place" for political discussion: "I do not favor American participation."

It was hair-splitting that took him to the isolationist side of Herbert Hoover, and among those angered by it was his wife. Eleanor, who had hosted peace activists for years at Hyde Park, refused to speak to him for days. Old friends were enraged. When he asked one of them, Agnes Leach, to arrange lunch to make amends, Leach not only declined but scolded him: "That was a shabby statement! I just don't feel like having lunch with you today."

Throughout early 1932, everyone, it seemed, was angry at FDR, even as he rolled up a big lead in delegate commitments. It was no surprise when Al Smith suddenly changed his mind and decided he was available as a candidate after all. Egged on by Belle Moskowitz and his top counselor, Joseph Proskauer, who called FDR "a mucker and a liar," Smith set forth to redeem himself. Why shouldn't he get a second chance against Herbert Hoover? With the economy bad, he figured he'd win this time, though he had neither a campaign theme beyond ending Prohibition nor a base outside the urban Northeast.

But Smith maintained control of the DNC—a powerful asset. He, not FDR, had the allegiance of the New York delegation. And Smith made headway against Roosevelt in some early primaries, though in those days primaries were much less important than today. While FDR won New Hampshire, Smith crushed him in the highly publicized Massachusetts primary by a margin of 3–1, in large part because of the ineptitude of Roosevelt's local ally, James Michael Curley, the legendary Boston mayor who had already served his first stint in jail. (One of Howe's few political mistakes that year was placing so much faith in the Irish Catholic Curley as a counterweight to Smith.) Mayor Frank Hague of Jersey City, one of the most important urban bosses in the party, supported Smith and insisted that Roosevelt was by far the weakest candidate and wouldn't carry any state east of the Mississippi against Hoover.

•   •   •

The Smith strategy, "the torpedo under the prow of the Roosevelt craft," was to make sure the DNC controlled the convention with its own handpicked chairman, who could wield the gavel so as to deprive FDR of the nomination. It's hard to imagine now, but in the days of contested conventions a chairman could make or break a nominee.

Here Roosevelt double-crossed his rival in a way that would sound familiar to his New Deal critics of later years. His move was cunning, shameless, and effective.

Smith wanted one of his loyalists, Jouett Shouse, who was then running the party day to day, to serve as convention chairman. The Roosevelt forces objected and a standoff ensued for weeks. Finally, the two sides worked out a compromise: An FDR backer, Alben Barkley of Kentucky,* would be the keynote speaker (also an important function in influencing delegates) and Shouse was to become the gavel-wielding chairman. One for Frank and one for Al. Not trusting Roosevelt, the Smith camp wanted the governor's personal commitment before sealing the deal. A young party official was dispatched to call FDR in Albany and he reported back that Roosevelt would "recommend" the compromise to the delegates once the convention opened.

Or would he? This would not be the last time that someone drew the wrong conclusion from a conversation with Roosevelt. Now the wordplay began. In April, the Roosevelt camp issued a statement that the governor had "commended" the compromise, including Shouse as chairman. After pro-Roosevelt newspaper reporters started speculating that FDR might want someone else for chairman—that "commending" was not the same as endorsing—Shouse piously said he couldn't believe that was true, that someone of Governor Roosevelt's high character would never play such appalling semantic games.

But he did. Roosevelt now proved himself a champion hair-splitter. He argued that "commend" meant something different than "*re*commend." When the convention opened two months later, FDR was ready with his double cross. He announced that his choice for chair-

---

* In 1948, Barkley was elected vice president under Harry Truman.

man was Senator Thomas Walsh of Montana, an influential Roosevelt supporter who had chaired the hearings into the Teapot Dome scandal a decade earlier. The Roosevelt forces put it to a test vote and won. So a pro-Roosevelt man would wield the all-important gavel from the podium.

The key parliamentary victory carried a price. FDR was developing a reputation as a man whose word was not his bond. When the head of the Indiana delegation, Thomas Taggert, phoned Albany to chastise him for it, Roosevelt tried to explain his way out of the "commending" gambit: "Tom, I was just pinning a rose on him [Shouse]," as if he had merely complimented Shouse instead of endorsing him as chairman. Taggert, whose word meant everything to him, was so disgusted that he hung up on Roosevelt midsentence.

Roosevelt was unperturbed by all of the criticism of his manuever- ing. "Have you ever stopped to consider," he wrote a friend in 1932, "that there is a difference between ideals and the methods of obtaining them?"

Chapter Sixteen

The "Corkscrew Candidate"

A S THE 1932 DEMOCRATIC NATIONAL CONVENTION got underway in late June, Chicago, like much of the country, was sinking fast. The weary, scavenging unemployed along Michigan Avenue reminded one reporter of a bunch of flies buzzing around any passerby. The city was broke and its schoolteachers had not been paid for five months. They taught for free and paid their bills with the help of loan sharks charging 40 percent interest. Of the 1.5 million Chicagoans employed two years earlier, 700,000 were out of work.

Over on LaSalle Street, former Vice President of the United States Charles Dawes was behind closed doors negotiating furiously for an emergency loan from Washington to save the bank he owned. More than forty local banks were already shuttered and the bank runs had become so ominous that they spoiled the political plans of Chicago mayor Anton Cermak, who was skeptical of Roosevelt and looking for an alternative.

Cermak—an immigrant from Bohemia still wedded to the 1920s idea that businessmen were the true leaders of society—wanted to nominate a prominent banker, Melvin Traylor, as Illinois's "favorite son" candidate for president. But Traylor was otherwise occupied. As the convention opened, the would-be candidate was busy standing on a pedestal in the crowded lobby of the First National Bank of Chicago pleading with a surging crowd of anxious depositors not to withdraw all of their money.

Roosevelt was the front-runner, but he faced a series of obstacles: the rule requiring the vote of two thirds of all delegates for nomination (which accounted for the frequency of multiballot nominations); the lack of delegate support from his base in New York; the residue of the bitter fight over convention chairman; his reputation as unprincipled; and most of all, the undying enmity of Al Smith, whose bitterness at watching FDR surpass him now galvanized him into action. The famed financier Bernard Baruch set up a secret meeting at the Blackstone Hotel between the old 1924 rivals who now made up what they called "the Combination"—Smith and California senator William Gibbs McAdoo, a Georgia-born dry who was Woodrow Wilson's son-in-law and former Treasury secretary.* Smith told Baruch beforehand, "I don't like him [McAdoo], I don't trust him, but in this fight I would sleep with a Chinaman to win." The agenda was simple: Stop Roosevelt. Smith made no secret of the fact that he would oppose him "to the last heartbeat" in Chicago.

At the meeting, Smith told McAdoo that even though he was second to Roosevelt in delegates, he knew he couldn't be the nominee himself. All he asked was that McAdoo let him know if the California delegation was planning to shift away from the candidate it was committed to, House Speaker John Nance Garner of Texas. If Smith had a heads-up, he said, he could put together a deal for someone else to beat Roosevelt. McAdoo apparently agreed, though he later denied it.

With their candidate at home in Albany (tradition dating back a century required the presumptive nominee to stay away from his nominating convention), the Roosevelt forces stumbled. They were inexperienced on the national stage, which became clear when they tried to change the rules. When southern allies rebelled at abandoning the two-thirds requirement, FDR backed off. Trapped in another fib, he

---

* The battle between Smith and McAdoo had split the 1924 Convention. Finally, on the 103rd ballot, a compromise candidate, John W. Davis, was nominated.

had to issue a statement from Albany saying he never had any intention of changing the rules, when everyone knew he did.*

The first night of the convention went badly for Roosevelt. Smith, whose valiant 1928 campaign gave him a lock on the hearts of many delegates, received a huge ovation for his speech supporting repeal of Prohibition. ("Who do we want? We want Smith!" chanted the delegates. "What do we want? We want beer!") During the speech, an aide at the podium offered Smith a glass of water. "Drinking water is not in the plank," Smith quipped, and the crowd roared. It cheered again when the organist played "How Dry I Am."

Howe and his FDR lieutenants did not have control of the floor. The New York delegation—dominated by Smith and Tammany Hall—was so hostile to its own governor that it conspired successfully to deny Jim Farley a seat with the delegation during roll calls.† At the same time, many delegates from other parts of the country still associated FDR with Tammany Hall and the embattled mayor of New York City, Jimmy Walker, then under investigation for corruption. Once again, FDR was trapped in the squishy middle—not pro-Tammany enough for New York; not anti-Tammany enough for reformers elsewhere.

In the middle of the convention, Heywood Broun wrote a widely read column about "Feather Duster Roosevelt," a "weak-willed," "corkscrew candidate." (The columnist Elmer Davis had memorably described Roosevelt as "a man who thinks that the shortest distance between two points is not a straight line but a corkscrew.") "I still remember that column," Leon Despres, a young Chicago lawyer in attendance, recalled decades later. "Nobody could work up much enthusiasm for Roosevelt." He was, in the argot of a later age, a "flip-flopper," who had gone back and forth not just on Tammany but on the League of Nations, Prohibition, and "sound money." The notion that FDR was "a phony and a weakling" soon "permeated the convention," remembered Samuel Bledsoe, a top political reporter. He and the rest of

---

* The two-thirds rule was abandoned in 1936 in favor of a simple majority, which is the main reason that only one Democratic presidential nomination in the years since—Adlai Stevenson's in 1952—has gone more than one ballot.
† This would be akin to Karl Rove being denied a seat in the Texas delegation at the 2000 Republican Convention that nominated George W. Bush—unimaginable.

the press pack "figured that [FDR] has no strength in him and not too much ability."

His "corkscrew" quality was, in fact, anything but weak. The best candidates and presidents are usually the best politicians, and smart politics is rarely about moving directly between two points in a straight line. But the public does not like to see that calculation. This political sleight of hand—making it *seem* as if one is being direct and straightforward, while in fact zigging and zagging toward the objective—still eluded FDR, but he would master it in the early days of his presidency.

It was around half past nine on the morning of July 1 when Roosevelt's campaign staffers came staggering back from the Chicago Stadium to their headquarters at the Congress Hotel. Unshaven. Smelly clothes. Blinking uncomfortably in the hot Chicago sunlight. Delegates had just adjourned after spending all night in session, and the big news was that the "Stop Roosevelt" forces had apparently stopped Roosevelt. The New York governor, whose campaign had promised a first-ballot victory, was in deep trouble after three ballots. FDR—once again derided by Mencken and many others as the "weakest candidate" available against President Hoover in the fall—was still nearly one hundred delegates shy of the two thirds needed for nomination.

The history of political conventions argued that front-runners who cannot close the deal after two or three ballots are finished. Some compromise candidate would now emerge, perhaps Governor Ritchie of Maryland or Newton Baker of Ohio, a former secretary of war under Woodrow Wilson who had electrified the 1924 convention with a brilliant defense of the League of Nations. Baker, a committed internationalist and economic conservative in the Hoover mold, was anathema to William Randolph Hearst (who supported Garner), but he was popular with pundits and much of the party establishment. Huey Long, elected in 1930 to the Senate, had decided to stick with FDR, though he had never met him. Now the Kingfish called Roosevelt at the Executive Mansion in Albany to tell him gratuitously that he was a "gone goose."

Farley was in a black mood. "Our situation was desperate," he said later. Up in Suite 1702, Louis Howe lay gasping for breath, one hand on a telephone receiver almost constantly in touch with Albany. He had not left the hotel in a week and didn't bother to get up to greet Farley. For the all-night session, he had moved his tiny five-foot-four-inch excuse for a body from the bed to the carpeted floor near the window overlooking Michigan Avenue, hoping for a breeze, with nothing but a pillow, two electric fans, and a radio to hear the convention proceedings. His high-collar shirt, out of fashion since at least 1910, was food-stained as usual but open now. His "trousers," noticed one reporter who dropped by earlier, "were confined perilously by a carelessly buckled belt."

Howe's young secretaries thought the man they called "the little boss" might die right there in Suite 1702. They were long since accustomed to the hacking and rasping as he dragged on his Sweet Caporal cigarettes, muttering his trademark "Mein Gawd" at life's passing absurdities. But never had they seen him this bad. A visiting newspaperman set them straight: "He's come this far, half alive, and you know damned well he isn't going to die until he sees Franklin Roosevelt nominated for president."

Whatever his condition, the man was always thinking. Before the convention started, Howe rigged up an amplifier to the specially outfitted switchboard. After important delegations were escorted to Suite 1702, Roosevelt's voice would come over the makeshift speakerphone from Albany almost as if he were on the radio. ("Hello, Nebraska!") The delegates loved it.

He also solved the theme song problem. Governor Ritchie's headquarters had "Maryland, My Maryland"; Al Smith's old standard was "The Sidewalks of New York"; House Speaker Garner used "The Eyes of Texas Are Upon You." Roosevelt had nothing so far. Someone suggested "Anchors Aweigh" because of his Navy Department experience, but no one knew the words.

A woman supporter from New York wandered into FDR's Chicago headquarters and mentioned a song written by Jack Yellin and Milton Ager for the 1930 MGM movie *Chasing Rainbows* that was getting some air play that year as a cigarette ad. Howe's secretary, Lela Stiles, ran up and down Suite 1702 singing the song, snapping her fingers, until Howe, groaning, motioned her to stop, and picked up the phone to rasp to the organ player at the convention hall to play "Happy Days

Are Here Again" when Roosevelt's name was placed in nomination. The tune, soon recorded by Bing Crosby, became the number one song of 1932 and the theme song of the Democratic Party ever since. It also fit FDR perfectly. He was the first presidential candidate since his cousin Theodore to smile regularly and act as if he were enjoying himself.

But now it looked as if Howe's twenty years of preparation had been in vain. Mayor Cermak, moving to Governor Ritchie, had offered sandwiches to hundreds of the unemployed if they would pack Chicago Stadium and shout against Roosevelt. Ray Moley feared violence at the stadium when the convention reconvened. Basil O'Connor tried to be philosophical about his law partner's loss: "Well, we'll have the governorship six months more anyhow and, boy, will we make those damned Tammany fellows wish they hadn't played this game!"

Inside the suite, Farley, more than twice Howe's size, asked the others to step back while he sprawled on the carpet to whisper in Louie's ear. Howe wheezed something back. Farley got up and left the room. They had only a few hours to prevent a mass desertion of delegates that would sink Roosevelt's chances for good.

As Howe lay on the carpet of Suite 1702, he had no idea how the convention would play out. At 5:20 that afternoon Roosevelt called from Albany to speak with Newton Baker, the Ohioan whose Wilsonian pedigree conservative internationalism made him the favorite of delegates searching for a compromise candidate. FDR, working on only an hour or two of sleep, was in despair; by some accounts, the long night before had been his darkest hour since the early years of polio.

Baker, by now emerging as the new front runner, recalled that FDR told him: "The Chicago convention is in a jam and they will turn to you. I will do anything I can to bring that about if you want it." This sounded sporting, but like so many of Roosevelt's statements, it hid the truth. At the time Roosevelt told Baker this, of course, he was constantly on and off the phone with Howe, scheming long distance to bring about the nomination for himself.

Amid all of the rasping and whispering as they sprawled together on the carpet, Howe and Farley had agreed that they must now stake everything on Texas and California. Both states were committed to Garner, the Speaker of the House who had earlier in the year obtained the support of Hearst. So, with FDR's approval by phone, they let the Garner camp know that he was Roosevelt's choice for vice president. Although he quickly accepted the offer, Garner didn't particularly want the second spot on the ticket, which was far less prestigious than in later years. If elected, he would have to give up a more powerful job and he had once famously said he didn't think the vice presidency was worth "a pitcher of warm piss" anyway. When the reporter he gave the quote to decided to change "piss" to the less offensive "spit" for his family newspaper, the Texan privately called him a "pantywaist."

More relevant, naming Garner would not necessarily bring along Texas. Many Texas delegates thought Roosevelt too liberal. And while many California delegates were also committed to Garner, in large part because of the efforts of Hearst, they were also committed to following the wishes of their Senator McAdoo.

After Roosevelt failed on the third ballot in the all-night session, Chicago bookies placed the odds against FDR being nominated at 5 to 1. The only thing that might save him, it was now clear, was not cutting a deal to put Garner on the ticket but the specter of the 103 ballots at the 1924 Democratic Convention in New York. At bottom, McAdoo didn't want to be held responsible for ripping the party apart for a second time in eight years when the chances were good to regain the White House. Although Smith loathed Roosevelt more than he resented McAdoo, McAdoo didn't reciprocate. He apparently loathed Smith enough that he could easily betray the commitment made to him in Baruch's suite four days earlier. McAdoo was sixty-eight years old but still harbored hopes that a brokered convention would turn to him. Once Hearst told him by phone from his estate at San Simeon that he would not have his support, McAdoo moved to Roosevelt.

Later, everyone from Hearst to Joe Kennedy to Huey Long claimed credit for securing the nomination for Roosevelt. But McAdoo was the indispensable man. "Boys, Roosevelt is lost unless California comes over to us on the next ballot," Farley told McAdoo's associates, tears streaming down his face. No one had a clue what California would do.

At a 7:00 p.m. California caucus shortly before the convention reconvened, McAdoo wanted to endorse FDR but the delegates were reluctant to commit and the caucus turned into a shouting match. To defuse
the meeting, McAdoo won caucus approval of a four-person steering
committee, headed by him, to decide when to switch California from
Garner. McAdoo and his three handpicked appointees immediately repaired to McAdoo's hotel suite, where they secretly voted to swing the
entire delegation to FDR. This was undemocratic. If all of California's
delegates had been polled, a plurality would likely have voted to stick
with Garner on the fourth ballot.

Basil O'Connor, trying to reconstruct the chaos, later joked that "Of
the 56,000 Democrats alleged to have been in Chicago, undoubtedly
62,000 arranged the McAdoo shift." Roosevelt did promise McAdoo
he could review his Cabinet selections, but this was hardly decisive.
More likely, McAdoo simply made up his own mind, still bitter over
Smith denying him the nomination eight years earlier and worried
about the consequences of another brokered convention. Jouett
Shouse complained after the convention ended that Roosevelt would
not have been nominated without McAdoo's double cross of Smith. "If
revenge is really sweet he [McAdoo] was sucking a colossal sugar teat,"
H. L. Mencken wrote later.*

"It's a kangaroo ticket," said one Texan, referring to the perceived
weakness of Roosevelt. "Stronger in the hindquarter than in the front."
Back in Washington, Garner slept through the proceedings, not even
bothering to listen to the radio. He didn't find out until the next day
that FDR was the nominee.

That evening, the roll call for the fourth ballot began. Almost as
soon as McAdoo took the microphone, the audience knew he would
seal the nomination for FDR and a thunderous demonstration
erupted—not for Roosevelt, but against him. "I intend to say what I
propose to say without regard to what the galleries or anybody else
think," McAdoo continued, before announcing that "California casts
44 votes for Franklin D. Roosevelt!"

---

* Hearst claimed in a letter to his wife that his role in nominating FDR was decisive and
many historians believed him. But Michelson, who had once worked for Hearst and was in
close touch with his lieutenants, said otherwise. He wrote that Hearst was "much put out
about the deal." Farley also insisted that Hearst was not pivotal.

It was all over. "Good old McAdoo!" Roosevelt exulted from Albany when he heard it on the radio. Eleanor, Missy LeHand, and Grace Tully embraced. Two sons, Elliott and John Roosevelt, tossed scratch paper in the air and shook hands, as if they hadn't seen each other in years. Eleanor retreated to the kitchen to make bacon and eggs, which she graciously offered to the reporters outside.

Even as delegation after delegation now dutifully jumped on the bandwagon, the Democrats weren't confident of victory in November. With the exception of 1912, when the Republicans split, no incumbent president had been defeated since Grover Cleveland in 1888, nearly a half century earlier. "It would be hard to find a delegate who believes seriously that Roosevelt can carry New York in November, or Massachusetts, or New Jersey or even Illinois," Mencken wrote that day. "How many delegates were honestly for him, I don't know, but certainly it could not have been more than a third." Another reporter wrote that "The Democrats have nominated nobody quite like him since Franklin Pierce."

A representative of the DNC asked Al Smith to do the generous thing: go down on the floor and request that the convention make the nomination unanimous. Smith just sat there, his arms folded in front of him, saying over and over: "I won't do it. I won't do it. I won't do it."

As all of the other candidates released their delegates, Smith announced that he was "taking a walk" and left for his hotel. The next morning, before Roosevelt got to town, Jim Farley caught a glimpse of Smith on the sidewalk turning the corner, shoulders back and head erect, strolling toward the Chicago train station. Alone.

Chapter Seventeen

Off the Reservation

ELEANOR ROOSEVELT FELT ALONE THAT CONVENTION week, too, even though she was at home with her husband in Albany. She came closer to acting on her unhappiness—and blowing up FDR's career at the very moment of his greatest triumph—than any but three or four people knew at the time. Her concerns, she later admitted, were selfish. Victory in November would mean moving to Washington and giving up the exciting new life she had built. The intellectual stimulation and creative ferment she had found in New York City would be hard to reproduce in the capital.

After Franklin was stricken with polio in 1921, Eleanor had taken a strong interest in politics and kept his career alive by appearing as his surrogate at countless functions. But what she truly loved was how it helped her to meet people from outside her suffocating social set. She knew there was a teeming country out there beyond society balls and proper charities; as a young woman, she had worked in settlement houses and later, during the war, she tried to stay active with the wives of other government officials. But until the 1920s, she was still a product of that insular world. She shared the offhand racism (her servants were "darkies") and anti-Semitism (she disliked attending a "Jew Party" with Bernard Baruch) of her class. In 1919, she even opposed the constitutional amendment granting women the right to vote. But by the mid-1920s, Eleanor hoped to move beyond all of that to find the fresh and unconventional. She yearned to escape to a more fulfilling life.

Her deliverance came in the form of a whole new group of dynamic friends—early feminists with whom she could exchange ideas and confide. She joined Molly Dewson and a small corps of political pioneers to build an organization for Democratic women within New York State. (Because women were new voters, this was an important effort for the party.) She invited scores of interesting guests to Hyde Park. She and two friends, Nancy Cook and Marion Dickerman, purchased the elite Todhunter School for Girls in New York City, where Eleanor became a popular teacher of history and government.

For more than a decade, the three women were so close that they embroidered towels "EMN" (Eleanor, Marion, Nancy) for the cottage they built with FDR's help at Val-Kill, the rustic hilltop property near Hyde Park where Eleanor often retreated. Together, they launched a small business, a bustling furniture reproduction factory called Val-Kill Industries. After her miserable childhood and unsatisfying marriage, Eleanor cherished this busy and independent life as a rare interlude of happiness.

At Hyde Park, she could take refuge at Val-Kill; in New York, at the Greenwich Village apartments of her friends; and in Albany, she drew great comfort from Earl Miller, a handsome state trooper and former middleweight boxer who became her bodyguard in 1929. Miller and Eleanor bonded, in part because they were both orphans and unlucky in love. He taught her how to dive gracefully, improved her tennis (eventually building her a court at Val-Kill), and gave her a horse she rode many mornings in Albany with Miller at her side. They spent so much time playfully enjoying each other's company that rumors of an affair were inevitable. (In 1947, Miller's third wife would name Eleanor as a co-respondent in her sealed divorce petition.) Miller vehemently denied it, and there's no documentary evidence that it was true. But Eleanor was clearly upset to be leaving her most loyal protector and defender behind when she moved to Washington, where the Secret Service was responsible for protecting the first family.

In the middle of the Democratic Convention, Nancy Cook—who had accompanied Louis Howe to Chicago—received a long and deeply troubling letter from her friend Eleanor in Albany. Eleanor had confided in Cook and Dickerman many times before, even telling them in 1926 about Franklin's affair with Lucy Mercer. But in the past she had always seemed detached about her personal feelings and aware that they must be subordinated to her public duties and her allegiance to her husband. This time, she let go of her self-discipline and poured her heart out in a stream of longing and petulance.

Eleanor wrote that she considered the prospect of FDR's presidency a death sentence for her. She simply could not bear being first lady, cooped up as a prisoner in the White House with all of the awful receptions, official dinners, and other obligations of a life she loathed. The job would prevent her from being herself and pursuing her own interests and she simply would not do it. She would run away with Earl Miller (never mind that he was recently engaged and Eleanor, over her mother-in-law's objections, was planning to hold his wedding at Hyde Park). She would refuse to move. She would divorce Franklin.

Shortly after Roosevelt was nominated, Cook and Dickerman, both of whom were great admirers of FDR, rushed to Suite 1702 with the letter and showed it to Howe, who was just then dictating his own draft of FDR's acceptance speech. Howe, they knew, was almost as close to Eleanor as he was to Franklin. As he read through Eleanor's letter, his face darkened. He knew that Eleanor would calm down, that this was simply a reflection of her frustration and heightened emotional state. But he couldn't take any chances. As Dickerman told the story years later, Howe abruptly tore the letter to shreds and threw the pieces into a wastebasket.

"You are not to breathe a word of this to anyone, understand?" he told the women. "Not to *anyone.*"

In her memoirs, Eleanor made no reference to the letter, but she did acknowledge that she hadn't wanted Franklin to be president: "It was pure selfishness on my part, and I never mentioned my feelings on the subject to him." Instead, she began to work hard for the campaign, not speaking for her husband directly but organizing a women's division of the Democratic National Committee and grassroots efforts in the states. By the end of the year, she had drawn close to another woman— a talented newspaper reporter named Lorena Hickok—who would offer a release from the burdens of Eleanor's new position and a way of contributing great substance to her husband's presidency.

Chapter Eighteen

Flight to Chicago

T HE NOMINATION IN HAND, it was time for theatrics. To bring
off his act and begin to change the psychology of American politics, Roosevelt knew he needed to enter with a dramatic flourish.

By long-standing tradition, candidates before 1932 did not accept
their nominations in person at the convention even if they were present in the hall. Acceptance speeches took place during something
called a "notification ceremony" that occurred, usually in the home-
town of the nominee, seven or eight weeks after the convention ended,
a throwback to the days when traveling took forever and candidates
had to pretend to be indifferent to high office. These were elaborate political set pieces, full of bunting and overblown rhetoric, but long since
out of date. The lag-time between nomination, notification, and acceptance was, as Roosevelt later told the delegates, among the party's
"foolish traditions."

So shortly after FDR went over the top in the balloting on July 1,
Chairman Walsh read a dramatic statement telephoned in by the nominee. If the convention would stay in session, he would fly to Chicago
the following day and accept in person. The galleries, so recently
stacked against Roosevelt, went wild with excitement. This was only
five years after Charles Lindbergh first crossed the Atlantic and only a

small fraction in attendance had ever been in an airplane. No American president or presidential candidate had ever traveled in one.

The plane trip was born of necessity; there was simply no time to arrive by train. But the larger idea of jettisoning tradition was FDR's brainstorm, originally supported only by the aging Colonel House among his advisers. Roosevelt understood the "drama" and "psychology" of it as a "symbol of new, bold and direct action," Rosenman remembered. And he loved milking it. A couple of days earlier, when the Albany press learned a Ford trimotor airplane was waiting nearby, FDR teased reporters. "I'll tell you what I'm going to do," he said with a straight face. "I'm going to bicycle out to Chicago. Sam [Rosenman] will follow—on a tricycle."

Roosevelt had flown a bit during World War I but most of the rest of his traveling party had not. Grace Tully stayed up all night talking with her mother about whether to make the frightening journey (she did). Originally, the party included a total of thirteen Roosevelt family members and aides, but FDR's superstition over that number led him to bump a couple of passengers and put in a desk instead so he could work on his speech. He didn't like flying and would not do so again until the wartime Casablanca Conference in 1943; ships were his first love and train travel let him see the country and learn from it.

But he managed to nap on the rough flight, even as his son John got sick. The only one who seemed to enjoy the ride was Eleanor, who would soon fly with Amelia Earhart and try unsuccessfully to convince her husband to let her earn a pilot's license. With stops for refueling in Buffalo and Cleveland, the plane, facing stiff headwinds, arrived three hours late in Chicago.

Although many Democrats would later write to scold him for taking such a risk, Roosevelt's reception at Chicago's tiny Municipal Airport (later Midway) was so tumultuous that his hat was knocked off his head and his glasses almost dislodged by the surging crowd. The hundreds of Chicagoans who turned out felt almost like Parisians greeting Lindbergh at Le Bourget. Present at the airfield were not just Jim Farley and his crew but Louis Howe, who had apparently made a miraculous recovery and left his suite at the Congress Hotel for the first time in a week.

Howe was on a mission to "save" the acceptance speech, which, like all Roosevelt speeches, was a mishmash. Ray Moley had written a draft that was then cut and substantially rewritten in Albany by Rosenman, who had stayed up until dawn eating hot dogs and working on the speech. Roosevelt himself had tried a few drafts of an eloquent peroration amid all the phone calls to Chicago, but when the candidate finished one and read it aloud, the group around him agreed unanimously that it was terrible and he sadly tore it up.

Rosenman's final section was much better. It contained two vague words that were to stretch and expand to the point that they came to symbolize an era in American political life. The phrase "new deal" had appeared as far back as Andrew Jackson's day, when Nicholas Biddle, the president of the Bank of the United States, called for a "new bank and a New Deal." It appeared in the novels of Mark Twain (*A Connecticut Yankee at King Arthur's Court*) and Henry James (*The Princess Casamassima*) and "A New Deal for Everyone" was David Lloyd George's campaign slogan when he ran for prime minister of Great Britain in 1919. It made a splash the very week of the convention in a June 29, 1932, cover story in *The New Republic* by Stuart Chase—entitled "A New Deal for America"—a dense piece of economic analysis arguing, in a sign of the times, that technological innovation was the cause of unemployment and should be stopped altogether. In his memoirs, Rosenman does not mention the *New Republic* article.

Moley made his own claim to the phrase, noting that he had referred to some kind of "new deal" in a May memo to FDR (the words had been used in passing). Others assumed it was a melding of Woodrow Wilson's "New Freedom" and Theodore Roosevelt's "Square Deal," but Rosenman recalled no discussion of those slogans. It was just another line on a scrap of paper, he recalled, and neither the candidate nor his counsel gave it a second thought.

When the final speech draft was read over the telephone and transcribed in Chicago, Howe's loathing of Rosenman boiled over. "Mein Gawd, do I have to do everything myself?" he grunted after reading it. "I see Sam Rosenman in every paragraph of this mess." Howe—whose jealousy over Rosenman's increased role knew no bounds—stayed up all night dictating an entirely new draft, which he tried to press into Roosevelt's hand at the airport. Rosenman walked over to the open car where Roosevelt was sitting just in time to hear Howe saying, "I tell you, it's all right, Franklin. It's much better than the speech you've got now—and you can read it while you're driving down to the convention hall and get familiar with it."

"Dammit, Louie, *I'm* the nominee!" FDR snapped. But the nominee then paid his weary longtime friend the respect of starting to read. Roosevelt later enjoyed describing how he would wave his hand and tip his hat to the thousands of well-wishers lining the route to the Chicago Stadium, as he stole glances down at Howe's draft.

With delegates itching to leave town after the long delay, there was no time for Roosevelt to go to the hotel to freshen up or change clothes after the exhausting nine-hour journey. As Roosevelt waited in the wings of the Chicago Stadium while the ecstatic crowd cheered his arrival, he took the Moley-Rosenman draft from his pocket and compared it to Howe's. Then, just moments before beginning the most famous acceptance speech in the history of American politics, he removed the first page from the Moley-Rosenman draft, replaced it with Howe's first page, and made his way to the rostrum. Like so much else in Franklin Roosevelt's future, this was slapdash, cavalier—and exactly the kind of improvisation that would serve him so well when he entered the White House the following year.

The delegates remembered that in 1924, he had dramatically hobbled to the podium on a crutch to nominate Smith. In 1928, they knew, he made another memorable entrance and stole some of Smith's limelight again. Now, straight from the thrilling plane ride, as foreign to most delegates' own experience as a trip on a rocket would be today, Roosevelt cranked up the theatricality to a new level.

"The whole hall was electrified as he came in on his son's arm," recalled Mary Bain, seven decades after she was an excited twenty-year-old school teacher from De Kalb, Illinois, attending her first political convention. "People were crying and hugging each other, even if they didn't really like him, just because it was so exciting."

When Moley and Rosenman heard him begin, they were dumbfounded. What's this? Was he reading Howe's draft? Then he switched to theirs and they relaxed. Howe was content to write the top:

Let it be from now on the task of our party to break foolish traditions.

And Rosenman the famous end:

I pledge you, I pledge myself, to a new deal for the American people. Let us all here assembled constitute ourselves prophets of a new order of competence and courage. This is more than a political campaign; it is a call to arms. Give me your help, not to win votes alone, but to win in this crusade to restore America to its own people.

The next day, a cartoon by Rollin Kirby in *The New York World-Telegram* showed a destitute farmer pausing to look in the sky at Roosevelt's airplane. On the wings were the words "New Deal." Until then, the campaign had done nothing to highlight the phrase. It just stuck.

Chapter Nineteen

The Bonus Army

H ERBERT HOOVER, FOR ONE, was not impressed with the governor of New York, and he missed no chance to rip Roosevelt
privately for concealing his disability. He insisted as late as the morning
after Roosevelt's nomination that the Democrats would do anything
possible to prevent his illness from being mentioned publicly. He was
mistaken. As his confidant, Jim MacLafferty, noted in his diary of July
2, "Mr. Hoover was wrong, for it has just been announced over the
radio that Mr. Roosevelt is being helped to arise to his feet so that he
may address the convention and the whole country is now hearing as to
his physical affliction." The next morning, several Hoover aides gathered on the South Lawn to play medicine ball and confidently predict
that the country would never elect a cripple as president.

Hoover, renominated in Chicago by the GOP only a few weeks earlier (with no opposition and no discernible enthusiasm), agreed. He
later wrote in his memoirs that he thought "it was a great mistake that
his [FDR's] friends insisted upon trying to hide his infirmity, as mani-
festly it had not affected his physical or mental abilities." This was
disingenuous, given that every time he saw Roosevelt in 1932 and 1933
he commented privately to aides afterward on how unfit for office he
thought the man was on physical grounds alone.

If Hoover believed that FDR was too weak physically to be elected, he was determined to go on the offensive anyway. By the end of July, vacationing at his wilderness cabin on the Rapidan River, he began to orchestrate a negative campaign. "We've got to crack him every time he opens his mouth. Now's our chance," he told his press secretary, Ted Joslin, before dictating exactly which line of attack his allies in the Senate should take.

But the end of July turned out to mark the effective end of the Hoover presidency, though it was not described that way at the time. The eminent Kansas journalist William Allen White, a friend of Hoover, called him "the greatest innocent bystander in history." But when you are president of the United States, that won't suffice. Hoover lost control of events, most conspicuously in the case of the Bonus Expeditionary Force, better known as the "Bonus Army."

The origins of the Bonus Army lay in the early 1920s in the aftermath of World War I, when Congress—which even then liked to postpone the day of reckoning—voted a bonus certificate (based on years of service) that wasn't redeemable until 1945, by which point most of the veterans would be in their late forties or fifties. As the economy worsened in 1931, a movement grew to allow veterans to get the money immediately by borrowing against their future bonuses. Congress declined to pass such a bill, which would have cost the Treasury billions. Neither Hoover nor Roosevelt supported an immediate bonus.

In Portland, Oregon, a jobless veteran named Walter Waters decided that if bankers could lobby, so could hungry veterans. He arranged a cross-country trip with just a handful of supporters. Publicity about railroads chasing scruffy war heroes off their cars drew sympathy and swelled the ranks of Waters's "bonus army." By early June, more than eight thousand men were encamped in Washington; eventually, twenty thousand or more showed up. Most of the veterans were law-abiding. When a new version of the bonus bill lost in Congress, the marchers sang "America the Beautiful" and returned peacefully to their encampments.

Hoover made the unfortunate decision not to meet with Waters, but he did win passage of a bill providing some new benefits and transportation home for the veterans. Many remained anyway, squatting in old government buildings that were scheduled for demolition that summer. Secretary of War Patrick Hurley and others began leaking word that the demonstrators were Communists, hoping to create a pretext for a crackdown.

It came on July 28, 1932, when two veterans were killed in a skirmish with police inside one of the unoccupied buildings where bonus marchers were squatting. The situation was quickly brought under control and the police agreed there was no need for more force. So why did Hoover order out the Army that afternoon? He never offered an explanation, though it seems as if he was talked into it by Secretary Hurley. General Douglas MacArthur, Army chief of staff, thought an armed rebellion was brewing. He sent an aide to Fort Myers to fetch his uniform with the idea that the sight of him on horseback with all of his medals would intimidate the veterans into submission. It didn't. So along with his two deputies, Dwight D. Eisenhower (a reluctant participant) and George S. Patton, MacArthur led seven hundred troops across the river and routed the veterans from their squalid encampments in Anacostia, setting fire to their meager belongings. A baby died from inhaling tear gas; scores of others were injured. Offering no resistance, the veterans fled the capital.

Hoover had swallowed the reactionary argument that the veterans posed a threat to the government; in fact, only a few were Communists. Most were patriotic Americans, fired upon by the very army they had served in. They resembled the thousands of other men drifting around the country in despair. Hoover had treated them with contempt, and he would pay for it.

Roosevelt was dead set against any bonus bill. During the Democratic Convention, Huey Long had called to tell him he could sew up the nomination if he just supported it and FDR still refused, a sign that on some issues he wasn't squishy at all. Unlike many Democrats who followed him in the presidency, he was generally opposed to what came to be known in later generations as "entitlement" programs, where belonging to a particular group entitled one to benefits, whether needy or not. In his mind, Social Security was the great exception.*

---

* By 1932, the number of veterans and their dependents drawing benefits had climbed to more that 853,000. That made veterans' benefits the greatest single expenditure of the federal government by far. The following year, after Roosevelt became president, the numbers were cut nearly in half, reflecting FDR's belief that even in a Depression most veterans' benefits should go to those with combat-related disabilities.

So FDR was vulnerable to being outflanked by Hoover for the support of veterans, but on the morning after MacArthur's crackdown, he knew that he would not have to worry about that anymore. As governor, Roosevelt had developed a habit of conferring with aides from his bed after he had been served breakfast and read several newspapers. Propped up on pillows, he told Rexford Tugwell that Hoover seemed to be following MacArthur, not leading him, which made him look weak. MacArthur, he added, was one of the two most dangerous men in America, the other being Huey Long.

But most of Roosevelt's scorn that morning was reserved for the president. He said facetiously that perhaps he should apologize publicly for having suggested Hoover for the 1920 ticket. He added that Hoover was a great humanitarian who became a sort of timid Boy Scout leader (could FDR have been thinking of Lippmann defining *him* along the same lines?). Hoover had been a figure of great respect, but now, FDR told Tugwell, he was surrounding himself with guards to keep away the revolutionaries. There was nothing left inside the man but jelly.

At this point, Roosevelt unfolded the newspapers, pointed to the pictures of the troops, and told Tugwell yet again how proud he was that as governor he not once had to call out the National Guard to quell disturbances. Suppression, he said, only makes matters worse. Hoover should have talked with Waters when his group arrived at the White House, sent coffee outside, then invited a delegation of veterans indoors out of the sun for a chat. FDR's final words to Tugwell that morning were that Herbert Hoover had been a very different man during the war years, or he hadn't known him as well as he thought.

Roosevelt was storing away the lessons of Hoover's mistakes in handling the Bonus Army. He would learn them, and respond much differently when he had the chance.

Chapter Twenty

The Trial of Jimmy Walker

M OST OF THE BOSSES OF THE DEMOCRATIC PARTY, and some of FDR's own aides, did not think he should actively campaign around the country in the fall. They argued that going to California would be a political mistake.* FDR knew what they were really thinking—that he didn't have the strength for it. He told them, "There is one reason in favor of my going which has not been brought to your attention and that reason is—I want to!"

But first FDR would have to bring Al Smith back into the Democratic fold. When he ran into Smith a week after the convention at a function, a wire service reporter did the Roosevelt campaign a big favor by inventing a colorful greeting from Smith—"Hello, you old potato!"—which, though untrue, was taken as a sign of rapprochement.

By this point, Al Smith was the least of Roosevelt's problems inside New York. As governor, FDR had to contend with the Jimmy Walker case, which threatened to derail his campaign. Much ink was spilled claiming that the case would lead to Hoover's reelection. Instead, it

---

* The 1916 GOP candidate, Charles Evans Hughes, had famously lost by a whisker to Woodrow Wilson after he campaigned in California without including Progressive Republican governor Hiram Johnson in his entourage. By 1932, Johnson was still in politics, representing California in the Senate, but he posed no threat to FDR.

showed the canny judiciousness of the man who would succeed him. FDR proved he could dodge a political land mine.

Jimmy Walker had been elected mayor of New York City in 1925, a charming ribbon-cutter who enjoyed warm relations everywhere, including with a showgirl mistress whom he squired around town without embarrassment. Mayor Walker was a part-time Tin Pan Alley songwriter and full-time dandy whose all-night carousing embodied the speakeasy glamour of the 1920s in New York. He changed outfits four times a day and was impeccably dressed each time, on a budget for clothes alone that exceeded what he made double-dipping as mayor and a state senator. For a man who wore as much cologne as Walker, he still stunk of corruption. The challenge was to prove it.

In 1930, after public reports of scandal, Governor Roosevelt had commissioned an investigation not just of Walker but of the entire municipal government and Tammany Hall. Now the results of the probe were complete and the papers were full of stories about corruption. The charter of the city of New York gave the governor the power to chair a trial-like proceeding to examine the evidence and remove the mayor, at least temporarily, for cause.

Tammany had seen governors and U.S. presidents come and go without hurting its power. The real question was not what Roosevelt could do to Tammany, but the reverse. Would the cold Tammany bosses sit on their hands and let Hoover take New York? This was a genuine risk if FDR removed Walker. At the same time, if he went too easy on the mayor, the rest of the country might think him timid: his equivocating on Walker and Tammany before the Chicago convention was what helped engender that impression of FDR's weakness in the first place.

The "trial" of Jimmy Walker, the honorable Franklin D. Roosevelt presiding, opened in Albany on August 11, 1932. It was a classic showdown that spurred interest across the nation: governor versus mayor; country versus city; reform versus machine; patrician Protestant versus up-from-the-streets Catholic. Most of all, it pitted a presidential nominee with little reputation outside New York against a wise-cracking politician with a rogue's charm and a better-than-even bet to make his inquisitor look foolish.

During the three-week trial, the governor showed reporters a side they had not seen. He was tough on Walker's lawyer for his "dilatory" tactics and showed a command of legal procedure that would have surprised his old law school classmates. Of course the quasi-legal nature of the rare proceeding gave Roosevelt the liberty to make up the rules as he went along, and he did so in a commanding fashion. *The New York Times* editorialized that he had won "nothing but admiration" for his "firm but impartial" handling of the matter.

As the trial wrapped up, Roosevelt was faced with the question of what to do about Walker. "How would it be if I let the mayor off with a hell of a reprimand?" he asked the Brain Trust. Most thought that would be the smartest move. Then Roosevelt answered his own question: "No, that would be weak." The governor was vacillating. According to Ed Flynn, who talked with him frequently about Walker, FDR felt the evidence would have to be overwhelming to remove him as mayor, and it wasn't overwhelming yet.

But the mayor got spooked. "I think Roosevelt is going to remove me," Walker told a friend. "Papa [FDR] made me eat my spinach." No one knows exactly what motivated Jimmy Walker on the last weekend of August 1932. It may have been news of the death of his brother from tuberculosis. Or perhaps Al Smith's dismissive advice—"You're through"—had sunk in. In any event, he telegraphed his resignation as mayor of New York.

Even this did not set FDR free of the case. As soon as he quit, Walker launched a verbal assault on his interlocutor, comparing him to King George III for his "assertions of arbitrary power" in the "mock trial." He immediately announced that he would take the matter to the voters by becoming a candidate for reelection in a special mayoral contest scheduled for November. James Hagerty of *The New York Times* (later President Eisenhower's press secretary) wrote that a Walker candidacy meant that FDR "may lose the Presidency entirely on the Walker issue." It was an example of how something that today is widely assumed to be a foregone conclusion—an FDR victory over Hoover— was not seen that way at the time. Polling was new, which made political prognosticating mostly guesswork.

At the end of the summer, Walker sailed for Europe to be with his mistress, intending to return for the state party convention. But while he was gone, the Catholic hierarchy of New York City, scandalized by his flagrant adultery, decided that it could not countenance another Walker candidacy. Like many other politicians, Walker's fate was sealed by sex more than money.

Because Walker had quit, FDR would not look strong for slaying "the Tammany Tiger." But he would not look weak, either. New York State would be solidly behind him in November. Herbert Hoover was finished, even if he didn't know it yet.

Chapter Twenty-one

"Hang Hoover!"

Economists now agree that in the late 1920s and early 1930s the United States and other countries did the absolute worst thing to revive their economies: They raised taxes and cut spending, depressing demand even further. They did this to keep their budgets balanced and avoid devaluating their currencies. Why did they so fervently seek to avoid devaluation? Because if they devalued their currencies and used inflation to get their economies moving again, they would have to go off the holy gold standard.

It was a self-contained theology of money, made worse by the image of Weimar Germany, where inflation got so bad after the world war that people pushed wheelbarrows full of worthless cash to the grocery store. Raising taxes, erecting trade barriers, and cutting spending in a depression was the equivalent of doctors bloodletting to cure disease (or Campobello doctors telling Eleanor and Howe to massage FDR's legs after the onset of polio): They made a bad situation worse.

But like most other major political leaders, Roosevelt adhered to the old economic orthodoxies. He sensed they were inadequate but was not yet ready to repudiate them. The Democratic Party Platform called for balancing the budget and a "sound" currency, a codeword for staying on the gold standard. So when Roosevelt started campaigning in earnest, his speeches were full of bromides; no sense, he figured, in risking his advantage by saying something unsound. He made not a single speech on foreign policy during the entire campaign. More astonishing, FDR said nothing about banking, though thousands of banks had already closed.

Instead, FDR scored points with offhand remarks calling Hoover, whom he never mentioned by name, "Humpty Dumpty," or mocking his lateness in responding to the Depression. When Republicans echoed Lincoln's 1864 slogan, "Don't change horses in the middle of a stream," Democrats chanted, "Change horses—or drown!" When Democrats spread the rumor that Hoover had exploited Chinese coolies while a mining engineer in Asia thirty years before, Republicans retaliated by whispering that FDR's polio was actually venereal disease that spread to the brain, a lie they would resurrect in the years ahead when battles over the New Deal turned bitter.

For the most part, FDR kept his speeches unspecific. One exception was a speech to the Commonwealth Club of San Francisco during his western swing in late summer. Written by Adolf Berle, the substantive address had the ironic distinction of being the campaign speech that the candidate himself had the least involvement in preparing; by one account, he barely even saw it until he reached the lectern. Because FDR had no time to sand down the edges and apply his usual caution, it reflected the thinking behind the early New Deal more explicitly than anything else he said in the whole period. The Commonwealth Club speech managed to combine all that was wrong and right about FDR's worldview.

The first theme, disturbing in its implication, was that "our industrial plant is built . . . overbuilt. Our last frontier has long since been reached." With growth and exploitation of natural resources at a dead end, the goal should be "administering" existing economic arrangements not "producing more goods." Even if FDR was by nature much more optimistic than Berle's text conveyed, this popular but false premise—embedded in the mind-set of New Dealers—would have serious consequences: until World War II, the Roosevelt administration offered no growth agenda besides public works. Policies were implemented without regard for their impact on productivity; "expanding the pie" was not much a part of the discussion. This was perhaps the central conceptual flaw of the New Deal.

The second, more inspiring part of the Commonwealth Club speech was its emphasis on an updated social contract whereby "every man has a right to life; and this means that he also has a right to make a comfortable living. He may by sloth or crime decline to exercise that right; but it may not be denied him." This was a revolutionary concept, which FDR expanded on in the years ahead, culminating in his landmark "Second Bill of Rights" speech in 1944.

Americans are still debating whether health care is a "right" and other ramifications of the deep philosophical shifts that FDR launched, almost inadvertently, in 1932. At the time, the emphasis was more negative, and focused on the villains who were depriving Americans of these rights. The reason the unemployed man was not getting work and access to the American horn of plenty, Roosevelt said in San Francisco, was "the lone wolf, the unethical competitor, the reckless promoter." These businessmen claimed to oppose government's involvement in their affairs but were always quick to ask Washington for a loan or protective tariff. Even if FDR didn't see the specific language until he reached the podium in San Francisco, he knew the thrust of the speech was to lower the boom on business for the first time in twenty years. Rex Tugwell believed the Commonwealth speech marked "the dividing line" in FDR's political evolution: "It was a real shocker for those who simply assumed that free competition was no more to be questioned than home and mother."

Roosevelt was in fact the originator of what President Bill Clinton and British prime minister Tony Blair sixty-five years later called "Third Way" politics. In a lesser known speech around this time, in Columbus, Ohio, FDR said that, in one sense, Hoover was right about the importance of "the individual," but that his definition was too limited. That individual, Roosevelt said, should "have full liberty of action to make the most of himself." But the invocation of "that sacred word"—individual—should not allow "a few powerful interests" to make "industrial cannon fodder of the lives of half the population of the United States." He added that he wanted neither a business elite nor the U.S. government to manipulate the individual or betray "the sacredness of private property."

Sometimes, Roosevelt's "Third Way" instincts reached almost comical proportions. In an address in September to Sioux City, Iowa, pig farmers, FDR—perhaps recalling how he had solved the Rosenman-Howe spat in his Chicago convention acceptance speech—again pulled the stunt of merging drafts. One draft, written in part by Charles ("the Molasses King") Taussig, represented the views of Senator Cordell Hull, whose single-minded goal in politics was a 10 percent across-the-board reduction in tariffs. Roosevelt liked Hull and would make him secretary of state, but he was addressing farmers who insisted on tariff protection. So another draft, by brain truster Hugh Johnson, pandered to protectionists. When faced with the choice of which one to give, Roosevelt instructed an exasperated Moley to "weave them together."

Fudging the trade issue—as Roosevelt would continue to do for years—was probably unavoidable during the Depression, when unilateral tariff reductions would have thrown millions more out of work. Hoover, playing the protectionist card, thought he smelled blood and grimly predicted that "the grass will grow in the streets of a hundred cities, a thousand towns; the weeds will over-run the fields of millions of farmers . . . their churches and schoolhouses will decay" if FDR and his nefarious free trade policy prevailed. Faced with the Democrats' "Roosevelt or Ruin" campaign, this line of attack didn't work for Hoover. Grass was *already* growing in the streets. Democrats would mock the remark by wheeling hand mowers in the Inaugural Parade the following March.*

At Pittsburgh's Forbes Field in October, FDR bid to neutralize the old guard fiscal conservatives. He blasted Hoover for "reckless and extravagant spending" in increasing government outlays by 50 percent, and for waiting too long before raising taxes to help balance the budget. This was a pro-business speech; businessmen in those days were willing to see taxes raised to close deficits. But in a more familiar vein, they wanted spending cuts. The speech also written by Johnson, included a pledge to fulfill the "economy" plank of the Democratic platform, which called for cutting the cost of government by a full 25 percent,

---

* Hoover was more on point when he compared Roosevelt's vague views on tariffs to "the dreadful position of the chameleon on the Scotch plaid." Sixty years later, in the election of 1992, President George Bush accused his challenger, Governor Bill Clinton, of having positions on trade and other issues that could best be described as "plaid." He lost, too. In politics, plaid pays.

far beyond any cuts proposed since. To accomplish this, FDR proposed abolishing many small agencies and promised to don a green eyeshade and "eliminate from Federal budget-making all new items except such as relate to direct relief of unemployment." This would eventually rank among the most violated campaign promises of all time.

One promise Roosevelt never dared make, even in Pittsburgh, was to "restore confidence." The whole idea had been so chewed over by Hoover that the public had lost confidence in confidence-building. Prosperity was not around the corner and there was no use pretending it was. So Roosevelt's task was a more daunting one—he would have to bring back hope in a way that gave meaning to platitudes. The confidence he would build during the opening Hundred Days was not faith in a stock market surge or a spurt in the GNP but confidence in the entire American system, in the idea that capitalism and democracy deserved to survive.

By the fall, it was dawning on people that FDR's positions on specific issues—to the extent that one could discern anything coherent—were not much different from Hoover's. To the chagrin of his Brain Trust, a Roosevelt victory would mean a mandate only to end Prohibition, to experiment with some farm relief and public works programs, and to balance the budget. That was about it. All proposals to raise prices and generate purchasing power were fuzzy at best. It didn't matter. Hardly anyone was paying attention to Hoover anymore.

The president was by turns morose and manic, stumbling over words in his speeches; some drafts ballooned to more than seventy typewritten pages of his own musings. Hoover was sure that an economic recovery had been underway but was aborted by, of all things, the election results from Maine. In those days, that state followed the unusual custom of holding elections for state and local candidates in September, two months before the national elections. A solid Republican state, Maine would end up going for Hoover in November. But in September, when voters elected a Democratic governor and two Democratic senators for the first time since the Civil War, the press considered the GOP losses there a shocking omen for the incumbent.

Hoover spent the rest of his life arguing that the Maine vote caused widespread fear of Roosevelt, which in turn caused the economy to sputter once more. This was special pleading. But he was right about some fleeting signs of economic improvement in the summer of 1932. Wholesale prices did surge in the third quarter, with cotton and wheat up 20 percent and wool consumption tripling. Cotton mill capacity went from 51 percent in July to 97 percent in October. Walter Lippmann wrote in late 1933 that Hoover had "arrested" the Depression in the summer of 1932.

But no one noticed. The only political campaign many Americans could stomach that fall was comedian Eddie Cantor's satirical run for president. The cry, "We want Can-tor!", was known throughout the country, the most famous line on the radio—far better known than anything the presidential candidates said.

Hoover could only dream of being Eddie Cantor. By the end of the campaign, the president was booed and his train was pelted with eggs and tomatoes. When the presidential party pulled into Detroit, a huge crowd began rhythmically chanting: "Hang Hoover! Hang Hoover! Hang Hoover!" Although Hoover couldn't bear to visit the soup lines or shanty towns, he bristled at the idea that he was uncaring: "No more cruel thing was ever said," he protested. By the time he arrived at his home in Palo Alto on the eve of the election, his old California friends thought he looked haggard and beaten, though he seemed genuinely surprised that reliably Republican states were apparently defecting from him.

The country was unsure about the challenger right through election day and beyond. Harry Hopkins, who three years later would enter FDR's inner circle and was already working for him in Albany running a relief program, felt it necessary to reassure his brother that fall that "all this business about his health is utter nonsense," a reference to the whispering campaign that had grown during the fall campaign to include the rumor that Roosevelt was deathly ill.

On election night at New York's Biltmore Hotel, Roosevelt sat with Jim Farley and Ed Flynn going over the happy returns, throwing back his head in exultation. Howe didn't want to sit at their table. He was off to the side, looking glum. "Losers always have a big spurt at the start before they finally begin to dwindle off to defeat," he said. When a newspaperman shouted, "Roosevelt wins! And Howe!" Louis finally reached down and broke out some sherry he had put away twenty-two years earlier when the Billy Sheehan fight was underway in Albany, swearing he wouldn't open it until Roosevelt was president.

Eleanor sat crying quietly in a corner, according to her cousin, Corinne Alsop. "Now I will have no identity. I'll only be the wife of the president," she said. Later, Eleanor wrote, "The turmoil in my heart and my mind was rather great that night." By contrast, Sara told her son elatedly, "This is the greatest moment of my life."

The final tally on November 8, 1932, marked what political scientists call a "realigning election." Republicans lost 12 seats (and their majority) in the Senate and a staggering 101 seats in the House. Roosevelt thrashed Hoover by 57.4 percent to 39.7 percent, carrying forty-two out of forty-eight states and becoming the first Democratic president since Franklin Pierce in 1852 to win a majority of popular votes. The Socialist candidate, Norman Thomas, and the Communist, William Z. Foster, won only 3 percent combined: most of those who talked of voting for them ended up with Roosevelt, not because they liked him but because they loathed Hoover more. The continued faith of the trade union movement in the Democratic Party was also pivotal. Had labor created its own party, as in Europe, the American two-party system might have fragmented under the pressure of the Depression.

Roosevelt went before the press to say that "two people more than anybody else are responsible for this great victory"—Jim Farley and Louis Howe. It was true, and it reinforced a point that the brain trusters and other talented people he had drawn around him often didn't understand. First, you had to win. And even then, to succeed, you had to play politics. The ones who played the game well would win again, and bend events to their will.

Even with a big victory, FDR was—like Lincoln in late 1860—still just another politician struggling against the storm, with no place yet in the hearts of Americans. Arthur Krock of *The New York Times* wrote that the electorate was playing national grouch, restless and angry. "All informed observers agree that the country did not vote for Roosevelt; it voted against Hoover," *The New Republic* concluded.

After FDR received Hoover's congratulatory telegram, he scrawled out a standard reply that he was prepared "to cooperate with you" in the months ahead. But something about that language gave him pause, and he replaced it with more vaguely gracious words about "common purpose."

Late on Election Night, FDR let down his hair a bit as his son James helped him into bed. "You know, Jimmy, all my life I have been afraid of only one thing—fire," FDR mused. "Tonight, I think I'm afraid of something else."

"Afraid of what?" James asked.

"I'm just afraid that I may not have the strength to do the job."

Then Franklin Roosevelt said he was going to pray to God for strength and guidance and asked his son to do the same.

"Pray for me, Jimmy."

PART THREE

The Crisis: Winter 1933

Chapter Twenty-two

The Perfect Foil

HERBERT HOOVER HADN'T CAUGHT A BREAK ALL YEAR. After his defeat in November, he went to Florida for vacation and as he boarded the train at West Palm Beach to return, the band leader on the platform gave a signal and the band struck up FDR's theme song, "Happy Days Are Here Again."

Franklin Roosevelt knew show business and knew he had, in vaudeville terms, "an easy act to follow." From his November election through his March Inauguration, Roosevelt used Hoover as a foil. He let the outgoing president hang himself—and the American economy—so that he could enter stage left as a hero. It's not that FDR could have ended the impending crisis; he didn't have power yet. And he certainly didn't like to see suffering. But he understood that the lower Hoover and the country slid, the better he would look upon assuming office. This theatrical and psychological insight was essential to his conjuring act when he finally took the oath.

The cordial relationship between Roosevelt and Hoover had ended during the 1928 presidential campaign, when a close friend of Hoover, Julius Barnes, the outspoken chairman of the U.S. Chamber of Commerce, passed along to Hoover a form letter FDR had written on behalf of Al Smith. It attacked the Republicans for their "materialism," which Hoover took as a personal affront he could never forgive.*

By the end of 1932, Hoover's views about Roosevelt had hardened further. He believed the economic paralysis the country experienced that winter was the direct result of his loss to FDR. He was at least partly right. If Roosevelt's election did not by itself halt recovery, it clearly contributed to a period of drift that worsened a grim economic situation. Uncertainty over what the new president might do shook confidence. The following year, FDR's agriculture secretary, Henry Wallace, concluded in an economic report that the economy had been recovering slightly in the fall of 1932, but that the "long interval" between the election and the Inauguration "proved unsettling to business" and was an important factor in impeding recovery.

The winter of 1932–33 was the last such "long interval" between the November election and the Inauguration on March 4, the day every president since George Washington had been sworn in. It was by far the worst such "interregnum," with the possible exception of 1860–61, on the eve of the Civil War. The uncertainty was excruciating. "By March 4 next we may have anything on our hands from recovery to revolution," Berle told FDR. "The chance is about even either way."

The awful economic conditions and long wait for Roosevelt were not, contrary to popular assumption, the reason all future inaugurations were moved up to January 20. For a decade, Nebraska senator George Norris, a Progressive Republican, had tried to move a constitutional amendment through Congress that would curtail its lame duck sessions (which Norris believed were subject to domination by special interests) and shorten the presidential transitions. He finally succeeded in early 1932. But with the time necessary for ratification by the states, the new Twentieth Amendment would not be effective until the election of 1936. It would have changed history had Norris prevailed earlier.

•   •   •

---

* He also showed no sense of humor about what he considered Roosevelt's "ungracious" remarks about him at the 1929 Gridiron Dinner, when FDR used the social occasion to criticize Hoover's record in a light vein.

If a rambunctious Roosevelt had had his way, he would have broken all precedent and been sworn in immediately after his election. The day before the election, Adolf Berle told him that with a huge victory—say, 25 million votes—the public would be impatient for economic action immediately. Roosevelt thought the margin would be closer to 10 million (it turned out to be 12 million), but he offered a startling scenario for taking power right away if the majority was very large. As Berle recorded in his diary, FDR said:

> There would be instant pressure on Hoover to fire [Secretary of State Henry L.] Stimson, appoint [Roosevelt] Secretary of State; have [Vice President Charles] Curtis resign to the President and then have the President submit his own resignation, whereupon Roosevelt would become President. He [Roosevelt] indicated that he thought there might even be some possibility of this happening, though he did not consider it probable.*

This was FDR at his most manic. If there were any possibility for such a scheme, he was the only one to raise it. Hoover was focused on doing his job until the end, which meant immersion in every policy issue. There's no sign he ever learned of Roosevelt's fanciful contingency, which he would have greeted with contempt.

The biggest issue of the moment was not unemployment surging past 20 percent but European debt repayment. Hoover was more of an internationalist than FDR. His inclination—attacked by Roosevelt—was to attribute the Depression to foreign causes. He argued, with some merit, that his June 1931 one-year moratorium on European debt repayment to the United States had averted economic destruction in Europe. But now the moratorium had expired and the payments—mostly to cover loans during World War I—were coming due. Two days after the election, Great Britain and France dropped what the press called a "bombshell," telling Washington that they wanted to renegotiate their debt and miss a key December 15 payment.

---

* In this far-fetched scenario, FDR forgot to mention that Garner, as House Speaker and second in line to the presidency, would have to resign, too, as well as the third in line, George H. Moses, president pro tempore of the U.S. Senate.

They weren't the only ones who felt no moral urgency to pay; most Europeans figured the United States had got off easy losing mostly money—not a whole generation of young men—in the war. These countries hadn't received full war reparations from Germany, which was in economic crisis and about to elect Adolf Hitler chancellor. So why should they repay the United States? Besides, their economies could not afford it. With public opinion in the United States overwhelmingly in favor of immediate repayment, the whole mess was Topic A in Washington and other world capitals.

To address it, Hoover cut short his post-election vacation and took the unusual step of requesting a meeting with his successor. Roosevelt thought all the talk about the foreign causes of the Depression was just blame-shifting and excuse-making. He wanted to focus on recovery at home and he wasn't going to let himself be drawn into agreements that could tie his hands for years. He was also suspicious of a trap—that Hoover was trying to embarrass him either by making him a party to his solutions, or by saying that Roosevelt had not done enough to stem the Depression. But he knew he must accept Hoover's invitation to this rare meeting of a president and a president-elect to the White House prior to Inauguration Day.

FDR asked Moley to accompany him to the November 22 meeting, and as they made their way through the streets of Washington, Moley was surprised to see soldiers everywhere. Did Hoover fear civil unrest? Inside the White House Red Room, the Republicans chomped on cigars while the Democrats smoked cigarettes; both drank Orangeade. Roosevelt tried to break the ice by twitting outgoing Treasury Secretary Ogden Mills, who had led the attack against his fellow Harvard man during the 1932 campaign. "The only thing I objected to in the campaign was when the Republican National Committee printed a picture of your private golf course and said it was mine," FDR said in his jocular way. Mills replied coolly that the golf course wasn't his, but belonged to a private club where he rarely played. The two men completed their small talk through gritted teeth.

Hoover didn't bother with banter. It was as if he and Roosevelt had never been friends during the war, had never corresponded, had never even met. The president spoke for an hour with scarcely any interruption, brilliantly explaining the complexities of international finance.

He could not bring himself to look at Roosevelt. When he wasn't staring at the Great Seal of the United States woven into the rug, he focused on Moley, whom he believed would influence the president-elect.

FDR, who knew little of the subject at hand, asked a few rudimentary questions jotted down on index cards.* Per earlier arrangement, Moley suggested that after insisting jointly on Britain's December 15 payment, the whole thing should be handled by normal diplomatic relations. Mills and Hoover were annoyed. They wanted the revival of a debt commission (Hoover loved appointing commissions for any problem), which would have led to renegotiating the amount owed. And they were "astonished" that FDR had not consulted Democratic members of Congress. The meeting adjourned amid strained conversation.

Afterwards, Hoover was dejected. He jotted down a memo of his impressions that characterized FDR as "amiable, pleasant, anxious to be of service [but] very badly informed." To his aides, he was even more scathing. "[The President] was shocked by his physical condition," Ted Joslin reported to his diary that evening. "He believes he is both physically and mentally unable to discharge the duties of the office he must so soon assume. He is surely disturbed more than I have ever seen him about anything."

The next day, FDR gave Hoover more cause for frustration. Moley, Bernard Baruch, and Charlie Michelson drafted a public statement for Roosevelt rejecting a commission and saying, in essence, that the whole debt repayment issue was up to the lame duck president and the lame duck Congress. Roosevelt later reinforced the point by telling reporters off the cuff, "It's not my baby."

This went over terribly in the press, where it crystallized the perception that the flip side of FDR's charm was irresponsibility. But the hands-off posture was critical to establishing a climate of hope when Roosevelt assumed office. Discerning aides were beginning to notice that it was not lassitude but calculation that led FDR to hold back. His political instincts told him that if he were enlisted by Hoover in No-

---

* On subjects where he was better informed, FDR did not use index cards, though Ronald Reagan famously did.

vember, he would not be able to break sharply from the past the following March.

The standoffishness also signaled that FDR would not play the internationalist. By saying that the debts would not be renegotiated (at least
not right away), he was pulling himself out of European power politics
and giving the early days of his administration an isolationist hue. A
more active American engagement with Europe in 1933 and 1934
might have told Hitler that he was being watched closely. As it was,
Roosevelt telegraphed early and often that his primary emphasis was
domestic. This vacuum was filled by accommodating European powers:
much of the internationalist engagement within Europe in this period
amounted to an early form of appeasement. The agreement by Great
Britain and France to cut German reparations would soon embolden
the Nazis to view them as paper tigers.

Whatever the long-term policy consequences, the personal relationship between Hoover and Roosevelt was now moving from bad to
worse. Usually outgoing and incoming presidents battle fiercely in the
campaign, then are polite during the transition. Not this time. Hoover
was determined to play pin-some-blame on the Democratic donkey;
Roosevelt wanted to make sure that the people remembered that it was
Republicans who had forgotten their interests. If this meant sitting by
idly while the economy sunk lower, FDR could live with that.

For an engineer who was supposed to be open to practical and flexible solutions, Hoover was beginning to seem surprisingly rigid. He worried that Roosevelt was unsound on the question of sound money. So
on December 17, he sent him a long telegram urging that they jointly
appoint delegates to the June 1933 World Economic Conference in
London, which by this time was a much-ballyhooed event that was expected to cure the global Depression and bring peace on earth in one
sweet package.

FDR was now ticked off. He figured that if he and Hoover began appointing delegates to the conference jointly, the world would assume
that the New Deal represented a continuation of Hoover's policies and
that he might even be locked into naming some of the delegates to his
Cabinet. The whole thing would look almost like a coalition government, which was the opposite of what Roosevelt wanted to convey. He
sent a cool, noncommittal response.

Rex Tugwell wrote in his diary that "the formal set up of government structure will, I imagine, never mean very much to Roosevelt. It means almost everything to Hoover." Even then, Tugwell understood that all of the New Deal commissions, agencies, and programs to come were just means to an end and of little importance to Roosevelt on their own.

The Hoover forces now believed that FDR was trying to sabotage their efforts to stabilize the world economy. Stimson called FDR's reply to Hoover's proposal "laughable and lamentable" in his diary. Hoover went even further. On December 22, in a petulant act, he released their correspondence to the press, with the comment: "Governor Roosevelt considers that it is undesirable for him to accede to my suggestions for cooperative action on the foreign proposals outlined in my recent message to Congress."

That round went to Hoover. Suddenly, Roosevelt was on the defensive, looking to the world as if he didn't want to cooperate to ease the Depression. He quickly told the press that he had offered to consult with Hoover freely between Christmas and March 4. He used his Harvard Law School contact, Felix Frankfurter, to invite their mutual friend Stimson to Hyde Park to "settle this damn thing that nobody else seems able to do." Stimson was eager to try to mediate between the two men, but Hoover was adamantly opposed. "My instructions to him were that he should have no communication at all with Governor Roosevelt," the president recorded in a private memo for the files.

But FDR knew how to get around that. On January 4 of the new year, he called Hoover. By now, the White House so mistrusted FDR that all contact with him, including phone conversations, was handled with a stenographer on the line. Roosevelt surprised Hoover by telling him that he wanted to come to Washington again to discuss ways to cooperate. Hoover, who had just finished railing to aides that any further contact with the man was pointless, quickly caved to the breezy charm and agreed. After hanging up, certain that Roosevelt aides had circulated negative impressions after their November 22 meeting, Hoover told Joslin bitterly: "I suppose he [FDR] will tell the press I called him up and invited him to come here."

With another Hoover-Roosevelt conference now scheduled for late January, the president could no longer prevent Stimson from having a preliminary meeting with FDR at Hyde Park. The Groton and An-

dover men got along well, spending six and a half hours alone, including the drive back down to New York City. FDR respected Stimson and
seven years later would bring him into his Cabinet as secretary of war.
Before this meeting, Stimson did not reciprocate the esteem, reflecting
the conventional wisdom in his circle. But now the outgoing secretary
of state found that despite having "strange advisers" and a "slapdash"
way of doing business, the president-elect was "quick and friendly."

The next day, FDR met secretly in New York with the French ambassador to assure him everything would work out. Deftly deploying his
knowledge of history, Roosevelt suggested that the French pay some of
the principal but not the interest on the loan, just as the Americans repaid the French for money lent to fight the Revolutionary War.

The Brain Trust felt FDR had been conned by Stimson. Moley described the Christmas holidays as "the most difficult period of my whole
association with Roosevelt." Both he and Tugwell believed that the
boss was going squishy on what they considered the central promise of
the 1932 campaign—to give priority to domestic recovery. How would
debt-ridden American farmers, small businessmen, and strapped families react to the "grand gesture" of reducing the debt of Europeans? Not
well, Moley reasoned. "For a time it was very doubtful whether we were
to have a New Deal or a continuation of the policies that had so sig-
nally failed in the Hoover years," Moley later wrote.

They needn't have worried. Roosevelt was just being Roosevelt—
appearing agreeable, calibrating his policy to fit the politics, finding cir-
cuitous means to achieve his broader objective. In this case, his goal
was to appear cooperative with Hoover without actually being so.

The second Hoover-Roosevelt White House meeting came on January 20 (which, had George Norris's constitutional amendment prevailed earlier, would have been Inauguration day). When FDR allowed
an ambitious diplomat, Norman H. Davis, to horn in on that meeting,
Moley could barely contain his rage. Instead of thinking about his turf,
he would have done better to take it as a sign that Roosevelt enjoyed
(and benefited from) playing aides off against each other: He knew that
Davis's presence would toss a bone to internationalists.

Hoover had decided that Roosevelt was beyond the pale. On the eve
of the January 20 meeting, photographers assigned to the White House
demanded that they get a chance to take pictures of the group in atten-

dance. When Joslin told the president that he had denied the request, Hoover replied: "That's right. I never will be photographed with him [FDR]. I have too much respect for myself."

The meeting took place again in the Red Room and not much was accomplished except to reinforce the disdain each side felt for the other. As they wrangled over debt relief, Stimson fumed. He thought he had prior agreement for a wide-ranging approach to the international crisis and that Roosevelt had become "rather wobbly again." Like Moley, Stimson still didn't fully appreciate the casual craftiness of the president-elect. Hoover stayed tactful and aloof, according to Stimson, because of rumors "about Roosevelt's personal dislike for him." Stimson was contemptuous of Roosevelt's failure to comprehend the subtleties of how to get the upper hand with the British on debt re-payment. He felt that Hoover's mastery of the complexities made FDR look like "a peanut." Such views had become commonplace among the financial elite of the country. Tommy Corcoran, a young Harvard-educated lawyer working for the Reconstruction Finance Corporation, was "angry and dismayed" that FDR would not join with Hoover to sta-bilize the economy. "Roosevelt seemed a villainous fool to me."

Hoover, for his part, was getting a bit cocky for a man who had just lost his job in a landslide. He figured that perhaps Congress could force Roosevelt to bend, so he convinced his main ally in the Senate, Repub-lican David A. Reed of Pennsylvania, to rip into the president-elect on the Senate floor. "I'll have my way with Roosevelt yet," Hoover told Joslin.

Chapter Twenty-three

Under the Mattress

ONE DAY THAT WINTER, Hoover's predecessor, Calvin Coolidge, came upon his old law partner sitting at his desk with his head in his hands. The man was financially ruined. "In other periods of depression it has always been possible to see some things which were solid and upon which you could base hope," the former president said ruefully. "But as I look about me I see nothing to give ground for such hope— nothing of man." By the first week of January, Coolidge—symbol of the lost prosperity—was dead.

Early 1933 was the nadir, though Americans had good reason to believe the economy could go lower still. At the beginning of the new year, thirty-six out of forty key indicators of economic activity hit their lowest point for the whole eleven years of the Depression. Stock prices were down 75 percent from 1929. National income was down more than half. Exports were down to their lowest levels since 1904, when the United States was not a global power. More than 600,000 properties—mostly American farms—were now foreclosed.

Revolution was in the air. One Chicago lawyer, Leon Despres, remembers a friend predicting that the Red flag with hammer and sickle would fly over some state capital by the end of the year, perhaps in radical Minnesota. In January, Senator James Byrnes and other congressional leaders emerged from a meeting in New York with FDR only to be chased back into the Roosevelt town house on Sixty-fifth Street by an angry mob of protesters shaking their fists and shouting, "When do we eat? We want action!"

Out in farm country, anyone connected to liquidation lived in fear of being lynched. A Kansas lawyer who handled a foreclosure was found dead in a field. An Iowa bankruptcy judge was dragged from the bench, stripped, and beaten. Soon, spiked telephone poles and logs blocked the entrances to Iowa cities. Armed farmers gathered at foreclosure auctions to threaten the lives of bidders, ready to buy their neighbors' possessions for a dollar or two, then give them back to the original owners. But with foreclosure so widespread, it was getting harder to feel so generous.

Perhaps the biggest surprise was that there wasn't even more unrest. The best explanation is the listlessness that accompanies despair: barricades are not easily manned by depressed people. A year later, when expectations rose under the New Deal, recruiters for various radical causes would have a more receptive audience; in 1934 alone, 1.4 million workers went out on strike. But for now, labor was quiet, wondering if management would even survive. The agrarian revolutionaries, Communist agitators, and homegrown fascists all held back, waiting for the final collapse that their dogma told them was their route to power.

Adolf Hitler became chancellor of Germany on January 30, 1933, Franklin Roosevelt's fifty-first birthday. He would complete the legal part of his ascension to power when the Nazis won an election on March 5, the day after FDR's Inauguration. That winter and spring came the suspicious Reichstag fire, widespread persecution of Jews, and Hitler's illegal consolidation of power. Hitler, while distrusted in Washington, was still mostly a curiosity.

In January, hearings began before the Senate Banking and Currency Committee that riveted the country. The target of the inquiry was Charles E. Mitchell, president of the National City Bank. Mitchell was so imperious that he had once fired a subordinate for being bold enough to tell him his pants were unbuttoned. "In those days the trousers of Charles E. Mitchell could no more be unbuttoned than Louis XIV's grammar could be at fault," the critic Edmund Wilson wrote. "He was the banker of bankers, the salesman of salesmen, the genius of the New Economic Era."

From the moment Mitchell took the stand, Ferdinand Pecora, the committee's young counsel, destroyed him. National City Bank was guilty of abuses that would be familiar to modern students of business wrongdoing: steering bank customers toward favored securities that proved worthless. Right up to the day of FDR's Inauguration, Mitchell remained in the dock on Capitol Hill, embarrassing American business. "If you steal $25, you're a thief. If you steal $250,000, you're an embezzler. If you steal $2,500,000 you're a financier," wrote one critic. *Colliers* magazine said the revelations shocked "the moral sense of the nation."

By the beginning of 1933, hoarding reached epidemic proportions. People hid their money under the mattress, in a sock, in a tin of baking powder, under the floorboard of a Model T. One family taped a thousand dollars in large bills to their young sons' chests so as not to leave it in a bank. Pulling money out of the bank and hiding it at home was not like a regular withdrawal because it didn't recirculate. So it wasn't surprising that from the peak in August 1929 to the trough in March 1933, the supply of printed money fell by a third, which was more than triple any recorded decline in a comparable period and an obvious source of crushing deflation. (Monetarism—controlling the money supply—barely existed in economic theory.) Each month, prices plummeted further.

House Speaker Garner made matters worse. In mid-1932, he had insisted that a "publicity clause" be inserted into the bill expanding the Reconstruction Finance Corporation (RFC). The amendment requiring public disclosure of all RFC loans sounded good, but it was like posting big DON'T TRUST US signs on the marble facades of ailing banks; any institution listed as receiving an RFC bailout was now at serious risk of a run.

Roosevelt supported the move. He and Garner felt they had to keep faith with an angry American public that was increasingly pointing the finger of blame at bankers. But FDR's refusal to adhere to financial orthodoxy on this point didn't help in the short term. "Fears that Roosevelt might devalue the dollar induced depositors to withdraw their balances," writes Barry Eichengreen in *Golden Fetters*, his seminal work on the gold standard. Here's an authority on economic history who thinks Hoover's faith in the gold standard deepened the Depression, but Roosevelt's unwillingness to utter a few reassurances about his commitment to "sound money" made it worse still. During one ten-day period in January, American banks lost in panicky withdrawals as much as they had gained in the previous ten months of RFC loans.

The chairman of the board of the RFC was Eugene Meyer, who was also chairman of the board of governors of the Federal Reserve.* Meyer called Garner's publicity clause "democratic sabotage." Although he has been second-guessed for not doing more, Meyer's hands were mostly tied; in those days, the Washington-based Fed—less than twenty years old—was an advisory body with little direct authority. Most of the clout resided with the New York Fed, which was not inclined to act.

The main problem, though, was that President Hoover would not intercede to stem the hoarding, despite warnings from Meyer and others. He chose instead to blame Roosevelt's election (and FDR's later unwillingness to endorse his policies) for the problem. There was some logic here. Businessmen with money in the bank had more likely voted for Hoover and feared FDR; those who were hurting and didn't have much to deposit in the first place tended to be Roosevelt voters.

Roosevelt was in a bind. The Democratic platform of 1932 called for "a sound currency to be preserved at all costs." But throughout the transition, FDR told prospective Cabinet members that he could not rule out devaluation of the dollar. To his left, Senators Huey Long of Louisiana and Burton Wheeler of Montana were talking about the virtues of printing money, pointing to the way the French and Italian economies soared in the early 1920s with only a little currency devaluation. To his right lay the entire financial establishment of the United States.

---

* Later in 1933, Meyer bought *The Washington Post* at a bankruptcy sale and eventually passed it on to his son-in-law, Philip Graham, who had married Meyer's daughter, Katharine.

Conservatives saw a series of disturbing omens they believed had caused the panic: A January 30 report in the *Washington Times-Herald* that Roosevelt was considering "reflation" (his handy euphemism for inflation); the gathering around FDR of advisers like Henry Wallace publicly committed to raising prices; a near majority in the Senate for the re-coinage of silver, which then looked like a hoary Populist-era pander getting a second wind; and incessant talk of Roosevelt's impending "revolution"—a word guaranteed to frighten investors.

The whole business elite now united once more behind the same conventional economic advice. Late in January, Treasury Secretary Ogden Mills published a long syndicated article reminding the public of the dangers of inflation. On February 13, Bernard Baruch, who would have been in FDR's Cabinet had he not worked so hard against him at the Chicago convention, testified that the government should "Sacrifice for frugality and revenue. Cut government spending—cut it as rations are cut in a siege. Tax—tax everybody for everything." This from a man widely regarded as the smartest investor in the country. He was followed by a stream of bank presidents, financial editors, and economists all saying the same thing.

For the next sixty years, these men were portrayed as hopeless mossbacks and, indeed, some of their advice—like raising taxes during a deep depression—looks more than faintly ridiculous in hindsight. But it's ironic in retrospect that the responsible conservative view of the day was that steep tax increases were essential to balancing the budget. At the time, genuine fiscal responsibility—whatever the political costs—still held sway inside the GOP, and much of the Democratic Party as well.

Resisting that, Roosevelt settled on an intentional strategy of passivity amid crisis. Lawrence Sullivan, a Hoover administration official, wrote in 1936 that FDR could have ended the panic at any time with "a single vigorous statement pledging unequivocal support of the existing gold standard" and a request that Congress balance the budget. Sullivan was probably right; a few words of orthodoxy from the president-elect might have stopped the bank runs. But those words would have also tied his hands in the presidency and rendered it much harder to make the essential decision to go off the gold standard and break with the past on many other economic issues. So FDR did what he knew how to do so well: He equivocated, issuing a vague call for "sound money," which was like supporting motherhood and apple pie.

Hoover officials later claimed that RFC loans and the outgoing president's behind-the-scenes efforts had averted bank panics in Cleveland, Chattanooga, Little Rock, Mobile, St. Louis, and Memphis. Probably so, but he hardly did so alone. The case of New Orleans suggests how strange—even humorous—this maneuvering to avoid collapse could be. To forestall a run on New Orleans's Hibernia Bank and buy time for an RFC loan, Senator Huey Long ordered his puppet governor to issue a proclamation at 4:00 a.m. that declared Saturday, February 4, a "holiday" in Louisiana in honor of the sixteenth anniversary of Woodrow Wilson's decision to sever diplomatic relations with Germany. ("Whereas, more than 16 years have intervened . . ."). The *sixteenth* anniversary? The German community in New Orleans was perplexed. It turns out this was the only anniversary or other excuse for closing the banks that Long could find in an almanac a friend consulted in the middle of the night.

February's crisis in Michigan was the tipping point in a national emergency. The bank holiday there led almost directly to suspension of banking in thirty-four other states within a month and eventually to FDR's March 6 proclamation of a nationwide holiday. It was one of the pivotal events of the Depression and, as usual with stories about Michigan, involved the family of Henry Ford. One could argue that without dysfunction in that family, there would have been no banking crisis and FDR would not have assumed the presidency with such a bang.

By 1933, Henry Ford was a hideously autocratic man, nearing seventy, and his son and heir-apparent, Edsel, had spent years chafing under him. To carve out his own identity, Edsel Ford invested heavily in a bank, the Guardian, started by his brother-in-law, a disgruntled former Ford executive. At first, the bank, which underwrote all borrowing for the purchase of Ford cars, was a phenomenal success. The imposing Guardian Building, which opened in 1929, still stands as one of Detroit's landmarks—"the Cathedral of Finance."

But after auto sales evaporated and Ford laid off two thirds of its workforce, the Guardian needed a huge bailout from the RFC. Edsel couldn't bear to tell his father the dreary financial details, and when Henry learned of them, he reacted so badly that Edsel suffered a depres-

sion from which he never fully recovered. Henry finally bailed out
Edsel personally—saving him from financial ruin—but he refused to
help the Guardian further, which doomed any reorganization plan. It
was as if a father had pulled his thirty-nine-year-old son off a lame pony,
then shot the pony dead.

For a brief moment, it looked as if President Hoover might save the
day. To secure the RFC loan, Hoover thought he had convinced Ford
to freeze the remaining Guardian deposits. He telephoned him from
the White House to ask that Ford receive his emissaries to work out the
details. But when they arrived at Ford's Dearborn office, Henry Ford
told Hoover's men that he had "not fully understood" the complicated
freeze proposal and in any case "had changed his mind." Even more
alarming, Ford barked that if the Guardian failed, he might yank his
money out of the First National Bank of Detroit, too, which would
bring down the other half of the state's banking industry. When told
that 3 million people would suffer directly, and the state and possibly
the country would be paralyzed, Ford seemed unperturbed. "I still feel
young," he said, and if the banks failed and his customers fell away, he
could just start all over again. Having stayed out of the market during
the 1920s, Ford had plenty of money still and was fatalistic. "If a crash
has to come, let the crash come."

After three days of round-the-clock meetings proved inconclusive,
Detroit's bankers asked Michigan governor William Comstock to step
in. On February 14, Comstock announced an eight-day bank "holiday."
It would actually last nearly a month, by which time FDR would apply
the holiday euphemism, which had originated during panics before
World War I, to the entire nation.

Hoover later wrote: "The governor of the state lost his head; if he
had not become panicky, that catastrophe would have been averted."
This was false. Everyone in Hoover's administration—including his
men on the scene—had urged Comstock to declare the holiday, or
"moratorium," as Hoover preferred. In fact, Comstock was the cautious
one. But finally, as he and an aide left the feverish Detroit negotiations
for a midnight visit to a hot dog stand, the governor made his momentous decision, which would set off the greatest financial crisis in American history.

The proclamation closed all 436 Michigan banks and marooned

900,000 depositors. Although the streets remained calm at first, the fallout was instantaneous. Detroit and other Michigan cities defaulted on bonds. Food grew scarce, as shelves were cleaned out in anticipation. Scrip issued by various institutions was used for months. Roads from Chicago were clogged with armored cars carrying cash to Michigan for payrolls. In fact, it was the payroll of Michigan companies that helped cause the problem to spread. Unable to draw cash from local banks, Michigan companies went to Chicago and New York banks, which were in turn drained of reserves. Even when liquidating mortgages and securities as fast as they could, American banks now had only about a seventh of what they needed in reserves to cover deposits.

The news, as the historian Charles Beard put it, "jangled the American system from center to periphery." When the country turned its eyes to Michigan, bankers joined gangsters in the American rogue's gallery. Father Charles Coughlin, "the radio priest" from Royal Oak, Michigan, just beginning to emerge as a well-known demagogue, called them "banksters."

As the Michigan "holiday" was extended from days to weeks, plan after plan to salvage the system surfaced and flopped. The energized Federal Reserve pumped more than ten times what Hoover had recommended into the state to no effect. The disease was moving fast now, with Maryland the next to go. Michigan was lost and would have to await a new president to find its way home.

Chapter Twenty-four

"Wooden Roof" and Other Cabinetry

B Y EARLY FEBRUARY, the president-elect was in political trouble. Despite his big win in the election, FDR's men knew that the old perception of him as a vague and hazy "trimmer" had returned since November. Even after leaving the governorship of New York on January 1, he had offered the nation no plans for easing the Depression, which was increasingly being printed with a capital "D." The impression of him as a vacillating politician had, in the words of one Roosevelt insider, "become strong again, feeding even on the sober judgment of many who had voted for Roosevelt."

Certainly Huey Long felt that way. In the fall, he had accepted an invitation to come to Hyde Park. He showed up wearing a loud suit, orchid shirt, and watermelon pink tie, the better to scare the swells. At lunch, Sara Roosevelt was heard to ask in a voice that Grace Tully remembered as practically loud enough to be heard all the way out on the Post Road, "Who is that *awful* man sitting to my son's right?" Long and FDR pretended not to hear. "By God I feel sorry for him," Long said later. "He's got more sonsofbitches in his family than I got in mine." But Long's conclusion was well short of enthusiastic. "I like him. He's not a strong man but he means well," he said with his patented formula for patronizing anyone he considered part of the elite.

Long pinpointed Roosevelt's affable impenetrability, which allowed the president-elect to soak up advice and give away nothing. In December, a few weeks after the election, the Kingfish had made a visit to Warm Springs. "When I talk to him, he says 'Fine! Fine! Fine!' " Long complained afterwards. "But Joe Robinson [the conservative Arkansas Democrat and soon-to-be Senate Majority Leader] goes to see him the next day and again he says 'Fine! Fine! Fine!' Maybe he says 'Fine!' to everybody."

While FDR's supporters and even many aides fretted over his declining reputation, the president-elect was patient. In January, he attended a dinner in his honor at the Harvard Club in New York. The president of the university, A. Lawrence Lowell, gave a talk in which he said that in his experience the most important principle for an American president to follow was to take and hold the initiative with Congress, not react to it. This was common sense, but rarely followed by presidents. As governor, FDR had hung back, sometimes waiting for the New York State Assembly to move. Hoover, of course, had done the same in Washington. Louis Wehle watched his old classmate listening intently to Lowell that night. If Roosevelt always applied this idea, Lowell said, he would not fail. So it was hardly a coincidence that the central organizing principle of his presidency became the written "message to Congress," which had earlier been a once-or-twice-a-year epistle to Capitol Hill from the president on legislative matters. FDR was to send fifteen messages to Congress in his first Hundred Days alone, or more than one a week.

But the substance of those messages was a long way off. "The notion that the New Deal had a preconceived theoretical position is ridiculous," Frances Perkins recalled. For now, FDR operated on pure instinct. The old sailor figured he would tack left, then right, then wait for a stronger wind at his back. He knew it was coming. Early in the year, he told Charlie Michelson that the bank crisis was due to culminate in early March, right around Inauguration Day, which left Michelson with the impression that he was calculating his route for dramatic effect.

The best place to sail (or drift) was on a boat, so on February 3, FDR embarked on an twelve-day Caribbean cruise aboard Vincent Astor's 263-foot yacht, the *Nourmahal*, one of the largest private yachts in the world. Astor was a student at Harvard in 1912 when his father, John Jacob Astor, went down on the *Titanic*. He had managed the vast family fortune competently and with some sense of public obligation. Now he hosted FDR, his retinue of secretaries and Secret Service men, and four other "boon companions," including a federal judge and Theodore Roosevelt's son, Kermit, the only member of the Oyster Bay branch of the family with anything nice to say about the new president. The president-elect's own family stayed home. They later wondered why "Father" went yachting when the country was scraping bottom and how, as Eleanor put it, he could relax with "those people."

Moley, who had emerged as FDR's top policy aide, wasn't happy about the cruise, either. It fed his growing suspicion that the president-elect was a lackadaisical administrator. Not only were banks closing all over the country, but key decisions about the Cabinet had not been made. To avoid excessive publicity, Roosevelt designated Moley to handle all of the confidential negotiations involved in staffing the senior levels of his administration. "Another reason for assigning the task to me was that he would be excessively busy," Moley noted sarcastically in the 1960s. "He was planning a vacation later on Vincent Astor's yacht." The logistics of the trip were a nightmare. Because the ship-to-shore radio was not secure, Moley and Howe would have to communicate from land with the boss in code.

One radiogram sent to the yacht read: PREFER A WOODEN ROOF TO A GLASS ROOF OVER SWIMMING POOL. LUHOWRAY. For any reporter who might stumble over it, this appeared to refer to a campaign by the *New York Daily News* to raise money to build a swimming pool for the new president in the White House West Wing (in the space now occupied by the press room). Vincent Astor believed as much, and didn't bring it to FDR's attention for a couple of days because it didn't look important. In fact, the message from "LUHOWRAY"—a combination of Louis Howe's first and last names and Ray Moley's first—referred to a series of sensitive discussions about the most important of Cabinet choices, that of secretary of the Treasury.

"GLASS" was seventy-five-year-old Senator Carter Glass, conservative Democrat of Virginia, legislative father of the Federal Reserve System in 1913, and widely respected as a great authority on banking. He mixed traditionalism with an instinct for reform and an understanding of how unpopular the money men had become. ("One banker in my state attempted to marry a white woman and they lynched him," he liked to joke, in a comment that would get *him* lynched today.)

Glass had served two years as Treasury secretary at the end of the Wilson administration and might have been willing to return to the job under the right circumstances. Given his stature, Roosevelt felt he had no choice but to offer him the plum, but the Virginian told Moley on January 19 that he had two conditions: He wanted Russell Leffingwell, a partner in the firm of J. P. Morgan, as undersecretary; and he wanted to know Roosevelt's views on inflation. If the new president pursued any inflationary policies, Glass threatened, he would be a "roaring lion in the Senate."

This was a pivotal moment in the history of the New Deal. Had Glass become Treasury secretary, he never would have allowed the inflationary New Deal legislation that lay ahead. Or he would have quit the government early on, wrecking Roosevelt's momentum. (As it was, he would be roaring against the White House by April.)

Here FDR showed some resolve. "Make it perfectly clear we simply can't go along with Twenty Three," he told Moley. This was a reference to 23 Wall Street, the address of Leffingwell and the powerful House of Morgan, symbol of capitalist power and source of a thousand conspiracy theories. On Glass's second condition, Roosevelt instructed: "So far as inflation goes, you can say that we are not going to throw ideas out of the window simply because they are labeled inflation." Then he added, "If the old boy doesn't want to go along, I wouldn't press it." The "old boy" got the message and Howe and Moley cabled Roosevelt aboard the ship that Glass was withdrawing from consideration for reasons of health.

Instead, FDR's first Treasury secretary was "WOODEN ROOF," actually William Woodin, the elfin president of the American (Railroad) Car and Foundry Company. Woodin, who was almost as short as Howe and wore a bad toupee, was unimpressive at first glance. He had made a $50,000 campaign contribution to Roosevelt—the only big business executive to pony up—but he looked so out of place among important people that the doorman at the Roosevelt campaign headquarters at the Biltmore Hotel had thought he was a salesman of campaign buttons or banners and barred him. He had to call Farley to get inside.

But Woodin had a way of growing on FDR—who called him "Wee Willie"—and not just because he was among the elite group who bragged they were FRBC ("For Roosevelt Before Chicago"). As an industrialist, he understood banking and had better perspective on the business of money than the bankers themselves, which would prove invaluable in the first critical days of the new administration. Modest and artistic, Woodin had reluctantly given up a career in music when he inherited the family business, though he still spent hours composing and playing piano, mandolin, and guitar. Before the Inauguration, this part of his background didn't inspire great confidence. He was best known to the public for a sunny children's song about bluebirds.

The other key appointment on economic policy was director of the Bureau of the Budget. With Glass out and Bernard Baruch passed over as Treasury secretary for opposing FDR in Chicago, FDR needed a smaller Glass to reassure the old guard. He found him in Lewis Douglas, the son of a mining magnate from Arizona who went east to school, was gassed in World War I, and returned home to be elected the state's only congressman at age thirty-two.* He bicycled to Capitol Hill every morning, where he dazzled older colleagues with his arcane knowledge of the budget. At home, he was pelted with eggs and oranges by Arizona constituents who thought him too stingy toward veterans. Douglas described the ordeal as "rather fun."

Douglas later realized how FDR had manipulated him out of a promising political career in Democratic politics and into his administration, in part by promising that the Budget Bureau would have Cabinet status for the first time since it was created a decade earlier under Warren Harding. In Douglas, FDR had a public symbol of economic rectitude, useful for carrying his message to Capitol Hill and helping to restore confidence on Wall Street. All Douglas had were Roosevelt's private assurances that he agreed with his basic anti-inflationary outlook, which were worth nothing.

---

* Douglas was an earlier, Democratic version of David Stockman, Ronald Reagan's first budget director, a whip-smart young congressman with classically conservative tightfisted views of government spending.

But FDR's manipulation was usually mixed with at least some sincerity. The Pittsburgh campaign speech that promised to cut government spending by 25 percent was not mere rhetoric. Riding by car from Hyde Park to Albany in December, he had asked Douglas, still in Congress, to introduce an amendment that would have amounted to huge new powers for the incoming president. Roosevelt wanted the lame duck Congress to vote him the authority to reorganize the government, slash departments, and cut functions—a proposal for what was referred to admiringly in the press as "dictatorial powers." More than half the savings would come from cutting nearly a billion dollars (real money in those days) from veterans. This "economy bill" didn't pass then, but later became a centerpiece of the Hundred Days.

Well before the yacht trip, Ed Flynn and Sam Rosenman had declined job offers in the new administration. Flynn was New York secretary of state and Rosenman a State Supreme Court judge, but the bigger reason was that they knew better than to get in Louis Howe's way at the White House. Besides secretaries Missy LeHand and Grace Tully, Stephen Early (the press secretary) and Marvin McIntyre (the appointments secretary), there would be no one on the premises to compete with Howe for the president's attention. Howe's position as "confidential secretary" didn't prevent FDR from seeing a wide variety of other advisers, but it did provide a perch for Howe to defend his turf.

Especially from Ray Moley, who had emerged in the press as the brains of the Brain Trust. Moley described himself as a "packhorse in his [FDR's] great affairs," but this was false modesty. In December 1932, Sam Rayburn, already a powerful Texas congressman (and future House Speaker), saw him on a train leaving Atlanta and said only half-jokingly: "I hope we don't have a goddamned Rasputin in this administration." Despite his central role in selecting the Cabinet, even Moley knew that Howe would never let him win a job on the tiny White House staff, which in those days numbered less than a dozen. Roosevelt convinced Moley that he could get around Howe and serve him directly by becoming deputy secretary of state, a position that FDR claimed would carry no particular responsibilities that would consume his time.

Typically, the president-elect brushed off concerns that this might not go over well with Moley's direct superior, Cordell Hull. The distinguished senator from Tennessee was the first choice of FDR and Howe for secretary of state; they respected him for his dignity and high-mindedness. (Though it didn't hurt that Hull was no choir boy; he had established his independence as a young man by winning $7,000 playing craps during service in the Spanish-American War.) If Garner hadn't agreed to run for vice president, Hull would likely have been FDR's running mate.

But Hull had felt rudely ignored by Roosevelt since Chicago—a feeling he would need to get accustomed to in the next decade—and he was surprised to be considered. Louis Wehle advised him to accept on the condition that he get Roosevelt's agreement that he be allowed to pick his subordinates. Hull sheepishly admitted that FDR had so charmed him in Warm Springs that he had forgotten to request that, and Roosevelt later scrawled on scrap paper and handed to Moley the names of Sumner Welles, William Bullitt, William Phillips, Breckenridge Long, and other choices to staff the second-tier ranks of the department.

These were to be critical appointments. Welles often seemed as if he were running the department; Bullitt helped engineer diplomatic recognition of the Soviet Union later in 1933; and Long (a floor manager for FDR at the 1932 Democratic Convention rewarded at first with an ambassadorship) proved to be a major impediment to the rescue of European Jews during World War II. From the start, FDR was circumventing Hull to deal directly with these men, which gave him indispensable backchannels to what was going on in his government. Unlike most presidents, Roosevelt knew enough about the details of governing to handpick his sub-Cabinet as well as his Cabinet. He had been disappointed as assistant secretary of the Navy not to have more contact with President Wilson and made sure his own subordinates had access to him.

About all Hull could do was request that he not have to exhaust himself attending tiresome diplomatic functions or pay for entertainment expenses out of his own pocket, as other secretaries of state had done. This led to a radiogram to the *Nourmahal* reading: FURTHER CONFERENCE ON TENNESSEE PROJECT INDICATES POSSIBILITY OF ADOPTION

PROVIDED SOME OTHER FOOD SUPPLYING AND CONSUMING MEANS CAN
BE FOUND. LUHOWRAY*

One day in Albany, Hull had almost lost the job to Senator Key
Pittman of Nevada, a subtle foreign policy expert despite his support
(per his mining constituents) for William Jennings Bryan–style free
coinage of silver. To his later shame, Moley sabotaged Pittman by
telling FDR that Pittman drank too much; the senator had gone on a
three-day binge at a New York hotel just after the election. Knowing
how such ideas could take root in Roosevelt's mind, Moley felt guilty
and took a taxi back to the Governor's Mansion, where he found FDR
in bed. But by urging the president-elect to forget what he had told him
earlier about the drinking, Moley feared that he was just driving home
the message further. Sure enough, Pittman was off the list to be secretary of state.

Hull was a single-issue man—free trade—and his long-winded
speeches on the subject had been known to empty the Senate floor. But
he was almost certainly right that "the half insane policy of economic
isolation" was "the largest single underlying cause of the present world
panic." And his views on the merits of trade, which seemed on the
fringe in 1932, are now accepted as mainstream gospel. Roosevelt
didn't care much about trade, and there's no evidence that he ever saw
the basic contradiction between the New Deal, with its emphasis on
domestic recovery, and Hull's global free market ideas. It mattered little. For the dozen years Hull served in the job, Roosevelt was essentially
his own secretary of state.†

---

* Hull's greatest asset was that he looked like a secretary of state and carried himself in a way
that conveyed gravitas and influence. Within a few years, an up-from-the hollow Tennesseean
named Albert Gore would pattern his political career closely on Hull's; his son, Albert Gore,
Jr., a future vice president, remembers Hull as a figure of reverence in his household growing
up. It could even be argued that Gore's stiffness and senatorial bearing, which helped cost him
the 2000 presidential election, trace back to the example of Cordell Hull.
† Later in 1933, this trait caused confusion. After James Cox turned down the job of ambassador to Germany, FDR cut Hull out of the search for an envoy. Louis Howe heard about a
Professor Dodd in Chicago who might be qualified. Unfortunately, there were two Chicago
professors named Dodd—Walter F. Dodd of the University of Illinois and William E. Dodd
of the University of Chicago—and neither knew much about Germany. The latter, an expert on the history of the American South, got the job, apparently on the basis of having
spent a summer traveling in Germany decades earlier as a student. Ed Flynn later wrote, "I
have always thought in the rush to get somebody appointed the wrong Dodd was picked."
Dodd was known for years in New Deal Washington as the "telephone book" ambassador.

Throughout the Cabinet selection process, it was never quite clear who had FDR's ear. Felix Frankfurter, the Harvard Law School professor (and future U.S. Supreme Court justice), thought he did. After spending the night with his wife at the Roosevelts over the Christmas holiday, he peppered FDR with memos on legislation and personnel, particularly his thoughts on recognizing the railroad industry. This aroused predictable jealousies. Adolf Berle concluded a letter to the president-elect, "Yours truly, in a mean state of mind, with considerable admiration of F.F.'s public career and an intense desire to see him shot." Frankfurter himself turned down the post of U.S. Solicitor General and spent much of the spring of 1933 on sabbatical in England. But he stayed in touch, in part because Justice Brandeis was secretly paying him $3,500 a year to keep him informed and promote the many causes that Brandeis, as a sitting justice, could not lobby for directly.

Farm policy was of great concern to the president-elect. With nearly half of all American workers still connected to agriculture, it was central to domestic recovery. FDR's Hudson Valley friend, Henry Morgenthau, a dairy and apple farmer, had hoped to become secretary of agriculture. Then Morgenthau made the mistake of talking to FDR about Henry A. Wallace. "It was no contest between a Protestant from Iowa and a Jew from upstate New York," as Morgenthau's son, Robert, put it many years later. Morgenthau, son of a respected banker and ambassador, settled for being head of the Farm Credit Administration, where he consolidated nine separate federal farm credit agencies and helped save thousands of distressed farms. By 1934, he was Treasury secretary, though he had never finished college and had little experience in high finance.

CORNBELT IN THE BAG. LUHOWRAY, read the radiogram. The new agriculture secretary would be Wallace, whose late father had held the post under Presidents Harding and Coolidge. Wallace was an expert on pricing and a brilliant innovator who revolutionized corn farming. With experiments begun when he was still in high school, he was the first to discover there was no relationship at all between how good an ear of corn looked and its yield. Although no one in the Roosevelt camp knew it at the time, Wallace also had an unorthodox spiritual side. Beginning in 1931, he became something of a mystic, developing intense and eventually embarrassing relationships with an Indian medicine man, a White Russian cultist, and an Irish agrarian revolutionary.

Summoned to Warm Springs in late November, the strapping farmer arrived at 9:00 a.m. and was astonished to find no one up. When Wallace was finally ushered in to meet FDR, the president-elect was shaving and eating breakfast in bed as if they had known each other forever. Wallace then met with Morgenthau, whose chief function, Wallace concluded, perhaps out of rivalry for the job, was "to get safe liquor for the evening cocktail."

Wallace listened to Roosevelt put off Key Pittman's pleas on silver coinage ratios with a long and involved story of searching for buried pirate treasure on Oak Island near Campobello. That FDR ever undertook treasure hunts was a reflection of his optimistic nature, but the story itself was part of Roosevelt's patented if often exasperating form of distraction, which he frequently employed to keep supplicants at bay. By the time FDR completed his tale, the time alloted for a particular meeting had elapsed. Pittman would hardly be the last favor-seeker to go away empty-handed, scratching his head about Roosevelt.

The selection of Harold Ickes as secretary of the interior, an aging Bull Moose Republican lawyer from Chicago, suggested the casual nature of much of FDR's Cabinet making. When Howe heard him recommended for Interior by western Progressive Republican senators, who were now part of FDR's coalition (six Republican senators had supported him in November), he commented: "There isn't any such name as Ickes. There must be some mistake." In February, Ickes came to New York anyway, where Roosevelt, peering around the waiting area of his Sixty-fifth Street town house, asked, "Which one of you is Ikes?" After less than five minutes of conversation, FDR—still garbling his name (it's pronounced "Ick-eze")—hired him. When Moley asked what happened, the president-elect said simply, "I like the cut of his jib."

Labor went to Frances Perkins, the insightful and skillful Mount Holyoke matron who became the first woman ever named to the Cabinet. Eleanor had urged the appointment, though she wasn't especially close to Perkins personally. Perkins at first declined, arguing that the job should go to someone with direct experience with unions. Her own background working in settlement houses (as a Jane Addams disciple) seemed wrong for the job. But Roosevelt, who admired her labor work in Albany, insisted. Although he later passed notes to Morgenthau during Cabinet meetings making gentle fun of her hats or other aspects of her appearance, FDR was proud to make history with his "Madam Secretary."

Perkins accepted the post on the condition that FDR endorse in broad outline what eventually became the most lasting contributions of the New Deal. Much of the modern-day American social welfare system came out of that first hour-long meeting. None of the ideas were radical; many had been tried in small ways by Hoover and more audaciously in progressive states such as New York, Massachusetts, Minnesota, and Wisconsin, or in Europe. But together, they represented something new in the United States: immediate federal aid to states for unemployment relief; more extensive federal public works than under Hoover; unemployment and old-age insurance (which became Social Security in 1935); and a commitment in future years to pursue federally mandated minimum wages, maximum hours, and abolition of child labor (not achieved until 1938).

Roosevelt quickly said fine to all of the progressive proposals. When Perkins had the foresight to predict that some would be declared unconstitutional, he was breezy. "Well, that's a problem, but we can work out something when the time comes."* Despite his insouciance, FDR knew that he was on the verge of proposing nothing less than a rewriting of the American social contract. Instead of every man being the captain of his own fate, he envisioned the ship of state carrying a safety net. In private conversations, he sounded more liberal than almost any mainstream politician today. He favored what he called "cradle to grave" coverage, including national health insurance. But he knew that trying to insulate average Americans from the ravages of the market was a long-term process. So, in public, he borrowed a term from the private sector and spoke vaguely of "social insurance."

The U.S. Attorney General–designee was Montana senator Thomas Walsh, hero of the 1923 Teapot Dome hearings, able chairman of the Chicago convention, and easily the most well liked member of the FDR team. Commerce went to an old South Carolina supporter

---

* The "something" turned out to be the disastrous "court-packing" scheme of 1937.

and former IRS commissioner, Dan Roper. With no combat on the horizon, the War and Navy Departments were thought to be relatively minor posts and were distributed as political payoffs to Governor George Dern of Utah and Senator Claude Swanson of Virginia. The new Postmaster General would be Jim Farley, the back-slapping Elks "Exalted Ruler," who handed out the jobs (local postmasterships were prized) and kept score of who was true-blue for Roosevelt.

In an inspired move, FDR decided to withhold filling the sixty thousand patronage jobs at the disposal of Democrats until well into the new administration. Because so many constituents wanted these posts, this gave him a whip over Congress to enforce party discipline and drive his agenda. The Hundred Days would not have been nearly as productive without it. He was determined to learn a lesson from Woodrow Wilson, who fell into a huge argument with fellow Democrats over patronage in 1913 and as a result had less to show legislatively for his first year in office than he had hoped. FDR would use patronage jobs as legislative carrots, dangling just over the horizon, which left legions of desperate job seekers in suspended animation.

Al Smith was among them. He probably would not have accepted an appointment, even Ambassador to the Court of St. James's, but he certainly wanted to be asked by Roosevelt, as so many southerners and Republicans who maligned him in 1924 and 1928 had been. The phone did not ring.

Instead, FDR selected a bipartisan Cabinet with a mix between conservatives and liberals. Hull, Woodin, and Roper were conservative Democrats; Wallace and Ickes long-standing Progressive Republicans. Over time, this became a pattern, as FDR looked beyond party to staff his government with the very best men (and occasional women) he could find. Many would go on to serve for eight or even twelve years, transforming their departments and reshaping American government.

Few would have had the chance, were it not for the poor aim of an ailing Italian immigrant who bought a cheap pistol one February day in Miami Beach.

Chapter Twenty-five

Nearly Martyred in Miami

AFTER THE *NOURMAHAL* SAILED INTO BISCAYNE BAY on February 15, Astor and his passengers held a farewell dinner. As dessert was served, reporters scurried aboard and the president-elect told them about the twelve "perfectly grand" days of fine swimming and bone-fishing. "And I didn't even open a briefcase!" he exulted, a carefree attitude at a time of crisis that might have caused some controversy had the evening proven uneventful.

Roosevelt didn't tell the press about the practical joke he had played on the cruise, a good example of the hijinks he enjoyed. The yacht contained a small mimeograph machine that produced a daily "newspaper" made up of news briefs obtained by radiogram to keep the passengers at least modestly informed of events. FDR added an item reporting that the U.S. Supreme Court had issued a ruling condemning quickie divorces and ordering all estranged husbands and wives to return to their spouses pending further review. One member of Astor's party had been divorced by his wife and was contemplating remarriage. As his friend blanched, FDR laughed uproariously and told him: "Forget it—it's all made up!"

The plan was for FDR to leave the port at 9:00 p.m. in a green Buick convertible for a short reception at the garish bandshell in Bayfront Park, then take an overnight train that would arrive in New York the following afternoon. Ray Moley had come down to meet the ship and brief FDR on the Cabinet. He was in the third car of the motorcade with Astor and Kermit Roosevelt when they saw the crowds already lining Biscayne Boulevard. Moley and Astor each remembered the other remarking how easy it would be to shoot FDR.

A few moments after this conversation, the motorcade pulled up to the bandshell. Darkness had fallen and the amphitheater was illuminated with red, white, and blue floodlights. An American Legion drum-and-bugle corps played patriotic songs. Local radio covered the event live. Gus Gennerich, FDR's powerfully built bodyguard, hoisted Roosevelt up on the top of the backseat of the car.

FDR spoke for less than a minute in the casual tones he favored. He talked about catching fish and how much weight he gained on his vacation: "One of my first official duties will be taking the ten pounds off." This was about as far as Roosevelt liked to venture off the cuff with a big crowd. Time was short and he wrapped it up by saying he looked forward to coming back to Florida the following year. Standing nearby was Mayor Anton Cermak of Chicago, who was vacationing in Miami and hoped to win federal help for his bankrupt school system and to mend fences after his disastrous treatment of FDR at the Chicago convention the previous summer.

The speech was briefer than anticipated—a disappointment, no doubt, for the throngs who had lined up hours in advance. After Roosevelt handed over the microphone, a member of a newsreel crew that had missed filming him climbed on the back of the convertible and asked him if he would repeat his remarks for the camera, a common request in those days of unreliable equipment. When FDR demurred, the man pleaded that he had traveled a thousand miles for the pictures. Roosevelt looked irritated and waved him off, before being helped back into his seat, where he made a smaller target.

"That unquestionably saved his life," Vincent Astor said later.

Giuseppe Zangara was a thirty-two-year-old unemployed New Jersey bricklayer who stood a mere five foot one and weighed only 105 pounds. He told anyone who would listen that his stomach hurt. He didn't intend it as a metaphor for the hunger and despair of the Depression, but it became one. Zangara had assassination in mind for years, having waited with a gun in his pocket for a glimpse of King Victor Emmanuel of Italy during a parade in 1923. But because the guards were over six feet tall, he could not even see the king, he recounted in a recently discovered jailhouse memoir.

This became a problem for him in Miami, too. Zangara had wanted to kill Herbert Hoover and had lingered around the fringes of the Bonus Army march in Washington the previous summer. But then he moved south and began plotting to kill the new president. He arrived only an hour and a half before FDR's appearance, not in time to stand or sit in front. When he tried to push himself there, he was rebuffed by H. L. Edmunds, a tourist from Ottumwa, Iowa, who reminded him that women and children were sitting at the front and told him sternly that he was showing bad manners.

Like the rejected newsreel request, that little lecture on crowd etiquette probably changed history. Zangara settled for the third row, less than ten yards from the back of the Buick. He was angling for a better view when the president-elect quickly finished his speech and sat down.

Standing just ahead and to the right of Zangara was Lillian Cross, a forty-eight-year-old housewife. Like Zangara, she was only about 100 pounds and five feet tall. When spectators began to leave their seats after FDR finished speaking, she and Zangara hopped up on the same rickety bench and stood on their tiptoes for a better sight line. Behind them stood Thomas Armour, a forty-six-year-old Miami carpenter, attending the event with his teenage son. Cross and Armour would each later claim to have saved Roosevelt, and they may both have been right.

Zangara got off five shots from twenty-five feet. They sounded to Astor like the popping of the magnesium flashbulbs still used by news photographers. One hit the back of the car, just inches from Roosevelt; the others wounded bystanders. "Stop that man!" a woman screamed. "Don't let him kill Roosevelt!"

"When I fired the first shot, the chair I was standing on moved and the result was that it caused me to spoil my aim," a frustrated Zangara recalled. That was apparently Cross's doing, though unintentionally jostling a bench (and getting her foot caught in it) was hardly the heroic act that later resulted in her being profiled in every newspaper in the country and nominated for a Congressional Medal of Honor.

Armour—a reserved man who made for a less tabloid-friendly hero than Mrs. Cross—had to fight for recognition, but a policeman and others who witnessed the shooting believed he deserved it. After the first shot, the spectators anywhere near the line of fire did what bystanders do in such circumstances—they ducked. This gave Zangara a clear view of Roosevelt's head. According to Armour, he grabbed the assassin's arm and broke his direct aim as he got off four more shots, then forced his arm into the air to avoid hitting people on the ground. Within seconds, another man helped him wrestle Zangara to the pavement.

Six people were wounded by the five bullets, including Mayor Cermak. Shortly after he began chatting with the president-elect by the side of the car, a shot penetrated his rib cage, and the crowd saw a red stain expanding across his white shirt.

By now, it was pandemonium. "Lynch him!" someone shouted as Secret Service agents moved in on Zangara. "Kill Him! Cut his throat!" Within moments, Zangara was handcuffed to the rack on the back of the car carrying Moley and Astor. Three policemen held down the suspect, with a fourth balanced precariously on the running board, secured to the sedan only by Moley's finger clinging to his belt-loop. Moley feared the car would capsize. Along the route, traumatized spectators asked: "Has Roosevelt been killed?"

In fact, Roosevelt was unscathed. "Get him out of here!" Gus Gennerich yelled as he threw himself over FDR's chest, giving him a case of sore ribs. The driver of the car, a Miami policeman, began accelerating out of the park. FDR, taking a risk that he might be shot by another hidden assailant, twice insisted that the driver stop and see whether Cermak needed help getting to the hospital. Finally, the wounded mayor was lifted into the seat next to him.

The president-elect was genuinely fearless that evening. It was almost a family tradition: His cousin Theodore was shot in 1912 while standing in the back of a car and went on to deliver his speech with a flesh wound. FDR also understood the importance of *seeing* fearless to the public—of investing an already harrowing tale with a mythic quality. Indeed, much of the public story of what happened in Miami came from Roosevelt himself, who the next day invited reporters into his private railroad car en route to New York. Between cigarette puffs, he described the events with a perfect understanding of the newspapermen's need for dramatic narrative. He also knew that the right depiction of his leadership under fire would offer him a heroic springboard into the White House:

> "Just then I heard what I thought was a firecracker, then several more
> . . . the chauffeur started the car. . . . I looked around and saw Mayor
> Cermak and Mrs Gill [another shooting victim] collapsing . . . I told
> the chauffeur to stop. . . . He did, about 15 feet from where we
> started. The Secret Service men shouted, 'Get out of the crowd.' The
> chauffeur started again and I stopped him again. . . .
>
> "Looking back, I saw Mayor Cermak being carried. . . . He was
> alive but I didn't think he was going to last. I put my left arm around
> him and my hand on his pulse, but I couldn't find any pulse.
>
> "After we had gone another block, Mayor Cermak straightened
> up and I got his pulse. . . . I held him all the way back to the hospital. . . . It seemed like 25 miles. . . . I talked to him all the way. I remember I said, 'Tony, keep quiet—don't move. It won't hurt if you
> keep quiet and remain perfectly still."

Eleanor told a friend, "That drive to the hospital must have been awfully hard on Franklin—he hates the sight of blood." But the story was public relations gold. The image of the next president of the United States cradling a wounded man in his arms, reassuring him that everything would be fine, made an indelible impression on Americans who were themselves wounded in some way that February. Like the flight to Chicago the summer before and the Inaugural Address less than three weeks away, the Miami shooting offered a chance to crystallize public impressions and shape his presidency—and Roosevelt knew it.

At Jackson Memorial Hospital, doctors credited FDR with helping to keep Cermak from going into shock. The tiny hospital staff had a shock of its own that night. When the motorcade arrived, the night resident on duty, with no radio at hand, still hadn't heard about the shooting. He was sitting with his feet propped up, reading a "girlie" magazine, when the loud voice of a Secret Service agent demanded: "Open the door for the President of the United States." Assuming it was a joke, the annoyed young doctor shouted: "Tell him to piss on the floor and swim in under it."

That story didn't make print at the time, but another received wide publicity and added to the Roosevelt mystique. It was reported as fact that when FDR went into Cermak's hospital room to check on him, the mayor looked up at the president-elect and said: "I'm glad it was me instead of you." This was the invention of John Dienhart, a Hearst reporter from Chicago who doubled as Cermak's drinking buddy and PR man. "Jesus," Dienhart said years later. "I couldn't very well have put out the story that Tony wanted it the other way around."

Zangara was quickly depicted publicly as an addled anarchist, though the jailhouse memoir he dictated shows no sign of mental illness. He was bent on regicide. "I see Mr. Hoover, I kill him first. Make no difference. President just the same bunch. All same. Run by big money," he testified. The fascism of Mussolini held no allure for him and the FBI was never able to find evidence of any Communist connections. And had he been a Mafia hit man aiming to kill Cermak—a popular notion for many years—he would not have made his attempt in front of a huge crowd. Of course none of this stopped the conspiracy theories. Just as Zangara was sure that the world was run by a few capitalists, many Americans were sure that Zangara himself must be the tool of larger interests. Although legally sane, according to the psychiatrists who examined him, Zangara was diagnosed as "perverse," "erratic," and "anti-social." But if his politics were strange and unfocused, so were those of thousands of people battered by the Depression. There was little organized communism or fascism in the United States in 1933, but plenty of confused anarchism and hatred of the wealthy. Zangara differed mostly in his willingness to act on it.

If the Iowa tourist hadn't insisted on manners, if the newsreel operator hadn't failed in his plea, if the five-foot housewife hadn't jostled the bench, if the alert carpenter hadn't grabbed Zangara's arm—then John Nance Garner would have become president of the United States. Under the newly ratified Twentieth Amendment (and by common agreement before that), the vice president-elect succeeded to the presidency on the death of the president-elect.

Like word of his nomination in Chicago, Garner did not hear the news until the following day, long after radio listeners around the world learned of it. His rule on not being disturbed at his Washington hotel after 9:00 p.m. was inflexible. At five feet one, with eyebrows he described as "like two caterpillers rasslin," "Cactus Jack" Garner of Uvalde, Texas, would have been FDR's polar opposite as president—a libertarian with little interest in dramatic action or the theatrics of governing. "The great trouble today is that we have too many laws," he said in 1932. "I believe that primarily a government has two functions—to protect the lives and property rights of citizens. When it goes further than that, it becomes a burden." He had made brief headway as a presidential candidate in 1932 because W. R. Hearst admired his isolationist views.

No one can know for sure whether Garner would have failed as president, but it's hard to imagine the sixty-four-year-old "Texas Coolidge"—a nickname he liked—inspiring the country over the radio in the dismal winter of 1933. As Roosevelt's running mate, he made only three campaign speeches all year, and the Democrats considered themselves fortunate he didn't deliver more. (In one, he pledged to "never do anything" as vice president.) The political scientist Richard Neustadt later speculated that "Garner's voice, had he become president, would have been as bad as Hoover's." More lackadaisical leadership would likely have led to serious social upheaval.* The consequences of a Roosevelt assassination, the *Literary Digest* concluded at the time, "might have been more disastrous than the imagination can picture."

Vincent Astor arrived at Jackson Hospital to find his friend sitting placidly in a white hospital jacket. He suggested that in view of the rumors on the street, FDR put out a statement. "Your mind, Vincent, works very slowly. I did that three minutes ago," Roosevelt replied.

Rumors were spreading fast. FDR's daughter, Anna Dall, had first

---

* William Manchester has written that with "another Hoover, the United States would have followed seven Latin American countries whose governments had been overthrown by Depression victims."

heard an erroneous report that her father had been shot five times. At the hospital, Franklin called Eleanor to tell her what happened. Years later, she remembered him saying that night that if someone wanted to kill him and didn't care if he was himself caught or killed, there was nothing the Secret Service could do. "You can't live with that on your mind all the time—you've got to forget it," he told her. "We will just have to force ourselves never to think of these possibilities, otherwise life will be impossible." Irvin McDuffie, FDR's valet, said he could "throw off anything," including an assassination attempt. "He believed what was to be would be."

But when it was Eleanor's safety at issue, FDR took a less fatalistic view. Some hours later, he called Eleanor again to tell her that he was dispatching Secret Service to protect her. "Don't you dare do such a thing," a friend heard her say over the phone. "If any Secret Service man shows up in New York and starts following me around, I'll send him straight back to where he came from." When Franklin insisted, she dug in. "Nobody's going to try to shoot me," she told her husband. "I'm not that important."

The president-elect remained at the hospital for two hours as Cermak's condition stabilized for the moment (all but one of the other five suffered only minor injuries). Then he returned for the night to the *Nourmahal*. Moley was mightily impressed that even when he was finally off-stage, FDR remained unperturbed: "There was nothing—not so much as a twitching of a muscle, the mopping of a brow, or even the hint of false gaiety—to indicate that it wasn't any other evening in any other place. Roosevelt was simply himself—easy, confident, poised, to all appearances unmoved." Seven years after the event, when he had turned sharply against the New Deal, Moley still averred that "I have never in my life seen anything more magnificent than Roosevelt's calm that night on the *Nourmahal*." A Secret Service agent, curious about the president-elect's nerves, looked into his cabin several times that evening. Each time, he was fast asleep. The next day, FDR himself made sure the reporters on his train knew he had "slept like a top." It was apparently true but also part of the aura he intentionally created.

If FDR wasn't nervous about his safety, the rest of the country had the jitters. When his train arrived in New Jersey, he was escorted to New York by a thousand policemen. Six days later, a crudely wrapped shotgun shell was found at a Washington, D.C., Post Office addressed to "Franklin D. Roosevelt, Washington, D.C." Sent by a crank, it was nonetheless the lead story in *The New York Times* and other papers, lending even more drama to the assassination attempt story.

The mail to Hyde Park suggested that many Americans believed Roosevelt had been spared by divine intervention. "God saved you, not only the dear God above, but that little lady Mrs. Cross," wrote Anne Bodek from New Haven. "Now you'll be one of our greatest presidents in history." Joseph Williams wrote: "Just as God made You the President of the American people, as He preserved You at Miami, I feel sure that he has destined You to be the Saviour of Our Country." Clergy took up the theme the following Sunday. The public reaction resembled the aftermath of the attempt on the life of President Ronald Reagan in 1981, just two months after he took office. By surviving assassination attempts, both FDR and Reagan established a warmth in their relationship with the American people that had not existed when they won landslide victories the previous November.*

Back in Miami, the aftermath of the shooting played out quickly. When Mayor Cermak died from a postsurgical infection during the first week of Roosevelt's presidency, Zangara faced more serious charges. He was tried and executed only a little more than a month after the February 15 incident, one of the shortest periods from crime to execution on record in the United States.

FDR was personally opposed to the death penalty, but he said nothing to influence the sentencing. After the Miami judge used his courtroom to preach for handgun control, Zangara was allowed to say a few words. "I want to kill the president because I no like the capitalists," he told the court. By the time of his execution, Zangara had convinced everyone who talked to him that he had acted alone. With his stomach still hurting, he welcomed his trip to "Old Sparky," the state of Florida's infamous electric chair. "Pusha da button!" he shouted just before dying.

---

* Like FDR in 1932, Reagan was elected in 1980 largely on an anti-incumbent tide. Then, two months after taking office, he was wounded by a bullet fired from the gun of John Hinckley, outside the Washington Hilton. The elan he displayed in the aftermath ("Honey, I forgot to duck," Reagan reportedly told his wife Nancy) was similar to Roosevelt's. Taking a bullet helped Reagan push his budget and tax proposals through Congress. Before the assassination attempt, the so-called Reagan Revolution did not have the votes to pass.

Miami was Franklin Roosevelt's first crisis, and his handling of it did much to set the tone for his entrance into the presidency. After experiencing some buyers' remorse following his election, many voters were coming to believe that here was the leader—even the dictator—they had been praying for. The people will "close ranks behind him to a degree that would have been impossible had not a crackbrained coward tried to kill him," editorialized the *New York Post*. "To a man, his country rose to applaud his cool courage in the face of death," wrote *Time* magazine. "He is a martyr president at the start of his term."

Chapter Twenty-six

"Damn the Secretary"

Hoover made one last try to rope FDR into the crisis. Just after returning from Miami, FDR attended the Inner Circle Club dinner in New York City on February 18, a night of drinking, skits, and easy rapport between reporters and the politicians they covered. As the clock neared midnight, the dinner at the Hotel Astor was still going strong. The nearly one thousand guests enjoyed a skit in which a reporter playing "Alfred E. Smith" as Ambassador to the Court of St. James ends up cutting a deal with the British for cancellation of Great Britain's entire debt in exchange for leasing six floors of the Empire State Building, better known, to the chagrin of part-owner Smith, as the "Empty State Building."

A Secret Service agent quietly approached Governor Roosevelt, attracting no notice. The agent, sent specially by the White House, bore an urgent handwritten letter from the president to the president-elect—so hastily written that "Roosevelt" was spelled "Rosevelt." Hoover had tried and failed to contact him while he was aboard Astor's yacht the week before. Now Hoover all but served his soon-to-be successor with a subpoena. He was sending the message through the Secret Service, he wrote, because the president feared "its misplacement would only feed the fire and increase the danger."

Hoover wrote that a "critical situation has arisen" of "steadily de-

generating confidence in the future" and "general alarm." He added
that a "tremendous lift" would be possible by "the removal of fear." In
that, Hoover and Roosevelt were in complete agreement. By this
point, debt repayment and other arcane international issues had been
eclipsed by the terrifying banking crisis. But Ray Moley remembered
that it was Hoover's letter announcing that the breaking point had
come that made the awful truth seem real for the first time. Could the
financial system of the United States be collapsing? It certainly looked
that way.

But as the letter continued, it became clear that Hoover was intent
on refighting the 1932 election. He concluded that Roosevelt could
help restore confidence if he promised right away that there would be
no inflation or tampering with the currency (that is, moving off the
gold standard, as some Roosevelt appointees were hinting), that "the
budget will unquestionably be balanced, even if further taxation is necessary," and that the president-elect would come out against the Democrats' idea of publicizing the names of the recipients of RFC loans.

Hoover's letter was polite but, as Roosevelt later said, "cheeky." The
outgoing president was trying to be clever and soon bragged of it. "I realize that if these declarations be made by the president-elect, he will have
ratified the whole major program of the Republican Administration,"
Hoover wrote to Senator Reed. "That is, it means the abandonment of
90 percent of the so-called new deal." Here was Hoover once again
showing that he was an inept politician. It's impossible to imagine FDR
proclaiming his own Machiavellian goals so baldly, even to a friend.

At the Inner Circle dinner, FDR scanned the letter quickly, then
passed it to Moley. Amid the laughter and revelry, he showed no trace
of anything amiss. What he did next reveals much about how Franklin
Roosevelt would operate in the White House. He felt with good reason
that he couldn't deliver the declaration Hoover sought without stran-
gling his own presidency in the cradle; nor could he reject Hoover's
entreaty completely without further panicking Wall Street. So FDR
chose not to respond at all for eleven critical days, before covering himself and buying time with what now seems to have been a convenient
little lie: he pretended that his reply to the hand-delivered Hoover letter had been lost.

When he received no reply from FDR, Hoover tried again. Ten days after his first impassioned letter, Hoover hand-wrote another letter that further explained the gravity of the crisis. Despite his growing fury at the Roosevelt camp, he kept it professional and diplomatic and asked nothing except that FDR consult with him once more. Roosevelt replied immediately on March 1 (three days before his Inaugural) to this second Hoover letter by apologizing for not having replied to the first. To prove he was not to blame, Roosevelt enclosed a vague letter he had claimed to have written to Hoover on February 21 (three days after Hoover's original missive had been brought by the Secret Service). It read as if it had been concocted at least several days after that date.

The ruse went like this: In his apologetic March 1 cover letter, Roosevelt blithely wrote that he just learned that the "inclosed, which I wrote in New York a week ago, did not go to you, through an assumption by my secretary that it was only a draft of a letter." The problem with this excuse is that the enclosed "February 21" letter includes an evaluation of the crisis that would have been hard to make on that date. The letter says that "a fairly general withdrawal of deposits [cannot] be prevented now." But how would FDR have been able to conclude that on February 21, when Michigan was the only state where the banks had been closed? The crisis there didn't become a "general withdrawal" until a week after the letter was supposed to have been written.

It's hard to imagine that either of FDR's frighteningly competent secretaries, Missy LeHand and Grace Tully, was actually at fault. But even as some historians suspected the "lost letter" was a fib, they had no proof until now. Deep within the files of FDR's years as governor, however, lies a previously undiscovered indication of what Howe and FDR had in mind.

Six months earlier, in the summer of 1932, a veteran and journalist named William Lee Mann wrote the Roosevelts asking that they join a new veterans' organization Mann was launching that favored not just the veterans' bonus but ending Prohibition and repealing all Sunday blue laws. The Roosevelt campaign did not want to appear hostile to veterans by rebuffing Mann, but his group's demands were political poison. So Louis Howe wrote FDR in June: "The net and unanimous opinion of everyone was to forget that you ever got it and if the matter ever came up afterwards to damn the secretary."

Now FDR used the same "damn the secretary" gambit with Hoover.*
It worked. By March 1, Roosevelt had nearly run out the clock, which
meant that he would have a free hand as president. It is hard to avoid
the conclusion that he intentionally allowed the economy to sink
lower so that he could enter the presidency in a more dramatic fashion.

The Hoover forces insisted this was so. On February 25, James Rand,
president of the Remington-Rand Corporation, undertook what
amounted to a spy mission for the Hoover White House. He called
Hoover's press secretary to say he had just had lunch with Rex Tugwell.
Rand claimed that Tugwell had said the "new dealers" believed nothing should be done to end the banking crisis enveloping the country.
Hoover wrote Rand personally to thank him for the espionage and
noted that Tugwell, "devoid of every atom of patriotism," would eagerly
"project millions of people into hideous losses for a Roman holiday."

FDR himself was too smart to be as indiscreet as Tugwell about his
strategy, even in private. But forces friendly to him later confirmed that
such thinking took place in the Roosevelt camp. Herbert Feis, a State
Department economist who served under both Hoover and Roosevelt,
quoted Tugwell as saying, "Let them [banks] bust—then we'll get
things on a sound basis." James P. Warburg, a shrewd banker from a legendary family invited into FDR's circle, later said that "they wanted it
to get as bad as it was going to get before he took office, so that he could
come in on the turn rather than in the continuing downward spiral."
And years later Henry Stimson alluded to the same in his memoirs.
Tommy Corcoran commented admiringly, "If he could acquire more
latitude for action—more power—by letting the roller coaster slide further down the hill, he would do just that."

Hoover was convinced that FDR and the Democratic Congress had
sabotaged him and the country. Shortly after leaving office, as he
stewed about his fate in Palo Alto, he dictated a 260-page manuscript
about the banking crisis "for publication in the distant future . . . as a
warning against demagoguery in public life." Starting in 1930, he had
taken more federal action than any president in any of the nation's

---

* John F. Kennedy's famous decision to pretend he had not received Nikita Khrushchev's
second, more hostile letter during the Cuban Missile Crisis resembled FDR's gambit, though
there is no evidence JFK knew of it.

twenty previous depressions, he wrote. The economy was recovering nicely in 1932, with a half million new jobs, when the Democrats insisted on publicizing RFC loans, which sent thousands of banks reeling, and refused to work with him to balance the budget and prevent inflation. The great banking panic of 1933 was "either deliberately fostered or at least brought on by refusal to do those things which would have prevented it." He wasn't buying FDR's line about his secretary losing the letter; the president-elect clearly "had not wished to make any reply." The crisis, he concluded, was used "to attempt revolution and not reform." Instead of publishing the account as a book, he incorporated elements of it in his later attacks on FDR's integrity.

When Hoover wrote his memoirs in the early 1950s, he contacted Moley—by then a conservative—to see whether he agreed. Moley would not fix FDR's motive specifically but offered a damning assessment nonetheless. "I feel when you [Hoover] asked him [FDR] on February 18th to cooperate in the banking situation that he either did not realize how serious the situation was or that he preferred to have conditions deteriorate and gain for himself the entire credit for the rescue operation."

In 1935, Hoover made a sensational public charge: "It was the most political and most unnecessary bank panic in all our history. It could have been prevented. It could have been cured by simple cooperation." Then he compared the New Dealers to the Nazis. "Closing the banks was a sign that the country was in a ditch," he wrote. "It was the political equivalent of the burning of the Reichstag [by the Nazis in 1933] to create an 'emergency.' "

Hoover was so blinded by his hatred of Roosevelt that he mischaracterized the history of the period. If the Reichstag was burning, the dozens of states that had already closed their banks by the time FDR became president must have lit the flame. So, ironically, did Hoover himself. As Moley and several of Hoover's own aides pointed out, he finally agreed that the banks should be closed by Washington but was so shaken and confused that he believed FDR, though he wasn't president, should also sign off on it. If Hoover had taken the action on his own, he would have left the presidency on a higher note.

As it was, Hoover couldn't admit that his vision had simply failed. His dream of men of goodwill voluntarily banding together to do the right thing was in tatters. "A sharp break with the past did in fact occur in March, 1933," Arthur M. Schlesinger, Jr., concludes in *The Cycles of American History*. "The essence of that break lay precisely in the changes from volunteerism to law as the means for ordering the economy."

That historic break between old and new would take months to become apparent. The sharper, more immediate transition was personal and presentational. Herbert Hoover, buried in the rubble of the economy, was determined that his successor join him there. Franklin Roosevelt, elected as the anti-Hoover, not only refused, he used the outgoing president's cascading failure to accelerate his own ascent. On the eve of the Inaugural, the personal animus between incoming and outgoing presidents would reach levels never seen since.

Chapter Twenty-seven

"Gabriel Over the White House"

WILLIAM RANDOLPH HEARST WAS RESTLESS. The previous summer in Chicago, he had failed to play kingmaker with Jack Garner, his handpicked "America First" candidate. When FDR won the nomination, the publisher scrambled to claim credit for cutting the deal that put him over the top. This was almost certainly untrue, but Hearst convinced himself otherwise. At the end of the fall campaign, he telegraphed all of his editors with firm written instructions that Hearst newspapers should endorse Roosevelt.

After the election, Hearst was determined to stay influential during what he considered the worst crisis of his lifetime. His own empire was crumbling under the weight of the Depression and would soon be restructured. But he still had control of a large media and entertainment empire and he resolved to use it to shape the future. Hearst believed that the country needed a dictator but he wasn't sure FDR knew how to fill the role. So in February 1933, he set out to show Roosevelt the way. Scratching out longhand changes in a film script he had purchased, Hearst put words into the mouth of "President Hammond," the dictator to be played by the star Walter Huston in the 1933 hit, *Gabriel Over the White House*. The film combines an implicit indictment of Hoover for mistreating the unemployed with a Hearst blueprint for how a benevolent despot would straighten out the country.

After a car crash that leaves him in a coma, President Hammond is visited by the archangel Gabriel. He awakens a new man, and refuses to call out the military against the camps of unemployed men patterned on the previous summer's real-life Bonus Army.

The fictional president proposes an "Army of Construction" to implement a "plan for the rehabilitation of America." He demands that his Cabinet of loud party hacks and stand-patters resign. When Congress tries to impeach him, he goes before a joint session to tell the country, "We need action—immediate and effective action," before dissolving the legislative branch. Then the president righteously declares martial law and approves the execution of his gangster enemies by firing squad in front of the Statue of Liberty, without the slightest indication in the film there is anything wrong with doing so. The movie ends with President Hammond dying of a heart attack. He is remembered by all as "one of the greatest presidents who ever lived."

Roosevelt liked the movie script so much that in the exhausting first weeks of his presidency he found the time to help put some finishing touches on it, changing one scene from a battleship to a yacht and another from Washington to Baltimore, so that the demonstrators massing against the government would not seem quite so threatening. (Because of jitters over the Zangara assassination attempt, a scene in which President Hammond is shot at while in a car was also changed.) "I want to send you this line to tell you how pleased I am with the changes you made in 'Gabriel Over the White House,' " Roosevelt wrote Hearst less than a month after assuming office. "I think it is an intensely interesting picture and should do much to help." That the Rooseveltian hero of the popular film was a dictator must have seemed an advantage to the real-life president. It would help pave the way for precipitous action, if the role required it.

This kind of bald-faced politics in a hit feature film was rare then, as it is today. Even those critics who called it a cartoon and a gross distortion of economic and political life in the capital recognized its importance. The oversimplification was seen as a sign of the American people's impatience. "It represents pretty well its public," Stark Young concluded in *The New Republic* when the film was released in April.

As Hearst sensed, the public—nearly catatonic that winter—was more ready than any time before or since to submit to a dictator. Mussolini was still widely popular in the United States that year. Hearst thought the Italian strongman was "a marvelous man [who] takes care of every detail of his job." The famous broadcaster Lowell Thomas narrated a film called *Mussolini Speaks* in 1933 that featured an ad campaign calling it "A HIT. Because it appeals to all RED-BLOODED AMERICANS. Because it might be the answer to America's needs." After Italo Balbo, Mussolini's Fascist air marshal, received a tumultuous welcome when he flew a squadron of warplanes from Rome to Chicago for the opening of the 1933 "Century of Progress" World's Fair, FDR invited him to lunch. Through the early 1930s, Fascism remained respectable.*

Communist Party ideology was also trendy in intellectual circles but never caught on with the masses. Despite intensive recruitment drives, the idea of the government seizing everyone's property didn't have much appeal. The Socialists under Norman Thomas fared only slightly better. The blue-blooded Thomas was not a dentist (Leon Trotsky had called Socialists a "party of dentists"), but beyond some cachet in churches and schools, his do-gooder socialism was seen as too tame for the times. Many Americans wanted a tangier political brew. It seemed that every dinner conversation among elites included some discussion of different ways to organize society. *Harper's, The Atlantic, Scribner's,* and other magazines debated the imminence of revolution, and the dean of the Harvard Business School admitted that capitalism itself was on trial. For a time that winter, a hare-brained futurist ideology called "Technocracy" had some cognoscenti discussing whether the whole government should be turned over to experts. Change was coming, but no one was quite sure when or how.

Some of the goals of these radical new approaches look prosaic in retrospect. The point of having a dictatorship, Bernard Baruch and others believed, was to balance the budget. The president needed the

---

* In mid-1933, retired U.S. Army General Smedley Butler reported that a New York bond salesman representing fascists offered him $18,000 to plan a coup against FDR if he proved an ineffective leader. Butler reacted indignantly to the overture and reported it to authorities. No treason charges were ever brought.

power to whip the government into shape—to cut through the meddling by bureaucrats and politicians and reduce government spending. In all its years of unpopularity, Congress had never been in such bad odor. Now maybe a new president would do something about it. Even a magazine like *Commonweal*, aimed at liberal Catholics, weighed in that Roosevelt should have "the powers of a virtual dictatorship to reorganize the government."

Walter Lippmann, usually a voice for sanity, might have been expected to resist the call to dictatorship, but he embraced it. "A mild species of dictatorship will help us over the roughest spots in the road ahead," he wrote in his column. On February 1, Lippmann had traveled to Warm Springs for a meeting with Roosevelt and told him privately that he might have to assume the powers of a dictator for an unspecified period. FDR cannot have been thrilled to see the man who had heaped so much abuse upon him in the previous year, but he knew the columnist spoke for the American political establishment.

Chapter Twenty-eight

The Hairy Hand

A S THE ROOSEVELT INAUGURAL SPECIAL made its way south through the chill air to Washington on the evening of March 2, the atmosphere aboard the train was less celebratory than funereal. Earlier in the day, word came from Miami that Mayor Cermak's condition had worsened, an unnerving reminder of why more than 2,700 uniformed and plainclothes police now secured the crowds along the Baltimore & Ohio rail line. Then came a shocking report. Attorney General-designate Thomas J. Walsh, easily the most respected member of FDR's new Cabinet, had died of a heart attack under titillating circumstances. The seventy-two-year-old Walsh was found on the floor of a Pullman car while returning on the Florida Limited from his honeymoon with his wife of one week, the beautiful young widow of a rich Cuban banker. His body was expected to arrive at Union Station in the sleet shortly after the Roosevelt party.

Midway, Jim Farley was invited back to chat with the president-elect in the last car. FDR told Farley that only Lincoln had faced such a challenge on assuming office, then talked quietly about religion, even recalling his own religious training as a child in Hyde Park. He assured him that the spiritual sense of the American people would see them through. The piety seemed genuine to the Catholic Farley. Roosevelt said simply that he believed that the salvation of all peoples depended on a proper attitude toward God. He told Farley that the measures he would adopt—whether legislative or executive—were far less significant than restoring shattered public confidence.

Eleanor later attributed her husband's own confidence in part to that simple faith. "He felt that human beings were given tasks to perform and with those tasks the ability and strength to put them through," she wrote. But if the faith was simple, the "ability" and "strength" were a complicated tangle.

Franklin Roosevelt was a rare mix. He somehow combined instinct with calculation, exasperating improvisations with what some of his contemporaries called "longheadedness"—a way of peering forward, fixing a point far away on the horizon, then tacking toward it without much worry about the day-to-day choppiness en route. This long-range thinking was not the same as long-term planning; he didn't waste a lot of time detailing it. But his focus on the bigger picture would serve him well.

In accounts of 1933, the causes of the final panic are myriad. Mass hysteria is one explanation. Herbert Hoover's failure to take decisive action is another. The underlying structural weakness of the banking system a third. But no explanation is complete without accounting for fear of Franklin Roosevelt, whose election and pre-Inaugural posture sent wealthy people to their banks to withdraw and hoard their currency and gold. Mostly Hoover voters, they were wrong about the gold standard and wrong about how Roosevelt would ruin them; as events would prove, he saved what was left of their fortunes. But their fears were genuine. The bank panic was not just the product of free-floating Depression anxiety. When FDR would soon proclaim, "The only thing we have to fear is fear itself," he was trying to calm not just the general public but the rich, by saying: *You* don't have to fear *me*.

The banking crisis peaked just before his Inauguration. With the upper Midwest in turmoil, Cleveland banks began to fold, threatening the Ohio banking structure. New Jersey passed an emergency law limiting withdrawals, causing a spread of panicky behavior in the East. In a three-day period starting February 23, Indiana, Arkansas, and Maryland declared holidays, kicking off a round of more closures the following week. By Saturday, February 25, the Hoover White House received word to expect rioting on Monday in Detroit, where the banks had been closed for nearly two weeks. People couldn't buy gasoline, milk, or bread. Railroad cars sat on sidings. Thousands of automobiles were abandoned, out of gas, in the middle of the road. The only good news was that this lack of transportation made starting a riot harder.

In the space of a few days, the whole system began to implode. "These bankers haven't any more notion of public psychology than a chicken," Roosevelt complained. On February 28, Nevada, which four months earlier had been the first state to declare a holiday, suspended banking operations for a second time, along with Alabama, Kentucky, and Tennessee. Most symbolically devastating, two Washington, D.C., banks, just a block from the Treasury, shut their doors. WASHINGTON BANK SUSPENDS! read tabloid headlines as far away as San Francisco. By the early evening of Friday, March 3, banks in thirty-two of forty-eight states were closed, with several more to come. Depositors had transferred more than $1.3 billion in gold and gold certificates to foreign accounts or just taken it home. The New York Fed said it didn't have enough gold left to open for morning business on Saturday, March 4—Inauguration Day.

Hoover makes no sense of these last, dizzying days of his administration in his memoirs. He argues at the same time that there was a severe crisis (caused by Roosevelt) and that the crisis was not severe enough to close the rest of the banks. When Ray Lyman Wilbur, the secretary of the interior, came calling at the White House, he told Hoover that everything humanly possible had been undertaken to avert disaster, but the Inauguration was only forty-eight hours away and little more could be done. Hoover exploded: "We will fight until 10:49 a.m. March 4, when I leave for the Capitol! We must try everything, not once but a dozen times!"

That suggests an instinct to act, but his own high command was frustrated at his inaction. The Treasury Department and the Fed both urged the president to approve deposit insurance and move forward with a national bank holiday. Because Hoover had no explicit power to close banks, the plan was to use the 1917 Trading with the Enemy Act, an obscure wartime provision that was intended to prevent gold transfers that could help the Germans. The original wartime measure was temporary and had long since expired. But when economic conditions worsened in 1932, a clever legislative draftsman at the Hoover Treasury had dusted off the bill and taken the legally questionable step of changing the "implementation language" to make the 1917 act permanent. This was probably illegal, but the Hoover men were frightened and not in the mood for legal niceties. They feared that if the president didn't act quickly, the whole system might vaporize. Treasury Secretary Ogden Mills told a banker planning to visit Bermuda: "If you go, don't get a roundtrip ticket—when you're ready to return, there'll be nothing worth returning to."

At the worst possible moment, Hoover got some bad advice. His attorney general, William D. Mitchell, at first decided that the Trading with the Enemy Act was fine to use as the basis for issuing an emergency proclamation. But before he advised Hoover of that, Mitchell backed off. If President-elect Roosevelt would not request the action, Mitchell reasoned, it didn't meet the test of an emergency. FDR demurred—no responsibility without authority. But he sent word through aides that he wouldn't object if Hoover acted alone. Hoover, spooked, felt that if he did move to shut the banks, the Democratic Congress would rebuke him after he left office for taking precipitous action on the way out the door, though there was no sign of any Democrats planning to do so.

As the board of governors of the Fed stayed in continuous seventeen-and-a-half-hour session from 10:00 a.m. Thursday, March 2, to 3:30 a.m., Friday morning, March 3, tempers began to fray. Up in New York, the New York Fed had thirteen teller windows paying out gold, with long lines at each one. In the Bronx, lines at banks were so long that a mother rented out her baby for twenty-five cents a trip to women who used the sympathy to move to the head of the line. By 3:00 p.m. on March 3, the Bowery Savings Bank across from Manhattan's Grand Central Station closed its doors with huge throngs still waiting outside.

Eight blocks north at Radio City Music Hall, the movie *King Kong* had recently opened. Across the nation, a giant hairy hand was closing around more than Fay Wray's throat.

Chapter Twenty-nine

Reluctant First Lady

ONE OF THE BIG HITS of the 1933 Broadway season was *As Thousands Cheer*, a musical revue by Irving Berlin and Moss Hart that ran for four hundred performances. The show featured a sketch entitled "Franklin D. Roosevelt to Be Inaugurated Tomorrow" that lampooned the Hoovers for stripping the White House bare and Eleanor for resenting the move from New York to Washington. Hart's hilarious skit was too hard on the Hoovers but understated the feelings of Mrs. Roosevelt.

Even on the eve of the Inauguration, Eleanor, at forty-eight, was still deeply apprehensive about what lay ahead. Her friends found it difficult to understand, but she was sure she was doomed to be a failure in Washington. "I'm just not the sort of person who would be any good at that job," she told one. "I dare say I shall be criticized whatever I do." She believed she would be a pallid copy of her aunt, Edith Roosevelt, a much-admired Washington hostess and first lady, and well behind Mrs. Coolidge, too. She loathed the hostess part of the job, anyway, and especially dreaded having her picture taken. She knew she had to smile, but when she did so, it accentuated her worst features. "If you haven't any chin and your front teeth stick out, it is going to show on a camera plate," she said.

Eleanor's greatest respect was reserved for women who made their own way in the world. "If I really had to go out and earn my own living, entirely on my own, I'd have to do it as a scrubwoman," she said, with the combination of ironic detachment and self-pity that characterized much of her pre-Inaugural mood. "And I'd probably not be very good at that. I have no profession—no training for anything." When reminded that she was an esteemed teacher at the Todhunter School in Manhattan, she replied that this was only because she held a financial stake in the school, and now she would have to give up teaching, too. She asked Franklin to hire her as a White House secretary to handle mail, just as Ettie Garner had done for her husband on Capitol Hill and would continue to do when he became vice president. FDR brushed her off, concerned that it would upset Missy LeHand.

The last night before boarding the train for Washington, Eleanor went alone for dinner to the apartment of a close friend, the reporter she had come to trust. It was, she told Lorena Hickok of the Associated Press, her last evening out of captivity. Hickok, or "Hick," was not just any friend. She was, perhaps, the great love of Eleanor Roosevelt's life, though for many years family members and retainers belittled her importance and cropped her out of most photographs. In late 1932 and 1933, Eleanor wrote Hickok almost every day they were not together, often ten pages or more, ending with expressions of longing and adoration. Over the course of their thirty-year friendship, they exchanged an estimated sixteen thousand pages of letters, most of them on substantive matters related to what they had seen and heard on their travels. After Eleanor's death, Hickok destroyed most of her early letters to Eleanor and edited and typed those the first lady sent to her, which were full of accounts of her time in the White House. Even these versions are often tender. Since the early 1980s, when their correspondence was disclosed, a spirited disagreement has taken place among historians over whether the women had a lesbian affair.*

The arguments over physical contact seem almost beside the point. It was the intense relationship between the two women that shaped Eleanor at a pivotal time in her life, and she, in turn, helped shape the life of the nation. Their love for each other was especially strong during 1933, when Eleanor was unsure of which course to take as she ventured into new territory. Shortly before Eleanor's death in 1962, Hickok pub-

---

* For instance, Blanche Wiesen Cook says yes, and Geoffrey C. Ward says no. See Notes.

lished a book called *Reluctant First Lady* that chronicles the trepidation felt by "Mrs. Roosevelt" (as Hick and almost everyone else called her) upon entering the White House.

Hickok eased those fears, suggesting a fresh path for the new first lady that influenced, to greater and lesser degrees, the roles that all women married to American presidents would play in the decades ahead. It was she who convinced Eleanor to hold the first press conferences ever undertaken by a first lady, to write a daily newspaper column, and to travel as her husband's eyes and ears. Without Lorena Hickok, Eleanor Roosevelt would not have ended up such a formidable historical figure. And without Eleanor's newfound strength, FDR would not have either.

The woman with such influence over Eleanor Roosevelt in 1933 sometimes claimed to be the great-granddaughter of "Wild Bill" Hickok. At five foot eight and nearly 200 pounds, "Hick" smoked cigars and pipes and could drink anyone under the table. She aspired to journalism at an early age, modeling herself on the great reporter (and playwright) Edna Ferber. While still in her early twenties, Hickok impressed her editors with her depth and range, covering opera for the *Milwaukee Sentinel* and football for the *Minneapolis Tribune*. She was gifted and funny, and accepted as one of the boys. By 1932, the reporter known to all as "Hick" had reached the top of the craft, assigned to cover the Lindbergh kidnapping trial and the presidential campaign for the Associated Press, the premier wire service in the world.

Almost from the start, Hick wrote puff pieces about Eleanor that— in a departure from her high standards—she agreed to clear first with Louis Howe. Their relationship deepened two weeks before the election when Eleanor asked Hick to accompany her to the funeral of Missy LeHand's mother. On the way home, the two women bonded over devastating childhood memories. Eleanor, normally reluctant to talk about her personal life, told Hick she had lost her mother, brother, and father by the time she was twelve, then was shunted to the home of a heartless grandmother and aunts who called her an "ugly duckling." Lorena's story was worse. After her mother died, her father whipped her and raped her. She was thrown out of the house at fourteen and raised herself in the streets before finding refuge in newsrooms. By the end of the long overnight train ride, each had a friend for life.

Hick was smitten. For Christmas 1932, she gave Eleanor one of her most prized possessions: a large sapphire and diamond ring she had received in 1916 as a gift from a European grand diva she had covered as a young reporter. Eleanor wore it on her left hand for the next four years.

But Eleanor was suffering from depression. "My zest in life is rather gone for the time being. . . . If anyone looks at me, I want to weep," she wrote Lorena that winter. "I get like this sometimes. It makes me feel like a dead weight and my mind goes round and round like a squirrel in a cage. I want to run and I can't and I despise myself."*

Before the Inauguration, Eleanor tried to hold onto as much of her old life as she could. She continued editing a magazine for young mothers, *Babies—Just Babies*, and edited a book of her father's letters about his life as a sportsman. She grew annoyed at the other women reporters now assigned to follow her every move, announcing in exasperation one day that she would not leave the train station until the reporters left first.

In late January, Eleanor was invited to the White House to meet First Lady Lou Hoover and the staff to make moving arrangements. The whole trip represented a defiance of protocol. At a time when few wealthy women drove, she motored down to Washington in her blue Buick convertible with Hick and a pair of dogs. Then she refused a government car to take her to the White House from the Mayflower Hotel, preferring instead to walk over with Hick. The reporter was blocked at the door by Hoover's staff but later got an exclusive interview for the AP, the first time in months she had printed anything close to what she knew.

By the time they returned to Washington on March 2, aboard FDR's special Inaugural train (Franklin had barred his wife from driving down), Eleanor was ready to bring Hick to a place of special meaning to her. En route, Hick had taken care of Eleanor's Scottish terrier, Meggie. This gave Eleanor an excuse to dodge the crowd of nearly two thousand waiting in the cold evening rain at Washington's Union Station. As she reclaimed her dog, she whispered to Hick to meet her at a side entrance of the Mayflower early the next morning with a cab.

---

* While Martha Washington was also unhappy about her husband becoming president, the only comparable emotional state for an incoming first lady was Jacqueline Kennedy's postpartum depression after the birth of John F. Kennedy, Jr., which followed the 1960 election.

At 7:45 a.m., Eleanor was already waiting at the DeSales Street side entrance to hop in the taxi with Hick. As soon as they were sure they were not being followed, Eleanor instructed the driver to show them the R Street house she had lived in during her wartime years in Washington, then proceed to Rock Creek Cemetery, to a clearing beyond the Soldiers Home that Lincoln used as his Civil War retreat. As they made their way through a grove of pines, Hick noticed that Eleanor knew the site well.

The haunting Sphinx-like sculpture they visited is a larger than life-size bronze by Augustus Saint-Gaudens of a seated woman enveloped in the folds of her robe. It is called *Grief*, but is better known as the Adams Memorial, commissioned by a grieving Henry Adams in memory of his brilliant wife, Clover. Eleanor had surely heard the story of how Clover Adams killed herself by swallowing photographic acid in 1885 after suffering from a prolonged depression. Thirty years later, during the Wilson administration, Eleanor became friendly with the aging Henry Adams in the years just before he published *The Education of Henry Adams*. He would come by the Roosevelts' Georgetown house in his carriage and visit with their young children. Once he pointed to the White House from his home across Lafayette Square and told Franklin and Eleanor that it didn't much matter what man lived there.

But the appeal of the sculpture went deeper. "Sometimes I'd be very unhappy and sorry for myself," Eleanor told Hick, remembering her difficult years in Washington, when she was suffering through her own confusion about her marriage. "When I was feeling that way, if I could manage it, I'd come out here, alone, and sit and look at that woman. And I'd always come away somehow feeling better. And stronger. I've been here many, many times."

Eleanor might not have felt better and stronger had she known that the cause of so much of her Washington pain, Lucy Mercer, now the wealthy Mrs. Winthrop Rutherfurd of Allamuchy, New Jersey, and Aiken, South Carolina, was about to arrive quietly back in the capital for the Inaugural ceremonies. "Lucy, I have just heard that Franklin Roosevelt was in love with you," a relative said to her that weekend. "Was that true, Lucy?" She brushed off the question, though one cousin, Mrs. Lyman Cotten, said later that FDR continued writing her secretly after their affair ended. In any event, Franklin had made discreet arrangements for her to have an unmarked car at her disposal and a seat for his swearing in.

With her parties canceled out of deference to Senator Walsh, her husband busy in meetings, and her children out, Eleanor had the night before the Inauguration free. The hundreds of other friends and relatives in town apparently did not interest her at the moment. The Howes and the Morgenthaus were the only nonfamily members given a place of pride on the seventh floor of the Mayflower. Eleanor liked Elinor Morgenthau but she found Grace Howe difficult.* "I'm alone," she told Hick on the phone. "Would you mind coming over and dining with me?" After dodging other reporters, Hick arrived through a side entrance. The room service food went untouched while Eleanor worried. "Anything can happen," she repeated over and over, as Jimmy Roosevelt and Louis Howe wandered in with reports of more states declaring holidays. "How much can people take without blowing up?"

After midnight, FDR, who stayed, as usual, in another suite, sent over a final draft of the Inaugural Address for Eleanor to read before it went to the mimeographers for copying in the morning. She read it aloud to Hick. "It's a good speech, a courageous speech," Eleanor said. "It has hope in it. But will the people accept it? Will they believe in him?"

The reading copy went back to Ray Moley, who knew nothing of Hick's presence and kept it under his pillow so that no newspaperman could see it. Hick later wrote that it hadn't occurred to her to call the AP desk with the gist of the speech and a few quotations: "Scoops and my career didn't seem important that night, even to me." Although she would remain at the AP several months longer, Hick admitted that "that night Lorena Hickok ceased to be a newspaper reporter."

At three or four in the morning, Jimmy Roosevelt came in to say that "Pa" was finally going to bed. When Eleanor returned from saying good night to Franklin, her fast friend was fast asleep. The next morning, Inauguration Day, they got up and walked the dog together.

---

* Grace Howe resented the Roosevelts and, for a time, believed without evidence that her husband and Eleanor had had an affair.

Chapter Thirty

"Like Hell I Will!"

I KE HOOVER, no relation to the president, was the longtime chief usher at the White House. In fact, Hoover, who had served happily under Theodore Roosevelt, was partial to Roosevelts and remembered Eleanor fondly from her teenage years. At 4:00 p.m. on March 3, the usher had greeted the president-elect as he entered the Executive Mansion for a traditional tea with the outgoing president.

"It's good to have another Roosevelt in the White House," Ike Hoover told him, and whispered to Roosevelt that Treasury Secretary Ogden Mills and Fed Chairman Eugene Meyer were on their way over. This was a surprise. With Eleanor, Jimmy, and daughter-in-law Betsey Cushing Roosevelt in tow, FDR had assumed this was to be a strictly ceremonial occasion. Now he knew he was mistaken. If Mills and Meyer were coming, it meant that the president planned to discuss a last-minute deal. FDR wanted no part of any joint action at this late hour. But the situation was growing increasingly grave. The news on March 3 was of long lines in New York and other financial centers as the people withdrew their gold and currency. What had begun as a regional problem a few weeks earlier was pulling down the entire financial system. Nearly three quarters of the states had closed their banks, with more likely overnight.

This would be the third meeting between the two men since the election, each more uncomfortable. At the earlier conferences, FDR had Ray Moley with him as backup. Now he told Ike Hoover to summon Moley from the Mayflower Hotel for what promised to be another game of chicken between two proud men. Moley was so exhausted from the round-the-clock crisis consultations and preparation of the Inaugural Address that he hadn't even taken off his coat before napping on his hotel bed. But awakened by a call from the White House, he rushed over.

Meanwhile, the tea with the president and Mrs. Hoover and the Roosevelt clan was not going well. In later years, the story was a Roosevelt family favorite, with President Hoover cast as the imperious prig. As FDR told the story:

> I decided to cut it short. It is customary for an outgoing president to return the [courtesy] call of an incoming one. I knew that I didn't want to go through the strain involved in this custom so I tried to give him a way out. I mentioned the custom to him, and then said: "I realize, Mr. President, that you are extremely busy so I will understand completely if you do not return the call." For the first time that day he looked me squarely in the eye and said: "Mr. Roosevelt, when you are in Washington as long as I have been, you will learn that the President of the United States calls on nobody." That was that. I hustled my family out of the room. I'm sure Jimmy wanted to punch him in the eye.

The "custom" FDR referred to didn't exist. There is no record of any outgoing president paying a courtesy call on an incoming president at his home or hotel. (In fact, even the courtesy call at the White House by the incoming president went back only to Woodrow Wilson in 1913.) After family members abruptly left the tea for an adjoining room, Hoover asked to see FDR alone for a few minutes.

It wasn't until nearly half a century later that an account of what transpired between the two men emerged. Hoover didn't mention it in his memoirs, and his comment was too barbed for FDR to make it part of his oft-told yarn about the courtesy call. In 1981, Dorothy Roe Lewis, a retired wire service reporter, wrote based on contemporaneous notes that Eleanor Roosevelt had returned to the Mayflower Hotel with a tale that was too explosive to print. As Eleanor explained it immediately afterward to the four women reporters who covered her, "They [Hoover and FDR] forgot to close the door and I could hear everything they said. Mr. Hoover said to Mr. Roosevelt, 'Will you join in a joint proclamation closing all of the banks?' Then she heard her husband say, 'Like hell I will! If you haven't the guts to do it yourself, I'll wait until I'm president to do it.' "

With the Inauguration only twenty hours away, Hoover's position was that he would only consider closing the banks if the president-elect joined with him. When Moley, Mills, and Meyer entered the room, the tense conversation turned to specifics. The issue was the legality of using the 1917 Trading with the Enemy Act to close the banks and control foreign exchange and withdrawals. Hoover said that he might try to invoke the old statute if FDR shared responsibility by guaranteeing that the new Democratic Congress would not object. Roosevelt's response was that the 1917 act could be legally invoked unilaterally and that his administration would view Hoover's decision to use it sympathetically, but that he could not speak for the Congress. He concluded: "I shall be waiting at my hotel, Mr. President, to learn what you decide."

When Eleanor told the women reporters back at the Mayflower about what she had overheard, she thought they would appreciate the scoop. But the reporters, including Lorena Hickok, decided that it would turn a national crisis into a worldwide panic if the public knew that the outgoing and incoming presidents were squabbling like children. Eleanor agreed, and they pledged to keep it a secret. Hickok's AP story reported simply that the Hoovers and Roosevelts had occasion to "chat quietly for an hour about picnics and camping."

Ed Flynn remembered that FDR was "visibly angry" when he returned to the hotel after this last encounter. It was, Flynn said, one of the only times in all of the years he knew Roosevelt that he had seen him that way. With others who angered him, Roosevelt would paper over his feelings with his patented bonhomie. But like his earlier meetings with the outgoing president, this one "cut deeply into Roosevelt's memory," Grace Tully remembered. He hadn't been prepared to be "treated like a schoolboy or to have his own integrity thrown into question by Hoover."

•   •   •

Thomas Walsh had been ready to use the Trading with the Enemy Act to close the banks once FDR became president. But now he was dead and Roosevelt didn't have any immediate ideas for a replacement as attorney general; nor did Howe or the other men around him. Missy LeHand piped up, suggesting that Homer Cummings, who was supposed to be the new governor general of the Philippines, might be a good choice. Roosevelt had no problem letting Missy weigh in on Cabinet selection. Within hours, Cummings both agreed to take the job and rendered a legal opinion that the 1917 statute could be twisted to allow for a national bank holiday.

As if the afternoon encounter between Hoover and Roosevelt at the White House had not been strange enough, there now commenced an unprecedented series of Inauguration eve contacts between incoming and outgoing presidents. At 8:30 p.m., Roosevelt called the White House from the Mayflower. He had calmed down. His concern was that his Inauguration would be overshadowed by the country's bankruptcy. Now he hoped to discuss once again the idea of Hoover closing the banks for a few hours, until the transfer of power. Hoover now argued that a joint proclamation against excessive withdrawals and restricting gold exports would be enough. A general bank holiday without a plan for reopening would be dangerous, he said, ignoring the fact that his own Treasury secretary had suggested just such a contingency plan.

Just before midnight, the call went the other direction. Hoover was concerned about huge bank runs on Saturday morning. He phoned FDR to ask once more if he would join him in a joint proclamation closing all banks. This time, it was Roosevelt's turn to say no. He wanted to study the idea after the Inauguration. He informed Hoover that Carter Glass didn't think a joint proclamation was worthwhile. He repeated that he would use the Trading with the Enemy Act to close the banks only after he became president and told Hoover that if he wanted to invoke the act on his last night in office, that would be preferable. FDR's message was clear: the incoming president wasn't going to give the outgoing president political cover.

Hoover asked FDR to hold the phone as he repeated Roosevelt's comments to Treasury Secretary Mills, Assistant Secretary Arthur

Ballantine, and the other Treasury officials gathered around his Oval Office desk. Because phones had no "hold" buttons in those days, Roosevelt heard Hoover, who was perhaps not aware he was being overheard, summarize his views to the others. Hoover got back on the line to make sure he understood FDR. No joint proclamation?

Right, said Roosevelt.

They spoke once more at 1:00 a.m. on Inauguration Day. Hoover called FDR to say that the Federal Reserve and some Treasury officials were still at work, monitoring the situation in New York, Illinois, and other states. Roosevelt thanked him and suggested they both "turn in" for the night.*

Will Woodin, FDR's puckish Treasury secretary–designate, was supposed to be in box seats that evening at the National Symphony Orchestra, which was scheduled to perform his special Inaugural composition, "The Franklin Delano Roosevelt March." Instead, he was in round-the-clock talks with Hoover officials and a group of sixteen of the nation's most important bankers, headed by Thomas Lamont of J. P. Morgan, who were gathered around a telephone at the New York Fed. Woodin and the bankers believed a joint proclamation was better than nothing; but at 11:15 p.m., Roosevelt had declined.

When Woodin relayed this to the Hoover camp, Hoover suggested issuing the proclamation with Hoover and *Woodin* signing—the president of the United States and the head of the American Foundry Car Co. Even the lateness of the hour—2:00 a.m.—couldn't excuse the absurdity of this idea. President Hoover was exhausted and not thinking straight. Woodin prudently declined. By this time, Hoover's own allies were growing frustrated with him. Fed chairman Eugene Meyer knew he would be up all night. His wife Agnes wrote in her diary: "World literally rocking beneath our feet . . . sound of crashing banks."

After its seventeen-and-a-half-hour session, the board of governors of the Federal Reserve system had met once more late on March 3—even pulling a sick member out of bed—and voted to urge Hoover to suspend all banking. That afternoon, while waiting to enter the Oval

---

* Not until the 1981 Inauguration of Ronald Reagan amid the Iranian hostage crisis would the outgoing and incoming administrations be in such close contact on the eve of the transfer of power, and then it was at the staff level.

Office to make the point, Meyer had been introduced to the young son of Ted Joslin, the president's press secretary, as "Governor Meyer."

"What state are you the governor of?" the boy asked.

"The state of bankruptcy," Meyer replied.

That night, Meyer told Hoover that the chairmen of both the New York and Chicago Feds were urging at least a three-day holiday. Once again, Hoover said no, unless Roosevelt requested it. At this point, Meyer told the president that he was "fiddling while Rome burns." "I can keep on fiddling," Hoover replied heatedly. "I have been fiddled at long enough and can do some myself."

In the wee hours, Meyer sent his secretary to the White House with the Fed board's letter recommending a national banking holiday and a draft executive order closing the banks for Hoover to sign. Hoover was finally asleep. When slipping the material under the door didn't suffice, Meyer insisted the president be awakened. Hoover was furious. Why was the Federal Reserve doing this to him in the last few hours of his term?

Because it was all collapsing. Michigan and Maryland were one thing. Now New York, center of banking for the nation, was in free fall. With huge bank runs on March 3, FDR's successor as governor of New York, Herbert Lehman, canceled his trip to the Inauguration of his political patron to stay in Albany and try to figure out what to do. For most of the day, he thought that declaring a bank holiday would worsen things. But after much prodding from the New York Fed, he finally issued a proclamation at 2:30 a.m. closing all banks in New York State.

If the New York banks had opened that Saturday, Ogden Mills told Henry Stimson as they rode to the Inauguration in the final moments of their official government service, they "would have gone bust, and the fault would have been lain at the president's door." As the economic historian Susan Estabrook Kennedy has written, it was ironic that FDR's protégé and successor had spared Hoover further ignominy, if that were possible.

At 3:22 a.m., Illinois governor Henry Horner followed Governor Lehman's example. That brought the total of states closing their banks to thirty-four out of forty-eight. But it meant that states without holidays would be subjected to ferocious bank runs unlike any yet seen. So, in the middle of the night, the Fed (which stayed in session until 4:00

a.m.) decided to instruct the ten regional Feds to contact state governors in their areas.

Most of the governors didn't get the word. As the large Philadelphia banks tottered, Pennsylvania governor Gifford Pinchot was in Washington for the Inauguration. The Progressive Era conservationist and Theodore Roosevelt's great friend had left home in such a hurry that he only had ninety-five cents in his pocket, not enough for a decent hotel. No one could reach him. Finally, at nearly 5:00 a.m., a high-ranking Treasury department official went over to the private home where Pinchot was staying, roused the household, and had Pinchot call his office in Harrisburg to give the order to close the banks that Saturday.

Moley had left FDR's suite at 1:00 a.m. to go to bed, but he ran into Woodin stepping out of the elevator at the Mayflower. Woodin said with a smile that he, too, had hoped to go to sleep but couldn't even get to the stage of undressing. "This thing is bad," he told Moley. "Will you come over to the Treasury with me? We'll see if we can give those fellows there a hand." Woodin and Moley joined the Hoover team in Secretary Mills's office, the beginning of a bonding between outgoing and incoming economic policymakers. Moley fell asleep in a chair until Woodin woke him to say that New York and Illinois were about to issue their proclamations. "It's all right," Woodin said. "Everything is closed. Let's go now." At 6:00 a.m., Herbert Hoover spoke to his aides with a tone of finality: "We are at the end of our string," he said. "There is nothing more we can do."

As dawn broke on Saturday, March 4, 1933, the United States resembled Franklin Roosevelt on that August day in 1921 at Campobello as he lay paralyzed with illness and fear. A few elderly men and women had dim childhood memories of the Civil War, seventy years earlier. No one else could bring to mind anything so frightening in the life of the nation.

PART FOUR

The Hundred Days

Chapter Thirty-one

"Fear Itself"

Asked years later what was the most memorable moment of her husband's presidency, Eleanor Roosevelt did not cite the attack on Pearl Harbor or D-Day or the Big Three summits. She spoke of the first Inauguration. For the country, the compelling part of the day was the Inaugural Address. For decades, historians have believed that FDR only pretended to write the speech and that it was, in fact, written by Ray Moley. But Roosevelt was probably the primary author, just as he claimed.

FDR had begun thinking aloud about his Inaugural Address as early as September 1932, more than six weeks before the election and nearly six months before the swearing in. Since his *Harvard Crimson* days, Roosevelt fancied himself a writer. During the grim period after he was stricken with polio, he wrote a couple of book reviews and dreamed of being an author. On several occasions, he began keeping a diary but always dropped it after a few dutiful entries. Even so, the ambition endured. As governor, he wrote Arthur Krock of *The New York Times* that a fortune-teller once told him that writing was his "forte." It was, he said, "the first event in my life that has given me a really swelled head."

The Democrats' top ghostwriter, Charlie Michelson, always thought FDR "a better phrase maker than anyone he ever had around him." Many of his best lines—"My friends," "a day which will live in infamy,"

"The Four Freedoms"—were unquestionably his. Like Winston Churchill and Ronald Reagan, he preferred reading written texts to speaking extemporaneously. This meant that the speechwriting process was central to his life in politics. But unlike Hoover, who often wrote alone, FDR pulled in so many people to review drafts and make suggestions that the provenance of his speeches was always in dispute.

FDR's First Inaugural began after a long day of campaigning with a three-hour conversation with Moley in San Francisco's Palace Hotel in September 1932. Roosevelt often enjoyed a burst of mental energy late at night. He told Moley that by March 1933 the situation he would face was likely to be something akin to a wartime emergency and that a strong show of presidential leadership would be needed. He began to talk of Lincoln, who expanded presidential power to meet the emergency in 1861. FDR outlined these ideas at a time when the economy was picking up a bit and few others, even within his campaign, would have thought in terms so dire.

For the rest of the campaign and most of the hectic transition, Moley didn't have a spare moment to work on the speech. It wasn't until February 4, when FDR was about to embark on the *Nourmahal*, that the two men had another conversation about the address, then a month away. Moley's scrap paper notes from this session are sketchy, with lists of themes mentioned by FDR: "Money changers," "the good neighbor," "disciplined action." These ideas made their way into the final draft, while others, such as "the Ten Points" (a variation on Woodrow Wilson's famous Fourteen Points) and "dictatorship" (a cryptic note without elaboration), were dropped. The idea of "giving them hell," also jotted down by Moley, would have to wait for Harry Truman.

As FDR was enjoying his voyage on Vincent Astor's yacht, Moley worked for two days in his office at Barnard College on a draft. He took what he had prepared to Hyde Park, where on the evening of February 27, Roosevelt, Moley, Missy LeHand, and a family stenographer dined and then repaired to the library for a long evening of work on the speech. At 9:00 p.m., according to Moley's contemporaneous notes, FDR sat before a roaring fire in a chair at a folding bridge table with a yellow legal pad and read over Moley's draft. As Moley lay nearby on a couch, Roosevelt took calls from Will Woodin and Cordell Hull, talked about the banking crisis, and drank a whiskey. He asked, "How

"Master Franklin," with Sara in 1887 (above left) and (above right, in top hat) in a school play where he showed an early instinct for theatrical performance. As president, he thought of himself as one of "the two best actors in America."

The "mama's boy" (sailing with his mama) was called "Feather Duster" by his own cousins and ridiculed in prep school for sounding British.

4

Courting Eleanor (with Sara between them). Even as he failed as a lawyer, balancing two strong women helped to bolster his self-confidence.

The assistant secretary of the navy with his wife, mother, and brood in 1919, not long after he and Eleanor nearly divorced. The early experience in the bureaucracy was essential to success in the White House.

5

6

With indispensable adviser Louis Howe, "the Medieval Gnome," (in cap) and old friend Tom Lynch in 1920, when FDR ran for vice-president.

Polio in 1921 left his legs withered, but in lifting the spirits of other patients in Warm Springs, FDR would be rehearsing the opening of his presidency, when he lifted the country from despondency.

With Al Smith, "the Happy Warrior," in a 1930 photo that—despite their bitter rivalry—hung in FDR's Hyde Park bedroom at his death. Smith was less forgiving and did everything to keep Roosevelt from becoming president.

7

8

9

The governor basks in congratulatory telegrams after his dramatic 1932 "flight to Chicago" to accept the nomination in person for the first time in history and unveil the "New Deal."

Pundits such as Walter Lippmann (below left) and H. L. Mencken thought he was lightweight, unprincipled, and would likely lose to President Herbert Hoover.

10

11

12

13

Greeting a farmer in Warm Springs, Georgia (top left). Whistle-stopping (top right) with Eleanor and Earl Miller (rear), her handsome bodyguard. Eleanor was so unhappy about the prospect of FDR becoming president that she told friends in the middle of the Democratic Convention that she would run away with Miller and wreck FDR's chances.

Offering his trademark smile to an ailing girl in Seattle (below). Even many aides thought Roosevelt too weak to travel widely during the 1932 campaign.

14

15

FDR's "Brain Trust," assembled by Sam Rosenman, included Raymond Moley (with FDR just before Inauguration), Rexford Tugwell (below left), Adolf Berle, Hugh Johnson, and others. Moley claimed, incorrectly, to have been the principal author of the famous Inaugural Address.

In the dismal four months between the election and Inauguration Day, cartoons commented on the obstacles facing the president-elect.

16

Can He Make It Spell National Confidence?

17

18

Riding in Miami, moments before assassin Giuseppe Zangara (below left, in towel) fired five shots at FDR from close range, killing the mayor of Chicago.

After his close call, reporters and cartoonists depicted FDR as a "living martyr," which powered his entrance into office two weeks later.

19

20

With 10,000 banks already closed and terrifying runs on the rest underway (above), the American financial system imploded on the eve of the Inauguration. President-elect Roosevelt had stalled and fibbed and let the crisis worsen rather than sign a joint proclamation with President Hoover.

William Randolph Hearst (below right) produced a hit movie starring Walter Huston that instructed the incoming president on how to be a good dictator. FDR offered some revisions to the script and told Hearst that the film would be a big help.

24

March 4, 1933: Hoover and Roosevelt squabbled into the small hours before ignoring each other en route to the swearing-in. Anticipated in a planned Peter Arno cover for *The New Yorker*, it was scrapped after the assassination attempt.

25

Suggestions:

2nd par. end of 1st line. "Exacting" instead of "serious".

We must battle to eliminate or subjugate these enemies
and to remedy the hovac they have wrought.   And from
the lessons taught and the experience gained in the war
upon which we now embark we will use these same forces
to build the fortifications to secure us against the
menace of future invasion.
We must enlist for that war the forces which recognize
the value of discipline and can teach others -- enlist
those who can take their designated places in the ranks
and sacrifice selfishness and greed in the inevitable
battle for the good of all.   And I can promise you that
the spoils of this war will be a spiritual happiness and
material prosperity incomparably greater than ~~thatxwhich~~
the meager dividends which victory has thus far paid or
ever will pay in "wars of death."
As ~~xaxr~~ new commander-in-chief under the oath to which
you are still bound I reserve to myself the right to
command you.in any phase of the situation which now confronts us.   That is the highest compliment within my power.

26

Casting the Depression as a war, FDR
briefly considered creating a Mussolini-
style private army of veterans, as indicated
by the final four lines of these unused draft
"suggestions" for his radio address to the
American Legion on his first day in office.

Many newspapers and opinion leaders in
fact urged the new president to assume
dictatorial powers. He declined to do so,
but he insisted on "action, and action
now" during his first "Hundred Days."

In Safe Hands!

27

Howe had cards printed up identifying him as "Colonel Louis Rasputin Voltaire Tallyrand Simon Legree Howe."

Leaving the White House after getting FDR's patented "fine, fine, fine" treatment: a frustrated Senator Huey P. Long (below left). Impish Treasury Secretary "Wee Willie" Woodin (below right, at right) was at first mistaken for a button salesman but he eventually designed FDR's banking rescue with Hoover's men and the senator he embraces, Carter Glass of Virginia.

In place of loud exhortation, FDR's first "Fireside Chat" made millions feel as if the president were sitting in their living rooms. His conversational radio style revolutionized how leaders spoke to the people.

Within hours of the first broadcast, the previous week's panicky hoarders began lining up to deposit their remaining money with patriotic confidence.

Eleanor and Lorena Hickok, a talented newspaperwoman, became close in early 1933. Hickok (above, wearing scarf, in Puerto Rico that fall) convinced Eleanor she could be a different kind of first lady. Later, she was cropped out of many photographs as an embarrassment.

When "Bonus Army" protesters returned to Washington, Eleanor offered them coffee, camp songs, and a chance to work. "Hoover sent the army and Roosevelt sent his wife," one veteran said admiringly.

35

The Civilian Conservation Corps was the fastest mobilization in American history, as FDR demanded that hundreds of thousands of unemployed young men be put to work by summer. Eventually, a civilian army of three million planted a billion trees and pioneered the idea of national service.

The president, with CCC chief Robert Fechner and Agriculture Secretary Henry Wallace at a camp in Virginia, knew all the levers of power. "He kept everyone's balls up in the air except his own," quipped Wallace.

36

37

Roosevelt signs the Social Security Act of 1935, the culmination of the social reform he launched in the Hundred Days. His labor secretary, Frances Perkins (behind FDR), the most acute observer of his character, had watched him grow from a supercilious "prig" in 1911 into a model of open-mindedness.

FDR believed in "cradle to grave" coverage but didn't push for it. He knew the only way to win passage was to work with conservatives instead of liberals.

38

FDR aboard the *Amberjack II* at the end of the Hundred Days. Back at Campobello in June 1933, for the first time since being stricken there with polio, he let the mask slip for only a moment before resuming his trademark ebullience.

do you spell 'foreclose'?"* Then, according to Moley, the president-elect, no doubt recalling the fight over the acceptance speech at the Chicago airport the previous summer, said he had better write out the text himself. If Louis Howe—who was arriving the next morning in Hyde Park—failed to see a draft in Roosevelt's handwriting, FDR said, he would "have a fit."

For two hours, FDR and Moley went over every sentence, every word. The session was interrupted by Roosevelt's musings on the founding fathers and presidents he respected, one of the only times on record that he did so. Benjamin Franklin was "shallow," he thought, and Thomas Jefferson "the best" president.† He talked of the range of Theodore Roosevelt's knowledge and apparently also felt a kinship with Woodrow Wilson, with whom he believed he shared some "artistic qualities." After they finished, Moley rose, took his initial draft from the table, and tossed it into the fireplace. "This is your speech now," he told Roosevelt.

Sam Rosenman ignited the struggle for credit when he wrote in his 1952 memoirs that "the speech was one of the very few of which the President wrote the first draft in his own hand." He dug up a memorandum for the files that FDR had written on White House stationery after his third week in office:

March 25, 1933
This is the original manuscript of the Inaugural Address as written at Hyde Park on Monday, February 27th, 1933. I started in about 9:00 p.m. and ended at 1:30 a.m. A number of minor changes were made in subsequent drafts but the final draft is substantially the same as this original.

The new president was clearly intent on history giving him sole credit for crafting his Inaugural Address. With no roaring fire, no whiskey, and, more important, no two-hour session with Moley's draft, the memo was a prideful bid for historical recognition. FDR's memo re-

---

* Vice President Dan Quayle might have wanted to cite this story in his own defense in 1992 when he was skewered for misspelling "potato."
† He would later act on this assessment by building the Jefferson Memorial in Washington, D.C., in 1943.

flects an insecurity about his writing at odds with his confidence in other areas and, if Moley is to be believed, an impulse to distort facts in his own interest. But the memo backfired. The unintended consequence has been that generations of historians incorrectly assume that FDR wrote almost *none* of the speech.

Moley was infuriated by Rosenman's publication of FDR's memo and determined to set the record straight. In a 1966 book, *The First New Deal,* Moley launched his own, more powerful myth: that FDR simply copied over Moley's draft in his own hand. He wrote bitterly that FDR's March 25 memo for the files "seems strange" after all of their conferences on the issue and "to say the least, misleading."

By responding so strongly Moley misled historians into believing the speech was mostly his. Because no Moley draft of the speech survives, Moley in 1966 made a point of reproducing the handwritten notes he used in the draft he tossed into the fire. This looks impressive on first glance but proves nothing. Indeed, a close reading of Moley's notes— both published and unpublished—actually weakens his case for having authored the speech. With the exception of the section on using wartime powers to meet the crisis (which originated in the San Francisco conversation with Roosevelt), the draft language in Moley's personal papers bears little resemblance to the final reading copy of the Inaugural.

In fact, Moley's draft passages disappear almost entirely in the final version, which is tight and direct. Some of that was probably Moley's editing. Some was Louis Howe's handiwork. But it's likely that the bulk of what was finally used was actually Roosevelt's. Not referring to this particular speech, FDR's longtime stenographer, Dorothy Brady, later said of his aides: "Some of them say he didn't write his speeches. They don't know what they're talking about. First, before any of them would say a word, FDR would ramble on and I'd take it all down. *Then* they'd go to work. Sometimes we'd do sixteen drafts before he was satisfied."

The origins of the Inaugural's most famous line—"the only thing we have to fear is fear itself"—remain unclear. Rosenman said the line was inserted on March 3, the day before the Inaugural, after the Roosevelt party had arrived at the Mayflower Hotel in Washington. He wrote that Eleanor Roosevelt told him that one of her friends gave FDR an anthology of Henry David Thoreau's writings and that the president-elect put it on his bedside table at the Mayflower and leafed through it as the speech was being polished. One of Thoreau's lines is: "Nothing is so much to be feared as fear."

Moley believed this story was preposterous, "a colorful fancy, but it could not possibly be true." He wrote that Louis Howe inserted that first paragraph, with the "fear itself" line, at Hyde Park on February 28, when he dictated a tighter version of the speech and added a new first paragraph, as was his habit, though he contributed almost nothing else.* As for FDR reading Thoreau at the Mayflower, Moley wrote: "I saw no books there. . . . I doubt whether during the many months since he first sought the nomination in the spring of 1932 he had read *any* book." Instead, Moley "clearly remembers" that Howe took the famous "fear" line from a department store advertisement that both Howe and Moley saw in a newspaper earlier in February 1933. Subsequent searches of various newspaper files and New York City department store records have failed to confirm Moley's recollection.

The idea behind the line was not new. Cicero, William Shakespeare, Francis Bacon, Daniel Defoe, Lord Chesterfield, and William James had all written about the debilitating effects of fear. And by the early 1930s, it was in the air. Two years before the Roosevelt Inaugural, in February 1931, *The New York Times* ran a front-page story on a job creation program begun by the U.S. Chamber of Commerce. The *Times* quoted the chairman of the chamber as saying, "In a condition of this kind, the thing to be feared most is fear itself."

The name of the Chamber of Commerce chairman was Julius Barnes, the same Julius Barnes who had received FDR's anti-Hoover form letter in 1928 and sent it on to his close friend, that year's Republican nominee for president, who was offended by Roosevelt's campaign gibe. The irony is delicious. Louis Howe and Franklin Roosevelt may have borrowed, or at least absorbed, what became FDR's most famous line from the Republican who launched his grudge match with Herbert Hoover.

---

* Howe died in 1936 and left no memoirs. Harry Hopkins, FDR's top aide during World War II, and Robert Sherwood, a wartime speechwriter, thought the First Inaugural was the best speech of Roosevelt's presidency.

Chapter Thirty-two

The Consecration

T HE MORNING OF SATURDAY MARCH 4, 1933, was cold and
gray, not what the press called "Roosevelt weather" a reference to
the sunshine that had seemed to bless each campaign stop the previous
fall. As Irvin McDuffie helped him into his formal morning attire, FDR
was not his usual cheerful self. The overnight news was grave. The
bank runs and bank closings and unprecedented suspension of trading
at the New York Stock Exchange and the Chicago Board of Trade were
not exactly votes of confidence in the new administration. Inaugurations are meant to be rites of hope. This one was draped in fear.

The official day began at 10:15 a.m. with a short private prayer at St.
John's Episcopal Church, the small "Church of Presidents" across
Lafayette Square from the White House. FDR asked the Reverend Endicott Peabody to come down from Groton to offer the blessing. The
president-elect didn't know that Peabody had voted for Hoover in
1932 as the "abler man" for the job. But soon after the election he had
become a loyal defender of his old student, and would continue to
argue his case against the large majority of Groton alumni who underestimated him then and loathed him later. (Harvard alumni agreed.)
With one hundred friends, relatives, and Cabinet appointees in attendance, the seventy-six-year-old rector prayed, "Oh Lord . . . most
heartily we beseech Thee . . . bless Thy servant Franklin, chosen to be

President of the United States." After Peabody's loud amen, Roosevelt remained with his head cupped in his hands for half a minute.

When FDR returned to the Mayflower, Moley and Woodin, both of whom had been up nearly all night, briefed him on the early morning news from the Treasury, where the teams from both administrations had worked well together. Roosevelt had decided on his immediate course of action. As soon as possible after taking the oath, he would invoke the 1917 Trading with the Enemy Act to declare a national bank holiday, then call Congress into special session to enact emergency banking legislation so that the solvent financial institutions could reopen. Bankers and governors from around the country would be invited to town to figure out how exactly to accomplish this end, and what to recommend next. There's no indication FDR himself had a plan in mind. He had what Rex Tugwell called "almost impenetrable concealment of intention."

Shortly before 11:00 a.m., Franklin and Eleanor arrived at the North Portico of the White House, where they remained in their open touring car until greeted with stony reserve by the Hoovers. Once the motorcade began, a peculiar security breach developed, unimaginable today. Behind the convertible with Hoover and Roosevelt was a Secret Service car and behind that was supposed to be the car carrying Lou Hoover and Eleanor Roosevelt. But as the cars turned onto Pennsylvania Avenue, a taxi cab appeared with three bewildered women passengers. The taxi had accidentally wedged itself between the cars carrying the Secret Service and the first ladies. With crowds pressing forward, it took police ten blocks to find a way to divert the cab from this place of honor.

The outgoing and incoming presidents were seated side by side, a symbol for the world of the peaceful transfer of power that had prevailed for nearly 150 years. But this time the traditional ride to the Capitol was more than awkward. After several minutes without a word being exchanged, they passed the Commerce Department building, which was still under construction. This had been Hoover's creation when he was secretary, though it was criticized for having offices laid out like jail cells. Unable to bear the silence any longer, Roosevelt pointed and said, "Lovely steel." Hoover grunted. These two words were the only ones uttered during the entire ride.

FDR noticed that Hoover was not acknowledging the polite applause of the large crowds that lined the avenue. He said later that, in fairness to Hoover, the outgoing president no doubt assumed the greeting was for the president-elect. But the tension had become excruciating. "After we passed the Commerce Building, I said to myself, 'Spinach!' [the expression was one of his and Eleanor's terms of disgust] 'Protocol or no protocol, someone has to do something.' The two of us simply couldn't sit there on our hands, ignoring each other and everyone else," FDR recounted. "So I began to wave my own response with my top hat and I kept waving it until I got to the Inauguration stand and was sworn in."*

The arrangements for this Inaugural were different from those held in the past. Retired Admiral Cary Grayson, the Navy doctor who at the end of Woodrow Wilson's term was practically running the government with Wilson's wife, Edith, while the president was ailing, had been placed in charge. Grayson and Edmund Starling of the Secret Service knew that Roosevelt could propel himself forward with the half-circular motion he had perfected for political conventions, but certainly not down steps. So Starling had ordered the construction of a series of ramps, two generations before they became standard in public places. To shield onlookers inside the Capitol from the sight of the president-elect in a wheelchair, he put up wooden barriers to create a private passageway from the Capitol rotunda to the east front, where Inaugurals were held until switched to the west front in 1981. That left another thirty-five feet for Roosevelt to "walk" in public view to the Inaugural stand.

Not everyone assigned a place of prominence made it there. The incoming secretaries of agriculture and labor, Henry Wallace and Frances Perkins, had failed to arrange rides from the church to the Capitol. Their cab took a wrong turn and they found themselves snarled in traffic. Finally, Wallace said: "I hope you have your rubbers on!" and the two began sprinting across the wet grass. They reached the platform to find their seats filled, and ended up far away, unable to see Roosevelt or hear anything but snatches of the speech. The diminutive new Trea-

---

* Peter Arno, the brilliant cartoonist for The New Yorker, had anticipated the moment perfectly by drawing a cover for the magazine of a smiling and waving Roosevelt sitting in the convertible next to a dour Hoover. But after the assassination attempt in Miami, with FDR in an open car, Harold Ross, the magazine's founding editor, scrapped the cover illustration. The Arno drawing was reprinted many times in the years that followed.

sury secretary, William Woodin, was also stuck in the throng, unable to see the swearing in. Mrs. Lillian Cross, the housewife still basking in her glory for reportedly saving Roosevelt's life the previous month in Miami, was seated on the platform with the honored guests.

As he sat waiting in his wheelchair in a Capitol hearing room, FDR seemed so lost in thought that when Huey Long peeked in, even the blustery Louisianan chose not to bother him. Roosevelt suddenly recognized that the wordy first sentence of the speech ("I am certain that my fellow-Americans expect that on my induction into the presidency I will address them with a candor and a decision which the present situation of our nation impels") was not sharp or spiritual enough for the occasion. So he took out his pen and wrote a new one to precede it: "This is a day of consecration."

Then, his face pale, he began the slow "walk" down the ramp to the Inaugural platform, leaning heavily on the arm of his son James. The crowd held its collective breath, as FDR drew on what one eyewitness called "bottomless reserves of physical and mental strength to make the short journey to the rostrum and the Presidency."

This would be the first of three Inaugurals at which Chief Justice Charles Evans Hughes, the 1916 Republican candidate for president, would administer the oath of office to FDR. Always one for breaking precedent, Roosevelt initiated a new style of oath-taking in 1933, though in a letter to the clerk of the Supreme Court he slyly made it seem as if it was the Chief Justice's decision. Instead of simply saying, "I do," after hearing the oath, as all of his predecessors had done, he repeated the oath after each phrase uttered by Hughes. And so, at 1:08 p.m., with his right hand raised, he repeated after the Chief Justice: "I, Franklin Delano Roosevelt . . ."

Roosevelt placed his left hand on a large old family Dutch Bible, opened to the thirteenth chapter of St. Paul's First Epistle to the Corinthians. He must have been especially taken with the verse, considering his superstition about the number 13. It reads: "And now abideth faith, hope, love, these three; but the greatest of these is love." Looking out over the radio microphones and apprehensive crowd, the man who had just become the thirty-second president of the United States still bore no smile. And he wore no overcoat against the chill wind, though a similar decision by William Henry Harrison at his 1841

Inauguration had famously caused his death from pneumonia a month later. FDR was determined to wear nothing over his formal morning coat, a signal effort to seem healthy and vigorous.*

Then, a last-second change. As he acknowledged "President Hoover, Mr. Chief Justice and my friends," Roosevelt added a word—"national"—to the opening line he had scribbled while sitting in the Capitol: "This," he began slowly, to add to the ecclesiastical meaning, "is a day of national consecration."

Roosevelt was infusing a civil ceremony of state with the moral authority of a religious rite. In the Gettysburg Address, Abraham Lincoln dedicated a large military cemetery and acknowledged modestly that "We cannot dedicate. We cannot consecrate. We cannot hallow this ground. The brave men, living and dead, who struggled here have consecrated it far above our poor power to add or detract." Roosevelt, by contrast, thought the American nation must assume whatever "poor power" it had left to consecrate this Inaugural ceremony. He would invest the American experiment with every atom of moral force that he could muster.

The material existence of the nation was at stake, which meant that the democratic system was as well. These stakes needed to be addressed more directly than Hoover had done, but not explicitly, which would be too frightening. So Roosevelt sought to be honest and optimistic at the same time, a challenging combination he had developed when counseling polio patients at Warm Springs. He told the nation:

> This is preeminently a time to speak the truth, the whole truth, frankly and boldly. Nor need we shrink from honestly facing conditions in our country today. This great nation will endure as it has endured, will revive, and will prosper.
>
> So first of all, let me assert my firm belief that the only thing we have to fear is fear itself—nameless, unreasoning, unjustified terror which paralyzes needed efforts to convert retreat into advance.

The "fear itself" phrase brought forth little crowd or press reaction. Within days it began being quoted more often but it didn't become fa-

---

* The effort to show vigor on Inauguration Day was later undertaken by another president with health problems, John F. Kennedy.

mous until the 1936 campaign, when Democrats emblazoned it everywhere as a way to show FDR's success in having rescued the country.
They knew it had resonated, especially in the mail received in the days
and weeks following the Inauguration.*

The line was a specimen of inspired nonsense, no different in substance than Hoover's jawboning, except for the fact that it came from a
different jaw, one jutting confidently. If FDR were truly showing "candor" and speaking "the whole truth, frankly and boldly," why would he
pretend that the only thing the United States had to fear was fear itself?
Some of the terror was irrational, but there were plenty of other real
things to fear: the loss of one's fortune or job or dignity, not to mention
the consequences to family and health. Some fears—like the panic of
the wealthy over what Roosevelt would do with their gold—were mis-
placed; others—worry over putting food on the table—were immediate. The widespread fear of a collapse of the banking system was neither
"nameless," "unreasoning," nor "unjustified."

All of this is true and irrelevant. Great leadership—like great theater—is often about the suspension of disbelief, the audience's surren-
der of questions, an embrace of hope and redemption. Though they
didn't immediately recognize the power of the "fear" line, tens of thousands of people on the Capitol grounds and tens of millions listening
on the radio sensed from the first paragraph that they and their country
might go somewhere better.

That was the message for the heart. More visceral were FDR's attacks on men of high finance. They had failed through "stubbornness"
and "incompetence" and they had now "abdicated." In what Arthur
Krock called a "fighting, Jacksonian speech," Roosevelt confronted
them. "They know only the rules of a generation of self-seekers. They
have no vision, and when there is no vision the people perish."

Then, in a phrase that came to him in church in Hyde Park, the
president evoked Mark 11:15: "The money changers have fled from
their high seats in the temple of our civilization. We may now restore
that temple to the ancient truths." By keeping his targets philosophical—"the falsity of material wealth as the standard of success," "the

---

* Seven decades later the line would still be widely invoked to fortify citizens against terrorism in the new century.

mad chase of evanescent profits"—FDR met the country's anger and dissipated its rage. Without mentioning his cousin Theodore, he conjured his turn-of-the-century ripostes against businessmen.

The scapegoats were pivots for his main theme, which he repeated three times: "This nation is asking for action, and action now." "We must act, we must act quickly." The people want "direct, vigorous action." In the argot of a later age, Roosevelt was relentlessly on message.

The action Roosevelt proposed was: put people to work, raise farm prices, boost purchasing power, prevent foreclosures, "national planning," "strict supervision of all banking and credits and investment," and "an end to speculation with other people's money." FDR knew that he would have to do more than urge action, however eloquently; he must act—and soon.

But act along which lines? To straddle inflationists and gold standard traditionalists, he added, without explanation, "there must be provision for an adequate but sound currency." In many accounts of the speech, this became a big headline, though "adequate but sound" was just a clever way of keeping his options open on currency issues. It was more of what Hoover had called "chameleon on scotch plaid." The speech contained a nationalist thrust, with trade relations rendered "secondary" to fixing the economy at home. Because he believed the national emergency demanded "the putting of first things first," foreign policy was covered only fleetingly with the platitudinous "policy of 'the good neighbor.'"

The next day's *New York Times* included just one front-page headline unrelated to the Inaugural: It was VICTORY FOR HITLER EXPECTED TODAY, a reference to the March 5 German elections, for which the new chancellor had made certain that all opposition to the Nazis was, as the *Times* put it, "verboten," in part because a suspicious fire had destroyed the Reichstag Building on February 27. Roosevelt had made no reference to fascism or other political trouble abroad. When he spoke of our "interdependence on each other," he was establishing a sharp contrast to the "rugged individualism" espoused by Republicans in the 1920s, not stressing global interdependence.

The most well received part of the speech was Roosevelt's embrace of wartime leadership. After suggesting that the times might call for "temporary departure from [the] normal balance" between the branches of government, he suggested the kind of authority he would seek. Avoiding the word "dictatorship," which he had weighed during his speech preparation, he established that first he would ask Congress to confront the crisis. But his threat was clear. If his plan failed, he would ask for "broad executive power to wage war against the emergency," power as great as to defend against a foreign invasion. It was at these words that the crowd burst into the loudest applause of the day. FDR had found the lever he might need to lead "this great army of our people dedicated to a disciplined attack." He was acknowledging congressional authority but putting the legislative branch on notice: Work closely with me or I'll make you irrelevant.

Finally, Roosevelt moved to unifying themes—"old and precious moral values" and the goal of "a rounded and permanent national life." Here, he was recognizing that a material critique of the status quo was insufficient if severed from a moral context. "Happiness lies not in the mere possession of money; it lies in the joy of achievement," he said. His aim was to tap the self-worth of his listeners. He praised the American people, he assured them that "the people of the United States have not failed." They had "registered a mandate" for action and they yearned for some "discipline and direction under leadership." They were sovereign. He was merely "the present instrument of their wishes. In the spirit of the gift, I take it."

Tommy Corcoran, the clever lawyer who had come to Washington under Hoover and was trying to decide whether to stay on, had begun the day, like many others, in "quiet despair," he remembered years later. All through the speech, he kept thinking to himself, "How? How? How?" When he heard Roosevelt utter, "I take it," he felt as if he had seen Arthur pull Excalibur from the stone. "This fellow talked as if he were 300 percent sure," he said. "That blast of the horn was worth 1,000 men."

When the president finished speaking at 1:34 p.m., the crowd was silent for a moment. Jimmy Roosevelt quickly grabbed his father's left arm and began to move him off. But not before he smiled brilliantly for the first time all day, just in time for a ray of winter sun that "broke through the gray mantle of clouds," as an enraptured supporter wrote in his diary, "and came to rest, like a friendly hand, upon his head."

Chapter Thirty-three

"An Injection of Adrenalin"

I N THE FIRST DAYS AFTER THE INAUGURATION, 460,000 letters and telegrams arrived at the White House. Even when the excitement passed, the intensity of the public's connection to the president was on a new level. Hoover had designated one person to sort and answer the mail; Roosevelt would employ a staff of fifty to answer more than eight thousand letters a day. As a measure of how much had changed in just two decades, President William Howard Taft had received fewer than thirty letters a day.

After Miami, many Americans believed that Roosevelt had been spared by divine intervention. Now they reached again for religious metaphors. "We have a Moses to lead us out of the wilderness into the Promised Land," wrote a businessman from California. Like millions of others, he was praying for the new president. A mother superior found that "since your Inaugural, peace seems to be coming to earth," Joe Kennedy wired Roosevelt after visiting a convent, with his usual mix of sincerity and ingratiation. "In fact, it seemed like another resurrection."

Now commenced a love affair between the president and the public that was fueled—like all such affairs—by infatuation and heartfelt vows of commitment. Saul Bellow, a poor Jewish high school student in Chicago, felt transported. "The secret of his political genius was that he knew exactly what the people needed to hear, a personal declaration by the president that took into account the feelings of the people."

The press reaction went beyond normal expression of good wishes for a new president. "There is something contagious about the cheery smile and innate confidence," editorialized the *Cincinnati Times-Star*. The *New York Daily News*, the largest-circulation newspaper in the country and often critical of FDR, vowed in its Sunday editions not to utter a negative word about him for an entire year. Two days later, the *News* ran an editorial entitled "The Dictatorship of Roosevelt" that began: "A lot of us have been asking for a dictator. Now we have one. His name is not Mussolini or Stalin or Hitler. It is Roosevelt. . . . Dictatorship in crises was ancient Rome's best era. . . . The impression we get from various quarters is that practically everyone feels better already. Confidence seems to be coming back with a rush, along with courage."

Rex Tugwell saw an irony. The speech, he wrote, was "directed single-mindedly to the reestablishment of confidence in the very institutions he denounced." But as presented by Roosevelt, it had worked at a level more powerful than the shifting of grand historical forces. The historian, Tugwell wrote, "dislikes admitting that the trite words of a man, flung out in the air for a listening people, could so change the course of events. Yet the change in those March days has to be admitted; and there is no explanation other than an access of hope."

Of the five presidents he had known and served, Secret Service agent Starling's favorite was Calvin Coolidge. His appraisal of FDR was mixed. But that day he felt "an injection of adrenalin in the veins of public morale. So far as the spirit of the thing was concerned, the Depression ended right there." After supervising security at the Capitol, Starling returned to the White House later in the day to find that "it had been transformed during my absence into a gay place, full of people who oozed confidence and seemed unaware that anything was wrong with the United States. The president was the most happy and confident of them all."

After a luncheon in the State Dining Room, Eleanor Roosevelt had consented to the first-ever interview with a first lady inside the White House. The reporter selected to conduct the interview was Lorena Hickok, whose idea it had been in the first place. While the Roosevelts had been all smiles in the open touring car that took them back from the Capitol, Hick noticed that Eleanor bore a sober expression now.

"It was very, very solemn," Eleanor said of the Inauguration, staring out the window as she pulled off her white gloves, "and a little terrifying." The crowds, she said, "were so tremendous and you felt that they would do *anything*—if only someone would tell them what to do." She had felt that particularly, she said, when they applauded so loudly after FDR announced he might have to assume wartime powers. Neither woman spoke for a moment. What they were thinking, Hick later wrote, was that if someone other than FDR had been elected—someone like Huey Long—American democracy might be now coming to an end. "One had the feeling of going it blindly because we're in a tremendous stream and none of us know where we're going to land," Eleanor said. Most of the exchange was published in newspapers across the country the following day, though in the rush of events it occasioned little comment.*

Eleanor had expected a thousand people for an afternoon tea in the Blue Room, but three times as many showed up and she shook hands for hours. Franklin joined her briefly before heading into meetings. He was especially glad to see the sixty patients and staff who had made the trip from Warm Springs at his invitation. A measure of the adulation that day can be found in the case of Ruth Sims, whose husband was joining the New Deal. As she left for the White House, Mrs. Sims put four handkerchiefs in her purse, one for each of her four children. Sims's intention was to shake hands with the new president, then immediately wipe her hand on each hanky, preserving traces of her hero's sweat for each child. But because security was especially tight that day, the Secret Service made her check her purse at the door.

---

* Lillian Rogers Parks, a White House maid, would write a lurid memoir making much of the fact that Hick and Eleanor finished the interview in Eleanor's bathroom, which she and others on the household staff considered "hardly the kind of thing one would do with an ordinary reporter. Or even with an adult friend." In their own books, written before Parks's, both Eleanor and Hick unself-consciously admitted they moved into the bathroom, the point being to avoid the repeated interruptions of the interview by family and friends in the upstairs sitting room.

That evening, Eleanor hosted a family dinner for the scores of relatives in town, including her cousin Alice, whom Eleanor had gener-
ously invited to the festivities. (Alice's stepmother, Edith Roosevelt,
Theodore's widow, who had also attacked FDR during the campaign,
didn't attend.) The White House facilities Eleanor inherited were appalling. According to Henrietta Nesbitt, the imperious chief cook and
housekeeper, the kitchen she and Eleanor found that day had cock-
roaches and "wasn't even sanitary." The refrigerator was wooden inside
and "bad smelling" and the electric wiring old and dangerous. The cup-
board lacked enough utensils to cook a fair-sized meal and the linen situation was "hopeless." The kitchen didn't contain any cookbooks.
Even so, Eleanor and Nesbitt, with their hopelessly bland and watery
meals, managed to take the White House cuisine down a few notches
from the Hoover years.

In the West Wing, FDR personally picked out the offices he wanted
Missy, Louis Howe, Grace Tully, appointments secretary Marvin McIntyre, and press secretary Steve Early—the bulk of his personal staff—to
occupy. Before having Associate Justice Benjamin Cardozo swear in his
entire Cabinet at once, another innovation, in "a small family party" in
his second-floor study,* FDR spent three and a half hours reviewing the
Inaugural Parade from a stand in front of the White House built to look
like Andrew Jackson's Tennessee homestead. It was led by the Army
Chief of Staff, General Douglas MacArthur, whom Roosevelt had privately denounced the summer before as one of the two most dangerous
men in America.

Edmund Wilson used the parade as a metaphor for the country. He
was unimpressed by the Inaugural Address, feeling "the old unctuous-
ness" inferior to Woodrow Wilson's eloquence. "The thing that
emerges most clearly [from the speech] is the warning of dictatorship,"
he wrote in The New Republic. But Wilson was struck by the collection
of Americana that made up most of the parade after the military units:
the man dressed as Abraham Lincoln, marching alone; the Indian War
Veterans in a big green bus; the clowns pretending to act drunk; the

---

* When, during the swearing in of the staff, the oath-takers swore to defend the republic
from its enemies, foreign and domestic, one shouted: "and Huey Long!" Howe was not
amused.

comic lodges and marching clubs, with their men in curled-up shoes and fezzes or "carrying the prong of an antler as if it were the Golden Bough"; the silk hats of Tammany, with Al Smith at the head.

Tom Mix, the Hollywood cowboy who had starred in seven movies in 1932, got the biggest cheers, as he rode a horse down Pennsylvania Avenue. The stars of the new film *42nd Street* also won a nice hand. Toward the end came the "Better Times Float," with its pretty girls sitting on wicker couches against a background of giant tulips. The critic was glad when the parade was over. "The America it represents had burst," Wilson wrote. "The America of the boom definitely died today, and this is the ghost it just gave up."

Wilson was right that the ballyhoo Twenties were finally in the past, but diversions from the grimness of everyday life were only beginning. The 1930s would be characterized by the power of entertainment and personality, from the popularity of Porky Pig to the Marx Brothers to the new president himself. As the Inaugural Ball got underway at the Washington Auditorium, the year's star crooner, Bing Crosby, was appearing at the Loews' Journal Square Theater in Jersey City, New Jersey. In the audience was a boy from Hoboken named Frank Sinatra, age seventeen, who had taken his girlfriend to the Crosby concert. Sinatra said later that was the night—March 4, 1933—that he decided to try show business.

Down in Washington, D.C., a politician was about to offer lessons in how to hold an audience.

Chapter Thirty-four

"Action Now"

O N SUNDAY MORNING, March 5, President Roosevelt decided to take a ride in his new presidential limousine. In 1933, presidents still lived by the same traffic rules as everyone else, but this was about to change. FDR found that one of Washington's traffic circles was jammed with the cars of visitors trying to get an early start out of town after the Inaugural. "Pull out and drive on the grass," he told Colonel Starling. "You won't hurt it." The Secret Service man took this as an indication that things were going to be different.

As the events of Inauguration Day sunk in, it didn't much matter to most Americans which specific policies Roosevelt had in mind for them. "It was enough to know that something was happening that had not happened before," Moley later wrote. "The American people wanted their government to do something, anything, so long as it acted with assurance and vigor." This fit perfectly with the background and sensibility of the new president. On arriving in the State Senate in 1911, he leapt into action on the disputed Tammany U.S. Senate nomination. At the Navy Department, it was all movement. And polio brought a tireless search for treatments, however unorthodox. Roosevelt's bias for action often didn't solve the particular problem at hand but it invigorated the people around him, which was half the point.

The presidency was no different, and that was why Roosevelt had seen the line about "action, and action now" as so central to his Inaugural Address. As usual, the nature of the action was up to FDR. All options were open. While his aides met around-the-clock with outgoing Hooverites on the banking crisis, the president went to church, got set up in his office, and toyed with whether to assume wartime powers, the line that had won him such applause the day before. Which way to go? He could easily have ruled by emergency decree; the country would have cheered. Instead, he would at least try to work with Congress, which remained unpopular but in his mind still essential to the credibility of any of his reforms.

The main decision that first Sunday—to close all the banks in the United States for four days—proved easy. FDR had simply been waiting to become president to make it. The closures by nearly four fifths of the states before he took the oath had rendered it practically a fait accompli anyway. FDR's simultaneous prohibition of the hoarding of all gold and gold bullion applied mostly to the wealthy, but it was a bolder decision, more resonant of the 1917 wartime legislation that legitimized it. In retrospect, it would be seen as moving the United States off the gold standard. And even this was merely a preliminary act. The men of the Hoover and Roosevelt administrations saw the closing of the banks as the anesthetic before the operation. After careful preparations for surgery, the real work would begin.

FDR summoned Wilbur Carr, a career State Department official for more than forty years, whom he knew from his Navy Department days. He asked Carr to determine whether these first actions should be handled by executive order or proclamation. Carr advised the latter. When he returned with the executed Banking Proclamation, Carr learned that FDR—on the advice of a Hoover holdover in the Treasury— decided to have it dated 1:00 a.m., Monday, March 6, so that no one would say the government had taken such momentous action on the Sabbath. That would have conflicted with the religious tone of the Inaugural.

The president was also determined to avoid being consumed by the seriousness of the crisis. As Carr turned to leave, FDR asked him to remain behind alone for a minute. Then, his mind relaxed enough on Day One to exploit his fresh power on behalf of his hobby, he said that he supposed the aging bureaucrat came across "a good many interesting foreign stamps." When Carr said yes, FDR asked if he would mind bundling them up and sending them over to him.

The light tone that would characterize his entire presidency was set from the start. As the proclamation was being prepared that evening, Steve Early invited a handful of reporters into the Red Room. "Roosevelt was in a good mood," remembered Raymond Clapper of the *Washington News*. "No atmosphere of tension." The president introduced himself, smiling, to the reporters. Then he requested that they label the proclamation a "modified bank holiday" or a "partial holiday"—not a "moratorium." The latter was Hoover's term, FDR reminded them. He would insist on the more festive name.

FDR must have been in the same frame of mind when contemplating what to say at 11:30 p.m. that evening in a short message to the American Legion, the first radio address of his presidency, less than thirty-six hours old. He had been offered a draft that gave him open-ended authority to, in effect, create a private army, a thrust for power that the nation would have readily accepted in its hour of peril. "I reserve to myself the right to command you in any phase of the situation which now confronts us," the draft read, echoing Mussolini and nearly every other crisis leader in world history. But in the end Roosevelt rejected the suggestion that he invoke dictatorial authority and gave the veterans a pro forma and entirely forgettable five-paragraph summary of his Inaugural Address of the day before. He would keep the mood urgent but light, patriotic but not extraconstitutional. He would act, not threaten.

The good news was that most states had closed their banks, which ended the hemorrhaging. The bad news was that this and the impending federal bank holiday would bring the financial system only a few days respite. Then what? No one knew.

On the evening of his Inauguration, Roosevelt had asked for some suggestions on what to do, so at 10:00 a.m. on Sunday, March 5, as FDR had his car driven up on the grass, more than a dozen representatives of the financial elite of the United States assembled in the main boardroom of the Treasury Building, across East Executive Avenue from the White House. Included were prominent bankers, congressional committee chairmen, members of the Federal Reserve, and the top Treasury officials of both administrations. This time, incoming Treasury Secretary Woodin sat in the position that his predecessor, Ogden Mills, had occupied the day before. Mills sat in Woodin's old chair.

There commenced a strange and unprecedented cooperation between administrations, little of which was recorded for posterity. In later years, the Hoover men had a vested interest in portraying everything about FDR as terrible; the New Deal historians were more preoccupied with the later glories of the Hundred Days. The two Treasury secretaries never wrote memoirs.

A few notes kept by Adolf Berle reflect the chaos at the top of the American government. The bankers seemed almost in a panic. Melvin Traylor, who eight months earlier had abandoned his favorite-son candidacy for president when he was forced to stand on a marble pedestal in the lobby of his Chicago bank and beg his depositors to be calm, proposed a total reorganization of the banking system under national charters. "I am not willing to go on being a member of a banking structure which is a stench in the nostrils of the world," he said. "Will you wipe out state banks?" Senator Carter Glass asked. "Yes," Traylor replied.

But there were more immediate problems. The men realized that the U.S. government had a "financing"—bills to pay—on the fifteenth of the month, which would be impossible to meet if the banks were closed. Moley suggested the president go on the radio and ask the people to pay the government's bills "out of the sock." (Many Americans kept their money in socks as well as under the mattress.) Mills argued persuasively that there wasn't a chance of the public coming up with the $50 million (small by today's standards) necessary to meet the payment. Mills's deputy, Arthur Ballantine, FDR's old Harvard adversary, argued that if the payment were missed, "it will ruin the government." At one point that Sunday morning a banker named Wayne Wing made a half-joking motion to "to do something." The minutes, kept by Berle, read: "Approved. (Futility! Gosh!)."

The afternoon session got off on a more authoritarian footing. Adolph Miller, a member of the Federal Reserve, suggested a single law that would put "the whole powers of the government in the hands of the President." He argued that "This is a war. Don't bother with the details. It isn't possible to formulate a plan of legislation." Eugene Meyer agreed, and Treasury Secretary Woodin said that the idea had already carried further than they knew. The governors of many of the forty-eight states were coming to Washington the next day and Woodin told the group confidentially that a committee of them was set to endorse the idea of the president assuming full wartime powers.

The meetings were inconclusive but they had a purpose. In the days that followed, Woodin, who knew the Federal Reserve folks because he was a member of the board of governors of the New York Fed, and knew the bankers through his railroad company, summoned many of them to his suite at the Carlton Hotel, where the amateur musician strummed his guitar and sang and worked hard to keep everyone feeling involved. His modest bearing and reputation as a dreamy poet did nothing to undermine the authority he brought to managing the crisis. The decision by FDR and Woodin to bring the bankers to Washington turned out to be a smart move. It got them out of their own communities, where disaster loomed, which improved their mood. Most of the "terribly important meetings" they held over the next few days amounted to nothing, but the very existence of such sessions helped hold the financial system together. In that sense, they mirrored FDR's preference for maintaining at least the impression of activity even if nothing much changed.

Meanwhile a smaller group of men, working around the clock, sleeping on couches, designed a banking rescue. The day before, as Roosevelt watched his Inaugural Parade, Ogden Mills had written a memo to Woodin on how to proceed. Mills kept an estate near Hyde Park and had loathed Roosevelt at least since Harvard. (A few years later, he would even build a model boat with its sails torn and lines tangled and playfully entitle the shipwreck "the New Deal.") But now he proved instrumental in FDR's first big success. Mills's "Tentative Outline of a Possible Line of Approach to our Banking Problem" became, after two all-nighters by the assembled group, no longer "tentative" and far beyond "possible." The Hoover men essentially designed the blueprint of FDR's rescue of the banks.

The idea was to distinguish three classes of banks: A, B, and C. The "A" banks were basically healthy and could be reopened quickly; the

"B" banks were shaky but could open in the weeks ahead if they were bolstered; and the "C" banks were insolvent and would stay closed unless they were reorganized. But even the "C" class banks were treated gingerly. To take the sting off, they decided to call the receivers of those banks "conservers."

When FDR adopted the Mills plan (without ever acknowledging its author), many progressives and radicals felt a rare moment for radical reform had been missed. Senator Bronson Cutting of New Mexico wrote with "a sick heart" about the failure to nationalize the banks when the opportunity arose, calling it "President Roosevelt's greatest mistake." It could have been accomplished, Cutting later said, "without a word of protest." Senators Robert LaFollette, Jr., of Wisconsin and Edward Costigan of Colorado paid a call at the White House to press the point, arguing that many other countries had nationalized banks. But they found the president firmly opposed to putting so much of the nation's wealth in the hands of the state. He always believed banks should be in private hands, he told them, even when they had just about wrecked the country.

Rex Tugwell had a scheme whereby post offices would handle deposits and checking transactions, with new corporations undertaking commercial lending. This would likely have proven a failure. Other countries have established postal banks, with unimpressive results. Within thirty years, the American postal system would be in a deep financial crisis, which would have probably brought another banking crisis. Taking entrepreneurship and competition out of the financial sector and bringing it under the political control of a postal patronage machine would have been disastrous for the U.S. economy over the course of the 20th century.

Roosevelt apparently sensed that, and he decided to use rhetoric in place of revolutionary thinking. The "moneychangers" line in his Inaugural Address turned out to be an effective bit of stagecraft. Although the biblical reference is directed against the Pharisees, who were Jews, there's no sign that FDR intended it that way. (Jesus and the others who chased them away were also Jews.) Roosevelt wasn't an anti-Semite and he didn't appeal to those elements in American society. But the line did give voice to the anger and resentment felt toward Wall Street without destroying the system. He believed tongue-lashing the money changers was sufficient, without actually driving them out.

Some bankers, for example A. P. Giannini, founder of the Bank of America, were forever grateful to FDR for allowing their ailing banks to reopen.* But most of the financial world eventually turned against FDR. In 1936, Roosevelt would tell the story of the drowning man in a silk hat who profusely thanks the lifeguard for saving his life, then returns three years later to ask what happened to his hat.

Many wealthy critics of FDR never admitted how close they had come to losing everything. If banking had been taken over by the government, the character of the New Deal would have been different. Instead of regulation, nationalization. Instead of reform, revolutionary change. The government would almost certainly have assumed control of other industries and pursued a much more radical course, with predictable bureaucratic and growth-killing results. For sparing them that, American millionaires should have felt indebted to Roosevelt.

On Monday, March 6, Will Rogers wrote in his syndicated humor column: "If he had burned down the Capitol, we would cheer and say, 'Well, at least we got a fire started anyhow.' . . . We have had years of 'don't rock the boat.' Go ahead and sink it, Franklin, if you want to. We might just as well be swimming as floundering around the way we are." The humorist knew FDR and would soon visit the White House, but he and his millions of readers had no way of knowing that their man might himself flounder a bit at the outset.

That Monday, the beginning of the first workweek of the Roosevelt administration, Irvin McDuffie wheeled the new president across the South Portico after his customary breakfast-in-bed, then withdrew. The work on Sunday had occurred upstairs in the family quarters, so this was to be his first time occupying the Executive Office, which later became known as the Oval Office. Roosevelt found it bare of all of Hoover's possessions but not yet containing his own naval prints and

---

* California bank examiners thought that the Bank of America, which then included 410 branches, was too weak to reopen, but Woodin overruled them, effectively saving what became the largest bank in the United States.

familiar desktop mementos. The drawers of the desk were empty, and the surface empty. There was not even a buzzer signal button to summon a secretary, which would be hooked up later in the day. The president felt cut off. He listened for some human voice and hearing none, found himself experiencing what was later described as a panic attack.

Rexford Tugwell was not an eyewitness, but this is the story he heard from those who were nearby: Unable to move about and find company, Roosevelt sat in a state of despair, his helplessness washing over him at what should have been his moment of triumph. His mind went blank for a moment. Then he leaned back in his chair and let out a loud shout that carried within it the trepidation, perhaps even the outright terror, he felt upon assuming office. Within seconds it was over.

Missy LeHand and Marvin McIntyre came running. In later years, both Grace Tully and FDR himself sought to make light of the incident, as if it had been a friendly bellow by a high-spirited man in search of his secretaries. Missy tried to blame herself for leaving him alone on his big day. But they knew something traumatic had happened. At the very beginning, the mask briefly slipped. When it went back on, it stayed for the rest of his life, at least when he was with other people. Henceforth, there would be no show of angst or even fretting. He would lay on a layer of insouciance—and act.

Chapter Thirty-five

That Temperament

A T 5:30 ON WEDNESDAY AFTERNOON, March 8, Franklin, Eleanor, and Jimmy paid a surprise call on retired Supreme Court Justice Oliver Wendell Holmes. FDR barely knew the great justice and he didn't really have time yet for socializing. But he accepted Felix Frankfurter's invitation to visit Holmes's Georgetown house for a little afternoon party to celebrate the justice's ninety-second birthday.

Here were two sides of the new president on display—the bon vivant who never missed a good party and the politician who never forgot a slight. Roosevelt was more than happy to honor Holmes with a half hour visit, but he left the White House at least partly to settle a score with Herbert Hoover. Five days earlier, on the eve of his Inauguration, FDR had been enraged by Hoover's haughty comment that "When you've been in Washington as long as I have, Mr. Roosevelt, you'll learn that the president calls on no man." Roosevelt must have known the former president would read of his visit to Holmes and get the message: *This* president pays calls on other men. *This* president shows respect.

Holmes, fortified by bootleg champagne, was in fine form. As reported by his former law clerks, Donald Hiss (brother of Alger) and Tommy Corcoran, the legendary jurist chatted with the new president about the boxer John L. Sullivan, and then recalled his Civil War days. The only thing to do when losing a battle, Holmes said, was to stop retreating, blow the trumpet, and give the order to charge. "And that's exactly what you are doing," Holmes said admiringly. "You are in a war, Mr. President, and in a war there is only one rule, 'Form your battalion and fight!' "

After FDR and his family left, Holmes reminded his clerks that it was the new president's cousin, Theodore, who had appointed him to the high court. Holmes then added, without specifying which Roosevelt: "A second-class intellect but a first-class temperament."

Alexander Woollcott, the critic and journalist, heard the line and began peddling it widely and it eventually became the most enduring of all descriptions of FDR, though historians now differ over which Roosevelt Holmes was referring to. These presidents shared more than a name. While their differences were significant, both projected immense vitality and a canny political intelligence. Henry Adams's distillation of Theodore as "pure act" applies as easily to Franklin, whose instinct was always to keep moving, even if he could not physically move himself. Instinct, that rarest and most precious of political gifts, is the mysterious offspring of temperament and timing. In the Hundred Days, his "first-class" temperament helped prove FDR nothing short of an instinctive political genius.

The great historian Richard Hofstadter wrote that "At the heart of the New Deal was not a philosophy but a temperament. The essence of that temperament was Roosevelt's confidence that even when he was operating in unfamiliar territory he could do no wrong, commit no serious mistakes." But Hofstadter's description of the "essence" of FDR's temperament is incomplete. A fine temperament reflects something more than immense confidence, a sunny disposition, and shrewd sociability. Whether the product of nature, nurture, or some combination, his temperament was what let him see around corners and into the hearts of people.

"Temperament is the great separator," wrote the political scientist Richard Neustadt in his classic text, *Presidential Power*. "Experience will leave its mark on expertise; so will a man's ambitions for himself and his constituents. But something like that 'first rate' temperament is what turns know-how and desire into his personal account." Both Hofstadter, who thought FDR was untrustworthy, and Neustadt, who revered him, appreciated just how rare this quality has been in American politics. A third historian, David Kennedy, neatly summarized how FDR saw his own gift: "His untroubled conception of the presidency consisted quite simply of the thought of him in it."

Well into the Hundred Days, that "untroubled conception" led some to continue to underestimate Roosevelt. How could someone so seemingly superficial be taken seriously? His rivals and even some of his aides still thought they could manipulate him. More often, "consciously or instinctively," as the columnist Joseph Alsop wrote, "FDR was deftly using them while they thought to use him."

A good temperament is multi-layered. Robert Sherwood, the playwright who later wrote speeches for FDR, concluded that his character was "not only multiplex, it was contradictory to a bewildering degree. He was hard and he was soft. At times he displayed a capacity for vindictiveness which could be described as petty, and at other times he demonstrated the Christian spirit of forgiveness and charity in its purest form. . . . He could appear to be utterly cynical, worldly, illusion-less, and yet his religious faith was the strongest and most mysterious force that was in him." About all that Sherwood could conclude was that FDR was "the most untemperamental genius I have ever encountered. That is one of the reasons he was able to sleep so well at night." By not agonizing over decisions, he could move quickly and experiment more than other politicians would dare. John Gunther once asked Eleanor, "Just how does the president think?" She responded, "My dear Mr. Gunther, the president never thinks! He decides."

Roosevelt didn't much care what others thought about his work habits. Where Coolidge and Hoover would arrive in the Oval Office before 8:00 a.m., FDR would be wheeled in closer to 10:00 or even 10:30 a.m. Because he had often conducted business past midnight the night before, he usually awoke around 8:30, put the first of thirty or forty Camels a day in his cigarette holder (necessitated by sensitive gums) and ripped through five newspapers while eating a big breakfast in bed.* Then he was briefed in his bedroom by a constantly rotating pair

---

* FDR liked to claim that as a young man his father had met Sam Houston, who, according to the president, received many visitors in his bedroom, dressed only in a nightgown and spitting tobacco into the fireplace.

of favored aides (Moley and Lew Douglas in the Hundred Days), who were expected to inform him about everything in the world of politics and government. If they didn't know all manner of scuttlebutt, they didn't last long in that role. Finally, Marvin McIntyre and Steve Early would appear to tell him about appointments and possible questions from the press. Some days, when his sinuses bothered him or he simply didn't feel like keeping his official appointments, he spent the whole day in bed talking to aides, transmitting and receiving information.

Gunther applied an electrical theory to FDR, describing him as a "switchboard," or "transformer" with a receptivity and energy that channeled ideas into action almost instantaneously. Just about any notion was worth receiving and at least exploring. "If one put to him such a stock question as, 'Do you believe that a purple elephant is flying at this minute around the top of the Empire State Building?'" Gunther wrote, "His reply would probably have been, 'It *might* be true—let's go out and see.'"

Beneath the loud motor of his energy lay a sensitive gauge, handcrafted by his own suffering. Like many disabled people, he developed a strong sense of how others reacted to him. Hofstadter argued that this fine instrument was put to no better use than a weathervane, that FDR was fundamentally directionless. But the historian mistook Roosevelt's feigns and stuttersteps and miscues for irresolution. He was always at least vaguely focused on bold, progressive, responsive government. The hesitations were usually the product of what his instincts were telling him about how far other politicians—and the American people—were willing to go. "He had to know, to a centimeter, the line that divides pity from compassion, condescension from cooperation, mere sympathy from real support," writes Garry Wills, arguing that FDR's polio-induced sensitivity to public opinion was his greatest asset—the very thing that allowed him to combine strong leadership with a commitment to democracy.

On a personal level, FDR's cheerful temperament proved deceptive time after time. His laugh—"as joyous, hearty, rolling, thunderous laughter as ever was heard on this sorrowful globe," the writer Fulton Oursler called it—could be unnerving. If meeting Roosevelt was "like opening a bottle of champagne," as Winston Churchill famously remarked, the taste was subtle.

Consider the case of Huey Long, who had already experienced FDR saying, "Fine! Fine! Fine!" to him and every other visitor during the transition—and called him on it publicly. By the spring of 1933, he saw Roosevelt take the technique to the next level. One afternoon during the Hundred Days, FDR told Farley to summon Long to the White House. It was going to be a showdown meeting, the president said. Long, playing his usual irreverent game, wouldn't remove his straw hat in front of the president, which enraged Farley. But Roosevelt didn't seem to mind. He had decided to place control of the growing federal patronage in Louisiana under Farley (his patronage chief) instead of giving it to the de facto dictator of the state, Long.

For Long, who had taken to calling FDR "Prince Franklin, Knight of the *Nourmahal*," this was a severe blow. Patronage was central to his control; without it, he was merely a populist rogue. FDR delivered the news by blandly telling Long that he was just interested in seeing good men in office. Because the maneuver was couched in a nonconfrontational platitude, it was hard for Long to react. The normally irrepressible Kingfish—watching his power base recede before his eyes—was reduced to his own platitude. "I understand the rules of war in politics," he murmured after leaving.

Long made no secret of his frustration. "What the hell's the use of coming down to see this fellow?" he complained to Farley on the way out. "I can't win a decision over him. He's hard to talk to." As Joe Kennedy had discovered during the struggle over Argentine destroyers (and would discover again in World War II) and as Al Smith and Herbert Hoover knew from their own bitter experience, Roosevelt was the wrong man to tangle with.

Senator Claude Pepper of Florida enjoyed telling a story about meeting with FDR in later years on a matter the president preferred not to discuss. Roosevelt talked the whole time about a man named Livingston. Pepper later reported that he had not had a chance to bring up the difficult topic, but he was now the second-best informed man in the world on the subject of Mr. Livingston.*

---

* This might have been a carousing or travel adventure story involving Livingston Davis, FDR's onetime best friend whom Roosevelt spent years trying to set up in business. Davis committed suicide in 1932.

Vice President Garner noted privately that FDR "utters 500 words for every one he listens to." But FDR was a good listener when it suited him ("every pore in his body was an ear," said the journalist Dorothy Thompson) and there was almost always a method to his chat. By telling a long story of dubious relevance—like the one about buried treasure in Nova Scotia—or jumping from topic to topic without much transition, the president could make sure the allotted time elapsed before his visitor got around to asking him for something. That allowed him to seem accessible and accommodating while relinquishing nothing. Because his schedule was rigidly divided into fifteen- and thirty-minute blocks, he could calculate exactly how long to prattle on before Marvin McIntyre arrived to usher the visitor out.

When he wasn't running out the clock, FDR employed his patented deceptive nod. Even after Long issued his public warning about this technique, most visitors still didn't get it. They assumed FDR's nod and "yes, yes, yes" meant he agreed with what they were saying, when, in fact, he just meant that he had heard and absorbed the information. It was a processing gesture that was of great manipulative use to Roosevelt and left everyone from aides to foreign heads of state confused about where they stood. Over time it became clear that Roosevelt's private meetings were often as much of a performance as his public speeches. The sentences he spoke were more like monologues or naturally delivered lines in a play than anything real. Even his friends knew they could not take his word to the bank. Moley noticed that whenever Franklin said "frankly" or "in all frankness," it was usually a tip-off that he was hiding something, just as when he used another favorite word, "definitely," it was a good bet that the decision was indefinite.

In his day-to-day interactions, Roosevelt seemed to take pride in his sense of timing. "I am like a cat," he once said. "I make a quick stroke and then I relax." Senator Alben Barkley once told him, "Mr. President, you play with men like a cat plays with a mouse." This feline quality may be what some friends found feminine in his temperament. If Bill Clinton was sometimes known as the first black president, FDR may have been the first woman president, not because he did so much for women's rights (though his respect for Eleanor's work helped) but as a result of an intuition rarely found in male leaders. Winston Churchill's son, Randolph, who studied FDR closely during World War

II, recalled him as "a rather feminine figure with visible prima donna traits of jealousy" (presumably toward Randolph's father). "But his voice—a great voice—instinct with courage."

"There was in the man a kind of narcissism," remembered Marquis Childs, an important syndicated columnist of the era. "I don't know if it was a feminine narcissism, but it was the quality of the actor." Childs remembered that FDR had the actor's ability to always be photographed from the perfect camera angle. On board a cruiser one day, he had his picture taken in his naval cape with the wind in his face: "He's standing with his head thrown back—now, don't tell me that's unconscious."

But Childs may have underappreciated FDR's talents. He was more of what in later years was called a "Method" actor—intuitive, improvisational, and once committed to a role, always in full character. In public and private, he consistently had one of his "faces" on, though it was often hard to tell which one. He certainly had the ego for show business: for years as president, he wore a Phi Beta Kappa key in his lapel even though he was only an honorary member.

Roosevelt believed in "acting" in both commonly accepted definitions of the word. He was, as Ronald Reagan often pointed out, a consummate actor, not just on the radio but in every dimension of his persona. And well beyond the Hundred Days, he possessed a strong bias for action. The acting and the action worked in combination to help FDR inhabit the role of president like no one before him or since. "You know, Orson," he once said to Orson Welles, "You and I are the two best actors in America." He understood the power of mystery in public life: "That was the Garbo in me," he said with a smile after seeing a newsreel one day. And his glow came to illuminate the glamour of the age. From the start, he seemed, in the words of the silent screen star Lillian Gish, "to have been dipped in phosphorus."

It was hardly a coincidence that Roosevelt adored all things Hollywood. When the actress and future California senator, Helen Gahagan Douglas, told him gossip about the actress Paulette Goddard making love under the table at Ciro's nightclub with the Russian-born director, Anatole Litvak, he roared: "I love it! I love it!!" He devoured movies—on cruises he would sometimes see one every day—and he wasn't choosy, though he preferred them to be cheerful. Anything starring

Myrna Loy was not to be missed. He was an unabashed fan of Walt Disney, especially Mickey Mouse.

His own stage presence was enormous. "God, how I'd love to see that man play Hamlet!" Edwin "Pa" Watson, later his military aide, once exclaimed. He was a president of many parts, but everyone knew his favorite. The actor Melvyn Douglas went barnstorming with him in Arkansas one day and found him "playing the role I think he liked best: leading man in a drama featuring People, Crowds, Speeches and the Spirit of Pioneering."*

Frank Capra, at the height of his power as a film director, visited the president in the Oval Office: He was "not the largest man in the world, nor even the largest president. Taft was. But FDR made you feel *he* was. At least he loomed large to me as I shook hands with all the aplomb of a man standing on his first pair of ice skates. His head was the biggest, his face the widest, and his smile the most expansive I had ever seen. By every measure he was a big man."

Size mattered to him. Displacement, to use a nautical term. "The president is at liberty, both in law and in conscience, to be as big a man as he can," wrote Woodrow Wilson, whom FDR continued to admire. But he also knew that weight of this kind is partly an illusion—an impression of strength and character no larger than the abilities of the person projecting it. To Dorothy Schiff, owner of the *New York Post* and one of what she called FDR's "back-door wives," his warmth and confidence were that of a "sun god." The same infatuation could also afflict men, though they tended to recover from it more easily. "My God!" Henry Luce said as he left the White House after a courtesy call during the Hundred Days. "What a man!"

Beyond cat and actor, FDR's other metaphor for himself was that of magician. "I am a juggler and I never let my right hand know what my left hand does," Roosevelt once said. Henry Wallace, not usually known for his wit, added that he "could keep all the balls in the air without los-

---

* During the war, Winston Churchill's presence accentuated the impression. They were "a pair of master showmen determined that no scenes would be stolen by the other," remembered Mike Reilly of the Secret Service.

ing his own." This could strike others as feckless. The British foreign secretary, Anthony Eden, later saw him as "a conjurer, skillfully juggling with balls of dynamite, whose nature he failed to understand."

More likely, he understood but did not explain. "His was an innate kind of reticence," Eleanor concluded. "It became part of his nature not to talk to *anyone* of intimate things." Eleanor might not be the best source for this; she was, after all, the wife who did not share her husband's bed for the last three decades of their marriage. But her impression is matched by others. One of the qualities he liked about the women he felt most comfortable with—like Missy LeHand and Daisy Suckley, the unmarried cousin with whom he spent countless hours from the mid-1930s on—is that they did not ask for intimacy, only company, which he was happy to provide, often on long picnics with FDR driving his hand-controlled car.

The president was endlessly convivial, from his sacred cocktail hour—when he would carelessly mix terrible martinis, then ask his guests, "How about a little sippy?"—to late-night poker, where he called himself "Pa," always played the banker and favored seven-card stud with one-eyed jacks wild. But the bonhomie shielded a cold and cutting side. After a visit, Dr. Carl Jung described him as "of impenetrable mind, but perfectly ruthless." FDR could be belittling, even—perhaps especially—to those in his own family. During the 1932 campaign, he developed a routine where he introduced various members of his family to the crowd and invariably ended with, "and this is my boy James. I have more hair than he does." The crowd always roared, but it left James forlorn. Like his other children, Jimmy revered his father but felt he rarely got beyond the cheerful exterior he presented to everyone.

Dean Acheson, who was pushed out as deputy Treasury secretary in 1933, found the president's indulgence in Damon Runyonesque nicknames condescending.* Acheson, who did not reveal FDR's nickname for him, compared the "patronizing and humiliating" experience of being teased to life on the manor. "It is not gratifying to receive the easy greeting which 'milord' might give a promising stable boy and pull

---

* Much as Treasury Secretary Paul O'Neill did when President George W. Bush bestowed patronizing nicknames on subordinates two generations later.

one's forelock in return." Sometimes the belittling went on behind the target's back. Harold Ickes never learned that FDR enjoyed calling him "Donald Duck."

Jim Farley felt there was bias behind it. After he broke with FDR in 1940, he famously complained that when talking politics with the president, he had never been invited to stay on for a social occasion. He quoted Eleanor saying, "Franklin finds it hard to relax with people who aren't his social equals," the suggestion being that FDR might have been anti-Irish. (Eleanor vehemently denied saying any such thing.) In fact, Ed Flynn, the Irish boss of the Bronx, whose interests were more broad-gauged than Farley's and whom Roosevelt simply liked better, socialized with FDR regularly. Even so, it was not true that FDR, as some acolytes claimed, treated everyone the same. Dorothy Schiff reported that "he was a snob—horrible word, and I wish I could think of a better one—and he liked women who were well brought up and well bred." Because she fit that category, it mattered nothing to FDR that Schiff was Jewish. The Morgenthaus and Rosenmans also fit this standard, and were part of the inner circle.

Roosevelt liked to think of himself as above snobbery. His only public remarks on the subject were in 1926, when he addressed schoolboys at Milton Academy. He told a story about an unnamed woman he had met. Referring to a mutual friend, she said, "I have not seen Jim for some time—you know he married a shop girl." Roosevelt found this story appalling and instructed the prep school students that "Poor Jim" is "a very lucky fellow with a much better mate than that woman would have found for him." He went on to ask the students: "How many of us lend a helping hand to people we do not like, people who do not 'belong to our crowd'?" But when it came time for his own children to marry, Roosevelt seemed pleased that they frequently chose socialites, even when, almost inevitably, the matches were ill-fated. When Daisy Suckley asked the president to check discreetly into the background of a friend's fiancé, he joyfully complied. Tommy Corcoran, who became an important White House aide and fixer, grew embittered with FDR because he believed that the president thought he was marrying down.

The experience of servants and other attendants suggests that if he liked someone, Roosevelt broke down the barrier between "the help" and "friends" more than many presidents. He always included Gus

Gennerich, his bodyguard in the early years, in whatever party, dinner, or activity was planned, instead of making him stand outside with the drivers and other security men. The Secret Service agents who spent the most time with FDR agreed. "He is as cold and hard as steel with everyone and anyone when it comes to the things he wants done," reported Ed Starling. "When it is a matter of ordinary relations with people he is the nicest, kindliest, friendliest person on earth. He is too easygoing, in fact. People take advantage of him." Starling's successor at the Secret Service, Michael Reilly, thought FDR sometimes tried too hard to mix it up. "He never was 'one of the boys,' although he frequently made a good try," Reilly later wrote. "It was such a good try it never quite came off."

But the try counted for something. Roosevelt's fundamental openness to new ideas and people helped him separate his personal preferences from what the country needed. George Biddle, the painter, once noted that "Roosevelt has almost no taste or judgment about painting [his tastes ran to pictures of ships], and I don't think he gets much enjoyment out of it; yet he has done more for painters in this country than anybody ever did—not only by feeding them when they were down and out but by establishing the idea that paintings are a good thing to have around and that artists are important." The openness extended even to moral questions, where he favored tolerance. If the homosexuality of Eleanor's circle ever disturbed Franklin, he showed no sign of it. He might well have been oblivious to it entirely.*

This seemingly easy and open approach to life co-existed with not just a cunning intelligence but a deep belief in God. Roosevelt had a simple faith, rarely expressed in a public forum, but one that he preferred as a label to the "isms" of the day. While he admitted to being "a little left of center" and helped popularize the word "liberal," that was as far as he would go in categorizing his political philosophy.

---

* During World War II, Summer Welles, his undersecretary of state, was caught making a pass at a black porter on a train. The rumor was spread partly by William Bullitt, an old friend of FDR and the first U.S. Ambassador to the Soviet Union. When Roosevelt learned that Bullitt was telling the story, he summoned him and began describing the parable of the two men on Judgment Day. One had a weakness that the other used to destroy him. At the Judgment Seat, FDR told Bullitt in a cold voice, the one with the weakness was forgiven, while the one who did him in was denied entrance through the Pearly Gates.

A young reporter once asked him, "Are you a socialist?"

"No."

"Are you a capitalist?"

"No."

"Well, what is your philosophy?"

"Philosophy? I am a Christian and a Democrat—that's all."

Perhaps so, but superstition was a greater presence in his daily life than religion. With the possible exception of Ronald Reagan, FDR was the most superstitious president in American history. He would never let the Secret Service set up a travel schedule that began on a Friday, even if it wasn't the thirteenth of the month. (Special presidential sleeper trains left at 11:59 p.m. on Thursday—usually to Hyde Park, where he visited at least once a month—or 12:01 a.m. on Saturday.) He would never have thirteen guests for lunch or dinner, so an addition or cancelation that left the number at thirteen meant a last-minute invitation to Grace Tully to fill out the table and lift the hex.

One of the few occasions Tully ever saw him abandon his nonconfrontational style and dress down someone was when a tutor to his sons had the temerity to light three cigarettes on a single match. This recalled a superstition dating to the trench warfare of World War I, where it was thought that the enemy could target cigarette-smoking soldiers if the match light lasted that long. The first time the tutor did so, FDR coldly noted that he didn't like the practice; the second time, the president exploded at the young man with uncharacteristic fury. When his "lucky hat," a battered fedora that got him through some tough campaigns, was mistakenly sold at a charity auction, Roosevelt insisted that his staff track down the movie actor who had bought it and make him give it back.

But if FDR's superstitions marked him as an eccentric, his collections better defined his temperament. Beyond rare books, Navy prints, ship models, donkeys, scrimshaw, and a whole desk covered with knickknacks, his famous stamp collection eventually came to 150 albums. His physician toted up that he spent an average of three to four hours a week during his presidency poring over the stamps, making sure that each was in its proper place. And so it was with the people and ideas of his time. He inspected, sorted, and pasted them—a collector at heart, determined to gather the world, then rearrange it.

Chapter Thirty-six

Holiday Spirit

FDR WAS HARDLY THE ONLY ONE TRYING to rearrange his world. In the winter of 1933, the big craze was jigsaw puzzles, with more than 6 million selling in just a few months. The underlying appeal went unexplained at the time but seemed obvious later. Puzzles, unlike the economy or the frightening future, can be mastered with a little perseverance. The pieces fit together.

With Roosevelt in the White House, Americans were feeling a little better than the week before but still confused, with the puzzle pieces of their institutions spread on the table before them. The Inaugural Address prepared people for the shock of the bank holiday but not for the reality of it. The country, as W. A. Sheaffer of the Sheaffer Pen Co. cabled his friend Ray Moley over the weekend, had come to a "standstill." Sheaffer's checks had already been refused and returned from twenty-four states, with the other twenty-four doing the same starting Monday, March 6. The magnate was not sure he could hold out a week or ten days. His business needed legislation now. The crisis upended the personal lives of everyone, even the Roosevelts. Eleanor fretted that the family had no cash to settle the large tab at the Mayflower Hotel. Franklin told her not to worry about it.

Woodin advised FDR that it was essential to get Congress back in special session by Thursday, March 9. He believed the necessary legislative package could be put together by then, allowing the reopening of banks the following week. This was decided upon at the emergency cabinet meeting on Sunday, March 5. But that left five or six business days for the public to fend for itself, without any means of exchange.

What most people remember from that week was that instead of bickering, a spirit of cooperation developed. A "holiday" mood set in. The new president, wrote *The New York Times*, which had often been critical of him, was now a "strong tower of hope" in Washington. "Instead of alarming the country, [the Banking Proclamation] seemed to cheer it up." The holiday worked "like a sharp slap in the face for a person gripped by unreasoning hysteria," wrote Charles Beard, the renowned economic historian who later became a New Deal critic. "It gave people the time to collect themselves."

For those who hadn't lost their money in bankrupt banks, the big practical problem was getting change. Many Americans were in the habit of carrying their wads with them, but they couldn't buy anything, because merchants quickly refused to offer big change for small purchases. Parents raided their children's piggy banks and Alaska gold miners swept up gold dust. Pesos, Canadian coins, and subway slugs were all used, but the shortage remained acute. When a New York man tried to purchase $3.52 in shaving supplies, he was told to grow a beard.

"Automats," like the one FDR had once invested in during the 1920s, found themselves besieged by well-to-do people with no intention of eating out of vending machines. They simply wanted to change a dollar for twenty nickels. New York's Hotel Commodore dispatched a bellhop to a neighboring church to exchange bills for silver from the collection plate. John D. Rockefeller, still the richest man in the country, was famous for handing out dimes to children but he didn't have any handy that week. So he splurged and gave his caddy a whole dollar.

A Baltimore man, Walter Sondheim, remembers the bank president of one of the biggest banks in town having to borrow money for lunch from a clerk, which caused smiles around the office. Although the banks didn't have any cash on hand, department stores fared better, and some people were able to get their checks cashed there. In New York, Macy's announced that it would offer credit for the first time in its history and Lord & Taylor saw a chance to expand its charge account

business. Sluggish business activity slumped further, but many retail es-
tablishments seemed to manage. "Do not declare a moratorium on your
appetite!" ran an ad for the Hollywood Cabaret Restaurant.

The famous radio stars "Amos 'n' Andy" (Freeman Gosden and
Charles Correll) wrote to Roosevelt offering to devote their broadcast
to explaining the holiday. One Salt Lake City man paid for a ride on a
trolley with a pair of pants (not the ones he was wearing at the time).
Reno, Nevada, suspended divorces because people couldn't pay the
fees. "A bank holiday is no time to hang a man," the governor of California announced, as he stayed an execution. The only politician who
seemed to have any cash on him was Huey Long. When Arthur Krock
of the *Times* ran into him in the Senate antechamber, Long asked, "Do
you need any money?" and pulled out a large wallet stuffed with high-
denomination bills. Krock demurred.

Personal checks—soon to be a permanent way of life—got a big
boost from the holiday, and informal IOUs sprung up everywhere. One
barter system that worked well took place outside the Golden Gloves
boxing semifinals at St. Nick's Arena on West Sixty-sixth street in
New York. The *New York Daily News*, sponsor of the tournament, announced that the admission price for balcony seats was being lowered
to fifty cents, payable in any household goods of that value, plus a
nickel to pay the tax. Neckties, spark plugs, a ham, sweaters, Bibles,
"step-in" shoes, and packages of hot dogs were offered and accepted,
with the police sometimes acting as good-natured appraisers. Nearby,
the famous Roseland Ballroom featured "taxi dancers" ("Ten Cents a
Dance!") who accepted the IOUs of customers able to show them their
bank passbooks. *Variety* reported a box office slump but added cheerfully that hens, fruits, and other edibles were being traded for admission.

The "funny money" alternatives weren't always so amusing. In Chicago, teachers who had gone unpaid for ten months finally began to be
compensated in city-backed scrip, which didn't offer full value. The
local currency situation was complicated by Colonel Robert Mc-
Cormick, owner of the *Chicago Tribune* and an FDR acquaintance at
Groton, who issued his own "dollars" with a picture of Theodore Roosevelt.

In Midland, Michigan, the Dow Chemical Company minted "Dow-

Metal Money" out of magnesium, with a value of twenty cents a coin, which was less than workers were charged for it. In Detroit, now in its fourth week of "holiday," more than one thousand city laborers found their paychecks useless. After several fainted from hunger, they were issued emergency food cards.

Almost everyone was touched. The previous week, W. R. Hearst had gone secretly to a Los Angeles bank for a loan to save his tottering empire, putting up his palace at San Simeon as security. Because of the confusion with the holiday, Harry Chandler, publisher of the *Los Angeles Times* and a member of the board of the bank, had to come up with the money personally, which he shifted into the bank. Hearst never found out that his rival now had a mortgage on him. At the other end of the income scale, James "Scotty" Reston, soon to be perhaps the best-known *New York Times* man of the century, was in the middle of his senior year at the University of Illinois when his hundred-dollar tuition check bounced because the Ohio bank on which it was drawn had failed. He barely avoided expulsion.

Man-in-the-street interviews turned into competitions over who was keeping the stiffer upper lip, with no one wanting to be seen as unduly troubled by events. But the pages of newspapers were full of encomiums for Roosevelt. "Now is the time for all of us to fall in behind this man and march toward wherever he is leading, whether it be toward Socialism, Fascism, Bryanism or simply old-fashioned Jeffersonism," wrote one man to the *New York Daily News*, signing himself "PATRIOT."

A more refined version of the same spirit greeted the president on Monday, when thirteen of the nation's most illustrious citizens—including Al Smith, Walter Lippmann, Newton Baker, and Nicholas Murray Butler—signed a letter to the conference of governors about to convene at the White House. After praising Roosevelt for building confidence, the letter argued that the ordinary operations of government "may be too slow" to meet the emergency.

With cash scarce, scrip now had its moment, as it had during the Panic of 1907. The New York state Assembly quickly gave Governor Lehman authority to issue scrip certificates, and he appointed Al Smith to run one of the clearinghouses issuing them. However, critics of scrip made the convincing point that it would quickly drive currency out of circulation, and people would start hoarding it the way they did gold and silver.

It wasn't as if Roosevelt had any better ideas yet. On Monday, March 6, after learning of Mayor Cermak's death in Miami and attending Senator Walsh's funeral, FDR hosted the governors' conference at the White House. He told the governors he couldn't be specific about how he would ease the crisis because it wouldn't be prudent. In fact, he couldn't be specific because he had nothing to say. The advisers who had met on Sunday were at sea, bereft of consensus on anything beyond reopening the banks. Woodin came to the Oval Office to tell Roosevelt that the group had no fresh ideas to offer.

The biographer Kenneth Davis compares FDR in this period to Kutuzov in Leo Tolstoy's *War and Peace*. He understood that there was "something stronger than his own will" and that his responsibility was "not to bring in any plan of his own" or to "devise or undertake anything" but to "hear everything, remember everything . . . put everything in its proper place."

But if FDR was mostly a sifter of the ideas of others, he occasionally threw out a wacky one of his own. Recalling his days selling bonds, he now suggested that all $21 billion in government bonds be immediately redeemable for cash, no matter what the maturity date. When word of this filtered back to the bankers and government officials, they were horrified. The resulting inflation would be so cataclysmic it would destroy the credit of the United States. Woodin explained this to Roosevelt and the "brainstorm"—like so many others over the years—was abandoned. FDR was always willing to listen to someone smarter tell him why his idea was no good.

The more immediate problem was the currency. There wasn't enough of it, but just printing more would kick off inflation. On Monday evening, Woodin and Moley agreed that the whole question of solvency depended on "make-believe," or public confidence. To bring that back, they decided to exclude from their deliberations all of the radical and visionary types who were everywhere that week. Some were old William Jennings Bryanites, dedicated to silver coinage as a magic elixir; others were college professors with intriguing but unproven new theories. But the new team's plan contained no radical or even unorthodox ideas. The only new thing was how boldly and quickly they moved. All of the frenzied motion masked the essentially conservative nature of the rescue operation.

As part of staying fiscally conservative, Moley and Woodin agreed that night that the first big bill to be introduced after the banking rescue should be what they called the "economy" bill. This would slash the budget, as Roosevelt had promised and his aggressive young budget director, Lewis Douglas, thought essential. The one thing they didn't resolve was the question of scrip.

The next morning at breakfast, Woodin told Moley that he had spent the rest of the night playing his guitar to clear his mind, read a novel for an hour or so and dozed, then come to a decision about what he would recommend to FDR.

"We don't have to issue scrip," Woodin told Moley. They would just print more money, as allowed by the 1913 Federal Reserve Act, but with a clever twist. Instead of Federal Reserve Notes (the line printed to this day at the top of every dollar bill), the Treasury would issue Federal Reserve *Bank* Notes, which looked the same but would be backed by the collateral of Fed-associated banks, not by gold. Over breakfast the next morning, he told Moley that unlike scrip, "It won't frighten people. It won't look like stage money. It will be money that looks like money."

By this time, Woodin was drawing close to the press, offering impromptu mandolin recitals and ready quips. He had to be dissuaded by Charlie Michelson from putting a big refrigerator stocked with beer in his Carlton Hotel room. Even so, the reporters looked out for him in ways that would be unimaginable today, piping up to warn that something sensitive Woodin said should be "off the record."

The bankers' deliberations were going badly, with Melvin Traylor almost dissolving into tears at one point. The financial types grew annoyed at Michelson's insistence that if he, a journalist, couldn't understand their proposals, neither would the public. Finally, at 11:00 p.m. on Tuesday, March 7, the Hoover holdovers at Treasury, Arthur Ballantine and Walter Wyatt, began to draft the Emergency Banking Act, which was to be submitted to Congress on Thursday. The bill offered the president unprecedented control over the financial system, ratifying not only what he had done in the previous days but what he *might do* "hereinafter." It reopened the banks Friday, gave authority to the Treasury to reorganize insolvent banks, authorized the Federal Reserve to issue more money (with Woodin's twist), and cracked down on gold hoarding.

Not that Congress cared about the specifics. Shortly after the bill was finished in the wee hours of March 9, Chairman Henry Steagall of the House Banking and Currency Committee was given a copy, one of only three or four in existence. (One story had it that he had only a napkin with a few provisions scrawled on it.) Steagall strode onto the floor of the House shouting, "Here's the bill. Let's pass it!" and his colleagues did so on a voice vote, without reading a word of it, as Eleanor sat watching placidly from the gallery, knitting. Bertrand H. Snell, the House Republican leader, who suffered under a 302–110 Democratic majority, admitted that it was "entirely out of the ordinary" that the bill had not even been printed and distributed before it was voted upon. But the urgency of the moment trumped any interest in reading the legislation, much less debating it.

Senate passage was a little more complicated, with Huey Long—defender of small banks—opposed to the bill and Carter Glass attacking Long's "ignorance." As the debate ended, Glass whirled on Long, who had been attacking him personally all day. "You damn sonofabitch!" Glass shouted. Long used the same expletive in reply and the two Democrats were about to exchange blows when Joe Robinson, the new majority leader, intervened. The bill passed 73–7 and was sent to the president and signed a mere seven hours after it was introduced, the first New Deal legislation written, though the public didn't know it, by Hoover's men. "The President drove the money-changers out of the Capitol on March 4th—and they were all back on the 9th," one congressman commented.

Franklin Roosevelt now had close to total authority over credit, foreign exchange, and gold purchases, arguably the largest peacetime grant of authority in American history. ROOSEVELT GETS POWERS OF DICTATOR read the headline in the March 11, 1933, *New York Times*. But he was given those powers by Congress; he did not assume them on his own based on some imperial reading of the Constitution. At the very moment when he could have pressed further, Roosevelt chose the path of restraint. Armed with new authority, his strategy for reviving confidence in the financial world nonetheless consisted mostly of not fulfilling the worst fears about him, at least not immediately. And of course he never assumed the worst aspects of dictatorship. "It is one of the great humanitarian qualities of the New Deal that it does not guillotine, imprison or exile the Public Enemies," the journalist John Franklin Carter wrote, without meaning it as a backhanded comment.

Contrary to myth, the initial surge of confidence in the banks that winter had nothing to do with bank deposit insurance, which had not yet been enacted. Ironically, this key to restoring long-term confidence in the banks was adamantly opposed by FDR at the time. "It won't work, John. You had it in Texas and it was a failure," he had told Garner before the Inauguration. "The weak banks will pull down the strong." Throughout the spring, Roosevelt argued that the insurance premiums forced on the healthy banks would cripple them. He repeatedly told Congress and the press that he would veto any bill with deposit insurance. The sincerity of that threat became one of the great guessing games of the Hundred Days.

More often than not, the new president made the right moves, especially when they involved the press and public. On March 8, he hit on a way to retrieve most of the gold that had seeped out of the banks in the previous weeks. At his direction, the Fed announced that it would publish a list of those who had withdrawn gold coins or bullion since February 1 and not returned the gold as of Monday, March 13. Suddenly, sheepish investors began to form lines at banks, determined to avoid having their names printed in the newspapers as unpatriotic hoarders. By Friday, March 10, an estimated four thousand people had passed through bank lines in New York City alone, bringing back $300 million in gold and gold certificates. With the Emergency Banking Bill completed and the fiscally conservative budget bill on the way, investor confidence was beginning to stir again.

Moley wrote in 1939 that the key moment of the Hundred Days was the rescue of the banks. "Capitalism," he concluded, "had been saved in eight days."

Chapter Thirty-seven

"Surpassing Charm"

In the days leading up to the Inauguration, Steve Early, who would serve for all twelve years of the administration as FDR's press secretary, passed the word that life for the press was about to change dramatically.

Warren Harding, Calvin Coolidge, and Herbert Hoover had become notoriously uncommunicative over the prior decade, usually requiring that questions be submitted in writing in advance, if they allowed them at all. Roosevelt was determined to redefine the relationship between the president and press by satisfying the correspondents' hunger for access—a hunger driven by both genuine professional need and the personal status that comes with uttering the words, "as the president just told me." The new president's aims were cunning. He expected that in exchange for access, White House reporters would have less time and motive to sniff around.

For the record, of course, FDR was interested only in accuracy and context. On March 8, at 10:10 a.m., the fourth full day of his presidency, about a hundred reporters trooped into the Oval Office, where they were greeted with a smile and an individual handshake by a seated man wearing a double-breasted blue suit, white shirt, and blue tie. With the greetings completed, the president began to explain his idea: "I am told that what I am about to do will become impossible, but I am going to try it." Then he outlined his plan to meet with the press twice a week—once in the morning for the afternoon papers; once in the afternoon for the morning editions—as he had done in Albany and at the Navy Department. This was the first of an astonishing 998 press conferences he held over the next twelve years, far more in an average month than many of his successors held in a year. Almost overnight, Washington replaced New York as the source of most national news.

From the outset, FDR laid down strict ground rules: He wasn't to be quoted directly (which meant no radio coverage) and wouldn't answer what he called "iffy" hypothetical questions; the press conferences would be "on background," meaning the president's comments could be used to inform the reporters' stories but without attribution to the president or the White House unless Early gave a verbal okay, as he usually did; and finally, some information would be "off the record," which he said meant that it couldn't be used at all. While "on background" and "off the record" were not unknown concepts in the Washington press corps of the 1920s, they now became the coin of the media realm, and they have remained so ever since.

On that day, after thirty-five minutes of cheerful discussion of everything from currency management to veterans' benefits, the reporters were enraptured. The president had started out by saying that he wouldn't be able to answer many questions, but he took a shot at almost all of them, in a manner that reminded one attendee of a friendly schoolmaster responding to eager pupils. Even when he dodged, it was illuminating. Asked whether the United States was now effectively off the gold standard, Roosevelt referred reporters to a column by "my friend" Ralph Robey in the *New York Post*. Robey's conclusion was that we were, leaving FDR with his point conveyed but no fingerprints. He went off the record to assure the gentlemen of the press that he was adamantly opposed to federal deposit insurance, then or in the future. The premiums, he reiterated, would overwhelm the healthy banks without providing enough money to help the weaker ones. On this, FDR was adamant—and wrong.

In a taste of things to come, some of what Roosevelt said in that first press conference was patently untrue; there would be no "two week breathing spell" before the introduction of more major legislation, and he already knew it. But the reporters now had something that many would find then and in the future to be more valuable than total candor—a sense of being on the inside, part of the action, privy to the president of the United States thinking out loud. It was heady and it would prove a powerful asset for Roosevelt.

Privately, FDR would come to be scathing about the press, which he viewed as a collection of uneducated hacks. With some exceptions, he treated them like children, teasing and humiliating them, giving out little favors or scolding them for printing things he didn't like. When columnists turned against him, he often sniped at them behind their backs, calling *The New York Times*'s Arthur Krock "that Tory Krock-pot."

But the first press conference was all charm. To add to the effect, Eleanor came in to whisper something in her husband's ear, then their twenty-two-year-old son Elliott entered to hug his parents good-bye; he was off to Arizona in a Plymouth Roadster, the reporters knew, and a few might have even heard that his father could give him no money for the trip since the president had only $8 in his pocket until the banks reopened. This was hardly the whole story. No reporter except Lorena Hickok realized that Elliott was ditching his wife Betty and their baby to light out for the territories. But there was a naturalness to this president and his family—a gaiety amid crisis—that offered a vivid contrast to the dour Hoovers.

Early, a former AP man and no-nonsense southerner descended from the Confederate cavalryman Jubal Early, interjected that he would "make an example" of any reporters who tried to wiggle out of the ground rules. But the mood stayed positive to the point of obsequious. When the press conference ended, Washington reporters who had written plenty of venomous, cynical copy in their careers—men whose bosses almost uniformly supported Republicans—broke into spontaneous applause.

A reporter for the *Baltimore Sun* wrote in his diary that FDR's handling of the occasion was "the most amazing performance of its kind the White House has ever seen. . . . The press barely contained its whoopees. . . . Here was news—action—drama!" Needless to say, neither he nor any of his colleagues reported that the performance had been conducted entirely from a seated position, because the new president could not stand up, much less walk, without the help of others.

Despite some later assumptions, the president's polio—almost always called "infantile paralysis"—was public knowledge. It had been reported many times and would continue to be mentioned throughout his presidency, especially on his birthday each year, when highly publicized "March of Dimes" fund-raisers were held to raise money for polio research. But by informal agreement, the extent of FDR's disability was not discussed, which left the American people under the wrong impression that he had mostly conquered his disability. The press went along with Early's insistence that FDR never be photographed in a wheelchair, being lifted out of or placed down in a seat, or trying to "walk" forward.

Instead, reporters twice a week gladly played bit parts in a display of presidential virtuosity and press manipulation unmatched by his successors. It's an unfair comparison; live coverage of press conferences on television made future presidents more cautious and less spontaneous. But had FDR allowed radio broadcasts of the news conferences or lived into the TV age, he almost certainly would have continued to dominate, even while sitting down. The sparring kept both the president and the press sharp and the rest of the country better informed about the ins and outs of government than it was before or has been since. Or so the detailed stories about public policy that appeared in many publications would suggest.

Soon, Roosevelt began the still-followed practice of preparing for these sessions with aides, cramming yet more facts and figures into his already prodigious memory. More important, this forced him to learn even more than he already knew about what was going on in his own government—a helpful prod in improving competence. (It follows that presidents who dodge the press are often less on top of their jobs.) Meanwhile, Cabinet members requested transcripts of these press conferences, the better to discover the policy of their government that week.

Roosevelt sometimes tried to rig the game by planting questions, which was unnecessary; he was perfectly capable of bringing up something himself if he wanted to discuss it. And he occasionally instructed Early to warn reporters not to broach certain sensitive topics. But usually the manipulation was good-natured and seductive.

Gardner Jackson of the *Montreal Star* explained FDR's gift for making each reporter feel as if he were Walter Lippmann. When he answered a question, Roosevelt usually went to great pains to dodge the head and shoulders of those in front of the questioner, craning his neck through the press pack until he had arrested the eyes of the poor hack, then pause for a critical moment of engagement. "He gave me the most beguiling smile before he uttered a word," Jackson remembered. John Gunther once stopped in on a press conference and in the space of twenty minutes saw Roosevelt expressing "amazement, curiosity, mock alarm, genuine interest, worry, rhetorical playing for suspense, sympathy, decision, playfulness, dignity, surpassing charm. . . . My first thought as I walked out of the White House was: 'Obviously, that man has never had indigestion in his life.' "

FDR could sometimes be testy, as when he told Bob Post of *The New York Times* to "put on a dunce cap and go stand in the corner." But more often the sessions featured self-effacing moments that would land other presidents in trouble. Merriman Smith of the AP remembered how Early "would whisper in the president's ear, and then FDR would throw out his big arms in a gesture of helplessness and say, 'Well, Steve tells me I'm wrong, it didn't happen that way. I'll have to accept Steve's version.' "

He was not a great wit, far less so than Churchill or JFK, but throughout his presidency he had a way of getting a laugh. Asked at an April 1933 press conference if he planned to forestall inflation with a public works program, he replied, "I wouldn't put it that way." Well, how would he put it? a reporter asked. "I won't put it at all," FDR replied to general laughter. In May, he broke up the press corps by recounting a presidential phony phone call. After three reporters serenaded him on the White House portico by singing a harmonized "Home on the Range," then repeated their performance on NBC, he disguised his voice and called the radio studio pretending to be a network sponsor offering the trio a singing contract on behalf of a company that sold laxatives. His diversions were legendary. When queried once about the money supply, he launched into a story about how Appointments Secretary McIntyre had his own money supply problems after his pocket was picked.

In his first week in office, Roosevelt hit on a device that would shape the news agenda for the rest of his administration. When the question-

ing got a little rough about the Agriculture Department, FDR exclaimed, "Really, this is not a cross-examination!" After some laughter,
the tone of the sessions changed for good. From then on, most of the
barbs were directed by Roosevelt, not at him. Each succeeding week,
month, or year brought a new set of issues that he could master, then
muster in shaping public opinion. For the duration, Roosevelt was the
teacher-in-chief, with the whole world as his classroom.

Eleanor's press conferences actually started two days before Franklin's—on Monday of the first week—and they, too, were revolutionary.
When Lorena Hickok first urged her to break precedent, Eleanor said
no. She didn't have enough to say and she didn't want unruly reporters
harassing her. Hick pressed the point. She would guide Eleanor. To
generate more favorable stories, Hick suggested that the session be limited to women correspondents. When Eleanor asked Franklin, he
thought it was a grand idea—a perfect way to woo and hold women
voters.

For months, Eleanor had assumed she would have to be a conventional first lady. As she put it in her final radio commentary for Ponds
Extract Cream before leaving for the Inauguration: "We women must
go about our daily task of homemaking, no matter what may happen,
and we needn't fear that ours is an unimportant part, for our courage
and our willingness to sacrifice may well be the springboard from which
recovery may come."

Eleanor still believed that, but it soon became clear that she believed a lot else, too, and wanted to express it. She stunned the White
House staff by her insistence on operating the White House elevator by
herself—a signal, she felt, that women could do most of what men
could. After the press conferences began to leave a mark, it was Hickok
who counseled her on how to reimagine her role. She urged Eleanor to
write a newspaper column, "My Day," which was syndicated in hundreds of newspapers and spread her influence for another thirty years;
and to venture into places where she met people never exposed before
to the wife of a president.

At first, Hick simply wanted to make sure her friend of six months
kept a written diary of her activities at the White House. Because of

their desire to stay in close touch, Eleanor's diary in the days immediately following the Inauguration took the form of daily letters to Hick that mixed descriptions of her activities ("I went to the station with them and left the Secret Service men at home!" "Back by 11 & moved furniture till 12") with sentimental passages.

From the start, Eleanor's letters that survive cover a great variety of policy matters and family issues, but are also full of ardor. On March 5, the day after the Inaugural and just hours after Hick returned to New York, Eleanor wrote her: "I feel as though a part of me was leaving tonight, you have grown so much to be a part of my life that it is empty without you even though I'm busy every minute. These are strange days and very odd to me. . . ."

The following day, Eleanor wrote that her son Jimmy's presence near the telephone meant that "I couldn't say 'je t'aime et je t'adore' as I longed to do but always remember I am saying it & that I go to sleep thinking of you & repeating our little saying." The day after, Hick's fortieth birthday, Eleanor called long distance again and wrote, "Oh! I want to put my arms around you, I ache to hold you close. Your ring is a great comfort, I look at it & think, she does love me or I wouldn't be wearing it!" She described kissing Lorena's picture each night before bed.

This correspondence continued every day for most of 1933. Whatever was happening between them personally, it was helping Eleanor think about how she might use her new position differently than she had imagined: "The only thing that reconciles me to this job is the fact that I think I can give a great many people pleasure & I begin to think there may be ways in which I can be useful. I am getting some ideas which I want to talk over with you."

It's clear from her letters that Eleanor had decided to use the Depression as an excuse to curtail White House social obligations. She told Hick there would be no entertaining until autumn except for the children's Easter egg roll and a garden party for veterans when they returned for a second Bonus Army march, which was part of FDR's plan to avoid Hoover's mistakes.

Eleanor made an exception by holding a large party for top government officials on March 17, which also happened to be her twenty-eighth wedding anniversary. Franklin did not forget entirely about the occasion, but the joshing tone of his letter to her is in sharp contrast to her correspondence with Lorena: "After a fruitless week of thinking and lying awake to find whether you need or want undies, dresses, hats, shoes, sheets, towels, rouge, soup, plates, candy, flowers, lamps, laxation pills, whisky, beer, etchings or caviar. . . . I GIVE UP!" Franklin apparently wanted some credit for thinking about Eleanor, but not too much. He asked her to pick her own gift.

In the meantime, Eleanor needed Hick's advice on serious family problems. "Anna is enjoying life, and I am a little afraid of gossip," she wrote on March 8. It would be more than a year before Anna filed for divorce from her husband, Curtis Dall, and her affair with John Boettiger, whom she would later marry, was still a secret. Eleanor was more concerned about Elliott, who began overdrafting at banks and showed no signs of growing up. She had Hick read Elliott's "unhappy" letters and practiced with her what she should say when she went out west to discuss his desertion of his young family. Eleanor told Hick she thought Elliott's wife Betty was "stupid," but she mostly looked inward: "I don't seem to be able to shake the feeling of responsibility for Elliott and Anna. I guess I was a pretty unwise teacher as to how to go about living. Too late to do anything now, however, and I'm rather disgusted with myself." This was only the beginning of what became an epidemic of divorce in her family: a total of nineteen marriages among Franklin and Eleanor's five children, with two of the spouses committing suicide and a third attempting to do so.* Yet before long, Eleanor had moved on from her family concerns.

By mid-1933, her letters to Lorena still included personal details of falling off her horse in Rock Creek Park or what she called her "unemployed emotions" about not having a real job. But she wrote more often about what she had seen and heard after taking Hick's advice to get out of Washington: the Allandale, West Virginia, subsistence farm experiment she sponsored, or the "tramp" she had picked up hitchhiking one day near Hyde Park and brought home and befriended. (He ended up

---

* Beyond the burden of famous parents and a family tolerance for divorce that was unusual for that era, no easy explanation for the epidemic presents itself. But the number of Roosevelt unions render ironic the articles and radio commentaries Eleanor wrote during the 1920s and early 1930s on how to have a strong marriage and family.

back on his feet.) In July, they got away together, taking a three-week trip in Eleanor's sporty light blue convertible "roadster" through French Canada, where they were barely noticed.

By then, Eleanor Roosevelt had come into her own, an indispensable source of intelligence for her husband, traveling incessantly (40,000 miles in 1933 alone) as a regular (often coach-class) passenger on trains and planes, and reporting back on the views of Americans she met and on the success or failure of New Deal programs. That spring, she descended into coal mines to check conditions,* went flying with Amelia Earhart, served a seven-cent lunch to her husband and White House guests (including stuffed eggs with tomato sauce, mashed potatoes, prune pudding, and coffee) to show that even those in difficult circumstances could eat balanced meals, and began speaking up for civil rights in her speeches. She criticized the common policy of firing married women from government jobs (the Depression-era assumption being that two-wage households were selfish). Nearly every day, she left fresh observations and ideas in an in-box by the president's bed, many of which he acted upon. "My Missus tells me . . ." became one of the most common refrains of FDR's Cabinet meetings.

After resigning from the AP, Lorena Hickok performed the same duty for Harry Hopkins (in charge of all relief programs), using her reporting ability and insight to tell senior officials what the bureaucrats beneath them would not dare disclose, especially out in the field. FDR thought Lorena's letters so good that he told Eleanor they should be published. Both women were observers of the first rank, and their reports became a means of backchannel accountability that proved essential to making FDR's presidency a success. That was inside the government. For the outside world, Eleanor was not the dreary policy expert of later caricature but a woman widely hailed for her guts, commitment, and charm.

If Eleanor's reputation soared, Sara's did not. She was praised in newsmagazine cover stories and politely applauded when she appeared in

* This prompted a famous *New Yorker* cartoon in which one surprised coal miner says to another: "For gosh sakes, here comes Mrs. Roosevelt!"

newsreels; the press liked it when she overruled the president and insisted that the family homestead continue to be known as "Hyde Park" and not "Krum Elbow" (the old Dutch name that FDR, in a post-Inaugural inspiration, inexplicably hoped to resurrect). But early on, reporters began to spread the image of a haughty and domineering sovereign. Confusion developed over which lady of the house should be called "Mrs. Roosevelt" (Eleanor disliked the title "First Lady"). The press decided to use that salutation for Eleanor and to call Sara "Dowager Mrs. Roosevelt." After she began signing her name that way, her son noticed and said: "Mummy is certainly getting grand." The *New Yorker* writer Brendan Gill recalled meeting her on a cruise and noticing her pleasure when Gill's father addressed her as "Your Majesty."

Sara took to walking around the grounds at Hyde Park muttering in disgust, "Newspaper men!" or "Secret Service men!" as she bent down to pick up one of the cigarette butts they had put out on her property. She went so far as to install a pay phone at Hyde Park so presidential aides wouldn't run up her phone bill doing government business. Reporters were struck by her "masculine drive" and photographs sometimes made her look less like an elegant dowager than a battle-ax.

The pattern was thus set from the outset: Eleanor, under Lorena Hickok's prodding, would transform herself from a sullen spouse deeply unhappy about moving to Washington into something the country had never seen before—a true partner in the White House. Sara, a frequent guest of her son, would serve as almost an ambassador to the Old Guard, an ever present reminder that for all the change afoot, this was no bomb thrower in the presidency, but the dutiful son of aristocratic privilege. Between them, fully comfortable with whatever familial oddities emerged, sat Franklin.

Soon, most Americans would feel that he was a member of their family, too.

Chapter Thirty-eight

That Voice

A FEW DAYS AFTER HE WAS SWORN IN, Roosevelt was sitting in the White House working on a radio speech about the banking crisis, scheduled for delivery on Sunday, March 12, when he glanced out the window. The new president saw a workman taking down the Inaugural scaffolding on the grounds of the White House. "I decided I'd try to make a speech that this workman could understand," FDR told Louis Howe. "I really made the speech to him."

Years later, he told Adolf Berle that he also conjured a workplace somewhere in the Hudson River Valley, where one man was painting a ceiling, another fixing a car, and a third sat at a cash register. FDR imagined them saying, "All of our money is in the Poughkeepsie bank, and what is this about?" The president told Berle this mental image helped him dictate the speech.

Without quite knowing it, Roosevelt was about to transform the ancient relationship between the government and the governed—to use a new medium in a new way to motivate new behavior in millions of people. Building on his 1930 "waffle-iron campaign" broadcasts, he would talk to people as individuals instead of as crowds, a revolutionary change in mass communications. The presidential broadcast was introduced by Robert Trout of CBS, who read from a folksy script written by his Washington bureau manager, Harry C. Butcher, and approved by

FDR: "The president wants to come into your home and sit at your fire-side for a little fireside chat."

FDR brought natural talent to this historic role. His speaking voice was a beautiful and relaxed tenor, not the contrived basso profundo of pompous politicians. It lent warmth and informality to his words and offered a soothing contrast to Smith's Lower East Side gravel or Hoover's dreary midwestern monotone. The Hudson Valley accent rang of money, but it lacked the languid and haughty lockjaw of the snobby rich. Instead, it registered nicely in the status consciousness of millions of stricken listeners—authoritative but not autocratic; persuasive but not coercive. A leader who began each radio speech by calling the people "my friends" must be . . . friendly.

This was the way much of small-town America liked to remember class before the Crash. Roosevelt's voice was different from ordinary folks' and different from other public officials', but it was familiar from the Hollywood "talkies." One young lawyer of the time called it "second-class aristocrat," less threatening than the self-satisfied platitudes of the millionaires of the twenties, with a touch of kindly paternalism. (To his staff, FDR sometimes referred to himself in the third person as "Father.") The voice conjured memories of a lost world, before the bitterness of economic ruin, a world where the well-liked scion of the well-to-do family on the hill went off to college, then returned to preside over the community with an easy benevolence. Those days were only three and a half years past, yet they might as well have been in another century.

But for all the resentment and despair, even the angriest citizens now craved comfort. The president's reassuring tones lingered in the mind long after the knobs of the RCA or Majestic wireless had been turned off and the children sent to bed. Years later, even the static felt comfortable, crackling through memory like the popping and settling of kindling in a family hearth.

Roosevelt owed much to technological good fortune. He benefited from the rapid penetration of radio into American homes. In 1921, only a few thousand radio receivers existed in the United States. By 1928, there were 9 million, and by 1932, 18 million, with more than half the households in the country owning at least one and most of the rest close enough to listen when it was important. The first president to speak on the air was Warren G. Harding, on KSD St. Louis in 1923. When Calvin Coolidge was president, his secretary of commerce, Herbert Hoover, organized the radio industry, first apportioned the public airwaves, and even appeared on one of the very first "telecasts" produced by an infant technology called television. But none of these men had the slightest idea of how to use the broadcasting medium effectively.

Roosevelt was different. As governor, he began a bit stiffly, but he eventually learned the art of radio communication, and by the time he reached the presidency, his voice resonated at an ideal pitch. This began to come through to Americans in his March 4 Inaugural Address, but the 10:00 p.m. speech on March 12, broadcast live coast-to-coast by six radio networks, was something fresh and astonishingly powerful.

All afternoon, workers busily removed the gold pieces and presidential china patterns displayed in the Diplomatic Reception Room on the White House ground floor. In their place came bulky electrical equipment and hundreds of feet of telephone cables, connected to a desk and built-in microphone rigged up by CBS. Sound-absorbing maroon curtains were hung at odd angles and someone remembered to bring along old quilts to muffle the whirling noise made by the newsreel film cameras.

Ray Moley understood the importance of the speech. After the blur of activity in the first week, the country needed everything explained. "There was magic, we knew, in that calm voice," he remembered. Moley was never one to give Roosevelt himself much credit; Michelson remembered FDR lying on a White House couch dictating speech revisions himself, but Moley insisted that it was entirely redrafted by Arthur Ballantine, who stuck around the Treasury Department for several days after the Hoovers left town. Ballantine himself claimed the same.

If true, this offered a rich irony, and not only because it meant that a Hooverite was at least partly responsible for one of the great speeches of the New Deal. Thirty years earlier, as ambitious undergraduate journalists, Roosevelt had defeated Ballantine in an election for the presidency of the *Harvard Crimson*; FDR later claimed that "Ballantine hated me ever since." Ballantine, for his part, was more arch: "As I watched [his] extraordinary career, there were times when I wished

Franklin Roosevelt had managed to spend more time in college on some of our excellent instruction in economics and government."

It turned out that FDR had been busy with a more valuable kind of learning. What he missed in classroom work, he more than made up for in human observation. The workman on the Inaugural scaffolding and the people in Poughkeepsie were only the first of many ordinary Americans whose shoes he tried to walk in. When the constraints of the presidency prevented him from engaging working people directly, Roosevelt learned to imagine them. He later said that before each Fireside Chat, "I tried to picture a mason at work on a new building, a girl behind a counter, a farmer in his field."

This was more than a conceit. "He saw them gathered in the little parlor, listening with their neighbors. He was conscious of their faces and hands, their clothes and homes," Frances Perkins, who witnessed many of the broadcasts, later wrote. "As he talked, his head would nod and his hands would move in simple, natural, comfortable gestures. His face would smile and light up as though he were actually sitting on the front porch or parlor with them. People felt this, and it bound them to him in affection."

Paradoxically, Roosevelt had few intimates. Like Ronald Reagan,* he kept other people at a pleasant but discernible distance. To compensate—or perhaps just because it was in their natures—both men often sounded more intimate to total strangers than to people in their own orbits.

---

* According to Michael Deaver, Reagan "idolized" Roosevelt, voted for him four times, and made sure as one of his last acts in office in early 1989 that an FDR Memorial would be built on the Mall in Washington, D.C. Reagan's biographer Lou Cannon wrote that "though Reagan's politics ultimately would evolve into opposition to some of the most enduring legacies of the New Deal, his style has remained frankly and fervently Rooseveltian throughout his life. His cadences are Roosevelt's, his metaphors the offspring of FDR's." To explain Reagan's success in office, the columnist Michael Barone in 1986 quoted a renowned historian: "His intellectual processes had always been intuitive rather than logical. He often thought lazily and superficially. But he felt profoundly. Some observers . . . condemned his oversimplifications and felt that portentous decisions were precariously reared on idiotic anecdotes. But the individual case was really more often the symbol rather than the source of his conclusion; it was the short-cut way to put over a vast amount of feeling, imagination and sympathy which the President himself could neither articulate nor understand, but which had a plunging accuracy of their own." After fooling the reader into thinking the reference was to Reagan, Barone revealed that the quote came from Arthur M. Schlesinger, Jr., analyzing Roosevelt.

It's hard to exaggerate the power of this impression of public intimacy that Roosevelt pioneered. For thousands of years, political leaders around the world delivered orations; in many places, these speeches
were even considered a form of popular live entertainment. But the
need to project one's speaking voice to the back of the audience made
public addresses formal. While the language itself was often homespun,
the effect was usually that of a harangue. A warm, conversational tone
was simply not technologically possible. Even after the invention of
radio, public figures continued to broadcast speeches in a loud, stentorian manner, as if they didn't quite understand that the microphone
had been invented. (Some present-day politicians have the same problem.) This orating could be effective, as Long showed in Louisiana and
Hitler and Mussolini proved in Europe. But it did nothing to break
down barriers between leaders and their people. Harnessed to the
power of mass media, these old-style speeches used emotion to control,
not reason to communicate. And they could be offputting to hear in
the comfort of one's own living room. Radio listeners found themselves
in agreement with the sentiments of Queen Victoria, who is said to
have asked Prime Minister Gladstone to stop speaking to her as if he
were addressing a public audience.

FDR found an opening for something original. Perhaps because he
couldn't wave his arms and strut the platform like other orators, he relied more on his finely tuned voice. What Bing Crosby did for singing,
Franklin Roosevelt did for speaking—use the microphone for a new,
softer connection to the hearts of his listeners. On that Sunday
evening in 1933, he changed not just his presidency and American politics but the whole way people communicated with each other in
public.

The ritual before a Fireside Chat usually went something like this: Upstairs, FDR put the finishing touches on the speech, studying how every
word and pause would sound. He had almost an obsession with punctuation. Grace Tully sometimes inadvertently inserted extra commas
when she typed up the draft, leading her boss to gently upbraid her for
"wasting the taxpayers' commas." His real concern was that the wrong
punctuation could throw off his timing, which was normally uncanny.

His reading speed was about 100 words a minute, but he also knew how to adjust his pace on certain paragraphs to speed up or slow down for effect, and to hit his "out cue" on the nose. Aides would shake their heads in amazement when, time and again, he finished exactly as the second hand passed 12 on the clock on the table.

At 6:00 p.m., Roosevelt was wheeled into the office of Admiral Ross McIntire, his physician, to get his throat sprayed for a sinus problem. Then it was time for cocktails and dinner, before he relaxed by putting in a little time on his stamp collection. The speech was typed on special limp paper that didn't rustle near the microphone. It was bound in a black leather looseleaf folder, which was usually unnecessary, for Roosevelt seemed to have memorized the text. Those in the room might see him glance down at the page, but his aides knew better; he was not looking at the words he was saying but at the next paragraph, to see which pauses and inflections to use, as he prepared to beam, grimace or nod toward the microphone as if he were on stage.

Quite often, "the Boss," as his personal staff called him, ad-libbed what he called "happy thoughts" into the text. When eyebrows were raised afterwards, he'd respond: "Papa just thought of it at the last minute." The felicitous "My friends" arrived that way on March 9, a salutation—borrowed perhaps from Shakespeare's Marc Antony—that set the tone of his presidency. For all the talk of a dictatorship in Washington, the man selected for the job wasn't dictating; in fact, he wasn't even orating. He was just explaining a few things to his 60 million friends.

That is, if he could manage to do so without whistling. After his boyhood friend accidentally knocked out one of his teeth with a stick on Campobello Island four decades earlier, FDR's voice emitted a slight whistle on the radio. So before many Fireside Chats, aides would listen for what they called the "pivot tooth" assignment. They could practically set their watches by it. Just minutes before broadcast, the president would absentmindedly dig in his pocket looking for the little heart-shaped jewelry box in which he carried his false pivot tooth, which he knew he needed for a flawless performance. When inevitably he couldn't find the box in his pocket, he would grin helplessly. Then Grace Tully or one of the Secret Service men would have to dash up to his bedroom and locate the tooth in its velvet box on the bedside table, before sprinting back to the microphones. Often Roosevelt would be screwing his tooth into his lower jaw even as Trout of CBS or Carlton Smith of NBC was counting down the broadcast.

On this night, the first Fireside Chat, the crisis involved not the president's tooth but his speech itself. Moments before airtime, no one could find the reading copy. Panic ensued for everyone except Roosevelt, who calmly picked up a smudged, single-spaced mimeographed copy prepared for the press. He sipped from a glass of water, stubbed out his cigarette, and read it perfectly on the air. The original reading copy, last seen on a White House hat rack, was never found, though the president's eldest son, Jimmy, was suspected of having snatched it as a souvenir.

The beauty of that first prime-time radio speech was its clarity. "He made everyone understand it, even the bankers," Will Rogers said. "He is the first Harvard man to know enough to drop three syllables when he has something to say. Why compared to me, he's almost illiterate." FDR walked the country through the basics of banking without being patronizing. He outlined the process for deciding which banks to open, though he skipped over the fact that some less than solvent banks would also be allowed to stay in business. He told listeners that at least some banks would reopen the following day, Monday, March 13, in Federal Reserve cities and elsewhere over time.

In the middle of the speech, Roosevelt said simply, "I can assure you that it is safer to keep your money in a reopened bank than under the mattress." By surfacing an issue that made so many feel shameful, he lifted the shame—and offered his listeners a way out, a way to strike a patriotic blow by simply depositing money into a solvent bank. Those who planned instead to withdraw money were gently thrown in with an unsavory lot. Hoarding, the president told his audience with perfectly wry disapproval, "has become an exceedingly unfashionable pastime."

Then he returned to the themes that were so popular in the Inaugural. "Confidence and courage are the essentials in carrying out our plan. Let us unite in banishing fear. . . . We have provided the machinery to restore our financial system; it is up to you to make it work. It is your problem no less than it is mine. Together we cannot fail."

Charlie Michelson, who hadn't thought much of it when it was being prepared, was stunned by how well that speech played on the radio: "They were ready to believe FDR could see in the dark." Even after his relationship with FDR became embittered, Jim Farley wrote that this speech may have been the greatest single utterance by an American president, if judged by its impact: "No other talk in history ever called forth such a wave of spontaneous enthusiasm and cooperation." Farley pointed out that it's easy to project back from FDR's success in restoring confidence and make it seem as if it was inevitable, "But it is just as easy to imagine the economic and financial chaos that would have resulted if the people had given way to fear and panic."

Edmund Wilson, as usual, was wrong about Roosevelt at the time. Although he expertly pinpointed Roosevelt's "slightly unnatural sunniness," he misheard his voice in some private notes he sketched that month. "Roosevelt's unsatisfactory way of emphasizing his sentences [seemed] fairyish, or as if there weren't real convictions behind them— in spite of his clearness and neatness—but regular radio announcers, I noticed later, did the same thing," Wilson wrote. In other words, FDR was in sync with what was becoming the informal, conversational professional standard that would dominate the airwaves because it worked better than the old stentorian style. Father Charles Coughlin, still a feverish FDR supporter, told McIntyre, "As far as radio is concerned, he is a natural-born artist."

Average Americans wrote with astonishing consistency that it felt as if the new president had somehow appeared in their living rooms—"a confidential conversation with me in the privacy of my home," wrote one Oklahoma man, summarizing almost word-for-word what appears in thousands of letters on file at the Roosevelt Library. For many, it was their first letter to a president; others confessed to having voted for Hoover but were now on the Roosevelt team. As one Brooklynite summarized, "It was homey and human and just what the nation needed."*

---

* The effect of Fireside Chats on future presidents was immense. Gerald Ford, nineteen years old at the time, remembered them as "big events—we would all stop whatever we were doing and listen very, very closely." Bill Clinton recalled hearing his grandfather talk about the Fireside Chats, how he sat in rapt attention on the floor, "then got up and went to work the next day feeling a little different about the country." Clinton himself felt he had become too formal in the early speeches of his presidency before realizing midway through his term that he needed to be more FDR-like: "We needed to be more direct—talk to the people the way they understand. I'd slash through the rhetoric of the speechwriters and just talk to them."

With 60 million people listening, the impact was immediate. The following day, Monday, March 13, newspapers reported long lines of Americans anxious to take their money from the mattress and redeposit it. The same people who only two weeks earlier had lost all faith in banks, who had seen their fortunes evaporate, were now waiting patiently to put their remaining money where their new confidence was. The New York Stock Exchange, closed for nearly two weeks, opened 15 percent higher, the largest one-day surge in more than half a century. Within a week, three quarters of the recently closed banks reopened. Thousands of others that went under in earlier months would stay shuttered, yet the number of banks that revived went far beyond the hopes of even the most optimistic New Dealers.

But even as he cemented his relationship with the people, Roosevelt understood the limitations of his gift. While some remember his speaking every week, he delivered only four Fireside Chats in 1933 and a total of twenty-seven in twelve years. FDR knew the actor's trick of always leaving the audience wanting more. "The public psychology and, for that matter, individual psychology, cannot, because of human weakness, be attuned for long periods of time to a constant repetition of the highest note in the scales," he wrote an old friend in 1935, explaining why he took to the airwaves much less frequently than Huey Long or Charles Coughlin.

After the first Fireside Chat, Roosevelt relaxed in his office with Howe and Rosenman. About 11:30 p.m. he said: "I think it's time for beer." Preparations for a bill to speed the end of Prohibition began that night. Speeches were fine, but the country was thirsty for more.

Chapter Thirty-nine

"The Chief Croupier"

I N 1937, GEORGE M. COHAN STARRED in a Rodgers and Hart Broadway smash hit called *I'd Rather Be Right* that featured the by now famous Hundred Days. Roosevelt never saw the musical, but he enjoyed hearing how Cohan, playing Roosevelt, would exclaim: "Mac, take a law!" In fact, Marvin McIntyre was responsible for appointments, not dictation. But Roosevelt liked to yell, "Grace, take a law!" to Grace Tully.

This wasn't so far off from how Roosevelt operated in the Hundred Days, and beyond. It didn't matter so much what the law was, as long as the country got the impression that something was happening. There was no design to it. "To look upon these programs as the result of a unified plan," Moley later wrote, "was to believe that the accumulation of stuffed snakes, baseball pictures, school flags, old tennis shoes, carpenter's tools, geometry books and chemistry sets in a boy's bedroom could have been put there by an interior decorator."

The anonymous author of a book written that first year said the new president was "the chief croupier, not the owner of the casino, the executor rather than the author of destiny." The croupier kept the action going, but within bounds. "His art," the author, known as "The Unofficial Observer" (later revealed as the Washington journalist John Franklin Carter), concluded, "is the combination of the familiar in such a way as to produce the new." Frances Perkins preferred the image of the artist "who begins his picture without a clear idea of what he intends to paint or how it should be laid out on the canvas, and then, as he paints, his plan evolves out of the materials." Another New Dealer, Elmer Davis, once said that FDR reminded him of a farmer with too many newborn puppies on his hands. He took them out in a boat, dumped them overboard, and kept those who could swim back to shore.

FDR, seeking credit for a game plan, favored a football metaphor. He described a captain or quarterback who knows the team's strategy and what the next play would be, "but they cannot tell you what the play after the next play is going to be until the next play is run off. If the play makes ten yards, the succeeding play will be different from what it would be if they were thrown for a loss."

The Hundred Days themselves have been so mythologized that the real ones are barely recognizable. The phrase was borrowed from the surprisingly short time period between Napoleon's triumphant escape from Elba and his final defeat at Waterloo in 1815. It was first used by FDR on July 24, 1933, to refer to the exactly 100 days (apparently a coincidence) that elapsed between the opening of the special session of the 73rd Congress on March 9 and its closing on June 17, a session that produced a record-breaking volume of new laws.*

There was nothing intentional about a session of this length. During the first week of his presidency, FDR had expected Congress to meet for two weeks to pass his emergency agenda, then adjourn. Nor was the volume of legislation anticipated. With a 196-vote margin in the House and a 23-vote margin in the Senate, Democrats in Congress have often been depicted as merely rubber-stamping FDR's agenda. But most of the southern Democrats were at least as conservative as Republicans, while some northern and western progressive Republicans were moving left. So while early emergency bills sailed through, most others were the product of the usual give-and-take on Capitol Hill. The urgency of the time made it horse-trading at a gallop.

Little of the major legislation remained in force for long. Some launched major social changes, while others spawned agencies that were quickly superceded by new ones (FDR often opened new agencies

---

* Later, Moley and others would use the phrase to refer to the period between March 4 and June 17, which was 105 days.

without closing the old bureaus). Most of the landmark New Deal accomplishments that endure to this day—the Securities and Exchange
Commission (1934), Social Security (1935), and the pro-union legislation like the Wagner Act (1935) that empowered the government to
fight unfair labor practices—date from later in the decade. In fact, one
could argue that if the actions of the Hundred Days had succeeded better and the positive economic trends of mid-1933 had brought full recovery in 1934 and 1935, the United States would not now have the
wide variety of social advances that it largely takes for granted. The
irony is that Roosevelt's failure to whip the Depression quickly may
have been a blessing for future generations.

The opening act of the Roosevelt administration also brought fewer
structural changes than is sometimes assumed. The banks were closed,
reopened, and reorganized yet the system was not overhauled. Regulation of Wall Street was begun, but it was not intrusive, despite the yelps
of publicly traded companies at the time. None of the bills that passed
could be considered radical. The early days of FDR's presidency were
marked as much by what did not happen as by what did. No martial law.
No constitutional amendments. No nationalization of the banks or
other key industries, though desperate coal mine operators actually
begged the government to take over their mines.

Some of the new laws simply extended Hoover's efforts. Reconstruction Finance Corporation loans were offered to small businesses as well
as large ones and used for job creation. Under the spirited leadership of
Jesse Jones, a Texas tycoon, the agency became a powerhouse. Public
works, a much larger feature of the Hoover administration than many
New Dealers acknowledged, were expanded, though it would take
months before dusted-off plans could be converted to large-scale construction jobs.

For all of the liberal reveries of later years, the first thrust of the Hundred Days was fiscal prudence. On the most fundamental economic
issue of the day—government spending—Roosevelt was still trying to
look conservative.* He thought balanced budgets would make it easier

---

* In 1980, Ronald Reagan said, "I didn't desert my party. It deserted me. [The 1932 Democratic Party platform] called for a restoration of states' rights and a reduction of the national
budget. You know what? I'm still for that." But Reagan's cuts were small next to FDR's.

for the federal government to borrow money and stay out of bankruptcy. Closer to home, deficit spending offended his Dutch thrift. Until the end of his life, FDR balanced his own checkbook (bolstered by subsidies from his mother) down to the penny.

The original centerpiece of the Roosevelt program was the so-called Economy Bill—officially designated "an Act to maintain the credit of the United States"—which was passed and signed by the end of March. In his famous October speech in Pittsburgh during the campaign, FDR had promised to cut government spending by 25 percent. In the end, with ninety-two Democrats dissenting in the House, this bill actually slashed federal outlays by an astonishing 31 percent, by far the largest reduction in government spending before or since.

Three quarters of the cuts came from veterans' benefits, the first of what are now called "entitlement" programs and the largest single source of federal spending at the time. Roosevelt was determined that those without service-connected disabilities fend more for themselves, even if they were unemployed and ailing. Civil War pensions were cut 10 percent and overall veterans' benefits slashed 50 percent, unimaginable in later years. Other savings came by cutting salaries of government workers (including the president and members of Congress) by 15 percent, a move that FDR dramatized by ostentatiously returning a portion of his first paycheck to the Treasury. He made a point of eliminating some boards and agencies—like the National Screw Thread Commission—altogether, and consolidating many others, ironic in view of what Al Smith disparagingly called "the alphabet soup" of New Deal agencies to come. All told, the cuts in government spending were far more than Herbert Hoover even dared to propose, and by the end of the Hundred Days they would cause a near rebellion on Capitol Hill.

FDR reveled in playing the hard-liner. Shortly after the Inaugural, Josephus Daniels, his old boss at the Navy Department, wrote him to urge that he join a campaign to prevent states from cutting teachers' salaries even further, the very issue that had brought Chicago mayor Cermak to beseech him in Miami a few weeks earlier on behalf of teachers who had not received a paycheck for nearly a year. Roosevelt's reply to Daniels was cool: "The past decade has seen a very large increase in teachers' salaries, and even if all the teachers were cut 15 percent like government employees, they would still be getting relatively more than in 1914!" In April, five thousand unpaid Chicago teachers occupied banks and City Hall in what later came to be known as a "sit-in." The president was unmoved.

At the beginning, Roosevelt was convinced that he must keep his campaign promise and actually balance the budget. Because donning the green eyeshade was of dubious fiscal relevance during a depression, this part of the New Deal probably delayed recovery. But it carried great symbolic importance. For the first time in memory, the country had a president who took on all the lobbyists and pressure groups angling for their slice of the pie and beat them decisively. The new budget showed that FDR was fully in charge and committed to the policy of "first things first" and the "discipline" he had outlined in his Inaugural Address.

But with Franklin Roosevelt, there was always another side, an angle to play. Just as he had hedged on the League of Nations and free trade and found the middle "damp" position on Prohibition before becoming president, he now hoped to spend money without being blamed for doing so. His have-it-both-ways solution was to pioneer creative bookkeeping in the federal government, a precursor to all of the "off-budget" spending in administrations to come. Meeting with reporters at the end of his third week in office, FDR drew a distinction between a "normal" budget and an "emergency" one. "You cannot let people starve, but this starvation charge is not an annually recurring charge," he explained, and so relief should not be counted as spending. The *Times* pointed out that according to such "painless arithmetic," Hoover would have been running a huge surplus instead of the deficit FDR had savaged the year before. No matter. The president had found his loophole, and he would push huge expenditures through it.

It would be more than three years before he admitted retreating from balanced-budget dogma. (When he fretted in 1936 about the 1932 Pittsburgh campaign speech calling for a balanced budget, Rosenman joked, "Just deny you were ever in Pittsburgh.") He slowly adopted Keynesian ideas that favored deficit spending to pump the economy, but even then he did so more from the gut than from adherence to any economic theory. When Keynes visited the White House in 1936, Roosevelt confessed to friends that he didn't understand a word the eminent British economist had to say and still favored submitting "conservative" budgets.*

FDR knew that the cuts would be painful. To make them go down more easily, he offered liquid refreshment. Immediately after delivering his first Fireside Chat on March 12, he reviewed the 1932 Democratic Party platform, which called for amending the Volstead Act to legalize 3.2 beer. The Eighteenth Amendment, which launched Prohibition in 1918, was aimed at hard liquor and permitted the legalization of beverages with less alcohol. So FDR issued a three-sentence message to Congress on legalizing beer. The next day, March 13, the House was preparing to recess when it received FDR's message. It stayed in session, immediately passed the bill on beer, and sent it to the Senate. As FDR knew, under Senate rules, senators could not consider modifying the Volstead Act until they voted on the Economy Bill, which was on the floor first. So they swallowed the bitter budget pill that afternoon and chased it down with a beer vote the next day, effective immediately.

The quick amendment of the Volstead Act is one of the least appreciated elements of how FDR changed the country's psyche during the Hundred Days. Although formal repeal of Prohibition would not come until the end of the year, beer parties were held all over the country starting in March. At 12:01 a.m. on the first day of legal beer, Hawaiian guitarists drew a crowd as a truck from Washington's Abner Drury Brewery pulled up at the White House with a sign: PRESIDENT ROOSEVELT, THE FIRST BEER IS FOR YOU. In Times Square, bands played "Happy Days Are Here Again." H. L. Mencken, tipping a few in Baltimore, decided that maybe Roosevelt wasn't so bad after all. "Something was happening immediately! Bars were opening overnight, with every other beer on the house!" recalled the author Studs Terkel, explaining how the news played for a young man growing up in Chicago. "In the midst of the Depression it was a note of hope that something would be better."

In truth, FDR wasn't sure what would make things better. He was throwing things against the wall to see what stuck. The process was almost always messy and rarely lived up to the idealistic dreams of reformers. But it moved forward nonetheless. For all the unacknowl-

---

* Keynes, for his part, admired FDR's program but thought him an economic illiterate.

edged continuity with the Hoover administration, the spirit of the Hundred Days did mark a sharp break from the past—a psychological jolt that helped convince people not to give up on the democratic system.

Consider the Securities Act of 1933, which grew out of public disgust with Wall Street, still pilloried daily on Capitol Hill. In December 1932, Moley had suggested FDR assign a crotchety lawyer named Samuel Untermyer to write a bill that addressed the abuses highlighted in the Mitchell hearings. Untermyer came back with a plan for Wall Street to be supervised by the U.S. Post Office, which would be empowered to withhold the mailing privileges of unscrupulous stock peddlers.

This was every bit as wrong-headed as Tugwell's plan to lodge all banks in post offices, maybe more so. But instead of immediately ditching Untermyer's plan, FDR did what he was to do so often in the years ahead—assign someone else the identical task. In early March 1933, a few days after he took office, he asked his secretary of commerce, Daniel Roper, for a proposal, and Roper asked an old Woodrow Wilson appointee, Huston Thompson, to draft one. When Untermyer and Thompson found out they had both been given the same time-consuming job, they were not pleased. Moley arranged for a meeting on March 19 with FDR, who apologized profusely and unconvincingly for having forgotten about Untermyer's assignment. Unable to "weave" the drafts together, as he had done on other ticklish issues, FDR fecklessly dumped the whole thing on Capitol Hill.

The key House committee was chaired by Sam Rayburn, who held hearings where the poorly drafted Thompson bill was savaged by Wall Street witnesses, including Averell Harriman, who would later serve as FDR's ambassador to the Soviet Union. Rayburn told Moley the bill would not fly. So the whole thing was turned over to Felix Frankfurter, who was informally staffing much of the administration. Frankfurter assigned a trio of his protégés—soon to be known in the press as "Felix's Happy Hot Dogs"—to the task.

The legislation was drafted over a long weekend in an apartment near the Carlton Hotel by three young Harvard Law School graduates, Tommy Corcoran, Ben Cohen, and Jim Landis, whom Frankfurter privately dubbed "the Three Musketeers." Corcoran drank endless cups of sugared coffee and he fell in love and later married the secretary sent over to help. Cohen chain-smoked. Landis complained. Together, they stayed up nearly around the clock writing the first-ever federal law regulating stock market transactions. The bill did not directly crack down on bankers and Wall Street speculators; that would have to wait until 1934 and the creation of the SEC. But the Securities Act of 1933 did require any company selling securities to the public to disclose its financial condition and register with the federal government. (At first, with the Federal Trade Commission.) These disclosure requirements are the foundation of what is now called "financial transparency."

Thompson was angered by the secrecy of the Frankfurter operation and he got some revenge by convincing the Senate—where he had many friends—to bottle up the bill. Only a parliamentary maneuver by Rayburn and Senator James Byrnes saved the Landis-Corcoran-Cohen handiwork. Even then, Rayburn, who chaired the House-Senate conference committee assigned to work out the differences, sat on the bill until receiving an urgent appeal from FDR, who had otherwise not bothered himself much with the legislative details. In the last week of May, the bill passed both chambers and was signed by the president.

For all the loose planning, bruised egos, and congressional shenanigans, an important threshold had been crossed. In his March 29 message to Congress introducing the Securities Act, FDR had written: "This proposal adds to the ancient rule of 'caveat emptor' the further doctrine of 'let the seller beware.' It puts the burden of telling the whole truth upon the seller."

Even if the bill did not have teeth, this was strong stuff for progressives who had been out of power for more than a decade. If these and other regulatory changes were reminiscent of turn-of-the-century trust-busting, much of the agenda suggested something new and bigger philosophically. Without directly saying so, FDR was beginning to redraft the American social contract, adding a clause in which the U.S. government acknowledged a duty at least to try to protect investors from ruin at the hands of unscrupulous players in the market. Exactly how such protection would work was less important to Roosevelt than that it was offered in the first place.

The same went for farmers. After the banking crisis, the devastation of the agricultural economy was widely considered the most pressing problem facing the country. The threat of rebellion in the farm belt was real. The president of the Farm Bureau Federation, Edward A. O'Neal, predicted in January that without federal action, "we will have revolution in the countryside within 12 months." Milo Reno, a charismatic agrarian rebel, announced in mid-March that a farmers' strike would begin May 3 if Washington failed to provide relief.

Although he knew the issues from talking to farmers near Hyde Park and Warm Springs, Roosevelt himself didn't have firm views on the complexities of agricultural policy. During the campaign, with his talent for useful simplification, he was fond of saying that the farmer now had to carry two wagonloads of his product to town to buy the same boots, plows, and other supplies that one wagonload bought before the war. He knew the problem—low prices—but not the solution.

As usual, this was no impediment to moving forward. FDR decided on an approach that reflected his sometimes casual but usually practical problem solving. On March 8, he summoned Agriculture Secretary Wallace and Rex Tugwell to the White House and asked them to assemble representatives of the farmers, the processors, and every other lobby connected to agriculture, put them in a room in Washington, and tell them to find a consensus. Whatever they agreed upon, he would recommend to Congress and sign. The idea was action, any action, with little or no thought given to the long-term consequences.

The resulting Agricultural Adjustment Act (AAA) was a hodgepodge improvisation with something for everyone. It dramatically increased the Department of Agriculture's authority to intervene in the farm economy. The core of the bill was a "domestic allotment" system that tried to boost prices by paying farmers not to produce wheat, corn, rice, cotton, tobacco, dairy, and hog products. The idea of subsidizing farmers had been around since the early 1920s (in the McNary-Haugen bill) but destroying crops while people were hungry was new and controversial. "These farmers are not producing too much," complained John Simpson of the Farmers' Union. "What we have is overproduction of empty stomachs and bare backs." *

The bill sailed through the House after less than a week of debate,

---

* Many critics couldn't get over the fact that Agriculture Department "planners" slaughtered more than 5 million hogs in September of 1933 and let the meat go to waste. FDR never figured out how to get surplus food to the hungry.

but it stalled in the Senate. The chairman of the Senate Agriculture Committee was Ellison D. "Cotton Ed" Smith, an ornery South Carolina racist who got his nickname when he proclaimed, "Cotton is king and white is supreme." Smith planned to take his time with the biggest reform of the farm economy since the abolition of slavery, but FDR had other ideas. On April 4, he invited Smith and his committee members to the White House, where he dressed them down for delaying the country's urgent business. As usual, Roosevelt mixed his vinegar with honey. To reward Smith for finally opening debate on the bill, the president passed the word that neither Agriculture Secretary Wallace nor Rex Tugwell, both already vilified for being too left wing, would run the huge new agricultural assistance program. First he would offer the job to Bernard Baruch, who had deep roots in South Carolina, owned a vast estate there, and still commanded great respect among fiscal conservatives. When Baruch unsurprisingly declined, the job went to one of Baruch's friends, George Peek. This made no sense bureaucratically: Peek opposed the idea of forcing farmers to take acreage out of production, one of the critical components of the farm bill. But the appointment appeased "Cotton Ed," and the measure was passed and signed in May.*

Almost overnight, FDR established the principle that Washington bore responsibility for farm prices and should pay farmers to create scarcity. Even after the AAA itself was declared unconstitutional in 1936, the idea has remained an article of faith in the farm belt to this day. The only ones left out of the original deal were sharecroppers, many of them black. Although FDR's liberalism helped convert hundreds of thousands of African Americans from their allegiance to the party of Lincoln, he offered them few tangible benefits.

The Agriculture Department was perhaps the hottest place to work in the early New Deal, with lawyers like future Supreme Court Justice Abe Fortas and future Democratic presidential nominee Adlai Stevenson leaving partnerships in fancy law firms to help revamp the farm economy. This drove agricultural experts crazy. "A plague of young

---

* FDR's relationship with "Cotton Ed" soon deteriorated. Smith walked out of the 1936 Convention because a black delegate was allowed to speak. In 1938, Roosevelt unsuccessfully tried to "purge" him by supporting his opponent in the Democratic primary.

lawyers settled on Washington," remembered Peek, who began feuding with Wallace and Tugwell almost immediately after arriving. "They floated airily into office, asked for papers and found no end of things to be busy about." Peek thought farm price supports were "communistic" and complained that Tugwell and the others "deeply admired everything Russian."

He was not entirely wrong. A young lawyer and Frankfurter protégé named Alger Hiss toiled there for a time. If Hiss was a secret Communist in those years, he wasn't alone. With the seeming success of the Soviet agricultural planning model, more than a few socialists settled in at the agriculture department. Roosevelt didn't seem to mind.

FDR's openness to new ideas extended even to his agriculture secretary's strange weakness for mystics. To "Roos, the medicine man," "Johndro the astrologer," and "AE the mystic poet," Wallace now added a mysterious Russian émigré painter and peace activist named Nicholas Roerich, whose ideas he peddled to Roosevelt. On March 12, just a week after starting his new job, Wallace wrote Roerich:

> Dear Guru, I have been thinking of you holding the casket—the sacred most precious casket. And I have thought of the New Country going forward to meet the seven stars under the sign of the three stars. And I have thought of the admonition "Await the Stone". . .
>
> May Peace, Joy and Fire attend to you always,
> In the great haste of this strange maelstrom which is Washington.

Through the late 1920s, Roerich had convinced wealthy New Yorkers to build him a twenty-four-story art deco museum to house his thousands of paintings (which he claimed had healing powers) and other dubious enterprises. Almost from the start, Wallace sought to bring Roerich into the government by sending him on a trip to Central Asia to promote his "Banner for Peace," a vague scheme to protect international cultural landmarks. Their letters, which were to prove hugely embarrassing to Wallace when a few of them leaked in 1940, were written largely in code, with Roosevelt called the "Flaming One" when referred to positively and the "Wavering One" when he would not commit. Because of State Department opposition, FDR wavered on funding the trip and eventually declined, but he later met with Roerich and consistently engaged with Wallace on this plane. From his mother, Roosevelt retained a deep interest in all things Asian. After the president sent Wallace a mystical book called *The Glory Road*, Wallace replied in October of 1933 by writing: "Mr. President, you can be the 'flaming one,' the one with the ever-upward surging spirit to lead us into the time when the children of men can sing again."

Roosevelt cannot have taken any of this too seriously, but he was developing a cast of mind that refused to rule out anything, no matter how outlandish. The president was not just buoyant, he was open-minded in a way that Washington had never quite seen before. The city crackled with anticipation and earnest conversation. Every day, hundreds would arrive beseeching Jim Farley for employment, often following him to his hotel or breaking down in tears. For those who got jobs, the feeling was euphoric. "Come at once to Washington," a legislator wired Donald Richburg, a Chicago lawyer who drafted large chunks of New Deal legislation. "Great things are underway." Catholics and Jews, long informally excluded from the upper reaches of the federal government, were now more often judged on their individual merit, a legacy of pluralism that quietly changed the country.

Richard Neustadt recalled that it felt as if the young New Dealers were floating down Pennsylvania Avenue several feet above the sidewalk. "I can only describe the change as physical, virtually physical," remembered Milton Katz, a young aide in the RFC who had arrived under Hoover. "The wind blew through the corridors [and] a lot of old air blew out the windows. You suddenly felt, 'By God, the air is fresh, it's moving, life is resuming. April may be the cruelest month, but now the world is beginning over again.'"

The backlash, which would soon flower into full hatred of Roosevelt, began early. Moley, who had disbanded the original "Brain Trust" after the 1932 election, scoffed at what the idea had become: "Everyone who had a college degree and carried a briefcase was regarded in the press not only as an 'intellectual' but as a 'brain-truster,'" he recalled after turning more conservative. "Many proved to be useful but many were nuisances." Appeals Court Judge Learned Hand went further, labeling the New Dealers "so conceited, so insensitive, so arrogant." A moderate neatly summarized the state of play: "The New Deal is simply the effort of a lot of half baked socialists to save capitalism for the dumb capitalists."

Some ideas did seem socialistic, especially after the laissez-faire style of the twenties. Even so, the unifying notion was not social control but social responsibility. Late in March, Roosevelt moved fast to make Washington the lender of last resort by issuing an executive order that consolidated nine farm loan programs under Henry Morgenthau, the director of the Farm Credit Administration, who both streamlined and greatly expanded agricultural lending. FDR also pushed through a Home Owners Loan Corporation to help those facing foreclosure, an example of a lesser known New Deal agency whose services struck so close to home that parents passed on to their children the story of how Franklin Roosevelt saved the very house they lived in.* And by laying the groundwork for a system centered on home ownership rather than the public housing popular in Europe, the New Deal made possible the great postwar housing boom that populated the Sun Belt and boosted millions of Americans into the middle class, where, ironically, they often became Republicans.

At the time, though, the social upheaval over the horizon was frightening even to Roosevelt's closest associates. Louis Wehle—the Harvard classmate who had helped keep the dream of an FDR presidency alive in the twenties—visited Roosevelt with a warning. Wehle predicted, correctly, that restricting farm production would send hundreds of thousands of country folk into the cities in search of jobs, thereby transforming the whole nation. "You are going too fast and too far," Wehle warned his old friend. The inspired Inaugural words about avoiding fear, Wehle said, had been replaced by actions reflecting fear. FDR was focused on the unrest in the farm belt. "Violence has become so widespread," he told Wehle, "that these measures are necessary to prevent revolution." To forestall it, required action, he thought. Any action.

Roosevelt was constantly driving home the importance of forward motion and change, even if it appeared to be dangerous. In mid-April, Senator Elmer Thomas of Oklahoma began winning support for a

---

* The Farm Credit Administration and Home Owners Loan Corporation eventually refinanced a fifth of all farm and home mortgages.

hyper-inflationist currency plan. FDR knew the Thomas amendment was a harmful idea that amounted just to printing more money. But Senator Byrnes and others he trusted on Capitol Hill told him the bill was going to pass and that if the White House resisted, FDR would suffer a highly publicized defeat that would jeopardize the rest of his agenda. So on April 18, Roosevelt brought Thomas to the White House, where he lavished praise on his plan. He hoped, of course, that the good senator would be kind enough to let him just fiddle a bit with the language of the bill as it related to timing and implementation. Thomas said that was fine as long as the "basic principle" was preserved, which was all Roosevelt needed to go ahead and do what he wanted in the first place.

Here FDR showed how to make a virtue of necessity. Late that evening, at a meeting to prepare for the arrival of British prime minister Ramsay MacDonald, he told Moley to handle the Thomas plan: "Have it thoroughly amended and then give them the word to pass it." But at the very moment he seemed to finesse a challenge, he issued another one. FDR turned to his assembled aides and congressional allies and said: "Congratulate me. We are off the gold standard."

If FDR was looking for shock value, he got it. In order to keep more assets in the United States, he had decided to prohibit the issuance of gold export licenses, at least temporarily. The net effect of this was to take power away from international bankers who had used their gold to control the dollar. James Warburg, the savvy adviser from the famous banking family, and budget director Lewis Douglas began "fighting like tigers" against the idea. "All of the men there agreed that it was the most momentous day since the war. We were letting the dollar fall— throwing out the sacred gold standard idol," Moley wrote in his diary.

Afterwards, Warburg and Douglas wandered the streets of Washington until dawn. "This is the end of Western civilization," Douglas said despondently. He and the rest of the financial establishment saw the decision as doubly bad: it simultaneously shattered the "good as gold" foundation of the economy and boosted the nationalism they feared would lead eventually to another war.

Later, FDR let Warburg and Douglas weigh in on the Thomas amendment so that the retreat from international monetary standards was less abrupt. The United States did not formally abandon the gold standard until President Richard Nixon decided to do so in 1971.* "There was a certain amount of naughtiness in Roosevelt," Warburg recalled years later. "The temptation to do something that would shock all of us was tremendous. Having had that fun, he was perfectly prepared to be more sensible about it." But it was more than a sense of "fun" that led FDR to reject hoary economic theory in favor of a pragmatic, nonideological approach. The president, Warburg added, was ignorant about the details of international finance but had a "marvelous sense of intuitive direction."

These thorny currency questions were supposed to be worked out at the World Economic Conference, scheduled for June in London. FDR's daily schedule during the Hundred Days was filled with get-acquainted sessions with foreign leaders and other preparations for what was assumed to be an historic meeting, though he had no intention of attending himself. His second Fireside Chat, on May 7, was devoted to outlining the aims of the conference, which he hoped would help stabilize the world economy and secure world peace. But he also explained why tariffs were necessary to help the American economy revive, an indication of the nationalist thrust of his early foreign policy.

Even as domestic recovery took precedence over foreign affairs, FDR already had his hands full with Japan and the new Nazi government in Germany. Although the United States was firmly isolationist, Roosevelt himself harbored illusions about neither. As Japanese troops were moving through Manchuria toward the Great Wall of China, an April lunch at the White House with the Japanese envoy, Yosuke Matsuoka, turned frosty; Matsuoka had told newspapermen that he thought the U.S. Fleet should leave the Pacific. Early in May, Roosevelt met with Hitler's representative in Washington, Hjalmar Schacht, and afterwards FDR told Henry Morgenthau that European leaders were "a bunch of bastards" and he saw "a very strong possibility" of war with Germany, which had begun rearming before Hitler came to

---

* As a technical matter, the U.S. abandoned the gold standard as early as March 6, 1933, when Treasury Secretary Woodin stopped making Treasury payments in gold. Those nations, like Great Britain, that went off the gold standard earlier, recovered earlier.

power and was now accelerating its production of war materiel. FDR felt he must respond to Hitler's jingoism.*

The opportunity came on May 16, when he issued a carefully prepared appeal to world leaders to stop building all offensive weapons systems, the idea being that war was caused by battleships, warplanes, and tanks, not defensive fortifications. With disarmament talks deadlocked in Geneva, Roosevelt hoped this would be a new formula for cooperation. The initiative was modestly successful. Leaders of other democracies praised FDR's leadership and Hitler replied with a surprisingly conciliatory speech, which led Roosevelt to claim to Morgenthau that "I think I have averted a war." (In truth it would be four years before Hitler was ready to fight.) But the offensive weapons ban went nowhere and FDR increasingly believed he was dealing with a menace in Berlin. All told, the president's peacemaking debut did little more than raise unreasonable expectations for the London Conference.

Expectations, Roosevelt now understood, were best raised at home. In late January, the president-elect and Senator George Norris had traveled to Muscle Shoals, Alabama, on the banks of the Tennessee River. After a two-hour meeting with Arthur Morgan, a visionary Antioch College professor, FDR started to think big and began musing to aides about "the widest experiment ever undertaken by a government." Why not use the Tennessee Valley as a pilot project to see if government planning could remake a whole region? The project could include dams, power plants, soil conservation, reforestation, navigational improvements. The cheap power could lure industry to the area, kicking off a boom for the desperately poor people in the valley.

This was an example of how Roosevelt went beyond hype. Moley believed for some weeks early in the presidency that the whole idea was part of a larger effort to provide "cheering headlines" to make the nation forget its funk. But in meeting with Roosevelt in May, he learned how serious the president was about moving forward. Three weeks later, Roosevelt delivered a message to Congress proposing a "Tennessee Valley Authority." The "Authority" part had never been used

---

* Shortly after assuming power, Hitler was already threatening England and France and his supporters began highly publicized book burnings and the purging of Jews from responsible positions in the professions.

before by the federal government (it was borrowed from the Port Authority of New York and New Jersey, which later received New Deal money to build the Lincoln Tunnel).

For several decades, the TVA served as an example of government planning that could work. It lifted wages throughout the region and saved three million acres from erosion. Although the concept of huge, publicly owned projects never spread beyond the region—a mix of private development with some federal support worked better and was less expensive for taxpayers—the TVA came to symbolize the spirit of the New Deal, the notion that government had the duty at least to think about how to improve local economic conditions. Most of the particular remedies did not survive, yet the larger idea did. By the 1950s, the example of the TVA inspired more than a thousand flood-control projects around the country, each radiating economic development. Most of the projects, usually built by the Army Corps of Engineers, were beneficial, though some dams and levees were ineffective or led to unintended environmental problems, like those constructed near New Orleans.

Even on a pet project like the TVA, Roosevelt refused to embrace any fancy theory of government to justify it. "What are you going to say when they ask you the political philosophy behind TVA?" Norris asked. "I'll tell them it's neither fish nor fowl but whatever it is, it will taste awfully good to the people of the Tennessee Valley," Roosevelt replied. He wasn't big on specifics, except when it came to politics and design. FDR fancied himself an architect, like his hero Jefferson, and he spent hours designing public buildings—mostly in the Dutch Colonial style he knew so well—for the village of Hyde Park. For government projects like the TVA, he loved poring over maps and plans, chatting on about the obscure topography and local politics of whatever area was under inspection.

His specific knowledge of politics, American history, and geography was vast. It was said that if you drew a line across a map of the United States, FDR could name every county traversed. A publisher heard him recite the average price of ten commodities in 1933 and how they compared to 1923; when he checked later, he found out that Roosevelt was wrong on only one. During World War II, he often knew more than the State Department experts about the obscure countries being discussed.

In the breadth of his knowledge of people and places, his only rival among modern presidents was Bill Clinton. But like Ronald Reagan, FDR preferred to keep all policy memos to a page or two, no matter how important. It wasn't until after the Hundred Days that Roosevelt, who hadn't served in a legislative body in more than twenty years, even familiarized himself with the outlines of legislation. In July 1933, he asked Sam Rosenman for suggestions on a document. "I am not very familiar with the form that a law should take and therefore do not feel adequate to give an opinion without your assistance," he wrote in a rare confession of inadequacy that Rosenman left out of his memoirs.

In the early New Deal, FDR left much of the hard work on Capitol Hill to Sam Rayburn and Jimmy Byrnes. One southern journalist likened Byrnes in the Senate to a black female cook in a kitchen slaving over a hot stove while Roosevelt and his liberal friends sat laughing in the dining room, calling out for more pie. But the president knew the recipes well, by dint of experience. Theodore Roosevelt and Franklin Roosevelt are the only modern American presidents to have served both in the federal bureaucracy (as assistant Navy secretary) and as governor. FDR served much longer than his cousin in both posts. He came to office knowing more about the process of government—the way power really works at the ground level—than any chief executive who followed. His style was to look over the shoulders of those below him, often talking to their subordinates, even their secretaries, to get the latest scuttlebutt. Cassandra Connor was Jimmy Byrnes's personal secretary. The president of the United States would call up the senator's secretary during the Hundred Days and say, "I don't want to talk to him [Byrnes]. I just want to know what he's up to."*

Harold Ickes had the same experience as Byrnes. He recorded his surprise in his diary that after a trip with the Roosevelts to the presidential hideaway on the Rapidan River, the president insisted on riding back with Ickes's subordinate at the Interior Department, not him, leaving Ickes to wonder what they talked about. In the same way FDR checked in with junior physicians to see what they thought of his doctors' recom-

---

* FDR spent about a quarter of every day on the telephone. More than a hundred associates knew they could call him and get connected directly without going through a secretary, though most knew it was ill-advised to call at night, when he was working on speeches or relaxing.

mendations regarding his polio, he was constantly checking and cross-checking advice on policy matters, building a more sophisticated, if informal, matrix of information upon which to make a sound decision.

By cultivating subordinates, pitting his top officials against each other, and assigning overlapping authority, Roosevelt was violating many of the tenets of modern management. But this technique, however exasperating, helped him keep tabs on his administration and keep his people on their toes. Only by circumventing the chain of command to find out what was truly going on in his government could FDR hope to implement the midcourse adjustments essential to making the New Deal work. "He would call you in," remembered James Rowe, an aide in later years, "and he'd ask you to get the story on some complicated business, and you'd come back after a couple of days of hard labor and present the juicy morsel you'd uncovered under a stone somewhere and *then* you'd find out he knew all about it, along with something you *didn't* know. Where he got his information from he wouldn't mention usually, but after he'd done this to you once or twice you got damn careful about *your* information."

On a nearly daily basis, "the chief croupier" melded this joyfully inquisitive nature with his intuitive understanding of the anthropology of Washington to produce a governing style that allowed him to stay well informed and entirely in control. His knowledge was power—for himself and for the country.

Chapter Forty

Roosevelt's "Tree Army"

T HE BEST EXAMPLE of how FDR's leadership style changed the
nation during the Hundred Days was the launching of the Civilian Conservation Corps (CCC), a tale of mobilization so rapid and so
competent that it almost defies belief for later generations. The lessons
for today could hardly be fresher.

The CCC brought together two of Roosevelt's most deeply held values: work and conservation. Although he greatly expanded relief aid to
the states in 1933, FDR never much believed in it. "What I am seeking
is the abolition of relief altogether," he wrote Colonel House the following year. "I cannot say it out loud yet but I hope to be able to substitute work for relief."

Roosevelt had always harbored a deep interest in conservation. In
his alumni report for his twenty-fifth Harvard reunion in 1929, he
wrote: "I find time at home to practice forestry, as I would rather plant
trees than cut them down." But his idea for combining that interest
with the need to put destitute young people to work immediately was
strictly practical, with no roots in theory—even the theory of pragmatism. When he outlined what would eventually become the CCC to
Moley in 1932, Moley—always reluctant to admit that his boss had a
truly new idea—asked if he had ever taken a course at Harvard with
William James, the great pragmatic optimist. The concept behind the
CCC seemed inspired by James's famous essay, "The Moral Equivalent

of War." FDR replied that although he never studied with James, he remembered him well in Harvard Yard for his whiskers.

FDR's obliviousness to theories of pragmatism was a blessing, for while his solution was practical, his means of getting there were not, or so thought those around him. Within three days of assuming office, he was already bending Harold Ickes's ear about having the governor of Florida take over some agricultural lands and use them to settle the unemployed. By March 10, when the governor told him it was impractical to move the men there with their families, FDR summoned Ickes and Henry Wallace to the White House at 9:00 p.m. for an emergency meeting. He told them he wanted to discuss a bill to enlist 500,000 for work on government projects by midsummer, a number he apparently plucked from thin air and later cut in half. And that was just the beginning of what he had in mind.

FDR didn't waste any time. Eleven days later, on March 21, he unveiled the idea in a message to Congress designed to tell the country that relief and job creation were on the way. The outlines of the CCC were accompanied by a call to create a Federal Emergency Relief Administration (FERA), under which Harry Hopkins supervised relief aid to the states, and a Public Works Administration (PWA), the first of several agencies devoted to developing big, labor-intensive construction projects. Because the CCC was focused on young workers, the PWA aimed to help out the middle-aged unemployed. Hopkins proved to be an exceptionally able administrator and a strong advocate of public compassion. "People don't eat in the 'long run,' Senator," he later told a congressional committee. "They eat every day."

Republicans accused Washington of "playing Santa Claus" instead of leaving the giving of alms to state and local authorities. Huey Long, favoring something even more radical, called the CCC "a sapling bill, a sapsucker's bill." Roosevelt laughed off the opposition and kept his focus. He knew that dams and other large-scale public works would take many months or years to get off the ground. By contrast, hiring a quarter of a million young men to clear trails, drain swamps, plant trees, fight forest fires, and build cabins in national parks and forests could begin immediately.

Roosevelt was told repeatedly that this was simply impossible, for all sorts of logistical reasons. Even Wallace, despite his reputation for dreaminess, sounded a hardheaded note and said the forestry service couldn't possibly handle such a large group. Frances Perkins was appalled by FDR's idea of paying the men only a dollar a day. Her constituency at the Labor Department, the unions, argued that this would bring down wages and that work camps amounted to "forced labor." The president of the American Federation of Labor, William Green, testified in March that the CCC "smacked of Fascism, Hitlerism, and Sovietism."

The more his Cabinet said no, the more Roosevelt said yes. Finally, Perkins, trying to be positive, proposed that the U.S. Army be ordered to care for the men in the woods, an assignment the Army didn't appreciate. Roosevelt approved the Army's role, but the unions and other liberals continued to object, this time opposing the "militaristic" component. FDR's solution was classic. "I'll tell you what," he said, "the Department of Labor will recruit these men." In other words, if labor doesn't like it—we'll make it labor's responsibility. "Mr. President," Perkins protested, "You know as well as I do that the Department of Labor has no facilities for recruiting, selecting and transporting these men. What's more, we have no tents, no cots, no kitchens."

In this, Perkins was like every exasperated subordinate pleading with a headstrong boss who doesn't have to worry about the details. But FDR didn't want to hear any more objections. From his days as assistant secretary of the Navy, when he overcame skepticism about his idea to plant sea mines, he understood how to work through bureaucratic obstacles. Now he became crisply executive: "Resurrect the United States Employment Service [a moribund agency] right away. Use the Labor Department to recruit and select these men."

FDR's message was: 250,000 men working in the forests by summer. Do it now and I won't take any excuses! There was management brilliance in this. "He put the dynamite under the people who had to do the job and let them fumble for their own methods," as Perkins later put it. This was the presidential leadership that eased the Depression and won World War II.*

---

* Comparisons of eras and presidents are speculative, but if such leadership had been present after September 11, 2001, it's a fair bet that it would not have taken more than four years for the FBI to fix its computer system and for the government to secure ports and chemical plants against terrorism. FDR would have demanded it be done in, say, four months.

But resoluteness was not enough. To achieve these results required something more than broad, ambitious goals by the president. After setting this seemingly unrealistic target, FDR worked on the gearing necessary to make it happen. From his days in the Wilson administration he remembered the names of obscure Interior Department bureaucrats who knew a lot about public lands. He invited members of the House and Senate labor committees to the White House, answered each of their objections, and dazzled them with his detailed knowledge of wage levels. He drew elaborate organization charts sketching lines of authority several levels down in the new agency. "I want *personally* to check on the location, scope etc of the camps, size [,] work to be done etc.," he scrawled under one executive order. After the War Department estimated the cost of food and shelter, he wrote, "This figure of $1.92 a day, not including transportation or wages is absurdly high—it must be greatly reduced."

The bill passed easily, with the only significant amendment coming in the House, where Republican Oscar De Priest of Chicago, the sole black member of Congress, successfully inserted an amendment barring discrimination. FDR signed it on March 31. To mend fences with organized labor, Roosevelt recruited a folksy machinists union vice president he barely knew, Robert Fechner, as director of the agency. When told that hiring a labor man would lead to inefficient administration, he said, "Oh, that doesn't matter. The Army and the Forestry Service will really run the show. The secretary of labor will select the men and make the rules and Fechner will 'go along' and give everybody satisfaction and confidence."*

This was a charade, because FDR planned to run the whole thing from the White House with Louis Howe. But when Howe insisted on signing off on practically every decision at every camp, paperwork stacked up on his desk. Campsites were not opening quickly enough for the impatient president, in part because most enrollees were in the East while most projects were in the West. To speed the already frenzied mobilization, Roosevelt instructed that more authority be delegated to the

---

* Robert Jackson, who later served as U.S. Attorney General and went on to the Supreme Court, was exasperated by FDR's administrative sloppiness but recalled how without his impatience and desire to "knock heads together" Washington would have faced many more problems winning World War II.

Army. The pace led to some bad publicity. Howe was summoned to Capitol Hill to explain why he had approved a contractor's bid of $1.40 each for 200,000 toilet kits when the Army could provide the same for corps members for 32 cents apiece. He was cleared of corruption, but the flap set a precedent for aggressive, bipartisan congressional over-sight of the New Deal. Unlike some later presidents, FDR often welcomed such accountability because it helped him improve his programs.

The urgency and resourceful problem solving paid off. By April 7, only thirty-four days into the administration, the first corps members were enlisted. By July 1, less than four months after Roosevelt made his outlandish demand, he exceeded his quarter-million goal. Nearly 275,000 young men were enrolled in 1,300 camps across the country, supporting their families and undertaking much-needed projects. Al-though no women were allowed in the CCC, blacks, housed mostly in segregated camps, eventually made up 10 percent of corps members and 14,000 American Indians were immediately included.* Colonel Duncan Major reported to Roosevelt that the speed of the mobilization had broken "all American war and peacetime records." And it has not been matched since.

Beyond providing work and improving the countryside, Roosevelt's "Tree Army" helped keep the peace. On April 29, Howe received word that the Bonus Army—the collection of ragtag veterans that had deliv-ered the coup de grace to Herbert Hoover—was coming back to town. This was troubling, as it came on the heels of reports of more unrest in the farm belt; a bankruptcy judge had been dragged from his court-room, beaten, and almost lynched in LeMars, Iowa. Within days, more than six thousand scraggly veterans showed up for the reprise, with more on the way. The men promised to be orderly, but with the cuts in veterans' benefits, tempers were short. They were all hungry.

J. Edgar Hoover, appointed in 1924 to head of the Bureau of Investi-gation, told Attorney General Cummings that this unrest was just the beginning. Hoover claimed that 333,000 delegates of "the oppressed people of the Nation" were about to show up in Washington, many of

---

* Several CCC camps were integrated, which set a precedent that President Truman later used to integrate the U.S. military.

them carrying arms. The young Justice Department bureaucrat, with no experience in the field, was grossly exaggerating. He was trying to hang onto his job and thought that the true-crime detective stories and ingratiating notes he sent over to Louis Howe might not be enough. If Thomas Walsh had lived, he intended to fire Hoover. Cummings was reserving judgment, in part because Harlan Fiske Stone, now on the Supreme Court, arranged for Frankfurter to write Roosevelt recommending that Hoover (a Stone protégé) be retained.

Hoover's reports on the bonus marchers got FDR's attention. First, the president ordered the Veterans Administration to set up a camp at Fort Hunt, Virginia, the site of the first CCC camp. The resulting tent city featured electric lights and running water, including showers for the men. FDR drove through the camp and waved his hat at the "bonus boys" but thought something more was necessary. Hoover, who won increased funding for what would soon be a newly restructured "FBI," was right about one thing: Tension was growing between left-wingers and right-wingers that threatened to split the veterans and break into violence.

While Howe worked with veterans' representatives to defuse political strife, FDR kept his eye on the simple, symbolic gestures. He instructed Howe to tour the area and make sure the men had plenty of the promised food and shelter—and above all, coffee. "There's nothing that makes people feel as welcome as a steaming cup of coffee," Roosevelt told him.

Howe had an idea of who should serve it. One rainy spring afternoon, he asked his old friend Eleanor if she would drive him out to Fort Hunt in her roadster. When they arrived, he told her he would nap in the car and pushed her out into the camp: "Talk to these men, get their gripes and be sure to tell them that Franklin sent you." Later, the Secret Service would insist that Louis and Eleanor each carry a gun when they traveled without a security escort, but this time, the agents assigned to protect Eleanor were left behind at the White House and she ventured into the camp unarmed and alone.

The Secret Service needn't have worried. The first lady, warming to her task, mingled winningly with the destitute veterans, talking of France in 1919. Soon they joined her in singing "Pack Up Your Troubles in Your Old Kit Bag," "There's a Long, Long Trail A'Winding," and other war songs. She visited the makeshift hospital. Here was Eleanor in her new, path-breaking role for a first lady and loving every moment of it. Afterwards, a vet said admiringly in earshot of a reporter: "Hoover sent the army. Roosevelt sent his wife."

That peace could reign in the camps was a surprising accomplishment, a reflection of how the Roosevelts' charm could soften a policy decision far harsher than Herbert Hoover's. Ever since the Economy Bill slashed veterans' benefits by 50 percent in March, members of Congress had been besieged by constituents urging that the cuts be at least partially reversed. Arthur Krock wrote in the *Times* that "down many main streets go armless veterans who used to get $94 a month from the Government and now get $36." Suicides among indigent veterans were reported around the country as front-page news. Finally, on May 10, FDR admitted error, acknowledging that the cuts to veterans with service-connected disabilities had been "deeper than originally intended." The president was hardly a humble man, but he knew the importance of avoiding the impression of infallibility.

To further defuse a volatile situation, Roosevelt and Howe hatched a plan to recruit Bonus Army marchers into the CCC, which was already a quasi-military organization, with Army surplus equipment and clothing, the playing of "Taps," "Reveille," and the rest. Here was the wartime metaphor of the Inaugural Address made real, but without the menace of Mussolini or the implied conscription threat of the radio address to the American Legion that FDR had discarded.

In one of the flexible midcourse adjustments he so frequently adopted, FDR waived the CCC's age requirement (originally eighteen to twenty-five) to allow enrollment of World War I and even Spanish-American War vets at least a decade older. There was plenty of grumbling over the dollar-a-day wage; "to hell with reforestation!" shouted one Bonus Army leader, to cheers. Another said, "It's like selling yourself into slavery." But about 25,000 marchers eventually enrolled. Those who didn't enlist in the CCC left Washington peacefully, their way home paid by a congressional fund. Within a few years, a quarter of a million veterans would serve their country in the CCC.

The bonus marchers who returned for a third time in the summer of 1934 were few in number and yesterday's news, another example of FDR's calculated finesse. Late in his life, he pointed with pride to the fact that through all the long years of Depression and war, no major civil unrest took place on his watch. It could easily have been otherwise. The columnist Ernest K. Lindley wrote in 1933 that "Mr. Roosevelt may turn out to be the Kerensky of the Revolution,"* a reflection of elite opinion that FDR's leadership was too mild to forestall something more violent. In fact, it almost certainly did prevent acts of rebellion. After the CCC was phased out in 1942, a victim of wartime needs, the final government report on the project explained that without the work provided to millions of men, the threat of revolution from the aimless and despairing unemployed might have become real: "They were ready victims for the moral dry rot that accompanies enforced idleness and its resulting dejection. Insidiously, there was spreading abroad in the land the nucleus of those bands of young predators who infested the Russian countryside after the revolution and who became known as 'wild boys.' "

This sounds overheated to modern ears but it reflected legitimate fears at the time. It helps explain why the CCC was the most popular New Deal program. When FDR wanted to cut enrollment to show he was fiscally responsible in his 1936 reelection campaign, he was stymied in Congress by both Democrats and Republicans. Colonel Robert McCormick, publisher of the *Chicago Tribune* and a fierce critic of his old Groton schoolmate, loved the CCC. After crime in Chicago dropped by 55 percent, a Chicago judge credited the agency with getting troublesome young men off the streets. Thousands of small businesses located near camps stayed afloat serving the needs of corps members. In the end, FDR's seemingly impractical brainstorm not only protected the country from unrest and eased suffering, it symbolized the spirit of rebirth and regeneration that he hoped to convey in his early days in office.

The future labor leader, Lane Kirkland, grew up in South Carolina, where the CCC was run by an Army officer named George C. Marshall, one of many distinguished officers in World War II who first served in the "Tree Army" at home. Kirkland later explained what the agency did for his state and region: "The southern U.S. was totally stripped of

---

* After the 1917 Russian Revolution, Alexander Kerensky proved too moderate for the Bolsheviks and was supplanted by Vladimir Lenin.

vegetation. Every river was thick with mud from erosion. Every farm had a gully. And every time it rained, the topsoil just washed away. You go down there now and you see millions of pine trees that are the basis of the timber and pulp industry, planted by the CCC."

Over nine years, more than 3 million men were given meaningful work. Corps members planted an astonishing 3 billion trees, developed 800 state parks, protected 20 million acres from erosion, and cleared 125,000 miles of trails, including those used for the first downhill skiing in the United States at Stowe, Vermont. (A president who could not use his legs indirectly launched the ski industry.) Perhaps most important, the Civilian Conservation Corps inspired programs over the next several decades such as the Job Corps, Peace Corps, VISTA, and Americorps and thousands of community projects, leaving no doubt that the father of national service in the United States was FDR.

Roosevelt's point was plain: Government counts, and in the right hands, it can be made to work. Strong federal action, not just private voluntary efforts and the invisible hand of the marketplace, was required to help those stricken in an emergency. The American people expected and deserved leadership in addressing their hardships, not just from state and local authorities but from the White House. This fundamental insight would guide politicians and help millions of people in the years ahead, but it was lost on others, who ignored the lessons of Franklin Roosevelt at their peril.

Chapter Forty-one

The Blue Eagle

Having addressed the banking crisis, Prohibition, Wall Street scam artists, low crop prices, foreclosures, and jobless young hobos within ninety days, FDR knew there was still something missing from his program. The industrial sector—including manufacturing, wholesaling, and retailing—remained under water. What to do?

As late as April, FDR had been prepared to do nothing until the next session of Congress. He thought an industrial recovery program would bust the budget. But action on Capitol Hill changed his mind. The idea for what became the largest and most complex bill of the Hundred Days was hatched almost by accident after legislation sponsored by Alabama senator Hugo Black for a mandatory thirty-hour workweek passed the Senate overwhelmingly and neared passage in the House in mid-April. This was a crude but popular bill; one House amendment even barred imports of any products that foreign workers had spent more than thirty hours a week making. *Time* magazine reported that the Black bill meant FDR "was dangerously close to losing control of Congress." The thinking behind Black's plan—a sign of the desperation of the times—was that if everyone was compelled to work fewer hours, there would be more jobs to go around.

Roosevelt sensed that this was a dangerous idea. It was one thing to break up sweatshop labor (which had made a comeback in the early 1930s) by giving Americans the right to refuse to work more than a certain number of hours per week. Why should someone be fired for saying no to a backbreaking schedule? But this bill had a different goal. It forced employers to prevent willing employees from working a full forty-hour week—and it applied to all industries engaged in interstate commerce. As usual, FDR had a way of making abstract problems concrete: "What will they do in the dairy industry, the milk evaporating and canning industry?" he asked his advisers about farming and seasonal occupations that required intense work. "How can they put that on a 30-hour week and still come out square?" Every time he raised objections to the Black bill, he talked about "the rhythm of the cow."

To stop Black's bill, Roosevelt needed something else, something big. With experts advising him that he must match agricultural assistance with a boost for the industrial economy, he cast his usual wide net, querying governors, business leaders, and anyone else he could think of for their ideas. Again, there was no master plan, only an instinct to improvise. In late April, Moley asked General Hugh ("Old Iron Pants") Johnson to pull together all of the industrial recovery plans floating around town. Johnson was a manic personality who fifteen years earlier had worked as Bernard Baruch's number two at the War Industries Board, which ran the domestic economy during World War I. In 1932, he had been part of the original Brain Trust but also helped Baruch in the "Stop Roosevelt" campaign at the Chicago convention.

It turned out that Baruch didn't think Johnson was the right man for this new job, which for a time would become the most important in the New Deal. "[Johnson's] a good number-three man, maybe a number-two man," Baruch told Frances Perkins. "But he's not a number-one man. He's dangerous and unstable. He gets nervous. Hugh needs a firm hand." But the financier never delivered the warning about Johnson directly to the president, who should have known better than to hire him. So Johnson got the assignment to design industrial recovery legislation and he ran with it, much to the consternation of Justice Brandeis and the other ideological opponents of centralized economic planning.

Hugh Johnson's omnibus bill—the National Industrial Recovery Act—established an important new principle: Washington would embrace a peacetime "industrial policy" to fight the Depression by directly supervising the economy and putting millions to work. The center-piece of the new law was the National Recovery Administration (NRA), which for several months after the Hundred Days became the biggest news in the country. The bill extended government further into the private economy than any wage and price controls before or since. Some of the changes would be permanent: The NRA created public works projects, abolished child labor, and set the first federal minimum wage ($12 for a 40-hour week). But the bill also eliminated antitrust regulation and established thousands of intrusive price and production codes for industry. The aim was to raise prices, but the persnickity rules would prove unhelpful to the economy.

The bill did not have an easy time on Capitol Hill. "Men have fol-lowed [FDR] upstairs without question or criticism," one Republican progressive wrote his family. "These men have about reached the limits of their endurance." Huey Long thundered that "every crime and fault" of both monarchy and socialism were contained in one bill, without any of their virtues. "It is worse than anything proposed under the So-viet [Union]." The rhetoric of other, more moderate senators was no less heated. In the end, Long voted for the bill, anyway, though on final passage it cleared the Senate by only seven votes.

At first, big business embraced the idea because the elaborate code-making process (meetings of industry representatives and bureaucrats) encouraged them to collude with their competitors to fix prices and drive out competition. Small business liked the protection afforded by official government affiliation. And the public loved the program be-cause it symbolized forward motion against the Depression. Pro-NRA marches in the fall of 1933 were at the time the largest demonstrations in American history, with 250,000 people marching down New York's Fifth Avenue and many thousands more gathered with great idealistic fervor in cities and towns across the country. Shopkeepers everywhere hung the NRA's emblem, a blue eagle, in their windows, with the leg-end: WE DO OUR PART.

Over time, the NRA led indirectly to the widespread adoption of humane working conditions and new safety standards. These advances grew partly out of the codes but were mostly the unanticipated result of a last-minute and little-noticed concession to unions in the form of vague language inserted by Senator Robert Wagner of New York into omnibus bill that officially recognized for the first time the right of workers "to organize and bargain collectively." After more than a half century of struggle, the American labor movement finally had the backing of Washington. This one clause, the famous section 7(a), eventually became the "Magna Carta" of labor organizing.

In retrospect, the NRA was a big, splashy bad idea that lasted only a couple of years. Hugh Johnson worked like a fiend and produced mostly red tape. The micro-regulation from Washington was perverse: hardware store owners operated under nineteen different codes, cork makers faced thirty-four sets of rules, and burlesque show proprietors were regulated as to how many times they could allow strippers to take off their clothes each night.

"The excessive centralization and the dictatorial spirit," wrote Walter Lippmann, regaining his powers of discernment, "are producing a revulsion of feeling against bureaucratic control of American economic life." The NRA boosted confidence in the short run, but it helped poison the well of the whole New Deal, and it gave conservatives an antiregulatory message that they exploited for decades. Even a loyalist like Harry Hopkins was moved to tell Johnson within months of the NRA's creation, "Your codes stink." By the time big parts of the program were declared unconstitutional by the Supreme Court in 1935, most New Dealers were secretly relieved.

But even such a misbegotten idea had a way of germinating something significant. The novelist Sherwood Anderson, attending a code hearing in the autumn of 1933, noticed it: "Here for the first time you see these men of business . . . coming up on the platform to give an accounting. It does seem the death knell of the old idea that a man owning a factory or store has a right to run it his own way." Anderson thought he was seeing the birth of "an entire new principle in American life"—corporate accountability to the community.

Although FDR championed the NRA, he didn't get involved in it directly, except for one key decision at a 2:00 p.m. Cabinet meeting on June 16, the same day he signed the bill setting it up. Just after the public signing ceremony, where he announced that the esteemed General Johnson would administer the program, he privately stripped Johnson of a good chunk of his authority. In a Solomonic move that also fit with his idea of dividing responsibility among his subordinates—the better to maintain control in his own hands—he took the public works part of the soon-to-be sprawling new bureaucracy out of Johnson's bailiwick and gave it to Harold Ickes. (Code-setting would remain under Johnson.) Johnson was shocked when he got the word that his baby had been cut in half before it was officially born. The ex-cavalryman turned purple and muttered to the president in a strange voice: "I don't see why. I don't see why." After the meeting, he angrily threatened to quit, but was talked out of it by Perkins, under instructions from FDR to "Stick with Hugh. Keep him sweet. Don't let him explode."

FDR's decision to clip Johnson's wings helped save the rest of the New Deal. Ickes, terrified of corruption, slowed down the public works portion of the NRA. This retarded recovery and infuriated restless New Dealers, but it also kept the hundreds of huge construction projects relatively clean. If they had become sources of scandal, later public works programs like the WPA would have faced stiffer opposition. It's doubtful Roosevelt understood this when he divided management of the recovery program, but his instinct proved sound, as Johnson not only confirmed Baruch's warning but by 1934 turned out to be a hothead with a weakness for bourbon and fascist ideas of social organization.*

Beyond that, the president's main contribution to the NRA was to help design the commemorative stamp. He thought the man depicted on it looked too much like himself, so he added a mustache and took off the gentleman's hat. The FDR look-alike on the original stamp, he said, just seemed too "stuffy."

Friday, June 16, 1933, the day Roosevelt simultaneously signed the bill establishing the NRA and recast its leadership, was also the final day of the special congressional session. All the loose ends of the Hundred Days came together in those final hours, though not exactly in the way FDR would have chosen. Pragmatism is inherently messy. When Congress the week before insisted on restoring some veterans' benefits (so that no veterans would have his check slashed by more than 25 per-

---

* In the meantime, the general provided great copy. Those who opposed the codes had "more than a trace of rodent blood" in their veins. If they resisted, Johnson told a newspaperman between sips of beer, "they'll get a sock right on the nose."

cent), FDR went along, though he wasn't happy about it. Moley later said that the only time he saw him lose his good humor during the entire Hundred Days was when Senator Cutting refused to compromise on veterans' cuts, casting FDR as a heartless skinflint. "He looked very tired and his face was drawn with fatigue," Morgenthau wrote in his diary. But after transacting so much legislative business, senators were tired, too, and anxious to go home. With Senator Black's help, the president finally got a veterans bill that he could sign.

A similar drama unfolded on the final negotiations of the Glass-Steagall Act, which for the next six decades would separate commercial from investment banking. In May, Republican Senator Arthur Vandenberg of Michigan teamed up with the Senate's presiding officer, Vice President Garner, to slip in an amendment that FDR vehemently opposed: deposit insurance. By mid-June, Roosevelt was still threatening a veto and hoped the whole banking reform bill would die. But with his own vice president and much of his party in full revolt on this issue, he knew that Vandenberg had the votes to override a veto and bloody him badly at the end of the session. So the provision for what eventually became the Federal Deposit Insurance Corporation (FDIC) stayed.

Within months, FDR's fears that high premiums would cripple healthy banks proved unfounded. The comfort of having deposit insurance (which covered the first $2,500 in deposits) so buoyed public confidence that only a handful of banks failed after 1933 and premiums stayed low. Today, even the strongest free market conservatives agree that the U.S. government had good reason to go into the bank insurance business in 1933. Milton Friedman called the FDIC the "single most important structural change" in the economy since the Civil War.

Roosevelt reluctantly signed the Glass-Steagall banking legislation containing that historic structural change at 11:15 a.m. on June 16. Fifteen minutes later, he signed a bill completely reorganizing the nation's railroad industry and fifteen minutes after that, he put his signature on the National Industrial Recovery Act, which contained the NRA, FERA, and PWA. At noon, he signed more farm credit legislation, bringing to fifteen the number of important bills that had reached his desk since the special session began. After having lunch with Garner and Farley, he chaired the momentous Cabinet meeting where authority for recovery was divided between Ickes and Johnson, met with more members of Congress, held a press conference, and was briefed on foreign policy issues. Finally, shortly after 8:00 p.m., he, Steve Early, and Missy LeHand left the White House for Union Station, where they boarded an overnight train north.

The first Hundred Days were over, with a new standard in place for all future presidents to measure themselves against. It wasn't just that Roosevelt, with the help of Congress, had pushed through the most legislation in the shortest time in American history. In a flash, he had transformed the presidency and the role of Washington, D.C. Presidents thereafter would have to perform the role of communicator in chief and legislator in chief, or risk irrelevance. Business would have to make room for government in influencing economic life. The American people would come to expect their presidents—from either party—to come to office with ambitious legislative agendas.

A week after his November 1932 election, FDR gave an interview to *The New York Times*. The presidency, he said, "is preeminently a place of moral leadership." He reviewed the work of great earlier presidents from George Washington to Woodrow Wilson and concluded that each of them were "leaders of thought at times when certain historic ideas in the life of the nation had to be clarified."

Now, a mere seven months later, the new president had already shown "moral leadership," proven himself a leader of "thought," and "clarified" some important ideas about the country. The results were spectacular. It wasn't just that a new bull market was underway and indices of industrial production were up sharply; the New Dealers all knew this was just another speculative bubble and that the underlying economy remained weak. The change, instead, was almost spiritual. Times were tough and would almost certainly remain so, but help was on the way. America would muddle through, just as it always did.

John Franklin Carter, as "The Unofficial Observer," concluded at the time that FDR, for all of his shortcomings, had accomplished "three magnificent things": hope, action, and self-respect. The country, he wrote, was no longer in a coma; the president "has saved us from chaos or revolution." Millions of Americans would still despair in the eight long years of the Depression that lay ahead and many of their individual dreams would be dashed on the rocks of economic hardship. But collectively, the country was in a new place, with a new confidence that the federal government would actively try to solve problems rather than fiddle or cater to the rich. Hope was no longer just for Pollyannas; the cynics about the American system were in retreat. Soon enough, politics would become viciously partisan once more, a luxury of democracy and a sign of civic health.

With Congress adjourned, FDR attended the graduation of his son Franklin Junior from Groton, then set sail in late June up the East Coast on the yacht *Amberjack II* with all of his sons except Elliott, whose Reno divorce was making headlines as the first ever in a first family. One more task awaited the president. The London Conference was not going well, in part because Secretary of State Hull, the head of the American delegation, was clashing with Ray Moley, whom Roosevelt had dispatched to London as his personal envoy when he feared that Hull's free trade internationalism would lead to the Americans getting suckered. Hull intercepted a cable that Moley had sent back to FDR that savaged Hull's leadership. "That pissant Moley," the secretary of state complained to James Warburg, another delegate. "Here he curled up at mah feet and let me stroke his head like a huntin' dog and then he goes and bites me in the ass."

For months, Roosevelt had gone back and forth on whether he favored addressing the Depression with international collective action. Now, feeling his oats after his legislative successes, he finally decided after consultation with Morgenthau that London was a distraction from domestic recovery. So sitting in the captain's cabin of the USS *Indianapolis* on July 3, he wrote a brusque and undiplomatic public message arguing that the conference was headed toward "a catastrophe amounting to a world tragedy" by focusing so much on the narrow issue of the gold standard and exchange rates. The so-called bombshell cable worked as planned and effectively blew up the conference. ("How could he have sent such a message to me?" Ramsay MacDonald complained.) FDR later said that European bankers and finance ministers with a vested interest in the gold standard were hijacking the meeting and that he was proud to have ruined it. At the same time, he was looking for a way to concentrate on implementing the New Deal unfettered by international obligations.

The "bombshell" was praised by nationalists at home and decried in Europe, except by the British economist John Maynard Keynes, who said FDR had been "magnificently right."* Roosevelt didn't much care about the reaction. He was on vacation, with the highlight a brief stop on Campobello. It was his first trip back since being carried off the island on a stretcher twelve years before. No letters or accounts reflecting his feelings survive; all we know is that he had left a broken man, his political career in ruins, and returned as the most dynamic new head of state in the world. Beyond that, the interior life of this man would remain a mystery.

But there was one glimpse—one fleeting insight into the off-stage Roosevelt, the one behind the banter and bonhomie. On a foggy morning at Campobello, a Washington correspondent was walking with a young lady in the woods on the island. The pair came to a clearing and saw the president's car, with bodyguard Gus Gennerich asleep behind the wheel.

That summer, the poet and essayist Archibald MacLeish wrote in a piece based on notes made by the Washington reporter:

> He [FDR] was sitting on the trunk of a tree, his legs folded out in front of him, his hands over his face. And suddenly, before they could move, the hands came down and there were his eyes looking straight into their eyes just a few steps off and not seeing them at all, the way a man's face will look at you not seeing you from a flash in the movies; there was a kind of drawn grimace over his mouth and over his forehead like a man trying to see something in his mind and suffering.
>
> And then all at once they could see the eyes focusing and it was like a shutter clicking down on a camera the way the smile came back over the look in his eyes and he called out: "Hello, there, Billy. Picking flowers?"
>
> They turned and got out of there. They could hear his big laugh back of them in the spruce.

---

* Eleven years later, FDR sponsored the 1944 Bretton Woods Conference, which stabilized international currencies and created the World Bank and International Monetary Fund. The British delegation was headed by Keynes.

Coda:
Social Security

THE NEW DEAL offered a cornucopia of new domestic ventures that changed the country, but the most far-reaching—and the one that made FDR most proud—was Social Security, which included not just old-age benefits but the first nationwide system of unemployment insurance. Social Security was the logical outgrowth of FDR's efforts to rewrite the American social contract. Over time, it transformed our definition of what we owe each other as Americans. While vaguely conceived during the Hundred Days, the idea didn't come to life until 1935. Even then, the bill barely made it into law.

The United States was late to the concept. The first modern social program was enacted in Germany in 1883 under Otto von Bismarck, who used national health care benefits to fend off more radical proposals. Other industrialized countries followed, but the United States clung to the idea that the elderly should be forced to fend for themselves or rely on private charity. Turn-of-the-century professors like economist John R. Commons of the University of Wisconsin, the "grandfather of Social Security," began agitating for pension reform. In 1933, Abraham Epstein changed the name of his old-age lobbying group to "the American Association for Social Security," the first time the phrase came into popular usage. By that time, half of the states offered tiny state pensions worth an average of 65 cents a day, but only about 3 percent of the elderly were covered. Louisiana, for instance, cut the pensions of elderly black men in half during the summer months in order to force them back into the fields to harvest cotton.

The Depression hit the elderly especially hard. Unemployment for those over age sixty-five seeking work was well above 50 percent—at a time when few had any other source of income. These were men and women who had worked to build the United States in the early part of the century and now had nothing to show for it. Even people employed by big companies with pension plans were usually out of luck; those pensions were long gone. Many elderly people gave what little food came their way to their grandchildren and joined soup lines.

As governor of New York, FDR, under prodding from Frances Perkins, first publicly advocated social insurance in 1930. But when he came to the presidency, FDR felt the country was not yet ready for such a big change. During the Hundred Days he decreed that first Perkins should begin an education campaign, inside the administration and out, and assemble experts to design a new system. Perkins took him at his word and brought the subject up at every other Cabinet meeting, about twenty-five times during 1933. That year, she made one hundred speeches across the country stressing social insurance as a way to assist the unemployed and soften future depressions.

As Perkins lit a fire within the administration, pressure was growing from without. In 1934, Francis E. Townsend, a retired dentist from Long Beach, California, found himself at age sixty-six unemployed and with no savings. So in a letter-to-the-editor to his local newspaper, he hatched a superficially appealing plan that would pay $200 a month ($2,900 in 2005 dollars) to every citizen over sixty, with the requirement that all of the money be spent in thirty days. (The original money was supposed to come from a 2 percent sales tax.) The idea spread like a chain letter. Within a year, five thousand "Townsend Clubs" across the country represented between 2 and 5 million members—a powerful new elderly lobby poised to take Congress by storm.

Senator Huey Long's "Share Our Wealth" plan was even more radical. In his book *Every Man a King*, Long proposed giving $2,000 a year (nearly $30,000 in 2005 dollars) to every family, plus a flat $5,000 to build and furnish a house, free college tuition, and pensions for the elderly. He proposed paying for it by confiscating all income over $1 million a year and all accumulated wealth over $5 million. By 1935, he had 7 million followers signed up. Long's plan was never realistic, but Representative Ernest Lundeen of Minnesota almost won congressional approval of a proposal that allowed elected committees of workers (known elsewhere as "soviets") to use the income tax to distribute unemployment benefits.

Even though FDR later imposed huge tax increases on the wealthy, he was appalled by these plans and alarmed by the political threat they posed to the New Deal.* "The Congress can't stand the pressure of the Townsend Plan unless we have a real old-age insurance system," he told Perkins. He would need to get out in front of these rival plans; but how?

His advisers were divided. Harry Hopkins advocated combining old-age benefits with new relief efforts. FDR said that smacked of "the dole," which he was trying to avoid. What interested the president— and had since at least 1930—was not "charity" but "insurance." Relief was meant to be curtailed when good times returned; insurance, which went back to medieval guilds, was supposed to be for life if one were eligible. He was insistent that the two concepts be kept separate. Justice Brandeis, working through intermediaries, was focused on implementation. He wanted all social reforms turned over to the states—which he called the "laboratories of democracy." Nearing eighty, Brandeis still wielded great influence on the Court, but he kept telling the New Dealers who flocked to Washington to go home and work in their state capitals.

Holding up the left, Rexford Tugwell, whose line to FDR was fading, agitated not just for national unemployment insurance but for national health insurance. Opposition to this idea from medical societies was so strong that Roosevelt never seriously considered it. Dr. Harvey Cushing, a socially prominent Boston physician and the father of Jimmy Roosevelt's wife, Betsey, lobbied him personally at the White House. FDR's policy on health care would take the form of earmarking federal public works money to build more hospitals, though many such facilities refused to treat the poor.

---

* Roosevelt was more sympathetic to the novelist Upton Sinclair's End Poverty in California (EPIC) campaign for governor, which was mostly a more radical version of FDR's own program. But Sinclair lost in November 1934 after being savaged by California industrialists.

All the while, vague ideas of "security" percolated. Even in its embryonic stage, everyone involved knew that the obstacles were formidable. First, the timing was terrible. Although aid to the disabled and to widowed mothers* would relieve immediate suffering, old-age pensions would do nothing to ease the Depression or help the elderly in the short term. The reserves would take a while to build up and no benefits would be paid until several years down the road. In fact, any such program might hurt the economy by taking money out of circulation.

When advised that social security taxes would be deflationary, FDR replied:

> We can't help that. We have to get it started or it will never start.
>
> You want to make it simple—very simple. So simple that everybody will understand it. And what's more, there is no reason why everybody in the United States should not be covered. I see no reason why every child, from the day he is born, shouldn't be a member of the social security system. When he begins to grow up, he should know that he will have old-age benefits from the insurance system to which he has belonged all his life. If he is out of work, he gets a benefit. If he is sick or crippled, he gets a benefit. . . . From the cradle to the grave they ought to be in a social insurance system.

After Perkins began shaking her head, he said emphatically, "I don't see why not—cradle to grave. I don't see why not."

But for all of Perkins's efforts to depict him in her memoirs as a true believer, FDR did, in fact, see why not. Despite his noble vision, Roosevelt was unwilling to use the phrase "cradle to grave" in public or to push for a comprehensive remedy. He didn't think the American political system could handle it.

In 1934, FDR appointed an interagency Committee on Economic Security (CES), with Perkins as chair, to study the problem. One big worry was that the U.S. Supreme Court would rule any national program unconstitutional. Article I of the Constitution allows Congress only those "legislative powers herein granted." Unless interstate com-

---

* This eventually became Aid to Families with Dependent Children (AFDC), the foundation of the federal welfare system that lasted until 1996.

merce is involved, all other powers are reserved for the states. Or so the Supreme Court was often ruling at the time. These concerns were eased when Perkins bumped into Justice Harlan F. Stone at a party and Stone whispered: "The taxing power of the Federal Government, my dear; the taxing power is sufficient for everything you want and need." His point was that as long as Congress imposed a national tax for it, social insurance was interstate commerce and constitutionally permissible. Perkins swore FDR to secrecy on this advance opinion from the Court, but it allowed them to proceed with more confidence.

The other contentious question was whether Social Security should be a Washington-run program or a federal-state arrangement. The arguments grew so loud and complicated that during Christmas week of 1934, Perkins locked the committee inside her house at 8:00 p.m. and announced that phone service would be discontinued for the evening and no one could leave until the federal-state question had been resolved. At two in the morning, the committee finally settled on a patchwork federal-state system for unemployment insurance (a sop to Brandeis) and a strictly federal system for old-age insurance. But within days another fight broke out over whether everyone should get the same old-age benefit or have it related to how much the recipient earned during his or her working life. The committee decided on the latter, which upheld the principle that this was "contributory" insurance, not welfare. Meanwhile, several Cabinet members were concerned that because of an aging population, the system would start running a deficit in 1980, forty-five years in the future. The prospect of having to dip into general revenues to keep the system afloat led Treasury Secretary Morgenthau to oppose the whole idea as fiscally reckless. FDR agreed.

By this time, Perkins was growing a little frustrated with a president who could not quite make up his mind whether he wanted Social Security or not. For a time it looked as if the bill would contain only unemployment insurance. He endorsed old-age insurance in his June 1934 message to Congress, then retreated from it in the fall by telling a conference that "I do not know whether this is the time for any federal legislation on old-age security." Barbara Nachtrieb Armstrong, the first female law professor in the United States, was on leave from Berkeley helping the CES. She was furious about FDR's comment and decided to "fix . . . that little wagon" by getting the liberal press to make a stink. FDR, reassessing the politics, told Perkins to make sure reporters knew that he favored the idea after all. She rationalized it as one of the "minor conflicts of logic and feeling which so often beset him but kept him flexible and moving in a practical direction."

By mid-1935, the president was determined to move forward. In May, he was enraged by the Supreme Court decision invalidating the NRA, which he derided as a "horse-and-buggy" interpretation of the interstate commerce clause of the Constitution. New Dealers in Congress then ended a period of drift and got busy with a summertime "second Hundred Days," which led to legislation on labor, banking, big tax increases on the wealthy (including a new inheritance tax), and, finally, Social Security. Fed up with attacks from conservatives, FDR was now more comfortable asserting his liberalism.

But the details remained vexing. A big problem was what to do about older workers who would only pay into the system for a short time before retirement. For them, there was no alternative to dipping into general revenues. So the president's initial message to Congress on old-age pensions stressed that Treasury funds would only be used to fund their retirement for a few years, which led to a long-standing conservative canard (resurrected in 2005) that FDR planned to phase out Social Security altogether once the Depression ended. In fact, he merely sought to phase out its transitional Treasury financing device.

To keep the system solvent, Morgenthau offered a painful compromise. He recommended excluding from old-age insurance all farm laborers, domestic servants, and anyone working in businesses with fewer than ten employees. This was in keeping with European social programs, though it was also convenient for the wealthy Morgenthaus, who ran both an estate and a farm, not to mention the Roosevelts. More important, excluding domestic servants and farm hands made the legislation more palatable among southerners who controlled the bill's fate. Senator Harry Byrd of Virginia made New Dealers promise that Social Security would do nothing to upset "The Negro Question."*

---

*As Ira Katznelson of Columbia University points out, Social Security, unemployment compensation, and the minimum wage were all established with occupational exemptions that discriminated against blacks.

"This was a blow," Perkins admitted, "[but] there was nothing for me to do but accept, temporarily at least." Her original goal had been reduced to a much more conservative Social Security plan, financed by a regressive tax, with no health insurance, an uneven form of unemployment insurance, and 9.4 million vulnerable elderly Americans excluded. At first, 40 percent of whites and 65 percent of blacks had no old-age coverage at all.

By now, FDR, like Morgenthau, was adamant that the program be funded over the long term by a special payroll tax on the earnings of workers, not from the income tax. He knew that it would be highly regressive, putting the same burden on poor workers as on rich ones, and that a payroll tax might retard recovery by removing billions in purchasing power from consumers, who would not receive benefits and recirculate the money for several years. (The first recipient of Social Security, Miss Ida May Fuller of rural Vermont, did not receive her first check, for $22.54, until January 1940.) But the president had good political reasons for structuring the system as he did. "We put those payroll contributions there to give the contributors a legal, moral and political right to collect their pensions and their unemployment benefits. With those taxes in there, no damn politician can ever scrap my social security program," FDR said privately, in his most revealing comments on the subject. His insight was that once recipients thought they had paid into the system for a few years, they would consider it *their* money—even though the Supreme Court ruled twenty-five years later that as a legal matter, it wasn't.

The whole thing was a bit of a semantic ruse. To appease the private sector, FDR sold the concept as "insurance," which resonated more of private business than "social benefits" or other vaguely socialist definitions. The original payroll tax of 1 percent of earnings (split evenly between employer and employee) was dubbed a "contribution," with the implication that, like a conventional contributory insurance plan, a worker got back his own money when he retired. In fact, the money went into a trust fund that would be used to pay retirees long before the "contributors" themselves retired—a direct subsidy from one generation to another. He even fuzzed up his message to Congress with a reference to the usefulness of supplemental private pensions. Seventy years later, this gave rise to a politically useful misimpression that FDR favored private accounts as part of Social Security. Nothing could be further from the truth. The bedrock of his plan was a word he used frequently: "guaranteed."

But if FDR was playing language games again, they continued to be effective ones. Even after a huge Democratic victory in the 1934 midterm elections, he knew that passage of Social Security would be a struggle. Organized labor was lukewarm, with some federation leaders still adhering to the dictum of their 19th century founder, Samuel Gompers, that benefits for the workingman should come from collective bargaining, not the government. Although most urban bosses didn't foresee it, FDR understood that Social Security would throw a wrench into their political machines, with Washington one day replacing the local ward heeler as a more reliable dispenser of grants to those in need. Most significant, much of the Democratic Party, and all of the GOP, was still fiscally conservative.

So, on the opening day of Congress in January 1935, when New Dealers Robert Wagner and David Lewis reintroduced their Social Security bills, Roosevelt, wary of overreaching, made a political decision to ignore them. Instead, he backed the versions introduced by the powerful southern chairmen of the Senate and House Finance committees, Senator Pat Harrison of Mississippi and Representative Robert L. Doughton of North Carolina (though the bill was still popularly called Wagner-Lewis). These were conservative men, leery of social programs. But both had seen their constituents devastated by the Depression.

Harrison came under pressure back home. The *Jackson Daily News* editorialized that "The average Mississippian can't imagine himself chipping in to pay pensions for able-bodied Negroes to sit around in idleness on front galleries while cotton and corn crops are crying for workers." Such commentary assured that farm hands and domestic servants would not be included.

As hearings got underway, elderly Senator Thomas P. Gore of Rhode Island raised the sarcastic objection that would underlay all of the criticism to come. "Isn't this Socialism?"

Secretary Perkins replied, "Oh, no." Then, addressing her as if she were a child, Gore asked, "Isn't this a teeny-weeny bit of Socialism?"

The final vote in the House, 371–33, was misleading. All Republicans but one on the House Ways and Means Committee voted to delete old-age insurance from the bill. If Chairman Doughton had not brought along the southern Democrats, Social Security would not have made it out of committee.

In the Senate, Huey Long filibustered the bill for fifteen hours, discoursing on everything from Frederick the Great to fried oysters and entertaining spectators by answering questions on the Senate floor shouted down from the press gallery. Bennett Clark of Pennsylvania almost scuttled the whole deal when a cantankerous constituent who peddled retirement plans to corporations convinced him to exempt any company with a private pension plan. After the Clark amendment was narrowly defeated, a carefully tailored bill proceeded to final passage. It was a close call. Had the original Social Security been a touch more liberal, Republicans and conservative Democrats would have halted it. Were any more benefits withdrawn, New Deal liberals would have pulled the plug.

After FDR signed the bill in August 1935, Long—who still wanted his share-the-wealth plan—began a second filibuster, this one of the appropriation that was necessary to fund the new Social Security Administration. It looked as if Congress would adjourn for the year without setting up the new agency. FDR was desperate to avoid calling members back into special session, so he came up with the idea of simply borrowing the NRA officials laid off when that agency was liquidated after the Supreme Court declared it unconstitutional. That meant the first Social Security employees in 1935 were the same bureaucrats who had been supervising codes for cork makers and strip clubs.

Enrolling 26 million people into the new system was the largest logistical undertaking in American history, bigger by far than the draft for World War I. When it was clear that each person would need a Social Security identification number, administrators decided that the fourth and fifth numbers on each card would indicate the year of birth. This was quickly shot down because thousands of people during the Depression had misstated their age to keep their jobs and many women simply did not like disclosing their age. To run the whole thing, Roosevelt named John G. Winant, a former Republican governor of New Hampshire, as the first chairman of the Social Security Board. But if

FDR thought this would convert most Republicans into supporters, he was mistaken. Herbert Hoover never even took a Social Security number.

When FDR ran for reelection in 1936, his Republican opponent, Alf Landon, called Social Security "a cruel hoax" and a "fraud on the working man." The Republican National Committee convinced employers across the country to put fliers into pay envelopes warning their workers that, starting January 1, 1937, a "New Deal law" would take 1 percent of their paycheck. "You're sentenced to a weekly pay reduction for all of your working life," read one inflammatory flier. "You'll have to serve the sentence unless you help reverse it Nov. 3, Election Day."

Roosevelt carried every state except Maine and Vermont, and Landon later confessed that attacking Social Security was the worst mistake of his campaign. The fearmongering failed. Americans understood that this new system FDR brought them would do nothing to relieve the despair of today. But they had faith now, and some hope for better days. They voted for the future.

When he signed the bill, Roosevelt described Social Security as "the cornerstone" of his administration—something to build upon that was "by no means complete." But he told associates in later years that even standing alone, it represented his greatest domestic achievement. Something fundamental had taken place. For the first time, a secure retirement was no longer reserved for people like FDR's aristocratic neighbors in Hyde Park. The promise of the Declaration of Independence was coming into fuller view, as the men and women who toiled to make America could now pursue happiness in their later years—not if they invested wisely or got lucky in the stock market or retired when the country was flush, but as a birthright. In that sense, the insurance concept was not a ruse but a deeply meaningful public commitment. The American government was telling the American people that their fates were not at risk but backed by the full faith and credit of the United States. This was the "ownership society" in its truest, fullest meaning, and one not likely to be forsaken without a fight.

Epilogue: "Dr. New Deal"

I N THE YEARS SINCE 1933, the idea of "the first Hundred Days" has rooted itself in American politics. Every new president hopes to use his honeymoon with Congress to enact big plans immediately after being inaugurated. For John F. Kennedy, this part of the Roosevelt legacy was a burden and he warned in his Inaugural that the work of his presidency would not be finished in the first hundred days or the first thousand days or "perhaps in our lifetime on this planet." Lyndon B. Johnson liked to boast that the fifteen bills he pushed through between January and April of 1965 achieved more than anything done in 1933. Jimmy Carter and Bill Clinton were also conscious of the hundred days' construct, though neither had much success early on. Ronald Reagan may have come closest to FDR's debut, with landmark victories on the budget and taxes.

For Franklin Roosevelt and the others, early success did nothing to guarantee later popularity. As soon as the economy began to recover a bit, the consensus of the Hundred Days—that FDR was a savior—broke down. All the way through World War II, fierce critics, some within his own party, pounded him. Many wealthy Americans could not even bear to utter Roosevelt's name and began calling him "that man in the White House." Others despised what they saw as his belief that he was indispensable, especially in running for an unprecedented third term. But the character and temperament that brought him to office and allowed him to restore hope in the dark domestic days would continue to inspire most of the country. Just as lifting up "polios" at

Warm Springs was a dress rehearsal for lifting the spirits of the whole nation in 1933, so the struggle of his early days in office prepared him for wartime.

This time, his mother would not be there for him. On September 7, 1941, Sara Roosevelt died at Hyde Park at eighty-six. Within hours of her death, a huge oak tree on the property fell without being hit by lightning, an omen that hardly went unnoticed by her superstitious son. The only time his aides ever saw him weep was when he opened a box of her mementos, including letters he had written her as a boy. Three months later came Pearl Harbor. The black armband he wore when delivering his "day that will live in infamy" speech before Congress on December 8 was not, as commonly assumed, to honor the dead in the Pacific, but a sign of mourning he had worn all fall for his mother.

Anna Roosevelt once said that her father as president "stood for self assurance . . . he spoke from security." And she knew why. While she conceded that her grandmother had controlled the family with money and sometimes played "the martinet," she also thought she changed the country by making FDR who he was. "She helped *save* it," Anna said. "I don't think anyone's given credit to Granny—the credit that she really is due."

In her "My Day" newspaper column the day after Sara died, Eleanor wrote: "There was a streak of jealousy and possessiveness in her where her own were concerned. The word *grande dame* was truly applicable to her." She had taken good care of Sara in her later years and gotten along with her reasonably well, but she confided to Joseph Lash: "I looked at my mother in law's face after she was dead and I understood so many things I had never seen before. It is dreadful to have lived so close to someone for 36 years and to feel no deep sense of affection or sense of loss. It's hard on Franklin and the material details [funeral logistics] are appalling and there, of course, I can be of some use."

She was already of more than "some use" to her husband and country, filling the in-basket by Franklin's bed with ideas and articles, inviting visitors who could broaden his perspective, and, most important, traveling widely to places a handicapped president could not easily go, then reporting back to him in vivid and insightful detail. This was all hugely valuable to the president, who depended for success on absorbing as much quality information as he could find. The political spouse who had been so reluctant about moving to the White House that she had threatened to run off with her bodyguard became the best known and most innovative first lady since Dolley Madison. She brought all of her energy and intelligence to the task of moving the country forward, or at least pointing the way. Franklin often said that they made a good team because, while he concentrated on what *could* be done, Eleanor looked further ahead to what *should* be done. So great was Eleanor's influence and popularity that after FDR's death, Harry Truman appointed her as representative to the United Nations, a post from which she helped launch the global campaign for human rights that keeps her legacy alive. By the time she died in 1962, she had become a model for the feminist moment just being born.

Through the years, Eleanor remained friends with Lorena Hickok, who even moved into the White House for a time. After more than two hundred letters from Eleanor to Lorena in 1933 alone, the passion between the two women cooled in the mid-1930s for no discernible reason, though as late as the early 1940s the first lady was still writing her friend every week or so. Despite this, Lorena was often treated as a nonperson by Roosevelt retainers who found her presence awkward. In their memoirs and oral histories, the Roosevelt children and Eleanor's other close friends, Nancy Cook and Marion Dickerman, acted as if Hickok didn't exist.

After Lucy Rutherfurd was widowed, she and FDR began to see each other again, thanks in part to the efforts of Anna Roosevelt, who wanted to be relieved of her duties as her father's off-hours hostess. Lucy was with him in Warm Springs in 1945 when he died, though she departed before the press could find out. Missy LeHand's health declined over the years and a debilitating stroke in 1941 left her barely able to speak. Roosevelt handled her hospitalization and left instructions that up to half the annual income from his estate be used to pay her medical bills, though she waited in vain for the president to visit her. At her death in 1944, FDR instructed the Navy to name a cargo vessel for her. Thirty years later, an ugly public spat erupted when Elliott Roosevelt wrote in a book that Missy and his father had been lovers and James Roosevelt flatly denied it.

Louis Howe lost authority after his hero reached the White House. He supervised the CCC and made sure that in mid-1933 J. Edgar

Hoover would be allowed to stay on in the Justice Department, where Hoover's "War Against Crime" would soon be fought from a newly empowered Federal Bureau of Investigation. But Howe was ailing and Roosevelt had less time to talk with him. Just as he outgrew Al Smith, FDR moved past Howe. "The Medieval Gnome" caused a flap in 1933 when he told journalism students at Columbia that "You can't adopt politics as a profession and remain honest." When asked how he himself would stay honest, he replied, "I'm not in politics. I'm just the handyman for Franklin Roosevelt."

Howe's ailments seemed to catch up with him in 1934, and his daughter, seeing him in an oxygen tent, wired her husband that he wouldn't last twenty-four hours. He lingered until 1936, once sending instructions, cheerfully accepted by FDR, that the president should go to hell. Roosevelt was attentive to his old friend, but he also made sure that Howe didn't get the direct telephone line to the White House that he had requested. The ostensible reason was to let Louis rest, but it also prevented him from meddling. On his deathbed, Howe told Vice President Garner: "Hold Franklin down!"

"After Louis' death, Franklin never had a political adviser who would argue with and give him unquestioned advice," Eleanor recalled. She saw Harry Hopkins as more of an errand boy and manipulator, who would try to rustle up allies to press a point on Roosevelt: "This was not as valuable a service as forcing Franklin, in the way Louis did, to hear unpleasant arguments." Roosevelt eventually drew as close to Hopkins as he had been to Howe, but it was more of a one-way relationship, and much of what FDR instructed Hopkins about politics, he had learned from Howe.

Eleanor was not alone in believing that if Howe had lived, FDR might have avoided the disastrous "court-packing" plan he launched in early 1937. The scheme was hatched after the Supreme Court invalidated the NRA and other New Deal programs, infuriating the president, who thought his overwhelming mandate in the 1936 election should not be stymied by "nine old men." The affair brought out the worst in FDR—his impulsiveness and temptation to deceive. First, he lied about the plan's intentions, stating publicly that he sought to expand the number of justices from nine to fifteen because the workload was too heavy for the Court, an assertion roundly denied. Then he tried to manipulate the vote in Congress, which aroused even his allies and led to an embarrassing defeat. His enemies and many in the middle believed he was acting like a dictator, and by this time the word was hardly meant as a compliment. It was not quite accurate; FDR never sought to circumvent Congress. But clearly the confidence of the early days had shaded over, at least temporarily, into arrogance. The following year, 1938, FDR attempted to purge eight conservative Democrats by withholding support for them in the midterm elections. This, too, was a political blunder. All but one was easily reelected. Even when the Supreme Court reversed course and began approving New Deal programs—"We lost the battle but won the war," FDR said—the period gave energy to conservatives and marked the low point of his presidency.

The first witness to testify against the court-packing scheme on Capitol Hill was Ray Moley, the original Brain Truster, once FDR's closest aide. Moley had stayed involved in speechwriting for Roosevelt as late as his 1936 acceptance speech at the Philadelphia convention (where the term "rendezvous with destiny" was first used), but he was upset by references in the speech to "economic royalists" "privileged princes," and "new despotism in the robes of legal sanction"—the very lines that thrilled liberals.

In truth, Moley's career in government effectively ended at the World Economic Conference in June 1933, when Cordell Hull, in London, discovered that his deputy secretary of state, Moley, had trashed him to FDR behind his back. Hull now had the ammunition he needed, and by the time Moley returned to the United States from Great Britain FDR and Howe had a new assignment for their erstwhile friend—investigating crime in Hawaii. Moley declined the distant posting, resigned as deputy secretary of state, and moved sharply to the right after launching a political magazine, *Today*, that soon merged with *Newsweek*. In 1939, he wrote what was then considered an explosive insider account of working with Roosevelt and his circle, *After Seven Years*. FDR called it a "kiss-ass-and-tell" book, suggesting that Moley could be a toady when it suited him. When FDR sought a third term, Moley compared him to Napoleon. He has served "two terms—the first was for the people, the second was for power," Moley said at an anti-FDR rally.

Rexford Tugwell became a lightning rod for conservative critics of the New Deal, a walking parody of the tweedy elitist liberal. He was dispatched conveniently to Europe during the 1934 midterm elections, muzzled entirely in 1936, and departed soon after to teach. His boss, Henry Wallace, was elected vice president under FDR in 1940, but his peace activism and association with mystics led him to be dumped from the 1944 ticket in favor of Missouri senator Harry Truman. Treasury Secretary Will Woodin was diagnosed with terminal throat cancer and gave way in late 1933 to Henry Morgenthau, who served as FDR's Treasury secretary thereafter. Only Frances Perkins and Harold Ickes from the original Cabinet stayed with Roosevelt until his death. Ickes wrote with brutal honesty about FDR and his circle in his secret diaries, published in 1953, but it was Perkins who offered the most acute personal insights into Roosevelt's character.

Lewis Douglas quit the Budget Bureau in 1934 in protest against FDR's abandonment of conservative economics. When Arthur Krock wrote about it extensively in *The New York Times*, FDR tried to get Krock fired from the paper. Joe Kennedy, who had provided campaign contributions and advice during the 1932 campaign, had felt shunted aside when Roosevelt had no job for him at the beginning of the administration. It turned out that Louis Howe sabotaged him. After the market surged at the end of the Hundred Days, Kennedy sold short on the expectation of a slide and made more money. When the SEC was created in 1934, FDR named Kennedy as its first chairman, figuring correctly that a Wall Street buccaneer would know all the tricks of the trade and how to crack down on them. Kennedy served with distinction and returned to government as FDR's ambassador to Great Britain.* On the eve of war, Kennedy was recalled from his post when he suggested publicly that a Nazi victory was inevitable.

Al Smith never received any appointment. In 1934, he helped form the Liberty League, the first of the major anti-Roosevelt organizations dedicated to fighting the New Deal. The Democrats won a big victory

---

* Even then, Roosevelt felt the need to humiliate him, just as he had over the Argentine warships during World War I. Before leaving for England, Kennedy appeared in the Oval Office, where FDR asked him to take down his pants. The president told Kennedy he was too bow-legged to wear the formal clothes required for the presentation of his diplomatic credentials to the king, then laughed uproariously.

in the midterm elections that year (with the help of an FDR line in a Fireside Chat: "Are you better off than you were last year?"),* but Smith never came back to the party. Roosevelt arranged for the RFC to rent space in the Empire State Building, easing Smith's financial problems and some of his resentment. In 1944, just days before going into the hospital to die, Smith was asked: "Governor, what do you think of Roosevelt?" Smith stopped, puffed on his cigar, and said: "He was the kindest man who ever lived, but don't get in his way."

Herbert Hoover would have thought that view too charitable. After the March 4, 1933, Inauguration, he and Roosevelt never saw each other again. (Hoover made a point of not visiting Washington unless FDR was out of town.) In 1936, Roosevelt privately put the odds at 12 to 1 that the Republicans would nominate Hoover once more. Not surprisingly, the GOP declined to do so, though the former president became a serious isolationist candidate for the GOP nomination in 1940. In 1943, FDR was still determined to strike back at his old adversary. He asked the War Department to look into Hoover's conduct during World War I and found that Hoover had opposed sending American soldiers to France in 1917. Senator Theodore Green of Rhode Island, a Roosevelt partisan, then argued publicly that if Americans had heeded Hoover a quarter century earlier, the Allies would have lost World War I.

Hoover spent the rest of his life refighting the 1932 election in several books. After FDR's death, Truman appointed him to a commission dedicated to Hoover's old specialty, helping war refugees. He was a success in that post, and brought his old energy to building the Hoover Institution and other projects until his death in 1964.

Walter Lippmann and H. L. Mencken both opposed FDR's reelection in 1936 and William Randolph Hearst became a fierce opponent of what he called the "Raw Deal" run by "Stalin Delano Roosevelt." By 1934, the publisher was linking the president publicly "to the Mussolinis, the Hitlers, the Lenins and all of those who seek to establish a dictatorial form of government." For Hearst and others, "dictator" had gone from a positive connotation to a piercing epithet.

---

* In 1980, Ronald Reagan used a variation on this line ("Are you better off than you were four years ago?") to take the presidency from Jimmy Carter.

Vice President Garner, while admiring some of what Roosevelt accomplished, also felt that FDR overreached, especially in extending diplomatic recognition to the Soviet Union in late 1933. He took pleasure from being right on deposit insurance. At a speech in 1936, when FDR ostentatiously included the FDIC on a list of his top New Deal accomplishments, Garner looked across the stage at his reporter friend, Bascom Timmons, and winked. He stayed on the ticket that year, but was appalled by the court-packing scheme and opposed a third term for FDR in 1940. On the morning of November 22, 1963, President John F. Kennedy called him in Uvalde, Texas, to wish him a happy ninety-fifth birthday. Garner was among the last people to speak to JFK before the president was assassinated.

As Garner moved right, FDR moved left, at least rhetorically. When Harold Ickes delivered a radio speech charging that the United States was dominated by a "ruling class" of one hundred families and Roosevelt said nothing to refute him, critics began to refer to the president as a "traitor to his class." This gibe boomeranged on Republicans and proved helpful to FDR with voters, many of whom were still intrigued by Huey Long. FDR was never in danger of losing to the Kingfish, who had publicly broken with the president and called him a liar as early as August 1933. But the Democratic National Committee commissioned a poll showing Long receiving 3–4 million votes running as a third-party candidate in the 1936 presidential election, which Jim Farley feared would be enough to tip the contest to the GOP. In September 1935, Long was shot and killed by an insane doctor in a corridor of the Louisiana state capital building.

Franklin Roosevelt served three full terms as the first major leader in world history who could not walk on his own. His illness was not a secret during his presidency; the fact that he suffered from polio was mentioned occasionally in print and on radio around the world. (In Italy, he was called "Il Paralitico.") The money raised publicly by "The March of Dimes,"* founded by Basil O'Connor, eventually funded a polio vac-

---

* It was no coincidence that when FDR was posthumously commemorated on a coin, it was the dime.

cine. But Roosevelt's "splendid deception," as Hugh Gallagher called it, was to minimize the extent of his handicap, so that most Americans thought he was a little lame but hardly disabled. When the British royal couple visited Hyde Park in 1939, the queen told Eleanor she had not the slightest idea that Franklin could not walk. With the press actively cooperating in this deception (unimaginable today), no close-up pictures of him handicapped were ever printed.

Only a single moving image survives of Franklin Roosevelt trying to walk. It is a home movie shot by a Dutchess County doctor, Harold Rosenthal, who caught him on film for only a few seconds being helped slowly from a building at Vassar College to his car in the fall of 1933. The early frames show an unsmiling president in discomfort as he holds bodyguard Gus Gennerich's arm and moves forward. When Secret Service agents spot Rosenthal, they successfully block his view, but not before FDR, aware of Rosenthal's movie camera, starts grinning. Eleanor also breaks into a wide smile. The film is interrupted for a moment and when it resumes, FDR has almost been secured in the backseat of a car. Then the party departs waving.

Roosevelt knew polio had changed him. Asked about his "serenity" in a crisis, he replied, "If you spent two years in bed trying to wiggle your big toe, after that anything else would seem easy!" The fortitude he showed in venturing back into a line of work where no other paraplegic had ever gone before astonished his contemporaries. After FDR's death, Winston Churchill told the House of Commons that "not one man in ten millions, stricken and crippled as he was, would have attempted to plunge into a life of physical and mental exertion and of hard, ceaseless political controversy."

John Gunther compared FDR's ordeal to that of politicians in other countries who went to jail early in their careers. He drew an analogy to Jawaharlal Nehru, India's first prime minister after independence, who spent fourteen years in prison before coming to power. Later, Nelson Mandela, South Africa's first president under majority rule, was in jail for twenty-eight years. All three men emerged from their suffering with greater vision and fortitude. Each of these figures also used his experience to establish a master political narrative, more powerful for being understated, even subconscious. FDR sold the idea that just as he had conquered the disease, so he could conquer the Depression. It deserves recognition as one of history's great half-truths. In the end, he conquered neither in fact, both in spirit.

In 1934, George Draper, Roosevelt's doctor during the worst of his polio and his old friend from Harvard, wrote the President that his bias for action against the Depression was harmful. Like so many in the president's orbit, he thought the New Deal needed a rest:

> There is a giant lying supine across the continent. He is paralyzed in arms and legs—a victim of infantile paralysis. He is in the hands of a most earnest and conscientious doctor. But the doctor is over-treating him. Would not the giant react more quickly and completely if the current prescription of massage and specialized exercise were interrupted for a period. Nature works in mysterious ways to heal wounds. The ideas of man often interfere with natural processes.

FDR's response captures everything he believed about trying to revive the economy and rescue the 16 million Americans who were suffering severe hardship. It was wrapped in another cheery medical metaphor that reflected his view that the New Deal's "gentle" treatment was of a piece with the various types of hydrotherapy he experimented with at Warm Springs, and the only thing preventing the United States from dying as a democratic society.

> I like your supine giant and I should like to stop treatment were it not for the fact that sixteen million little cells out of the one hundred and twenty million cells in his body would lose their circulation, starve and die, if we were to stop the very gentle massage which keeps some blood running through these sixteen million little cells. That is the only treatment being given at the present time. Also, in cases like this medical history proves that if treatment is suddenly stopped the giant is very apt to leap from his bed and either commit suicide or die of an epileptic fit.

To give the patient a chance, Roosevelt conceived of government programs the way he had once viewed untested polio treatments. After the CCC, PWA, and NRA of the Hundred Days, came the REA (Rural Electrification Administration, which tripled the number of farms with electricity), the CWA (Civil Works Administration), the WPA (Works Progress Administration), and dozens of other "alphabet soup" agencies. The changes they wrought—39,000 new schools (70 percent of all new schools built during the 1930s), 2,500 new hospitals, 325 airports, and tens of thousands of smaller projects—helped build the nation's infrastructure and transform the American landscape.

Few Americans today understand how many of the roads and public projects they take for granted began with FDR, from the Triborough Bridge in New York to the Outer Drive in Chicago to the University of Texas Library and college football stadiums across the South. Almost every city in the nation contains several roads and public buildings that were constructed under one of his federal programs. And most later public works are at least spiritually descended from the New Deal. Even as the Tennessee Valley Authority itself polluted the land and became embroiled in scandal, the idea behind the TVA led to local and regional planning in rural and, later, urban areas, and to the economic development projects that dot the country today.

Unlike some of his successors, FDR was not adamantly attached to any program. The "spirit of bold experimentation" he adopted in 1932 led him quickly to shuffle most in and out of existence. The great exception was the "second New Deal" of 1935, which produced the Social Security Act and the National Labor Relations Act. Social Security was amended slightly in 1939 to begin the dispensing of checks sooner and to make it more of a pay-as-you-go system. The years since have seen many payroll tax increases, cost-of-living hikes, and, more recently, structural adjustments. But the system has remained largely intact since 1935. It has rightly been credited with virtually wiping out poverty among the elderly, making Social Security the most successful single social program in American history.

Many of FDR's other initiatives yielded positive long-term results. The principles of transparency established in the Securities Act have been essential to stable markets and the growth of the global economy. For all of their shortcomings, the crop supports launched in the AAA eventually helped stabilize prices, kept food affordable, and established conditions that have made the American farm economy the most productive in the world. The backing for home mortgages brought tremendous economic gains after World War II. In a broader sense, the New Deal helped Americans begin to see their responsibilities to each other more clearly. Infant mortality, for instance, actually declined during the 1930s, despite the grim economy. The New Deal yielded a legacy of commonality and community that filtered down to the local level and lasted for decades.

Even in public, Roosevelt had a habit of looking back on the Hundred Days in a wry medical context. "Some of these people really forgot how sick they were," he said in 1936 of the millionaires who opposed him. "But I know how sick they were. I have their fever charts. I know how the knees of all our rugged individualists were trembling four years ago and how their hearts fluttered." Many of his strongest critics were doctors. By 1935, the medical establishment thought Roosevelt was some kind of Bolshevik. Syndicated columnists and even the Democratic governor of Georgia began accusing the family of profiting off the Warm Spring Foundation and running the resort as a racket, which was untrue. But the attacks stung. They were symbolic of what was happening to the New Deal, only more personal.

FDR was bitterly amused that his Dutchess County neighbors, who never voted for him for governor or president, thought he had betrayed them.* That was ridiculous, he felt; he had *saved* capitalism. Without him, the plutocrats who, in the famous *New Yorker* cartoon by Peter Arno, went "down to the Trans-lux to hiss Roosevelt" would have been broke or swinging from a lamppost after the revolution. But in convincing himself of that, Roosevelt may have missed the irony: By extending security—democratizing it—he was inevitably eroding the comfortable, insular world of Warren Delano and James Roosevelt, and of Sara, the most important woman in his life.

In the heat of the 1936 campaign, Roosevelt addressed a Madison

---

* The journalist Dorothy Thompson was crossing the Atlantic in the early 1930s and struck up a conversation with Harry Sinclair, one of the plutocrats implicated in the Teapot Dome scandal of the Harding administration. Sinclair told her that big business still owned all of the presidents but made a "slight error" with FDR, whom he knew would attack the rich rhetorically, "but we did not expect him to take action."

Square Garden rally and famously said: "They are unanimous in their hatred for me—and I welcome their hatred." After winning nearly 61 percent of the vote that November, and a majority of the black vote for the first time in the history of the Democratic Party, his liberalism reached its high-water mark.* In his second Inaugural the following January, Roosevelt said: "Here is the challenge to our democracy . . . I see one-third a nation ill-housed, ill-clad, ill-nourished."

But the days of bold New Deal ventures were largely over. After signing the Social Security Act in August 1935, FDR called for a "breathing spell" in new legislation—and got it. Even though Social Security and other New Deal programs were now routinely upheld by the Supreme Court, which before long was dominated by FDR appointees, fewer new ideas were turned into legislation. FDR's second term was his least successful, though liberalism was embedding itself in American life at the very moment that actual reform diminished.

Because Roosevelt raised such expectations, it's easy to see where he fell short. Although Eleanor prodded him, he never pushed hard for a federal antilynching statute or took on the southern Democrats over Jim Crow segregation. Health insurance remained a dream. Although labor and consumers won a seat at the table once reserved mostly for corporate interests, they were often stymied in later Congresses. Moreover, for all the inspirational rhetoric and industrial planning, the New Deal did not end the Depression. The key benchmark was the unemployment figure, which dropped from 25 percent in 1933 to 21.7 the following year, and slowly down to 14 percent in 1937, a welcome but hardly spectacular result. The fall of 1937 brought a major setback, with unemployment surging to 19 percent and the Dow losing 50 percent of its value. By 1940, the economy was headed up (before the boost in arms production), but unemployment did not move into single digits until factories begin churning out war materiel. A modern-day conservative critic of FDR, Jim Powell, makes a good case that the

---

* After a half century run in elective politics, the New Deal coalition eventually cracked. Blacks, women, and urban reformers stayed Democratic, but by the beginning of the 21st century, the electoral map had flipped. FDR's rural voters in the South and West were now going heavily to the GOP, while the once Republican Northeast was more solidly Democratic.

Roosevelt Administration never figured out how to stimulate business with a strategy of incentives for growth.

In the short term, some of Roosevelt's programs may have even delayed recovery. Although it was favored by many industries seeking to stifle competition, the NRA laid a heavy burden of regulation on business that discouraged investment. The introduction of a payroll tax to pay for Social Security arguably helped send the economy back down, with the money collected sitting idle in a reserve fund until the pay-as-you-go system was inaugurated in 1939. Had war not broken out in Europe late in 1939, Roosevelt would have left office in early 1941 having reduced unemployment from a quarter to a fifth of the workforce—and would likely have been viewed by historians as a far less significant president.

But to argue that the shortcomings of the New Deal undermine FDR's achievements reflects a narrow view. It's like saying that because the "polios" who went to Warm Springs were never fully cured, they should not have made the trip in the first place. There is no record of any patient with such regrets. Even marginal improvements in their physical conditions helped boost their confidence, and their spirits were replenished. The result of FDR's efforts was a new social contract that has informally bound his successors to confront major domestic and international problems, rather than leave them entirely to the marketplace or to other nations. For all of their antigovernment rhetoric, even the most conservative of his successors, Ronald Reagan and George W. Bush, presided over an expansion of government and could never fully repeal the obligations FDR began redefining in 1933.

The greatest of those obligations remains to the less fortunate, an idea that cleaves American politics to this day. "The test of our progress is not whether we add to the abundance of those who have much," FDR said in his second Inaugural Address, perhaps his clearest statement of principle in domestic affairs. "It is whether we provide enough for those who have too little."

If that living "New Deal" was to be FDR's enduring legacy, his greatest accomplishment was more immediate. During the 1930s, he succeeded in keeping a fractious country from giving up on its ideals and offered a world darkened by fascism and communism an alternative vision of the future. Sinclair Lewis may have been right in his 1935 novel

It Can't Happen Here that it could—that a demagogue using radio could seize power in the United States, just as Hitler and Mussolini did in Europe. But it didn't happen, and the best explanation is no more complicated than the presence of Franklin Delano Roosevelt in the presidency. Especially at the beginning, when hope was a dying ember, he succeeded brilliantly in restoring faith in democratic institutions and establishing a legacy of innovation. Eventually, the same flexibility that allowed Roosevelt to confront that crisis led him to scrap most of his domestic program in order to face another historic challenge.

FDR began laying the groundwork for intervention as early as 1937, when, in a Chicago speech, he employed a medical metaphor yet again by urging that the Allies "quarantine the aggressors" in Europe and Asia. After the fall of France to the Nazis in 1940, Roosevelt broke George Washington's two-term tradition and decided to run for an unprecedented third. With the crucial help of the GOP candidate, Wendell Willkie, an internationalist who gave FDR cover, he executed a high-wire act that tested all of his political skills—instituting a draft and rearming Great Britain against the Nazis without alienating the largely isolationist American public.

After the 1940 election, the Lend-Lease program was the fruit of the same semantic games ("commend" versus "recommend" at the 1932 convention) he had used earlier in his career. By making it seem as if the United States were simply "lending" weapons and supplies to Britain (there was never much chance they would be returned or paid for), FDR beat back "America First" opposition and rescued England and Europe, and he did so with the explicit approval of Congress. Then, prior to Pearl Harbor, he retained enough political capital to reauthorize narrowly the unpopular draft (which he, classically, called "mustering"), raise taxes, and prepare his reluctant nation for war. Rarely have the black arts of political intrigue been put to such good use.

For all of his skill in handling the Allies and choosing the right men to win the war—particularly General George C. Marshall, whom he knew from CCC days—Roosevelt has been criticized in recent years for not moving more aggressively to rescue the Jews of Europe. FDR was not entirely negligent. In the face of an isolationist Congress and polls showing that more than 80 percent of the American public were opposed to easing immigration quotas, he raised the specter of the Nazi threat early, and sponsored international conferences on refugees. But Roosevelt did not bring the activist spirit of the Hundred Days to rescuing the Jews. It was never a priority. His 1944 War Refugees Board came years too late. FDR was not an anti-Semite; he employed more Jews than any other president. But he also promoted his friend the anti-Semite Breckenridge Long to a key position in the State Department.* And he made the mistake of listening to military advisers who said that bombing the rail and communications lines to the Nazi concentration camps in Hungary was impractical. (Although bombing the camps themselves would have killed more prisoners, hitting the rail heads—while unlikely to save many Jews—was worth a try.) At the same time, his support for the military's internment of Japanese-Americans was one of the worst civil liberties decisions in U.S. history.

Nonetheless, FDR was indispensable in the Allied victory, and his gift for communicating helped to explain the stakes, just as it had in 1933. His press conference of December 28, 1943, was quintessential Roosevelt, down to the medical "allegory" he cooked up with Steve Early. That day, he announced to reporters that they should no longer use the term "New Deal." Times had changed, he said, and the slogan should be retired:

> How did the New Deal come into existence? It was because in 1932 there was an awfully sick patient called the United States of America. He was suffering from a grave internal disorder. . . . And they sent for a doctor.

FDR went on to explain how "the illness of ten years ago was remedied." Then he noted that on December 7, 1941, the patient got into another scrape, this one with a foreign power. "Old Doc New Deal" didn't know how to treat these new injuries, he said, and had to be replaced by his partner, "Dr. Win the War." So now "the patient is back on his feet and has given up his crutches. He has begun to strike back—

---

* The refugee ship St. Louis was turned away in 1939 under great congressional pressure. FDR thought that the refugees would be resettled in other countries, but most ended up dying in the holocaust.

on the offensive." But if FDR seemed to abandon many of the programs of the New Deal—programs that constituency groups would battle fiercely to keep, whatever the merits—the idea behind it took root in his mind and grew. The postwar world, he believed, must be based on the idea of security—the same security he first noticed was so important to voters back in 1910. In his 1944 State of the Union address, he outlined an "Economic Bill of Rights" to match the founders' Bill of Rights. Its aim was "not only physical security but economic security, social security, moral security."

The next year, the most destructive war in human history was won, Roosevelt's second monumental triumph. The medicine of "Old Doc Roosevelt" had worked again. In April 1945, the ailing president traveled to Warm Springs. His plan was to rest before giving an important speech. As he sat for his portrait, Lucy Rutherfurd and Daisy Suckley by his side, Roosevelt complained of a headache and died shortly afterwards from a cerebral hemorrhage. The unused draft of the speech—so different in tone from the call to arms he pulled back from delivering to the American Legion in 1933—conveyed his vision of the world we inhabit still: "If civilization is to survive, we must cultivate the science of human relationships—the ability of all peoples, of all kinds, to live together and work together in the same world, at peace."

Franklin D. Roosevelt was laid to rest in a courtyard of the house at Hyde Park. In a funeral service in the East Room of the White House, Bishop Angus Dun led the mourners in hymns and prayer, then, respecting the wishes of the first lady, he recited the line that had rung through the chilly capital twelve years before: "The only thing we have to fear is fear itself."

Beyond our human interest in the lives of other human beings, why study the history of individuals, even powerful ones? Several generations of historians have argued that technology, geography, economics, and culture are better instruments for probing the past. There is merit in this argument. History is a river and people—even presidents—are twigs. The bends in the river are shaped by mighty forces working slowly over many lifetimes. Some of those forces are simple accidents.

But even if one rejects a "great man theory of history," the contributions of a few world leaders are exceptions. They defy the power of impersonal forces. The last hundred years have brought us negative examples—Stalin, Hitler, and Mao—and several positive ones that compel our attention to the role of particular human qualities in the unfolding of momentous political events. Among them must be Franklin Roosevelt.

Playing historical "What If?" is a hazardous game; the variables are too numerous and fluid for solid assessments. Hindsight clouds the plausibility of other historical figures who might have been summoned to greatness had the timing been right. But cosmic odds makers could make some good bets. Roosevelt was not nearly the smartest or even the firmest American president, and his judgment, as we have seen, was far from unerring. Others were sturdier pillars of integrity. But it's hard to imagine anyone negotiating the complexities of rearming the Allies during World War II, wearing down the Axis powers, and envisioning a postwar world more skillfully than he did.

The case for FDR as the only man for the crisis of 1933 is even more compelling. Neither Herbert Hoover nor John Nance Garner possessed the inspirational abilities necessary to carry the nation through the Depression. Newton Baker and Albert Ritchie, FDR's main rivals for the 1932 Democratic nomination, are blanker slates. But it's unlikely anyone else would have emerged with the perfect mixture of charm, guile, and instinct—that first-rate temperament—to energize the country without sending it off the rails. Another president might well have heeded the calls for dictatorship or proven so conservative as to divide the Democratic Party in two and leave the nation prey to demagogues like Huey Long. Even if one accepts the argument that the United States was always infertile soil for communism or fascism, the very idea of a peaceful, stable democracy did hang in the balance that winter.

By itself, no single quality possessed by FDR in the Hundred Days was exceptional. It was a magical alloy of attributes: his ebullience after the dour Hoover, his theatricality upon entering the big stage, and his pragmatism in a time of destructive dogma. These combined into a new vision of security for the American republic—the ideal of a more benevolent state no longer "trapped," as he later put it, "in the ice of its own indifference."

Our template for crisis leadership in the media age comes from Roosevelt. The idea of strong presidential authority extended from Washington through Jackson, Theodore Roosevelt, and Wilson. They established that effective presidents dominate the public debate, with the help of what TR called the "bully pulpit." But FDR was the first to understand how that notion could be harnessed to technology and magnified in ways that transformed the office. The refinement of presidential stagecraft comes from him, with its mixed legacy of image-making and media manipulation.

For all of his transformative influence, FDR was, at bottom, a vessel president—a carrier of all the qualities, admirable and less so, that presidents need to chart a course in choppy waters. The vessel held not just personality traits but the essential elements of the American character: our faith in ourselves, our spirit of experimentation, and our hope for the future. When each of these seemed nearly extinguished in 1933, Franklin D. Roosevelt restored them in a matter of months, with an elixir of leadership we are only beginning to understand. This was the work not of social forces, but of a man.

‑ APPENDIX ‑

Inaugural Address, March 4, 1933

This is a day of national consecration. I am certain that my fellow Americans expect that on my induction into the Presidency I will address them with a candor and a decision which the present situation of our Nation impels. This is preeminently the time to speak the truth, the whole truth, frankly and boldly. Nor need we shrink from honestly facing conditions in our country today. This great Nation will endure as it has endured, will revive and will prosper. So, first of all, let me assert my firm belief that the only thing we have to fear is fear itself— nameless, unreasoning, unjustified terror which paralyzes needed efforts to convert retreat into advance. In every dark hour of our national life a leadership of frankness and vigor has met with that understanding and support of the people themselves which is essential to victory. I am convinced that you will again give that support to leadership in these critical days.

In such a spirit on my part and on yours we face our common difficulties. They concern, thank God, only material things. Values have shrunken to fantastic levels; taxes have risen; our ability to pay has fallen; government of all kinds is faced by serious curtailment of income; the means of exchange are frozen in the currents of trade; the withered leaves of industrial enterprise lie on every side; farmers find no markets for their produce; the savings of many years in thousands of families are gone.

More important, a host of unemployed citizens face the grim problem of existence, and an equally great number toil with little return. Only a foolish optimist can deny the dark realities of the moment.

Yet our distress comes from no failure of substance. We are stricken by no plague of locusts. Compared with the perils which our forefathers conquered because they believed and were not afraid, we have still much to be thankful for. Nature still offers her bounty and human efforts have multiplied it. Plenty is at our doorstep, but a generous use of it languishes in the very sight of the supply. Primarily this is because rulers of the exchange of mankind's goods have failed through their own stubbornness and their own incompetence, have admitted their failure, and have abdicated. Practices of the unscrupulous money changers stand indicted in the court of public opinion, rejected by the hearts and minds of men.

True they have tried, but their efforts have been cast in the pattern of an outworn tradition. Faced by failure of credit they have proposed only the lending of more money. Stripped of the lure of profit by which to induce our people to follow their false leadership, they have resorted to exhortations, pleading tearfully for restored confidence. They know only the rules of a generation of self-seekers. They have no vision, and when there is no vision the people perish.

The money changers have fled from their high seats in the temple of our civilization. We may now restore that temple to the ancient truths. The measure of the restoration lies in the extent to which we apply social values more noble than mere monetary profit.

Happiness lies not in the mere possession of money; it lies in the joy of achievement, in the thrill of creative effort. The joy and moral stimulation of work no longer must be forgotten in the mad chase of evanescent profits. These dark days will be worth all they cost us if they teach us that our true destiny is not to be ministered unto but to minister to ourselves and to our fellow men.

Recognition of the falsity of material wealth as the standard of success goes hand in hand with the abandonment of the false belief that public office and high political position are to be valued only by the standards of pride of place and personal profit; and there must be an end to a conduct in banking and in business which too often has given to a sacred trust the likeness of callous and selfish wrongdoing. Small wonder that confidence languishes, for it thrives only on honesty, on honor, on the sacredness of obligations, on faithful protection, on unselfish performance; without them it cannot live. Restoration calls, however, not for changes in ethics alone. This Nation asks for action, and action now.

Our greatest primary task is to put people to work. This is no unsolvable problem if we face it wisely and courageously. It can be accomplished in part by direct recruiting by the Government itself, treating the task as we would treat the emergency of a war, but at the same time, through this employment, accomplishing greatly needed projects to stimulate and reorganize the use of our natural resources.

Hand in hand with this we must frankly recognize the overbalance of population in our industrial centers and, by engaging on a national scale in a redistribution, endeavor to provide a better use of the land for those best fitted for the land. The task can be helped by definite efforts to raise the values of agricultural products and with this the power to purchase the output of our cities. It can be helped by preventing realistically the tragedy of the growing loss through foreclosure of our small homes and our farms. It can be helped by insistence that the Federal, State, and local governments act forthwith on the demand that their cost be drastically reduced. It can be helped by the unifying of relief activities which today are often scattered, uneconomical, and unequal. It can be helped by national planning for and supervision of all forms of transportation and of communications and other utilities which have a definitely public character. There are many ways in which it can be helped, but it can never be helped merely by talking about it. We must act and act quickly.

Finally, in our progress toward a resumption of work we require two safeguards against a return of the evils of the old order: there must be a strict supervision of all banking and credits and investments, so that there will be an end to speculation with other people's money; and there must be provision for an adequate but sound currency.

These are the lines of attack. I shall presently urge upon a new Congress, in special session, detailed measures for their fulfillment, and I shall seek the immediate assistance of the several States.

✓ Through this program of action we address ourselves to putting our own national house in order and making income balance outgo. Our international trade relations, though vastly important, are in point of time and necessity secondary to the establishment of a sound national economy. I favor as a practical policy the putting of first things first. I shall spare no effort to restore world trade by international economic readjustment, but the emergency at home cannot wait on that accomplishment.

The basic thought that guides these specific means of national recovery is not narrowly nationalistic. It is the insistence, as a first consideration, upon the interdependence of the various elements in and parts of the United States—a recognition of the old and permanently important manifestation of the American spirit of the pioneer. It is the way to recovery. It is the immediate way. It is the strongest assurance that the recovery will endure.

In the field of world policy I would dedicate this Nation to the policy of the good neighbor—the neighbor who resolutely respects himself and, because he does so, respects the rights of others—the neighbor who respects his obligations and respects the sanctity of his agreements in and with a world of neighbors.

If I read the temper of our people correctly, we now realize as we have never realized before our interdependence on each other; that we cannot merely take but we must give as well; that if we are to go forward, we must move as a trained and loyal army willing to sacrifice for the good of a common discipline, because without such discipline no progress is made, no leadership becomes effective. We are, I know, ready and willing to submit our lives and property to such discipline, because it makes possible a leadership which aims at a larger good. This I propose to offer, pledging that the larger purposes will bind upon us all as a sacred obligation with a unity of duty hitherto evoked only in time of armed strife.

With this pledge taken, I assume unhesitatingly the leadership of this great army of our people dedicated to a disciplined attack upon our common problems.

Action in this image and to this end is feasible under the form of government which we have inherited from our ancestors. Our Constitution is so simple and practical that it is possible always to meet extraordinary needs by changes in emphasis and arrangement without loss of essential form. That is why our constitutional system has proved itself the most superbly enduring political mechanism the modern world has produced. It has met every stress of vast expansion of territory, of foreign wars, of bitter internal strife, of world relations.

It is to be hoped that the normal balance of Executive and legislative authority may be wholly adequate to meet the unprecedented task before us. But it may be that an unprecedented demand and need for undelayed action may call for temporary departure from that normal balance of public procedure.

I am prepared under my constitutional duty to recommend the measures that a stricken Nation in the midst of a stricken world may require. These measures, or such other measures as the Congress may build out of its experience and wisdom, I shall seek, within my constitutional authority, to bring to speedy adoption.

But in the event that the Congress shall fail to take one of these two courses, and in the event that the national emergency is still critical, I shall not evade the clear course of duty that will then confront me. I shall ask the Congress for the one remaining instrument to meet the crisis—broad Executive power to wage a war against the emergency, as great as the power that would be given to me if we were in fact invaded by a foreign foe.

For the trust reposed in me I will return the courage and the devotion that befit the time. I can do no less.

We face the arduous days that lie before us in the warm courage of national unity; with the clear consciousness of seeking old and precious moral values; with the clean satisfaction that comes from the stern performance of duty by old and young alike. We aim at the assurance of a rounded and permanent national life.

We do not distrust the future of essential democracy. The people of the United States have not failed. In their need they have registered a mandate that they want direct, vigorous action. They have asked for discipline and direction under leadership. They have made me the present instrument of their wishes. In the spirit of the gift I take it.

In this dedication of a Nation we humbly ask the blessing of God. May He protect each and every one of us. May He guide me in the days to come.

First Fireside Chat, March 12, 1933

My friends, I want to talk for a few minutes with the people of the United States about banking—with the comparatively few who understand the mechanics of banking but more particularly with the overwhelming majority who use banks for the making of deposits and the drawing of checks. I want to tell you what has been done in the last few days, why it was done, and what the next steps are going to be. I recognize that the many proclamations from State Capitols and from Washington, the legislation, the Treasury regulations, etc., couched for the most part in banking and legal terms, should be explained for the benefit of the average citizen. I owe this in particular because of the fortitude and good temper with which everybody has accepted the inconvenience and hardships of the banking holiday. I know that when you understand what we in Washington have been about I shall continue to have your cooperation as fully as I have had your sympathy and help during the past week.

First of all let me state the simple fact that when you deposit money in a bank the bank does not put the money into a safe deposit vault. It invests your money in many different forms of credit—bonds, commercial paper, mortgages and many other kinds of loans. In other words, the bank puts your money to work to keep the wheels of industry and of agriculture turning around. A comparatively small part of the money you put into the bank is kept in currency—an amount which in normal times is wholly sufficient to cover the cash needs of the average citizen. In other words the total amount of all the currency in the country is only a small fraction of the total deposits in all of the banks.

What, then, happened during the last few days of February and the first few days of March? Because of undermined confidence on the part of the public, there was a general rush by a large portion of our population to turn bank deposits into currency or gold—A rush so great that the soundest banks could not get enough currency to meet the demand. The reason for this was that on the spur of the moment it was, of course, impossible to sell perfectly sound assets of a bank and convert them into cash except at panic prices far below their real value.

By the afternoon of March 3 scarcely a bank in the country was open to do business. Proclamations temporarily closing them in whole or in part had been issued by the Governors in almost all the states.

It was then that I issued the proclamation providing for the nationwide bank holiday, and this was the first step in the Government's reconstruction of our financial and economic fabric.

The second step was the legislation promptly and patriotically passed by the Congress confirming my proclamation and broadening my powers so that it became possible in view of the requirement of time to entend [sic] the holiday and lift the ban of that holiday gradually. This law also gave authority to develop a program of rehabilitation of our banking facilities. I want to tell our citizens in every part of the Nation that the national Congress—Republicans and Democrats alike—showed by this action a devotion to public welfare and a realization of the emergency and the necessity for speed that it is difficult to match in our history.

The third stage has been the series of regulations permitting the banks to continue their functions to take care of the distribution of food and household necessities and the payment of payrolls.

This bank holiday while resulting in many cases in great inconvenience is affording us the opportunity to supply the currency necessary to meet the situation. No sound bank is a dollar worse off than it was when it closed its doors last Monday. Neither is any bank which may turn out not to be in a position for immediate opening. The new law allows the twelve Federal Reserve Banks to issue additional currency on good assets and thus the banks that reopen will be able to meet every legitimate call. The new currency is being sent out by the Bureau of Engraving and Printing in large volume to every part of the country. It is sound currency because it is backed by actual, good assets.

A question you will ask is this—why are all the banks not to be reopened at the same time? The answer is simple. Your Government does not intend that the history of the past few years shall be repeated. We do not want and will not have another epidemic of bank failures.

As a result we start tomorrow, Monday, with the opening of banks in the twelve Federal Reserve Bank cities—those banks which on first examination by the Treasury have already been found to be all right. This will be followed on Tuesday by the resumption of all their functions by banks already found to be sound in cities where there are recognized clearinghouses. That means about 250 cities of the United States.

On Wednesday and succeeding days banks in smaller places all through the country will resume business, subject, of course, to the Government's physical ability to complete its survey. It is necessary that the reopening of banks be extended over a period in order to permit the banks to make applications for necessary loans, to obtain currency needed to meet their requirements and to enable the Government to make common sense checkups.

Let me make it clear to you that if your bank does not open the first day you are by no means justified in believing that it will not open. A bank that opens on one of the subsequent days is in exactly the same status as the bank that opens tomorrow.

I know that many people are worrying about State banks not members of the Federal Reserve System. These banks can and will receive assistance from member banks and from the Reconstruction Finance Corporation. These state banks are following the same course as the national banks except that they get their licenses to resume business from the state authorities, and these authorities have been asked by the Secretary of the Treasury to permit their good banks to open up on the same schedule as the national banks. I am confident that the state banking departments will be as careful as the National Government in the policy relating to the opening of banks and will follow the same broad policy.

It is possible that when the banks resume a very few people who have not recovered from their fear may again begin withdrawals. Let me make it clear that the banks will take care of all needs—and it is my belief that hoarding during the past week has become an exceedingly unfashionable pastime. It needs no prophet to tell you that when the people find that they can get their money—that they can get it when they want it for all legitimate purposes—the phantom of fear will soon be laid. People will again be glad to have their money where it will be safely taken care of and where they can use it conveniently at any time. I can assure you that it is safer to keep your money in a reopened bank than under the mattress.

The success of our whole great national program depends, of course, upon the cooperation of the public—on its intelligent support and use of a reliable system.

Remember that the essential accomplishment of the new legislation is that it makes it possible for banks more readily to convert their assets into cash than was the case before. More liberal provision has been made for banks to borrow on these assets at the Reserve Banks and more liberal provision has also been made for issuing currency on the security of those good assets. This currency is not fiat currency. It is issued only on adequate security—and every good bank has an abundance of such security.

One more point before I close. There will be, of course, some banks unable to reopen without being reorganized. The new law allows the Government to assist in making these reorganizations quickly and effectively and even allows the Government to subscribe to at least a part of new capital which may be required.

I hope you can see from this elemental recital of what your government is doing that there is nothing complex or radical in the process.

We had a bad banking situation. Some of our bankers had shown themselves either incompetent or dishonest in their handling of the people's funds. They had used the money entrusted to them in speculations and unwise loans. This was of course not true in the vast majority of our banks but it was true in enough of them to shock the people for a time into a sense of insecurity and to put them into a frame of mind where they did not differentiate, but seemed to assume that the acts of a comparative few had tainted them all. It was the Government's job to straighten out this situation and do it as quickly as possible—and the job is being performed.

I do not promise you that every bank will be reopened or that individual losses will not be suffered, but there will be no losses that possibly could be avoided; and there would have been more and greater losses had we continued to drift. I can even promise you salvation for some at least of the sorely pressed banks. We shall be engaged not merely in reopening sound banks but in the creation of sound banks through reorganization. It has been wonderful to me to catch the note of confidence from all over the country. I can never be sufficiently grateful to the people for the loyal support they have given me in their acceptance of the judgment that has dictated our course, even though all of our processes may not have seemed clear to them.

After all there is an element in the readjustment of our financial system more important than currency, more important than gold, and that is the confidence of the people. Confidence and courage are the essentials of success in carrying out our plan. You people must have faith; you must not be stampeded by rumors or guesses. Let us unite in banishing fear. We have provided the machinery to restore our financial system; it is up to you to support and make it work.

It is your problem no less than it is mine. Together we cannot fail.

~ NOTES ~

ABBREVIATIONS

COHP—Columbia Oral History Project

ER—Eleanor Roosevelt

FBP—Family, Business Personal, FDRL

FDR—Franklin Delano Roosevelt

FDRL—Franklin Delano Roosevelt Library

MN—Meyers-Newton Documents, Herbert Hoover Presidential Library

NYT—New York Times

PPA—The Public Papers and Addresses of Franklin D. Roosevelt, Vols. 1–5, ed. Samuel Rosenman

PPF—President's Personal File, FDRL

RFP—Roosevelt Family Papers, FDRL

SDR—Sara Delano Roosevelt

TNR—The New Republic

WM—Walch-Miller Documents, Herbert Hoover Presidential Library

AUTHOR'S NOTE

xiii   a "defining moment": The earliest citation in Nexis of the title of this book is in a November 13, 1983, article in *The New York Times* by Howell Raines about presidential candidate Walter Mondale rallying the Democratic establishment against the candidacy of John Glenn. Raines later said, "The phrase was in the political air that year. I can't claim it as my own." William Safire goes beyond the standard definition of a "defining moment" as a "turning point." He writes that it "centers on the expression of character, or lack thereof, in a person or organization facing a crisis"— *NYT*, September 23, 1990.

xv   "His most dazzling successes": Saul Bellow, *Esquire* (December 1983).

PROLOGUE: SUNDAY, MARCH 5, 1933

1   new president's schedule: Pare-Lorentz Chronology, FDRL.

3   it lasted four-hundred years and was called the Dark Ages: John Maynard Keynes quoted in Nathan Miller, *FDR: An Intimate History*, 252.

3   "Capitalism itself was at the point of dissolution": Earle Looker, *The American Way: Franklin Roosevelt in Action*, 5.

3   "It was just as traumatic as Pearl Harbor": Author interview with Richard Neustadt, September 25, 2002.

3   press coverage: Lawrence W. Levine, and Cornelia R. Levine, *The People and the President: America's Conversation with FDR*, 61.

3   "a beleaguered capital in wartime": *NYT*, March 5, 1933.

4   Founding of the American Legion: Among the other founders was Harold Ross, founding editor of *The New Yorker*.

4   "As new commander-in-chief under the oath": Speech Files, FDRL. There is no indication of who in the tiny Roosevelt inner circle wrote this draft, though Louis Howe and Ray Moley are the likeliest authors, with press secretary Steve Early also a possibility.

5   "The situation is critical": Lippmann quoted in Ronald Steel, *Walter Lippmann and the American Century*, 300.

5   a "benevolent dictator": Eleanor Roosevelt quoted in Frank Freidel, *FDR: Launching the New Deal*, 205.

5   "storm troopers": The Unofficial Observer [John Franklin Carter], *The New Dealers*, 143.

5   "concentration camps": Louis Howe Papers, FDRL. The phrase goes back at least to the Boer War.

5   "If ever this country needed a Mussolini": Senator David Reed quoted in Arthur M. Schlesinger, Jr., *The Crisis of the Old Order*, 268.

6   "There was a thunder in the air": Looker, 19.

6   "If it fails . . . I'll be the *last* one": FDR quoted in Unofficial Observer, 144. There is no corroboration for this story, nor a name for the visitor, which may mean either that the visitor was the reporter John Franklin Carter himself or that the story is apocryphal. But it was repeated so often at the time that the public certainly believed it to be true.

7   "sacrifice and devotion" of wartime: Speech Files, FDRL. The reading text of the American Legion speech shows no signs of deletions or additions.

8   a "laughing revolution": Quoted in Unofficial Observer, 25.

Part One

CHAPTER ONE

13   Delanos: The family was so prominent in whaling in New Bedford, Massachusetts, that the American protagonist in Herman Melville's novella, *Benito Cereno*, is named Captain Amasa Delano.

14   all horse thieves were Democrats: Rita Hall Kleeman, *Gracious Lady*, 100. Warren Delano was a tough character, who once dismissed an employer with a reference to "our slut of a cook." He excused his opium dealing by arguing that the Peabodys, Russells, Forbeses, and Lows—all the best families—took part in the trade.

14   more like the lord's coachman: Geoffrey C. Ward, *Before the Trumpet*, 37. Delano had good antennae. White was a philanderer who was later famously shot and killed by Harry K. Thaw after Thaw discovered White was having an affair with his wife.

15   FDR's birth: Kleeman, 126.

CHAPTER TWO

16–17   Baby Franklin "crows and laughs all the time": Sara Roosevelt in Ward, *Before the Trumpet*, 112–13.

17   "Laura flashed down the stairway": Ibid., 117–19. Ward has the first and fullest account of this tragic accident.

17   "We seem to be going down": Kleeman, 152.

17   "I never get frightened": Ibid.

17   he recalled it often: Kleeman, 152. FDR spoke of the ship experience to his sixth cousin, Daisy Suckley. See Geoffrey C. Ward, ed., *Closest Companion*, 305. Suckley, twenty years younger than FDR, first met him in 1922, but they did not become close friends until 1934. For the final decade of Roosevelt's life, Daisy, who loved him deeply, saw the president constantly, and they wrote each other tenderly and often. After her death in 1991, friends discovered a suitcase beneath her bed containing diaries and more than three dozen previously undiscovered letters from FDR.

18   "secondary characters in Edith Wharton novels": Richard Hofstadter, *The American Political Tradition and the Men Who Made It*, 318.

18   it was a "fallacy" that anyone could be too refined: SDR quoted in Patrick J. Maney, *The Roosevelt Presence*, 5.

18   "My little man": See Davis, *The Beckoning of Destiny*, 63. Richard Flynn, son of Ed Flynn, recalls President Roosevelt telling him this story when Flynn was a boy. Author interview with Richard Flynn, November 8, 2005.

18   "A child will shake and tremble": See Anna Freud, and Dorothy T. Burlingham, *War and Children*, 32–35.

19   "He looked surprised": Mrs. James Roosevelt, *My Boy Franklin*, 16.

19   "self-conscious when he talked": Ibid., 4.

CHAPTER THREE

21   Franklin saw Mr. James: Ibid., 20, 26.

21   "perfectly awful": Ibid., 25.

22   He put on a cap to cover the bloody wound: Kleeman, 192.

22 "of course Roosevelt had an Oedipus complex as big as a house": John Gunther, *Roosevelt in Retrospect*, 162.

23 Freud . . . did not focus much on mothers: Peter Gay, *Freud: A Life for Our Time*, 505–06. See also Bonnie Angelo, *First Mothers: The Women Who Shaped the Presidents*, 1.

23 "power devil": C. G. Jung, *Memories, Dreams, Reflections*, 48–52.

23 the baths of Bad Nauheim in Germany: Ward, *Before The Trumpet*, 148; Roosevelt, *My Boy*, 35.

25 "He was the kind of boy whom you invited": Alice Roosevelt Longworth quoted in Joseph Lash, *Eleanor and Franklin*, 103.

25 "All that is in me goes back to the Hudson": FDR quoted in ibid., 116.

25 a family code word for "all is well": Ward, *Before the Trumpet*, 82.

25 sledding . . . Hyde Park: Doris Kearns Goodwin, *No Ordinary Time*, 13. This story comes from Betsey Whitney, FDR's daughter-in-law.

25 "illusive inner islands of strength": Susan Vaughan, *Half Full/Half Empty*, 5. See also Daniel Goleman, *Emotional Intelligence*.

25 "Whether he excelled at what he tackled": Roosevelt, *My Boy*, 40.

26 FDR's Spanish-American War fib: Ward, *Before the Trumpet*, 200.

26–27 "a snob—he did not have": Ibid., 240.

27 "an inferiority complex": Frank Freidel, *Franklin D. Roosevelt: The Apprenticeship*, 57.

CHAPTER FOUR

28 She worked with poor Jewish immigrants: Bernard Asbell, *The FDR Memoirs: A Speculation on History*, 238.

29 "Please don't make any more arrangements": FDR-SDR, FRDL. Franklin was not well liked at Oyster Bay but enjoyed visiting.

29 "I am the happiest man": FDR, *Letters, Early Years*, 518.

29 a "sense of security I had never known before": Eleanor Roosevelt, *This Is My Story*, 128.

30 "the groom at every wedding": Carol Felsenthal, *Princess Alice: The Life and Times of Alice Roosevelt Longworth*.

31 Eleanor sank into a deep depression: Ibid., 164–65.

31 Eleanor maintained a pleasant correspondence with her mother-in-law: Frank Freidel, *Franklin D. Roosevelt: A Rendezvous with Destiny*, 14. Freidel interviewed Eleanor on the subject in 1948.

31 "He lived in an atmosphere": Gunther, 167.

CHAPTER FIVE

32 "it was no use": Ledyard quoted in Geoffrey C. Ward, *First-Class Temperament*, 77.

32 "Once you're elected governor": FDR quoted in Kenneth S. Davis, *FDR: The Beckoning of Destiny, 1882–1928*, 214.

33 "a poor little rich boy": FDR quoted in Charles Hurd, *When the New Deal Was Young and Gay*, 53. Ward agreed in an interview with the author that the story that follows sounds apocryphal.

33 "Every individual wanted security": Quoted in Looker, 108.

33 "With his handsome face": *NYT* quoted in *Ward, First-Class Temperament*, 131.

34 "hopelessly stupid" children of "hillbillies": FDR in ibid., 144.

34 "bristling with the conceits": FDR in ibid., 153.

34 "an awfully mean cuss": FDR in Frances Perkins, *The Roosevelt I Knew*, 12.

35 "penetrated into his personality": Ibid., 26.

CHAPTER SIX

36 "presidential timber": Howe quoted in Lela Stiles, *The Man Behind Roosevelt*, 33. Stiles was a young journalist who went to work as Howe's secretary and took contemporaneous notes that she later used in her book.

36 "If you say a thing often enough": Howe quoted in Alfred B. Rollins, Jr., *Roosevelt and Howe*, 14. Howe was raised in Saratoga Springs, New York, the son of a down-on-his-luck newspaper editor. Saratoga was a lively town, famous for its baths. Like Roosevelt visiting European spas, Howe spent much of his youth in the presence of invalids. He worked for the local newspaper as a young man and directed and acted in scores of plays, which also proved helpful for FDR's theatrical entrance to the presidency. His father suffered a nervous breakdown, ending Louis's hopes for college and beginning many years of financial worry. While still working for the *New York Herald*, Howe went on the payroll of Thomas Mott Osborne, a wealthy upstate mayor. In 1912, he finally quit journalism and began writing hundreds of letters on behalf of Osborne's campaign for governor. Then Osborne decided not to run, which left Howe facing unemployment. It was his desperate need of a paycheck that finally brought him into FDR's employ. Osborne was later implicated in the Newport homosexuality scandal that threatened FDR's career and was found dead in the street in 1926 wearing a bizarre woman's disguise—Howe Papers, FDRL; Ward, *First-Class Temperament*, 549.

36 "immense confidence": Rollins, 14.

37 "one of the four ugliest men": Howe quoted in Looker, 166.

37 Howe had cards printed: Stiles, 224.

37 "Beloved and Revered Future President": Howe Papers, FDRL.

38 "Keep that temperature down": Howe quoted in Stiles, 37.

38 "provide the toe-weights": Ibid., 40.

38 "to hold Franklin down": Rollins, 251.

38 "Dear Old Louis": Ibid., 3.

39 "At heart . . . I am a minstrel": Howe quoted in Stiles, 270. Howe also wrote reverent poetry, some of which he addressed to FDR.

CHAPTER SEVEN

41   "Young Roosevelt knows nothing": Lane quoted in Ward, *First-Class Temperament*, 216.

41   "unbent, laughed with them, swapped yarns": Perkins, 20.

42   "You should be ashamed of yourself": Lane quoted in Ward, *First-Class Temperament*, 223.

42   "Sharpen your pencils": Daniels quoted in ibid., 227.

42–43 FDR's standoff with Joseph P. Kennedy: Michael Beschloss, *Kennedy and Roosevelt: The Uneasy Alliance*, 44–47. FDR wanted to enlist in the war, as Theodore Roosevelt had urged him to do (TR, in his late fifties, even tried to get in himself). But Franklin never pressed the point and Howe made sure Eleanor and the rest of the family knew that men with children were not being accepted as volunteers, and that President Wilson himself didn't think Franklin should go. So he stayed out.

44   "The bottom dropped out of my own particular world": Eleanor Roosevelt quoted in Lash, 220. The best sources on the sketchy details of FDR's affair with Lucy Mercer are books and oral histories of Lash, Alsop, and Daniels, all of whom later knew the family.

44   "He might have been happier": Eleanor quoted in *Time*, February 2, 1998.

45   Social calendars of FDR, Herbert Hoover: See WM, 210.

45   "I had some nice talks with Herbert Hoover": FDR quoted in Timothy Walch, and Dwight M. Miller, eds., *Herbert Hoover and Franklin D. Roosevelt: A Documentary History* (cited hereafter as WM), 6.

45   Hoover-FDR ticket: Louis B. Wehle, *Hidden Threads of History: Wilson Through Roosevelt*, 85–86.

46   "This young Roosevelt is no good": Charlie Murphy quoted in Arthur Krock, *Memoirs*, 152–53.

46   "You know, I had something to do with": Ward, *First-Class Temperament*, 535.

CHAPTER EIGHT

49   "is a well-meaning, nice young fellow but light": Lodge quoted in Davis, *FDR: Beckoning of Destiny*, 616.

49   Newport Scandal details: See ibid., 642–45; Ward, *First-Class Temperament*, 569–75; and *NYT*, July 20, 1921. The Republican National Committee had raised the scandal briefly during the 1920 campaign. Arthur Krock, working at the time for the Democratic National Committee, was dispatched to Hyde Park to work on a statement of reply—Krock, 152.

50   he would never walk . . . again: James Roosevelt, and Sidney Shalett, *Affectionately, F.D.R*, 41–42; Davis, *FDR: Beckoning*, 650. A good overall analysis of the effect of polio on FDR is Hugh Gregory Gallagher's *FDR's Splendid Deception*. Gallagher himself survived polio and spent time as a child at Warm Springs.

50 "I know that he had real fear": Eleanor quoted in Gallagher, 14.

50 He . . . now felt abandoned: Perkins, Columbia University Oral History Project (COHP).

50 reminded him of a tomb: This apparently comes from a personal interview Frank Freidel conducted with Perkins. Quoted in Davis, *FDR: Beckoning of Destiny*, 656.

50 massage . . . worsened the paralysis: Gallagher, 13.

50 "cured him permanently of any belief": Max Lerner, *Wounded Titans*, 48. In 2003, Dr. Armond S. Goldman of the University of Texas, Galveston, wrote an article in the *Journal of Medical Biography* asserting that it was more likely that FDR suffered from Guillain-Barré syndrome than polio. Goldman cited FDR's short-term partial facial paralysis, extreme pain, numbness, and bladder dysfunction as more common symptoms of Guillain-Barré (which was little known at the time). But the fever and vigorous exercise that preceded the onset are more typical of polio, and the pain was likely exacerbated by the massages administered by Eleanor Roosevelt and Louis Howe. Dr. Marinos Dalakas of the National Institute of Neurological Disorders called the Guillain-Barré theory "a significant stretch." In any event, there was no effective treatment for either disease in 1921—Associated Press, Reuters, November 1, 2003.

51 "has been such a comfort to all who tried to help": Ward, *First-Class Temperament*, 606. Ward, also a polio survivor, offers an especially complete narrative of FDR's experience with the disease, 576–649.

51 "I realized that I had to be courageous": SDR quoted in Gallagher, 118.

52 "he definitely will not be crippled": *NYT*, September 16, 1921.

52 "now that I have seen": FDR to Adolph Ochs, September 16, 1921, FDRL.

52 more than a thousand times: *NYT* search, ProQuest.

52 "he has almost completely recovered": *NYT*, February 23, 1928.

52 List of institutions for invalids: See Gallagher, 29.

52 Letter from Dr. Draper: Quoted in Ward, *First-Class Temperament*, 604–05.

53 "all light and no darkness": Milton MacKaye quoted in Patrick J. Maney, *The Roosevelt Presence*, 39.

53 "totally immobile, like a doll": Author interview with Robert Rosenman, October 7, 2002. Rosenman, son of Sam Rosenman, saw FDR on many occasions as a child.

53 "Fix the God-damned brace!": Quoted in Ward, *First-Class Temperament*, 784.

54 Even those close to him were consistently surprised: Robert W. Merry, *Taking on the World: Joseph and Stewart Alsop—Guardians of the American Century*, 54.

54 "Jonathan, look, I'm on the make here now": Daniels, COHP.

54 "by next autumn I will be ready to chase": FDR quoted in Ward, *First-Class Temperament*, 670.

55 "I am very much disheartened": Ibid, 675

55 Details of Anna Roosevelt's wedding: Curtis Dall, *FDR: My Exploited Father-in-Law*, 17, 101. The groom, Curtis Dall, became a far right-winger after his divorce from the president's daughter.

55 FDR's time with Missy LeHand: Described by Asbell, 261–93. Asbell calculated the days away from Eleanor.

56 "Missy was the only woman Franklin ever loved": Laura Delano quoted in Ward, *First-Class Temperament*, 710. The FDRL contains no indication in correspondence of an amorous relationship.

56 Hugh Gallagher on sex and polio: Gallagher quotes a doctor's report from 1931 that says FDR was capable of having sex but speculates that his polio contributed to his repressing his sexual desire and shutting down his emotion life—Gallagher, 130–44.

57 "he must have been psychoanalyzed by God": Gunther, 33.

57 "There were days on the *Larooco*": Frank Freidel, *Franklin D. Roosevelt: The Ordeal*, 191. Geoffrey C. Ward pointed out to the author that this is the only direct evidence that FDR suffered from depression in this period.

CHAPTER NINE

58 "go over and shake": James Roosevelt, and Bill Libby, *My Parents: A Different View*, 93. The "Happy Warrior" line was written by Smith's aide, Joseph M. Proskauer, who later become a well-known New York judge.

59 John Paul Jones screenplay, history of world: FDRL. The underdeveloped screenplay treatment consists of Jones and other characters entering and leaving rooms, but with no dialogue and little action. The few pages of the world history that FDR managed to write before abandoning his efforts are well-written but don't seem to reflect much research.

59 business ventures: Ward, *First-Class Temperament*, 658–59; FDRL.

60 "There I was, large as life": *Macon Daily Telegraph*, April 14, 1925, FDRL.

61 "You no doubt think me very fussy": SDR to FDR, March 25, 1928, FDRL.

61 "I undertook": Ward, *First-Class Temperament*, 722.

62 "You're not an orthopedist": Looker, 148.

63 "Beyond comparison, the finest man": Durant quoted in Ward, *First-Class Temperament*, 785.

63 "rare combination of stoicism and chronic buoyancy": Wehle, 89.

63 "purged the slightly arrogant attitude": Perkins, 29.

64 "No, no, I won't hear of it!": Ibid., 11. Frances Perkins was the only close FDR associate who knew Roosevelt over the whole course of his public life. She could compare the arrogant young man of 1911 to the statesman of 1945.

64 "If you can't use your legs and they bring you milk": Perkins, COHP.

64 "he would certainly have been president": Eleanor quoted in Gunther, 243.

64 "Having handled that": Author interview with Robert Morgenthau, November 2, 2002.

65   a "playboy": Early's description as noted in Harold Ickes, *The Secret Diaries of Harold Ickes: The First Thousand Days*, 699.

65   "You couldn't pin him down": Howe quoted in Stiles, 82.

CHAPTER TEN

67   "Frank Roosevelt just threw me out of a window": Robert A. Slayton, *Empire Statesman: The Rise and Redemption of Al Smith*, 360.

68   "were so deeply buried in his subconscious": Perkins, COHP.

69   Relationship with Robert Moses: Robert Caro, *The Power Broker: Robert Moses and the Fall of New York*, 289–91.

69   FDR-Alfred E. Smith correspondence: Slayton, 354.

69   "Smith considered Franklin a little boy": Stiles, 119.

70   Smith didn't want FDR to be his successor: See Slayton, 356. Notes from the meeting were found in Jim Farley's papers.

70   "You are raising up a rival": Ibid.

70   many people "believed": Elliott Roosevelt, *FDR: His Personal Letters*, Vol. II, 771–72.

70   "If ever a man": *Time*, February 1, 1932.

70   "If I could campaign another six months": FDR quoted in Gunther, 253.

71   his shirt was soaked with sweat: Arthur M. Schlesinger, Jr. *The Crisis of Confidence*, 384.

71   Flynn's gambit: Edward J. Flynn, *You're the Boss*, 71–72.

71   "The time hasn't come": Jack Beatty, *Pols*, 206.

72   "You know, I didn't feel able": FDR in Perkins, 52–53. See also Oscar Handlin, *Al Smith and His America*, 144. For correspondence over arrangements for FDR's swearing in, see Governor's Files, FDRL.

Part Two

CHAPTER ELEVEN

77   "I am 100 percent": John M. Barry, *Rising Tide*, 268.

77   "the most unceasing mental energy": Henry L. Stimson, and McGeorge Bundy, *On Active Service in Peace and War*, 285.

77   "Facts are as water to a sponge": Baruch quoted in Eugene Lyons, *Herbert Hoover: A Biography*, 219. See also Richard Norton Smith, *An Uncommon Man: The Triumph of Herbert Hoover*. Smith explains many of Hoover's overlooked attributes.

77   "like sitting in": *Time*, February 1, 1982.

77   "clammy": Robert E. Sherwood, *Roosevelt and Hopkins*, 47.

78   "many persons left their jobs": Herbert Hoover, *Memoirs: The Great Depression, 1929–1941*, 195.

78   "purge the rottenness out of the system": Treasury Secretary Andrew Mellon quoted in Gene Smith, *The Shattered Dream*, 57.

78 "We didn't admit it at the time": Rexford Tugwell quoted in Robert. A. Wilson, ed., *Character Above All: Ten Presidents from FDR to George Bush*, 158.

78 baseball game: *TNR*, March 16, 1959.

79 "if you put a rose in Hoover's hand": Gutzon Borglum quoted in Grace Tully, *FDR: My Boss*, 60.

CHAPTER TWELVE

80 "that he just doesn't have . . . amiable boy scout": Lippmann quoted in Steel, 291.

80 "He is an amiable man": Ibid.

81 "People aren't cattle, you know!" FDR quoted in Perkins, 108.

82 "Roosevelt is one of the most charming": Mencken quoted in Herbert Mitgang, *Once Upon a Time in New York*, 15.

82 "men of far greater intelligence": Nicholas Murray Butler quoted in Schlesinger, *Crisis of the Old Order*, 204.

82 T. S. Eliot lecture: *NYT*, March 1, 2003.

82 "to bring on the revolution": F. Scott Fitzgerald quoted in Schlesinger, *Crisis of the Old Order*, 205.

82 Lewis Mumford voting for Communists: Steel, 294.

83 John Dos Passos's "This Is All Bullshit": Dorothy Wickenden, ed., *The New Republic Reader*, 7

84 a hit on the "wireless": No audiotapes of the gubernatorial radio speeches survive, so it's impossible to assess his tone. But the transcripts are mostly dull. It would take time to make FDR into a gifted communicator.

84 "The Democrats nominated their 1932": *NYT*, November 6, 1930.

84 Looker's "challenge": Looker, 188–89.

85 "a glass eye": Krock, 158.

85 "Come on, Sam": Samuel Lambert quoted in Krock, 159.

85 "Well, here's the helpless, hopeless invalid": FDR quoted in Ward, *First-Class Temperament*, 196.

85 "I proposed this for the annual message": Rosenman private papers.

86 "Remember this: You're nothing": Howe quoted in Gunther, 86. Robert F. Kennedy gave a speech with the same message to JFK campaign workers in 1960.

87 "Franklin, you damned, idiotic fool": Howe quoted in Stiles, 161. Lela Stiles's notes for her book on Howe are on file at FDRL.

87 "doesn't really think of him as an equal": Colonel Edward House quoted in Slayton, 351.

87 "requires a man of great vigor": Al Smith quoted in *Saturday Evening Post*, June 10, 1932.

CHAPTER THIRTEEN

88   "Here is a subject for a campaign cartoon": FDR memo in WM, 34.

88   Michelson's role: Charles Michelson, *The Ghost Talks*, 91; see also Lyons, 234. Michelson literally wrote the book on how to oust an incumbent president. When Hoover himself complained that his enemies "came out of the smear departments of yellow journalism," he was accurate. Michelson went all the way back to W. R. Hearst's first paper, the *San Francisco Examiner*, where he drank with Ambrose Bierce and Rube Goldberg. He helped invent yellow journalism covering the Spanish-American War and other adventures with Frederic Remington and Stephen Crane. After reports surfaced that the assassin, Leon Czolgosz, carried a Hearst newspaper in his pocket when he shot William McKinley in 1901, Michelson was dispatched to Buffalo, where he unsurprisingly reported that Czolgosz never read Hearst papers, only "communistic literature." He covered Harry Thaw's trial for killing Sara Delano's old beau, Stanford White, and the Scopes Trial, where he asked William Jennings Bryan if he thought the world was flat. Bryan was so angered by the question that he never spoke to Michelson again.

89   "bury the hatchet—in Al Smith's neck": Tennessee senator Cordell Hull quoted in David Robertson, *Sly and Able: A Political Biography of James F. Byrnes*, 122.

89   Smith vs. FDR: Handlin, 153–55.

90   "the Al of today is no longer a politician": Mencken quoted in Jonathan Daniels, *The Time Between the Wars*, 220. In 1928, a prominent New York City lawyer named Thomas L. Chadbourne turned against Smith and wrote an unpublished memoir detailing how he had given Smith $400,000 in stock and cash over several years, in part to win his help in raising the subway fare over a nickel. Chadbourne, a major investor in the subway, was bitter and claimed that Smith—who enjoyed a reputation for honesty that was rare among Tammany Hall politicians—pocketed the money without getting the fare raised. Ward, *First-Class Temperament*, 507.

90   Sumner's original "forgotten man": Daniels, 214.

90   "Attacking me?": FDR quoted in Looker, 33.

91   "Whaddya mean—'progressive'?": Raymond Moley, *After Seven Years*, 9–10.

91   "definite obligation to prevent the starvation": FDR quoted in Bernard Bellush, *Franklin D. Roosevelt as Governor of New York*, 147.

92   "Well, if your fellows think": Samuel Rosenman, *Working with Roosevelt: FDR and the Era of the New Deal*, 65–66; see also Rexford Tugwell, *The Brains Trust*, 103–05.

94   "Dragging his legs from his hips": David Grubin Productions, *FDR*. Field was interviewed on a WGBH *Frontline* documentary.

94   Hoover watching FDR arrive: WM, 44.

CHAPTER FOURTEEN

95 with piercing black eyes: Moley had been a small-town elected official as a very young man in Ohio. FDR's cousin Daisy Suckley described him as "strange and unattractive and impossible socially, but he had a strange depth in two black, piercing eyes, and his mouth is scarred and twisted to one side when he smiles." Quoted in Geoffrey C. Ward, ed., *Closest Companion*, 23.

96 "Do you think these professors can be trusted": Howe quoted in Rosenman, 58.

96 matching his blue shirt to the color of his eyes: Merry, 77.

96 "Rex was like a cocktail": Moley, *After Seven Years*, 15.

97 an "intellectual ransacking of his visitors": Ibid., 20.

97 Moley wrote his sister Nell: Ibid., 11.

98 "He was a progressive vessel yet to be filled": Rexford Tugwell, *The Democratic Roosevelt*, 36.

98 Memo on the Roosevelt view: Raymond Moley Papers.

98 Ed Flynn and Pope Leo XIII: Author interview with Richard Flynn, November 8, 2005.

CHAPTER FIFTEEN

99 Hearst calls FDR's bluff: David Nasaw, *The Chief: The Life of William Randolph Hearst*, 453.

100 "That was a shabby statement!": Agnes Leach quoted in Kenneth S. Davis, *FDR: The New York Years, 1928–1933*, 260.

100 "a mucker and a liar": Joseph Proskauer quoted in Slayton, 366.

100 James Michael Curley: By the convention, Curley only got into the hall by finagling a seat with the Puerto Rican delegation.

101 "the torpedo under the prow": Michelson, *Ghost Talks*, 5.

101–102 commending versus recommending gambit and Thomas Taggert's disgust: Krock, COHP; Arthur Krock, *Memoirs*, 7–14.

102 "Have you ever": Wallace, *Character*, 174.

CHAPTER SIXTEEN

103 Chicago as the convention opened: Charles Bledsoe, COHP; Jonathan Norton Leonard, *Three Years Down*, 287.

104 "I don't like him": Smith quoted in Rosenman, 246.

104 oppose him "to the last heartbeat": Smith quoted in Bascom N. Timmons, *Jesse H. Jones: The Man and the Statesman*, 156.

104 Smith's meeting with McAdoo: Rosenman, 248.

105 "How Dry I Am": Edwin P. Hoyt, *Jumbos and Jackasses*, 341.

105 "a man who thinks that the shortest distance": Elmer Davis quoted in Steel, 291.

105 "I still remember that column": Author interview with Leon Despres, September 13, 2002.

105 "a phony and a weakling": Bledsoe, COHP.

106 the "weakest candidate" available: H. L. Mencken, *The Vintage Mencken*, 210.

106 "Our situation was desperate": Farley, COHP.

107 His "trousers were confined perilously": Stiles, 179.

107 "He's come this far" and "Happy Days": Ibid., 177–82.

108 "we'll have the governorship six months more": Basil O'Connor quoted in Moley, *After Seven Years*, 7, 30.

108 Howe sprawled on the carpet: James A. Farley, *Behind the Ballots: The Personal History of a Politician*, 144.

108 "The Chicago convention is in a jam": Rosenman, 258; Davis *FDR: The New York Years*, 332. This was Baker's account to a friend. Apparently FDR consulted with neither Howe nor Farley before making this commitment. See Eliot A. Rosen, *Hoover, Roosevelt and the Brains Trust*, 113.

109 "a pitcher of warm piss," which a reporter changed to "spit": Robert Cowley, ed., *What If? 2: Eminent Historians Imagine What Might Have Been*, 250. Timmons's depiction of Garner and his profanity would tend to confirm this version.

109 "Boys, Roosevelt is lost": Farley quoted in Rosenman, 262. See also *Chicago Tribune*, July 1, 1932.

110 "Of the 56,000 Democrats": O'Connor quoted in Steve Neal, *Happy Days Are Here Again*, 294. For details of the switch of the California delegation, see ibid., 273–94; also, Rosen, 243–75.

110 "If revenge is really sweet": Mencken, 212.

110 "It's a kangaroo ticket": Quoted in James McGregor Burns, *Roosevelt: The Lion and the Fox*, 138.

110 "I intend to say what I propose to say": McAdoo quoted in *NYT*, July 2, 1932.

111 Hearst wrongly claiming credit: Nasaw, 456. Michelson, 9. Farley, *Behind the Ballots*, 149.

111 "Good old McAdoo!": FDR quoted in Tully, 52.

111 "It would be hard to find a delegate": Mencken, 210, 213.

111 "The Democrats have nominated nobody quite like him": Maney, 40.

111 "I won't do it": Smith quoted in *NYT*, July 2, 1932.

111 Smith walking toward the Chicago train station: James A. Farley, *Jim Farley's Story*, 26. This was the genesis of Smith's reputation for "taking a walk" from the Democrats.

CHAPTER SEVENTEEN

114 "You are not to breathe a word": Howe quoted in Davis, *FDR: The New York Years*, 330–31. See also Lash, 351. No copies of the letter were ever recovered and Dickerman did not reveal this story until after Eleanor's death in 1962.

114 "It was pure selfishness on my part": Eleanor Roosevelt, *This I Remember*, 68.

CHAPTER EIGHTEEN

116 "I'll tell you what I'm going to do": FDR quoted in Rosenman, 68.

116 flight from Albany to Chicago: *Chicago Tribune*, July 3, 1932.

116 tumultuous reception at Chicago's tiny Municipal Airport: Moley, *After Seven Years*, 29.

117 "New Deal" acceptance speech details: Rosenman, 69.

117 Origins of phrase "New Deal": See William Safire, *Safire's New Political Dictionary*, 485–87; *TNR*, June 29, 1932; Moley, *After Seven Years*, 146; and Rosenman, 71–72. Moley told Safire that the phrase was in the original draft of the acceptance speech he delivered to Albany, but there is nothing in his books or papers to prove it. He used it in his May memo as an afterthought ("It is not the pledge of a new deal it is the reminder of broken promises"). One point all parties agree on is that no one planned the "new deal" as the frame for FDR's program. The first to raise that idea was apparently Herbert Bayard Swope, who wrote to Moley immediately following the speech that it should be made the keynote of the campaign.

117 "Mein Gawd, do I have to do": Ibid.

118 "Dammit, Louie, *I'm* the nominee!" FDR quoted in Rollins, 348.

118 "The whole hall was electrified": Author interview with Mary Bain, September 12, 2002.

119 FDR's speech: Moley, *After Seven Years*, 33; Rosenman, 76–79.

CHAPTER NINETEEN

120 "Mr. Hoover was wrong": Jim MacLafferty's diary quoted in WM, 45.

120 Hoover aides gathered on the South Lawn: Gene Smith, 119. Medicine ball, a game where players bat around a large cloth ball, had become popular at the White House in the 1920s.

120 "it was a great mistake": Hoover quoted in WM, 211.

121 "We've got to crack him": Ibid., 52.

121 "the greatest innocent bystander in history": White quoted in Joan Wilson, *Herbert Hoover: Forgotten Progressive*, 163.

121 the "Bonus Army": For the full story of the Bonus Army, see Paul Dickson, *The Bonus Army*.

122–23 FDR on the Bonus Army and Hoover: Tugwell, *In Search of Roosevelt*, 193–94.

CHAPTER TWENTY

124 "There is one reason in favor of my going": Stiles, 208; Michelson, 12.

124 "Hello, you old potato!": Farley, *Behind the Ballots*, 177.

124   the Jimmy Walker case: See Mitgang, 167–204. Mitgang provides the most complete recent treatment of the trial.
125   the stakes in the trial: *NYT*, August 22, 1932.
126   "How would it be": FDR quoted in Mitgang, 202.
126   the evidence would have to be overwhelming: Flynn, *You're the Boss*, 121.
126   "I think Roosevelt is going to remove me": Walker quoted in Mitgang, 201.
126   "may lose the Presidency entirely on the Walker issue": Hagerty quoted in Mitgang, 211. Arthur Krock of the *Times* wrote in his memoirs that if FDR had not proven himself independent of Walker and Tammany with the hearings, "I am not sure that Roosevelt would have been elected President"—Krock, 148.

CHAPTER TWENTY-ONE

128   the holy gold standard: the best explanation of the gold standard's connection to the worsening of the Depression is in Barry Eichengreen's *Golden Fetters: The Gold Standard and the Great Depression, 1919 to 1939*. Governments around the world believed that protecting their gold reserves was second only to protecting their homelands from attack. So powerful was the dogma of "good as gold" that it wasn't until late 1931, when Great Britain went off the gold standard, that the old orthodoxies began to crack. In the meantime, a vicious cycle developed. After the Federal Reserve, fearing more speculation, fatally tightened the money supply in 1928, U.S. lending fell off, which led to retrenchment abroad. That sparked a new international credit crisis, with Germany and Austria in default, which brought a new round of trade barriers, including the infamous Smoot-Hawley Tariff, signed reluctantly by Hoover in 1931, which led to a further decline in demand worldwide.
130   "the lone wolf": *PPA*, Vol. 1, 755.
130   the Commonwealth speech marked "the dividing line": Tugwell, *In Search of Roosevelt*, 176. Tugwell believed the speech's importance had little to do with FDR himself, whom he said scanned it only briefly before delivering it.
130   "It was a real shocker": Ibid., 175.
130   the originator of "Third Way" politics: In 1991, Bill Clinton quoted the Commonwealth Club speech when launching his own candidacy for president; he later argued that changing with new circumstances "was what being true to the spirit of the New Deal meant, not sticking with every last bit of the old [New Deal] policies"—Michael Waldman, ed., *My Fellow Americans: The Most Important Speeches of American Presidents*, 99.
131   to "weave them together": FDR quoted in Moley, *After Seven Years*, 48.
131   At Pittsburgh's Fordes Field: *PPA*, Vol. 1, 809.
131   "chameleon on the Scotch plaid": Hoover quoted in Davis, *FDR: The New York Years*, 362.

132 importance of results from Maine: Gene Smith, 179.

133 some fleeting signs of economic improvement: Lyons, 310.

133 that Hoover had "arrested" the Depression: *New York Herald-Tribune*, November 14, 1933.

133 "Hang Hoover!": Gene Smith, 210.

133 Hopkins's letters to his brother: Sherwood, 41.

133 "Losers always have a big spurt": Stiles, 216.

134 Eleanor's unhappiness: David B. Roosevelt, *Grandmere: A Personal History of Eleanor Roosevelt*, 148; Eleanor Roosevelt, *This I Remember*, 77.

134 "This is the greatest moment": Manchester, *The Glory and the Dream*, 54.

134 Krock on national grouch: See William E. Leuchtenberg, *The FDR Years*, 215.

134 "All informed observers agree": *TNR*, November 16, 1932.

135 "to cooperate with you": Manchester, *The Glory and the Dream*, 54.

135 "You know, Jimmy, all my life": Roosevelt and Libby, *My Parents*, 142.

Part Three

CHAPTER TWENTY-TWO

139 "Happy Days Are Here Again": Edmund W. Starling, *Starling of the White House*, 301.

139–40 Barnes passed along FDR's form letter on "materialism": WM, 211. More than thirty years later, Hoover was still steamed about it, writing in a peculiar memo for the files entitled "My Personal Relationship with Mr. Roosevelt" that FDR's 1928 letter to Barnes showed "less than fair play in political debate from a personal friend."

140 "proved unsettling to business": Henry Wallace quoted in Lyons, 310.

140 "By March 4 next": Adolf Berle quoted in Freidel, *FDR: Launching the New Deal*, 73n.

140 FDR's "ungracious" Gridiron remarks: WM, 32.

141 "There would be instant pressure on Hoover": FDR quoted in Berle's diary, WM, 68–69. FDR was usually politically practical, but this was an example of his wishful thinking.

142 Inside the White House Red Room: Moley, *After Seven Years*, 27–30.

143 "amiable, pleasant": Hoover memo quoted in Freidel, *FDR: Launching the New Deal*, 34.

143 "He believes he is both physically and mentally unable": Ted Joslin's diary in WM, 77.

143 "It's not my baby": FDR quoted in Gene Smith, 220.

145 "the formal set up of government structure": Tugwell's diary in WM, 97.

145 "laughable and lamentable": Stimson's diary in ibid., 85.

145 "Governor Roosevelt considers that it is undesirable": Ibid., 97.

145 "settle this damn thing": FDR in ibid., 95.

145 "My instructions to him were": Ibid., 96.

145   "I suppose he will tell the press": Hoover quoted in ibid., 100.

146   "strange advisers": Stimson, 295.

146   FDR met secretly with the French ambassador: Robert Dallek, *Franklin D. Roosevelt and American Foreign Policy*, 28.

146   "the most difficult period of my whole association": Moley, *After Seven Years*, 42.

146   "For a time it was very doubtful": Ibid., 42.

147   "That's right. I never will be photographed": Hoover quoted in WM, 111.

147   rumors "about Roosevelt's personal dislike": Ibid., 115.

147   "Roosevelt seemed a villainous fool": Thomas Corcoran quoted in Lash, *Dealers*, 100.

147   "I'll have my way with Roosevelt yet": Hoover quoted in WM, 126.

CHAPTER TWENTY-THREE

148   Coolidge's despair: Gene Smith, 204.

148   Red flag flying over Minnesota: Despres interview; Gene Smith, 221. Smith conveys the mood of the country that year in colorful detail.

149   "When do we eat?": Robertson, 125.

149   Descriptions of Mitchell: Edmund Wilson, *Travels in Two Democracies*, 1936, 52–62. Susan Estabrook Kennedy, *The Banking Crisis of 1933*, 110.

150   "If you steal $25, you're a thief": Susan Kennedy, 126.

150   hoarding reached epidemic proportions: Ibid., 133. *US News & World Report*, February 24, 2003.

151   "Fears that Roosevelt might devalue the dollar": Eichengreen, 326.

151   clause "democratic sabotage": Meyer, COHP.

151   Businessmen with money in the bank: Eichengreen, 328

152   "Sacrifice for frugality and revenue": Baruch quoted in Schlesinger, *Crisis of Confidence*, 457.

152   "a single vigorous statement": Lawrence Sullivan, *Prelude to Panic: The Story of the Bank Holiday*, 43, 74–75.

153   Louisiana bank "holiday": T. Harry Williams, *Huey Long*, 615–16. When the *New Orleans Times-Picayune* got wind of Long's scheme and reported on it on February 4, Long called the head of the state militia and told him to occupy the newspaper's offices. Only a promise by the publisher to recall every edition of that paper from the streets averted a military showdown in the newsroom.

153   February's crisis in Michigan: This account is drawn largely from Susan Kennedy, 77–102, and Robert Lacey, *Ford: The Men and the Machine*, 343–57.

155   "jangled the American system": Quoted in Susan Kennedy, 82.

CHAPTER TWENTY-FOUR

156 "become strong again": Looker, 6.

156 "Who is that *awful* man": SDR quoted in Tully, 324.

156 "By God I feel sorry for him": Huey Long quoted in Alan Brinkley, *Voices of Protest*, 58.

157 "When I talk to him, he says 'Fine! Fine! Fine!' ": Ibid., 58.

157 Harvard Club dinner: Wehle, 134.

157 "The notion that the New Deal had a preconceived": Perkins, 167.

157 the bank crisis was due to culminate in early March: Michelson, 50.

158 with "those people": Roosevelt and Shallet, 277.

158 "Another reason for assigning the task": Moley, *After Seven Years*, 75.

159 "One banker in my state attempted": Susan Kennedy, 133.

159 a "roaring lion in the Senate": Glass quoted in Moley, *After Seven Years*, 81.

159 "Make it perfectly clear we simply can't go along": FDR quoted in ibid.

160 Woodin's sunny children's song: "Let us be like bluebirds/Happy all day long/Forgetting all our troubles in/A sunny song," quoted in William Manchester, "The Great Bank Holiday," *Holiday* magazine, 61.

160 Lewis Douglas's background: James E. Sargent, *Roosevelt and the Hundred Days*, 70; *NYT*, February 24, 1933.

161 "I hope we don't have a goddamned Rasputin": Raymond Moley, *27 Masters of Politics*, 243.

162 Hull was no choir boy: Hurd, 95.

162 Louis Wehle advised him: Wehle, 130.

162 Roosevelt later scrawled on scrap paper: Raymond Moley Papers.

162 "Tennessee Project" radiogram: Moley, *After Seven Years*, 91.

163 Pittman's drinking: Ibid., 89.

163 "the largest single underlying cause": Unofficial Observer, 290.

163 the "telephone book" ambassador: Flynn, 148. Dodd's daughter, Martha, became a well-known Communist and heiress. See Philip Metcalfe, *1933*.

164 "Yours Truly, in a mean state of mind": Berle quoted in Lash, *Deal-ers*, 90.

164 $3,500 a year from Brandeis to Frankfurter: Bruce Allen Murphy, *The Brandeis/Frankfurter Connection*, 42.

164 "It was no contest between a Protestant from Iowa": Morgenthau interview.

164 Wallace's background: See John C. Culver, and John Hyde, *American Dreamer: A Life of Henry A. Wallace*, 29.

165 "to get safe liquor for the evening cocktail": Ibid., 106.

165 "Which one of you is Ikes?": FDR quoted in Moley, *After Seven Years*, 94; Conrad Black, *Franklin Delano Roosevelt: Champion of Freedom*, 262. Ickes was later the father of Harold Ickes, who served in the Clinton administration.

166 making gentle fun of Perkins in Cabinet: Morgenthau interview.

166 "Well, that's a problem, but we can work": Perkins, 152.

CHAPTER TWENTY-FIVE

168   hijinks on the *Nourmahal:* Unpublished Vincent Astor interview, October 18, 1958, FDRL.

168–69 scene at Bayfront Park: Ibid.

169   "That unquestionably saved his life": Ibid.

169   Zangara's background: Blaise Picchi, *The Five Weeks of Giuseppe Zangara,* 241. Picchi dug up Zangara's unpublished jailhouse memoir and many other previously unknown details of the assassination attempt.

170   Zangara had wanted to kill Hoover: Paul Dickson, and Thomas B. Allen, *The Bonus Army,* 330.

170   H. L. Edmunds, a tourist: Robert J. Donovan, *The Assassins,* 146.

170   Lillian Cross's story: Picchi, 252.

170   Thomas Armour's story: Author interview with Armour's daughter-in-law, Mrs. Susan Armour, whose late husband was a witness, August 5, 2002, Picchi, 209.

170   "Stop that man!": Astor interview. See also Picchi, 15.

172   FDR's description of the scene: *Time,* February 27, 1933; *Detroit Free Press,* February 17, 1933.

172   "That drive to the hospital": Lorena Hickok, *Reluctant First Lady,* 82.

172   doctors credited FDR with helping: *Newsweek,* February 25, 1933.

173   "Tell him to piss on the floor": Picchi, 25.

173   "Jesus. I couldn't very well have put out": Deinhart quoted in Len O'Connor, *Clout: Mayor Daley and His City,* 46–47. Paddy Bauler, a legendary Chicago alderman, had urged Cermak to go to Miami and make peace with FDR after the bad feelings associated with the previous summer's convention, when the bohemian immigrant mayor known as "Pushcart Tony" had attacked the country squire as a "clubman Caesar" and declined to come on board the Roosevelt bandwagon until it didn't matter anymore. In the months since, his feelings hadn't changed. "Cermak said he didn't like the sonafabitch," Bauler later recalled. "I sez, 'Listen, for Chrissakes, you ain't got no money for Chicago schoolteachers [who had been working without pay for months] and this Roosevelt is the only one who can get it for you. You better get over there and kiss his ass, or whatever you got to do. Only you better get the goddamn money for them teachers, or we ain't goin' to have a city that's worth runnin.' So he goes over and Christ Almighty, next thing I hear on the radio is that Cermak's got shot."—

173   "I see Mr. Hoover, I kill him first": Zangara quoted in Picchi, 150. In later years, the gossip columnist Walter Winchell peddled the conspiracy theory that Zangara was a Mafia hit man and Cermak his actual target. As a young *New York Mirror* columnist, Winchell happened to be in Miami the night of the shooting. He bribed an elevator operator to take him to the nineteenth floor of the county jail, where Zangara was being held. The police chief let him interview the assassin even before the official interroga-

tion in exchange for making him and his department famous around the world. Nothing Zangara said that night suggested the Mafia theory—besides being Italian, he didn't fit the profile. And Cermak wasn't a known Mafia target; as mayor, he both challenged the Chicago crime syndicate still run by Al Capone's capos and occasionally cooperated with it. Winchell (and, later, the television series *The Untouchables*) reinforced the myth, anyway.

173   Zangara was diagnosed as "perverse": Robert Donovan, 200.

174   Garner background, eyebrows "like two caterpillers rasslin": Cowley, ed., 250–51. See also Bascom Timmons, *Mr. Garner of Texas.*

174   that "Garner's voice": Neustadt interview.

174   "another Hoover": Manchester, *The Glory and the Dream*, 56.

174   "might have been more disastrous than the imagination": *Literary Digest*, February 25, 1933.

174   "Your mind, Vincent, works very slowly": Unpublished Vincent Astor interview, FDRL.

175   "You can't live with that": Eleanor Roosevelt Oral History, quoted in Jon Meacham, *Franklin and Winston*, 182.

175   he could "throw off anything": Irvin McDuffie quoted in Gunther, 83.

175   "Don't you dare do such a thing": Eleanor Roosevelt quoted in Hickok, 83.

175   "There was nothing—": Moley, *After Seven Years*, 139.

175   FDR made sure the reporters on his train: *Time*, February 27, 1933.

175   a crudely wrapped shotgun shell: *NYT*, February 22, 1933.

176   "God saved you": Anne R. Bodek to FDR, February 22, 1933, FDRL.

176   "Just as God made You the President": Joseph Williams quoted in Houck, 13. Most scholars have viewed the Miami shooting as a curious footnote. The author's interpretation differs by attributing much greater importance to the event and its aftermath, which were essential to FDR's success in the Hundred Days.

176   "I want to kill the president:" Zangara quoted in Picchi, 144.

176   personally opposed to death penalty: *NYT*, November 11, 1933.

177   The people will "close ranks behind him": *New York Post*, February 16, 1933.

177   "To a man, his country rose": *Time*, February 27, 1933.

CHAPTER TWENTY-SIX

178   Inner Circle Club festivities: *NYT*, February 19, 1933.

178   Hoover's letter and reaction: Moley, *After Seven Years*, 140; WM, 130.

179   "I realize that if these declarations": MN, 338–41.

179   What he did next: See WM, 134; Sullivan, 111.

180   "The net and unanimous opinion of everyone": Howe to FDR, June 22, 1932, RFP, FDRL. It's not clear whether this was the only prior occasion where Howe and FDR used the "blame the secretary" excuse.

181   "devoid of every atom of patriotism": WM, 133.

181   "Let them bust": Tugwell quoted in Herbert Feis, *1933: Characters in Crisis*, 104.

181   "they wanted it to get as bad": Warburg, COHP, unpublished manuscript, 68–69. Also see Stimson and Bundy, *On Active Service*, 295.

181   "If he could acquire more latitude": Corcoran quoted in Lash, *Dealers*, 100.

181   "for publication in the distant future": In 1947, Hoover sent the unpublished manuscript to a journalist friend, and during the 1980s it ended up in the Hoover Library, where Frederic Alan Maxwell brought it to the author's attention. The manuscript is a one-sided chronology of the 1932–33 period, but it does reflect Hoover's command of the details of the crisis.

182   "I feel when you asked him": Moley, *First New Deal*, 213.

182   "It was the most political and most unnecessary": Lyons, 318–19.

182   "A sharp break with the past did in fact occur": Schlesinger, *Cycles of American History*, 379.

CHAPTER TWENTY-SEVEN

184   *Gabriel Over the White House:* Walter Huston, most famous for the film *September Song*, was the father of John Huston and grandfather of Anjelica Huston. He visited FDR in the White House and wrote him supportive notes over the years. Letters in FDRL.

185   "I want to send you this line": FDR-W. R. Hearst, April 1, 1933, PPF, FDRL.

185   "It represents pretty well its public": *TNR*, April 16, 1933.

186   "a marvelous man takes care": W. A. Swanberg, *Citizen Hearst*, 430.

187   "the powers of a virtual dictatorship": Charles Grant Curtis, Jr., *Franklin D. Roosevelt and the Commonwealth of Broadcasting*.

187   "A mild species of dictatorship": Lippmann quoted in Steel, 299.

CHAPTER TWENTY-EIGHT

188   FDR on the train: Farley, *Behind the Ballots*, 208–09.

189   "He felt that human beings": Eleanor Roosevelt, *This I Remember*, 69.

189   Details of the banks' collapse: Sullivan, 108.

190   "These bankers haven't." Lindley, *The Roosevelt Revolution*, 75.

190   "We will fight until 10:49 a.m. March 4": Hoover quoted in ibid., 113.

191   "If you go, don't get a roundtrip ticket": Ogden Mills quoted in Susan Kennedy, 147.

191   Bank run details: See Manchester, "The Great Bank Holiday," *Holiday* magazine, 60.

CHAPTER TWENTY-NINE

192   Eleanor's apprehension: Hickok, 86–88.

193   a spirited disagreement has taken place: Blanche Wiesen Cook, author of a
      multivolume biography of Eleanor, argues yes—and not just because
      Hickok lived with other women both before and after meeting Eleanor (in
      what were then called "Boston marriages") and made little secret of her ho-
      mosexuality. She cites specific passages as unambiguous. "I wish I could lie
      down beside you tonight and take you in my arms," Eleanor wrote in one.
      Lorena wrote: "I remember your eyes, with a kind of teasing smile in them,
      and the feeling of that soft spot just northeast of the corner of your mouth
      against my lips. . . ." Cook argues that there was nothing ambiguous or
      coded in their words. "Sigmund Freud notwithstanding: A cigar may not
      always be a cigar, but the 'northeast corner of your mouth against my lips' is
      always the northeast corner." See Blanche Wiesen Cook, *Eleanor Roo-
      sevelt. Vol. I, 1884–1933*, 479; Rodger Streitmatter, ed., *Empty Without
      You: The Intimate Letters of Eleanor Roosevelt and Lorena Hickok*, 22.

      Geoffrey C. Ward, hardly an apologist for the Roosevelts, doesn't be-
      lieve it. He explains that Eleanor, starved for affection as a child, wrote
      many friends with considerable ardor and could not possibly have had
      affairs with all of them. Ward cites a letter that Eleanor sent to Hickok
      in 1935 saying: "I know you often have a feeling for me which for one
      reason or another I may not return but I feel I love you just the same."
      He adds that Eleanor once confessed to Hickok that "something locked
      me up and I cannot unlock it." In the 1920s, Eleanor talked with her
      daughter Anna about sex as "an ordeal to be borne" and found herself
      reacting with horror to an André Gide novel about male homosexual-
      ity ("She couldn't bring herself even to consider homosexuality," Esther
      Lape, her lesbian friend, told Joseph Lash). After weighing various ac-
      counts of her discomfort with sex, Ward concludes that Eleanor's life-
      long need for self-control and sense of guilt conspired against her
      enjoyment of it. See Ward, "Outing Mrs. Roosevelt," *New York Review
      of Books*, September 24, 1992, and March 3, 1993.

194   "My zest in life is rather gone for the time being": Eleanor Roosevelt
      quoted in David B. Roosevelt, 152.

195   Hickok was blocked at the door: Streitmatter, 10.

196   visit to the Clovis Adams Memorial: Jonathan Daniels, *Washington
      Quadrille*, 247.

196   "Sometimes I'd be very unhappy": Eleanor quoted in Hickok, 92.

196   "Lucy, I have just heard that Franklin Roosevelt was in love": Daniels,
      Washington Quadrille, 251.

197   Details of Inauguration eve: Hickok, 95. Nowadays, if a close friend of a
      first lady wrote a book about spending the night before her husband's inau-
      gural in a room with her, it would likely set off a scandal.

197   "It's a good speech, a courageous speech": Hickok, 95.
197   end of Hicks's AP career: Moley, *First New Year*, 115; Hickok, 96.

CHAPTER THIRTY

198   "It's good to have another Roosevelt": Ike Hoover quoted in Tully, 64.
199   "I decided to cut it short": FDR quoted in ibid.
199   history of courtesy calls, Wilson to Harding: *NYT*, March 4, 1921.
200   "They forgot to close the door": Eleanor quoted by Lewis in *NYT*, March 13, 1981.
200   "I shall be waiting at my hotel": FDR quoted in Moley, *After Seven Years*, 146.
200   to "chat quietly for an hour": *NYT*, March 4, 1933.
200   FDR was "visibly angry": Flynn, 125.
200   "cut deeply into Roosevelt's memory": Tully, 64.
201   there now commenced an unprecedented series: For details of these final negotiations, see Moley, *After Seven Years*, 147.
202   "World literally rocking beneath our feet": Agnes Meyer quoted in Black, 266.
203   "What state are you the governor of?": Meyer quoted in Merlo J. Pusey, *Eugene Meyer*, 235.
203   "I can keep on fiddling": Hoover quoted in Sargent, 88.
203   they "would have gone bust": Susan Kennedy, 150.
204   Contacting Pennsylvania governor Gifford Pinchot to close the banks: Moley, *After Seven Years*, 128.
204   "This thing is bad": Ibid., 147–48.

Part Four

CHAPTER THIRTY-ONE

207   most memorable moment: ER draft, Eleanor Roosevelt Papers.
207   "first event in my life that has given": FDR quoted in Krock, 142.
207   "a better phrasemaker than anyone": Michelson, 13.
208   Account of Hyde Park evening: Moley, *First New Deal*, 113.
209   "the speech was one of the very few": Rosenman, 89–90.
210   Rosenman-Moley dispute: Although Rosenman reprinted Roosevelt's self-serving memo in 1952, Moley writes that he wasn't aware of it until 1964. This is peculiar, considering that Moley wrote Rosenman a complimentary letter about Rosenman's memoirs after they were published in 1952—Raymond Moley Papers.
210   the draft language bears little resemblance: Moley, *First New Deal*, 111–17. Any convincing evidence of authorship would likely have gone into one of Moley's books, probably *The First New Deal*, which contains photocopies of speech notes and two pages of an early draft. But of the portion of his

early draft that he reprints, only one sentence—"The means of exchange have become frozen all along the channels of trade"—survives intact in the reading copy of the Inaugural. Perhaps his later drafts would be more consistent with the reading copy, but Moley preserved no copies of them. When he threw his draft into the fire at Hyde Park, he apparently immolated any proof of his authorship of the speech. An examination of Moley's papers by the author failed to find any more documentation.

210   "Some of them say he didn't write his speeches": Dorothy Brady, FDR's stenographer, quoted in Ward, ed., *Closest Companion*, 23.

210   Rosenman on "the only thing we have to fear is fear itself": Rosenman, 91.

211   Moley on the "fear" line: Moley, *First New Deal*, 118–99.

211   Moley "clearly remembers": Ibid., 115. The author and research assistants conducted an exhaustive search of newspapers in New York and Washington that Howe might have read—and searched several databases and department store archives—but failed to find any such advertisement containing the "fear itself" line or anything approximating it. Seven decades later, the line is still widely invoked: See *NYT*, July 10, 2005, and *New York Post* in the days after 9/11. The catchiness of the line itself and the charm of the man who used it give the phrase greater importance than it perhaps deserves. Richard Hofstadter wrote: "When Hoover bumbled that it was necessary only to restore confidence, the nation laughed bitterly. When Roosevelt said, 'The only thing we have to fear is fear itself,' essentially the same threadbare half-true idea, the nation was thrilled"— *The American Political Tradition*, 312.

211   "fear itself" line in Chamber of Commerce story: *NYT*, February 9, 1931. There is no direct evidence that FDR or Howe saw the Chamber of Commerce story in *The New York Times*. The origin of the famous line thus remains unconfirmed.

CHAPTER THIRTY-TWO

212   the "abler man": Peabody quoted in Goldberg, 169.

213   "almost impenetrable": Tugwell, *The Brains Trust*, 62.

213   taxi cab story: *NYT*, March 5, 1933. Accounts of FDR's official day gleaned from the *Times*, the *New York Herald-Tribune*, and other publications.

213   "Lovely steel": FDR quoted in Tully, 68.

214   "After we passed the Commerce Building": Ibid.

214   "I hope you have your rubbers on!": Ibid.

215   "bottomless reserves": Phillip Hamburger, *The New Yorker*, March 13, 1933.

215   FDR's new style of oath-taking: In a February 25, 1933, letter to Charles E. Cropley, clerk of the Supreme Court, FDR wrote that "the question has been raised" as to whether he should repeat the oath and asked Cropley to "talk it over with the Chief Justice," who agreed. FDR, *Letters, Early Years*, 331.

216 adding "day of national consecration": Rosenman, 91. Because the conse-
     cration line was not in the prepared text, it appears in few, if any, printings
     of the speech. But it is included in the version in the Appendix.
217 attacks on men of high finance: See Tugwell, *In Search of Roosevelt*, 223.
218 VICTORY FOR HITLER EXPECTED TODAY: *NYT*, March 5, 1932.
219 "How? How? How?": Corcoran quoted on CCNY TV, Roundtable on
     FDR, 1963.
219 a ray of winter sun that "broke through the gray": Kleeman, 296.

CHAPTER THIRTY-THREE

220 "We have a Moses": Thousands of letters about the speech are on file at
     FDRL. Many make reference to his polio, another indication that it was
     hardly a secret.
220 "since your inaugural, peace seems": Joe Kennedy quoted in Beschloss,
     Kennedy and Roosevelt, 80.
220 "The secret of his political genius": Bellow, *Esquire* (December 1983). The
     diplomat George Kennan, also from the Midwest, noticed that the locus of
     accountability seemed transformed in a moment. In the past, "when times
     were hard, as they often were, groans and lamentations went up to God,
     but never to Washington": George F. Kennan, *Memoirs: 1925–1950*, 4.
221 "There is something contagious about the cheery smile": *Cincinnati Times-
     Star* quoted in Levine and Levine, 61. Jim Pinkerton argues that the inau-
     gural spurred a "Hawthorne Effect." He explains that at Western Electric's
     Hawthorne Plant in Cicero, Illinois, post-war researchers decided to see if
     they could improve productivity by making the lights brighter. It worked.
     Output increased. But then productivity settled back to where it was.
     Next, the researchers tried reducing lighting in the plant. Strangely, this
     worked, too. Productivity went up again. The lesson the researchers took
     away—later called "The Hawthorne Effect"—was that almost any change
     in the work environment will bring forth improved effort, at least for a
     time. Pinkerton argues that this "organizational equivalent of adrenaline"
     was at work in 1933 after the Inauguration. The speech spurred hope and
     economic activity even before the legislation of the Hundred Days took
     effect—James P. Pinkerton, *What Comes Next*, 78.
221 "The Dictatorship of Roosevelt": *New York Daily News*, March 5, 1933,
     and March 7, 1993.
221 "directed single-mindedly to the reestablishment": Tugwell, *In Search of
     Roosevelt*, 222, 231.
221 "an injection of adrenalin": Starling, 306–07.
222 "It was very, very solemn": Eleanor Roosevelt quoted in Hickok, 103–04.
222 "hardly the kind of thing one would do": Lillian Rogers Parks with Frances
     Spatz Leighton, *The Roosevelts: A Family in Turmoil*, 5. See also Hickok,
     104; Eleanor Roosevelt, *This I Remember*, 78. Parks seems to have been
     trying to create a scandal, but it didn't work.

222   Mrs. Ruth Sims attempting to preserve traces of FDR's sweat: Neustadt interview.

223   The White House facilities . . . "wasn't even sanitary": Henrietta Nesbitt, *White House Diary: FDR's Housekeeper*, 30–31. For the next twelve years, the president and his guests complained about Nesbitt's starchy and flavorless meals. Some fell into the habit of eating a sandwich before coming to the Roosevelt White House for dinner. Their best hope was to be invited for informal supper on Sunday night in the family quarters, when Nesbitt was off and Eleanor would cook scrambled eggs in a chafing dish. Wine was not served until long after the end of Prohibition, and when it was, the sherry was passable but the champagne, according to Harold Ickes, "undrinkable." Whether the bad food and drink resulted from Eleanor's submerged hostility to her husband or simple inertia, Nesbitt survived until Bess Truman finally fired her for insubordination—Goodwin, 198–99; Ickes, 249.

223   "The thing that emerges most clearly": *TNR*, March 22, 1933.

224   Sinatra at the Crosby concert in Jersey City: See Malcolm Mcfarlane, *Bing Crosby: Day by Day*, March 4, 1933.

CHAPTER THIRTY-FOUR

225   "Pull out and drive on the grass": Starling, 307.

225   "It was enough to know that something": Moley, *First New Deal*, 337, 339.

226   "a good many interesting foreign stamps": Katharine Crane, *Mr. Carr of State*, 308.

227   "Roosevelt was in a good mood": Raymond Clapper, *Washington News*, quoted in Sargent, 93.

228   Minutes of FDR's meeting with bankers, officials: Adolf Berle Papers, FDRL.

229   Mills's model of a shipwrecked boat he called "the New Deal": Author interview with Diane Bryce, National Park Service guide at Hyde Park, 2003.

231   FDR's story of the drowning man with a silk hat: Quoted in Freidel, *FDR: Rendezvous with Destiny*, 205.

231   "If he had burned down the Capitol": Will Rogers's column, March 6, 1993, from the Clippings File, FDRL.

232   FDR's panic attack: See Tugwell, *Democratic Roosevelt*, 270–71; Davis, *FDR: New Deal Years*, 40; and Freidel, *FDR: Launching the New Deal*, 213–14. Grace Tully tells a different story of FDR at his desk on March 6. She writes that he caused panic in the office by playfully pushing all the buzz buttons at once, which summoned all five of his aides simultaneously—see Tully, 71. Tugwell gets the date wrong but his version is more believable.

CHAPTER THIRTY-FIVE

234 "And that's exactly what you are doing": Retired Supreme Court Justice Oliver Wendell Holmes quoted in Hickok Papers, FDRL; Katie Louchheim, ed., *The Making of the New Deal*, 23.

234 "A second-class intellect but a first-class temperament": It was long assumed that Holmes was referring to Franklin, who had not been a standout student or author of books but knew how to lift the mood of any room he entered. Over time, of the thousands of descriptions of FDR, Holmes's assessment has become the most quoted. Now, however, Holmes scholars Gary Aichele and Richard Posner believe that Holmes was, in fact, referring to Theodore, whom he knew much better and whose intellectual acuity he had questioned on prior occasions (see Black, 1150). Edmund Morris, a noted Theodore Roosevelt scholar, told the author on June 14, 2005, that he believed Holmes had FDR in mind after all.

234 "At the heart of the New Deal was not a philosophy": Hofstadter, 316.

234 "Temperament is the great separator": Neustadt, *Presidential Power*, 172.

235 "His untroubled conception of the presidency": Kennedy, *Freedom from Fear*, 95.

235 "FDR was deftly using them": Alsop quoted in Merry, 8. Alsop's mother was Eleanor's cousin.

235 "not only multiplex, it was contradictory": Sherwood, 11.

235 "the most untemperamental genius": Ibid., 269.

235 "My dear Mr. Gunther": Quoted in Eric Larrabee, *Commander in Chief*, 644.

235 Sam Houston story: Tully, 12.

236 FDR as a "switchboard": Gunther, 79.

236 "He had to know, to a centimeter": Garry Wills, *Certain Trumpets: The Call of Leaders*, 31.

236 "joyous, hearty, rolling, thunderous laughter": Oursler quoted in Gallagher, 134.

237 Long and FDR: Williams, 637–39. Farley, who thought FDR showed himself to be "all backbone and brains," thought Long was admitting FDR's political skill, but Williams says not. See Farley, *Behind the Ballots*, 241–43.

237 "utters 500 words for every one": Garner quoted in Timmons, 202.

237 "every pore in his body was an ear": Dorothy Thompson quoted in Gunther, 63.

238 "in all frankness": FDR quoted in Moley, *First New Deal*, 254.

238 "I am like a cat": FDR quoted in Goodwin, 608.

238 "Mr. President, you play": Gould, *The Most Exclusive Club*, 132.

238 "a rather feminine figure": Randolph Churchill quoted in Meacham, 352.

238 "There was in the man a kind of narcissism": Marquis Childs, COHP.

239 "You know, Orson": FDR quoted in Michael F. Reilly, *Reilly of the White House*, 59.

239   "That was the Garbo in me": FDR quoted in Gunther, 62.

239   "to have been dipped in phosphorous": Lillian Gish quoted in Piers Brendom, *The Dark Valley: A Panorama of the 1930s*, 101.

239   "I love it! I love it!!": FDR quoted in Goodwin, 39. This story comes originally from the director Billy Wilder.

239   "God, how I'd love to see that man": Watson quoted in Hedley Donovan, *Roosevelt to Reagan*, 21.

240   "playing the role I think he liked best": Melvyn Douglas quoted in *TNR*, April 15, 1946.

240   "not the largest man in the world": Frank Capra, *The Name Above the Title*, 344.

240   FDR as a "sun god": Unpublished interviews with Jeffrey Potter; and Jeffrey Potter, *Men, Money and Magic: The Story of Dorothy Schiff*, 135. Schiff had a long flirtation with FDR during World War II that she later reported fell just short of an affair.

240   "My God! What a man!" Henry Luce quoted in Swanberg, 106.

240   "I am a juggler": FDR to Henry Morgenthau, quoted in Michael Beschloss, *The Conquerors: Roosevelt, Truman, and the Destruction of Hitler's Germany, 1941–1945*, 217.

240   "could keep all the balls in the air": Wallace quoted in Leuchtenburg, *FDR Years*, 25.

240   FDR as "a conjurer": Anthony Eden, British foreign secretary, quoted in ibid., 17.

240   "this was an innate kind of reticence": Eleanor Roosevelt, quoted in Ward, *First-Class Temperament*, 18.

240   "a pair of master showmen": Reilly, 124.

241   "of impenetrable mind": Manchester, *The Glory and the Dream*, 82.

241   "patronizing and humiliating": Dean Acheson, *Morning and Noon*, 164.

241   Jim Farley felt: In 1940, Farley grew embittered with FDR when the president refused to step aside after two terms and let Farley himself have the Democratic nomination. After this, Farley wrote a second memoir, far more critical than his first, in which he accused FDR of being a snob.

242   "he was a snob": Schiff quoted in Potter, 136.

242   Milton Academy speech mentioning snobbery, 1926: Speech Files, FDRL.

242   FDR looking into background of friend's fiancé: Ward, ed., *Closest Companion*, 14.

242   Corcoran embittered: David McKean, *Tommy the Cork*, 126. Corcoran's fiancée was Peggy Dowd, a working-class Irishwoman from Washington, D.C., and the aunt of *NYT* columnist Maureen Dowd.

242   "He is as cold and hard as steel": Starling, xiv.

242   "He never was 'one of the boys' ": Reilly, 57.

243   "Roosevelt has almost no taste or judgment about painting": Biddle quoted in Perkins, 76.

243   "Are you a socialist?": Reporter quoted in Perkins, 330.

243   the most superstitious president in American history: Tully, 22. Tully fre-

quently noted that Roosevelt would have been glad that he died in Warm Springs on Thursday, August 12, 1945, only a few hours before a Friday the 13th, though he would have been appalled that his funeral train embarked on such an unlucky day. See also Gunther, 111.

244   his "lucky hat," a battered fedora: Reilly, 60.

CHAPTER THIRTY-SIX

245   the big craze was jigsaw puzzles: First connected to the Depression in Manchester, "The Great Bank Holiday," *Holiday* magazine, February, 1960, 60. Manchester's magazine piece effectively depicts the mood that week.

245   Shaeffer's cable: Moley, *First New Deal*, 161.

245   Eleanor fretted over Mayflower tab: Eleanor Roosevelt, *This I Remember*, 79.

246   a "strong tower of hope": Quoted in *Literary Digest*, March 18, 1933; Susan Kennedy, 163.

246   "like a sharp slap in the face": *Literary Digest*, March 18, 1933.

246   Rockefeller gave his caddy a dollar, not a dime: *Time*, March 13, 1933.

246   bank president borrowing change for lunch: Author interview with Walter Sondheim, October 2, 2002.

247   Huey Long's wad of bills: Krock, 175.

247   holiday details: Susan Kennedy, 161; *Time*, March 13, 1933.

247   bartering outside St. Nick's Arena: *New York Daily News*, March 7, 1933.

247   box office slump: *Variety*, March 7, 1933.

248   "Dow-Metal Money": Davis, *FDR: New Deal Years*, 43.

248   Hearst's money problems: Swanberg, 521.

248   Reston's bounced check: John F. Stacks, *Scotty: James B. Reston and the Rise and Fall of American Journalism*, 33.

248   "Now is the time": *New York Daily News*, March 7, 1933.

248   "may be too slow" to meet the emergency: Letter to the conference of governors quoted in Davis, *FDR: New Deal Years*, 36.

249   FDR compared to Kutuzov: Ibid., 39.

249   FDR's "brainstorm": Susan Kennedy, 173.

250   "We don't have to issue scrip": Moley, *First New Deal*, 172.

251   "You damn sonofabitch!": Senator Carter Glass quoted in Williams, 628.

251   "The President drove the money-changers": Susan Kennedy, 136.

251   ROOSEVELT GETS POWERS OF DICTATOR: *NYT*, March 11, 1933.

251   "It is one of the great humanitarian qualities": Unofficial Observer, 389.

252   "It won't work, John": FDR quoted in Timmons, 179.

252   "Capitalism had been saved in eight days": Moley, *After Seven Years*, 155; Moley, *First New Deal*, 208.

CHAPTER THIRTY-SEVEN

253–54   First press conference: Clippings File, FDRL.

255   "That Tory Krock-pot": FDR quoted in Stacks, 93.

255   "the most amazing performance of its kind": *Baltimore Sun* reporter quoted in Sargent, 101; Leuchtenberg, *FDR Years*, 144.

257   "He gave me the most beguiling smile": Sargent, 101

257   "amazement, curiosity, mock alarm": Gunther, 23.

257   "put on a dunce cap": Reilly, 87.

257   " 'Well, Steve tells me' ": Gene Smith, 96.

257   Well, how would he put it?: Sargent, 124.

257   McIntyre getting his pocket picked: Betty Houchin Winfield, *FDR and the News Media*, 33.

258   "Really, this is not a cross-examination!": Ibid.

258   Hickok's recommendation that ER hold press conferences: Streimatter, 11.

258   "We women must go about our daily task": Eleanor Roosevelt quoted in Daniels, *Washington Quadrille*, 249.

259   Eleanor Roosevelt–Hickok correspondence: See Streimatter, 16–25; Hickok File, FDRL.

260   "After a fruitless week": FDR quoted in Jan Pottker, *Sara and Eleanor*, 268.

260   "I don't seem to be able to shake": Eleanor Roosevelt letter to Lorena Hickok, FDRL.

262   "Your Majesty": Brendan Gill, *Here at The New Yorker*, 156.

262   "Newspaper men!": SDR quoted in Reilly, 82.

262   Sara's "masculine drive": See Hurd, 49. The 1939 visit of the king and queen of England to Hyde Park didn't help Sara's image. Word leaked that she was appalled that her son and daughter-in-law served the royals hot dogs, a decision highly popular with the American public. Before the visit, Sara made arrangements for the accommodations to be upgraded in the hardly luxurious part of the house where King George and Queen Elizabeth were to stay. After they left, she refused to pay the bill, thinking it too high. The local Dutchess County plumber went to the estate, ripped out the plumbing and toilet seat, and hung the seat in his store with a sign attached: "The King and Queen Sat Here"—Gunther, 263.

CHAPTER THIRTY-EIGHT

263   "I decided I'd try to make a speech": FDR quoted in Stiles, 245.

263   "All of our money is in the Poughkeepsie": Berle diary, September 19, 1939, quoted in Davis, *New Deal Years*, 681. FDR was angry that Moley in his book *After Seven Years* (published in 1939) took credit for writing the first Fireside Chat. He told Berle this story to show that Moley was mistaken and he had dictated the speech himself.

264   FDR's speaking voice: A new machine, called a "voice-o-graph," used science to chart voice modulations. It found that FDR had a richer, steadier voice than any other politician of the day—*NYT*, May 14, 1933.

264   FDR's radio persona as a "second-class aristocrat": Author's interview with Leon Despres, August 24, 2002

265 All afternoon, workers busily removed: Curtis, unpublished manuscript, 1.

265 "There was magic, we knew": Moley, *First New Deal*, 172.

265 FDR on couch: Michelson, 57.

265 Moley insisted that the speech was entirely: Moley, *First New Deal*, 194.

265 "As I watched [his] extraordinary career": Ballantine quoted in Ward, *Before the Trumpet*, 238.

266 "I tried to picture a mason at work": FDR quoted in Stiles, 245.

266 "He saw them gathered in the little parlor": Perkins, 72.

266 Reagan "idolized" Roosevelt: Author interview with Reagan aide Michael Deaver, 2002. Barone column, *Washington Post*, September 17, 1986; Cannon, *Reagan*, 18.

267 Queen Victoria and Gladstone story: Robert T. Jackson, *That Man*, 159.

267 "wasting the taxpayers' commas": Tully, 93

268 The ritual of FDR's "pivot tooth": Reilly, 76; Tully, 100.

269 no one could find the reading copy: Tully, 92.

269 "He made everyone understand it": Will Rogers columns, FDRL.

270 "They were ready to believe FDR could see in the dark": Michelson quoted in Cabell Phillips, *From the Crash to the Blitz*, 108.

270 "No other talk in history": Farley, *Behind the Bellots*, 210.

270 "Roosevelt's unsatisfactory way of emphasizing": Edmund Wilson, *The Thirties*, 362.

270 "As far as radio is concerned": Coughlin to McIntyre, quoted in Brinkley, *Voices of Protest*, 109.

270 Letters from average Americans: PPF, FDRL.

270 Gerald Ford remembered: Author interview with former President Gerald Ford, July 19, 2001.

270 Bill Clinton recalled: Author interview with former President Bill Clinton, August 9, 2001. The best account of FDR's influence on his other successors is contained in Leuchtenberg's *In the Shadow of FDR*.

271 "The public psychology": FDR, *Personal Letters, Early Years*, 466.

CHAPTER THIRTY-NINE

272 "To look upon these programs": Moley, *After Seven Years*, 369–70.

272 "the chief croupier": Unofficial Observer, 5.

273 "who begins his picture without a clear idea": Perkins, COHP.

273 FDR as a farmer with newborn puppies: Elmer Davis quoted in Gunther, 82.

273 FDR favored a football metaphor: *PPA*, Vol. 2, 138.

273 FDR's first reference to the 100 days: Arthur Krock, *NYT*, July 26, 1933.

274 "I didn't desert": *Time*, February 1, 1982.

275 Three quarters of the cuts came from veterans' benefits: Dickson, 208–09. For FDR's fury at the cutting, see Moley, *After Seven Years*, 191.

275 "The past decade has seen a very large increase": FDR, *Personal Letters, Early Years*, 340.

276   "painless arithmetic," *New York Times*, March 26, 1933.

276   "Just deny you were ever in Pittsburgh": Rosenman, 87.

277   Details of beer legalization: *Time*, April 17, 1933.

277   "Something was happening immediately!": Author interview with Studs Terkel, August 15, 2001.

278   the Securities Act of 1933: See Lash, *Dealers*, 130–36; McKean, *Tommy the Cork*, 38.

280   "we will have revolution in the countryside": Quoted in Davis, *FDR: New Deal Years*, 71.

280   "These farmers are not producing": Simpson quoted in ibid., 74.

281   Baruch offered the job: Leuchtenberg, *FDR Years*, 328. This comes from the diary of John O'Connor.

281–82 "A plague of young lawyers": George N. Peek, *Why Quit Our Own?*, 20. Peek also asserted that visiting businessmen and farmers from the West and South complained of all of the Jewish lawyers in the department. If so, this was another sign of the bigotry that would lead anti-Semites to call it the "Jew Deal"—Unofficial Observer, 322.

282   Peek thought farm price supports were "communistic": Peek, 14–15.

282   Wallace and the guru: Culver and Hyde, 130–36.

283   "Come at once to Washington": Quoted in Maney, 47.

283   New Dealers were floating down Pennsylvania Avenue: Neustadt interview.

283   "I can only describe the change as physical": Katz quoted in Louchheim, 121.

283   "Everyone who had a college degree": Moley, *First New Deal*, 336.

283   "so conceited": *Time*, February 1, 1982.

283   "The New Deal is simply the effort": Quoted in Gunther, 281.

284   "You are going too fast and too far": Wehle, 140.

284   For details and discussions of the Thomas amendment, see Lindley, *The Roosevelt Revolution*, 119; Davis, *FDR: New Deal Years*, 105.

285   "All of the men there agreed": Moley, *After Seven Years*, 156–61; Moley, *First New Deal*, 298–305.

286   "There was a certain amount of naughtiness": James Warburg, COHP, 514–15; Feis, 124–30.

286   "a very strong possibility" of war: See Robert Dallek, *Franklin D. Roosevelt and American Foreign Policy*, 57–58.

287   "I think I have averted a war": Ibid., p. 57.

288   "What are you going to say": Norris quoted in Alan Wolfe, *Return to Greatness*, 41.

289   "I am not very familiar with the form": FDR letter to Rosenman, July 31, 1933, Rosenman private papers.

289   likened Byrnes in the Senate to a black female cook: Quoted in Robertson, 153.

289   "I don't want to talk": FDR quoted in ibid., 148.

289   FDR rode with Ickes's subordinate: Ickes, 18. The diaries of Harold

Ickes do not contain much revealing information about the first Hundred Days.

290   "He would call you in": Quoted anonymously in Neustadt, *Presidential Power*, 150. Neustadt disclosed in an interview with the author that it was Rowe.

CHAPTER FORTY

291   "What I am seeking": FDR to Edward M. House, November 27, 1934, FDRL.

291   "I find time at home to practice": Quoted in Daniels, *Washington Quadrille*, 229.

291   FDR's contact with William James (or lack thereof): Moley, *First New Deal*, 5.

292   emergency meeting with Ickes, Wallace: Ickes, 4–5.

292   Long called it "a sapling bill": Daniels, *The Time Between the Wars*, 231.

293   the CCC "smacked of Fascism": William Green, quoted in *Time*, April 3, 1933.

293   "I'll tell you what": FDR quoted in Perkins, 180–81. Perkins offers a lively description of the origins of the CCC.

294   he remembered the names of obscure Interior Department bureaucrats: Diary of Horace Albright, assistant secretary of interior, FDRL.

294   "I want *personally* to check": Quoted in Freidel, *FDR: Launching the New Deal*, 263. See also Rollins, 404–05.

294   "Oh, that doesn't matter": FDR quoted in Perkins, 180–81.

294   FDR's administrative sloppiness and World War II: Jackson, 48.

295   Major reported to Roosevelt: John A. Salmond, *The Civilian Conservation Corps, 1933–42*, 40–45.

295   J. Edgar Hoover's role in facing Bonus Army: See Dickson, 213; Burrough, 15. After a series of copycat Lindburgh kidnappings and the killing of federal agents in the "Kansas City Massacre" in June 1933, Hoover's job was safe.

296   "There's nothing that makes people feel": FDR quoted in Stiles, 265.

296   "Talk to these men, get their gripes": Stiles, 263.

297   "Hoover sent the army. Roosevelt sent his wife": Quoted in Dickson, 216.

297   "down many streets go": Ibid.

298   "Mr. Roosevelt may turn out to be": Lindley, 327.

298   "They were ready victims for the moral dry rot": J. J. McEntee, *Final Report of the Director at the Civilian Conservation Corps*, 3–4.

298   "The southern U.S. was totally stripped of vegetation": Kirkland quoted in Pinkerton, 314.

299   CCC and skiing: Ibid.

CHAPTER FORTY-ONE

300   "was dangerously close to losing control": *Time*, April 17, 1933.

301   "What will they do in the dairy industry?": FDR quoted in Perkins, 194.

301   "a good number three man": Baruch quoted in ibid., 200–01.

302   "Men have followed [FDR] upstairs": Senator Hiram Johnson quoted in Freidel, *FDR: Launching the New Deal*, 447.

302   "every crime and fault": Long quoted in Davis, *FDR: New Deal Years*, 143.

303   "The excessive centralization and the dictatorial spirit": Lippmann quoted in Susan Kennedy, 186.

303   "Your codes stink": Quoted in Daniels, *Time Between the Wars*, 251.

303   "Here for the first time": Anderson quoted in Leuchtenberg, *The FDR Years*, 244.

304   "I don't see why": Johnson quoted in Perkins, 202.

304   FDR alters the picture on the NRA stamp: Gunther, 88.

304   "they'll get a sock": Walter Johnson, *1600 Pennsylvania Avenue*, 68.

305   "He looked very tired": Morgenthau diary, June 12, 1933, FDRL.

305   the "single most important structural change": Friedman and Schwartz, 454.

305   Chronology of June 16: Pare-Lorentz Chronology, FDRL.

306   "is preeminently a place of moral leadership": FDR quoted in *NYT*, November 13, 1932.

306   "three magnificent things": Unofficial Observer, 21–23.

307   "That pissant Moley": Daniels, *Time Between the Wars*, 241. Hull was friends with Robert Bingham, the Kentucky newspaper publisher who served as FDR's ambassador to England. Moley sent his critical cable from the ambassador's residence. Bingham, home with a cold, discovered it and passed it on to Hull.

308   "He was sitting on the trunk": Archibald MacLeish, quoted in Jonas Klein, *Beloved Island: Franklin and Eleanor and the Legacy of Campobello*, 147. The story was originally published in *Fortune* magazine in December 1933, then excerpted in Don Wharton, ed., *The Roosevelt Omnibus*, 92–93. The names of the couple were never disclosed.

CODA

309   History of social insurance: See Michael A. Hiltzik, *The Plot Against Social Security*, 29.

312   "We can't help that": Perkins, 281. Perkins devotes a whole chapter of her memoirs to the origins of Social Security, 278–302.

313   "The taxing power of the Federal Government": Stone quoted in ibid., 286.

313–14 to "fix . . . that little wagon": Armstrong quoted in Nancy Altman, *The Battle for Social Security*, 52. Altman offers a complete account of the origins of the program.

314 "minor conflicts of logic and feeling": Perkins, 294.

314 exclusion of domestics in keeping with European plans: See *Boston Globe*, August 14, 2005.

314 to upset "The Negro Question": Byrd quoted in Ira Katznelson, *When Affirmative Action Was White*, 43–44.

315 "This was a blow": Perkins, 294.

315 "We put those payroll contributions": FDR quoted in Maney, 67.

316 "The average Mississippian can't imagine": *Jackson Daily News* quoted in Asbell, 320.

316 "Isn't this Socialism?": Senator Thomas P. Gore quoted in Perkins, 29.

317 Logistics of enrolling 26 million people: Louchheim, 155.

318 Social Security's role in 1936 campaign: Hiltzik, 41.

318 FDR described Social Security as "the cornerstone": Perkins, 301. Social Security was the centerpiece of what came to be known as the "Second New Deal." By 1944, historians and political scientists were dividing the era into the "First New Deal," extending from the Hundred Days through 1934, and a "Second New Deal," which began with FDR's message to Congress on January 4, 1935. Basil Rauch and many other historians thought the First New Deal was conservative and the Second New Deal was liberal; Rexford Tugwell and Arthur M. Schlesinger, Jr., argued that, despite the more liberal rhetoric, the policy moved in a more conservative direction, away from national planning. The author endorses the view of William E. Leuchtenberg, who has noted that the cross-currents of New Deal policies defy easy categorization—See Leuchtenberg, *The FDR Years*, 216–18.

EPILOGUE

319 the idea of "the first Hundred Days" for presidents post-FDR: See Safire, 345.

320 "stood for self assurance": Anna Roosevelt quoted in Angelo, 37.

320 "I looked at my mother in law's face": ER quoted in Lash, *Eleanor and Franklin*, 642–43.

321 Cook and Dickerman acted as if Hickok didn't exist: Cook, Vol. I, 489.

321 an ugly public spat erupted: See Elliott Roosevelt, *An Untold Story: The Roosevelts of Hyde Park*; Roosevelt and Libby, *My Parents*.

322 Howe as FDR's "handyman": Stiles, 233.

322 "Hold Franklin down!": Howe quoted in Rollins, 251.

322 "After Louis' death": Eleanor Roosevelt, *This I Remember*, 167–68.

322 "This was not as valuable a service": Stiles's notes for her book, FDRL.

322 court-packing seen as dictatorial: See Stimson Diary, April 7, 1937.

323 a "kiss-ass-and-tell" book: Quoted in *Newsweek*, April 5, 2004.

323 FDR as Napoleon: Moley quoted in Jackson, 225.

324 It turned out that Louis Howe sabotaged him: Unofficial Observer, 355.

325 "Governor, what do you think of Roosevelt?": Question to Smith quoted in Slayton, 398. By 1934, Lewis Douglas, James Warburg, and Dean Acheson all resigned, in agreement with Smith that FDR was moving too far left.

325 "to the Mussolinis, Hitlers, Lenins": Hearst quoted in Nasaw, 482.

326 Garner looked across the stage and winked: Timmons, 180.

327 the queen told Eleanor she had not the slightest idea: Ward, ed., *Closest Companion*, 132.

327 "If you spent": FDR quoted in Wallace.

327 Only a simple moving image survives: FDRL.

327 "not one man in ten millions": Churchill quoted in Meacham, 339.

327 Gunther analogy to Nehru: Gunther, 275.

328 Draper-FDR correspondence: Excerpted in Lisa Grunwald, and Stephen J., Adler, eds., *Letters of the Century*, 220–21.

332 some of Roosevelt's programs may have even delayed recovery: This is the argument made by Jim Powell in *FDR's Folly*. The problem is that Powell's alternative—conventional conservative economics—probably would not have worked either. Hoover tried it, minus the tax cuts. No economist has persuasively argued that deep tax cuts (from a much lighter overall level of taxation) would have made much difference in improving purchasing power in the late 1920s and early 1930s, though it would have at least represented part of a growth agenda that was otherwise lacking.

333 FDR and Lend-Lease: See Charles Peters, *Five Days in Philadelphia*, 174–98.

334 "Old Doc New Deal" becomes "Dr. Win the War": Quoted in Goodwin, 481–82.

~ BIBLIOGRAPHY ~

Acheson, Dean. *Morning and Noon*. Boston: Houghton Mifflin, 1965.

Altman, Nancy J. *The Battle for Social Security*. Hoboken, NJ: John Wiley & Sons, 2005.

Angelo, Bonnie. *First Mothers: The Women Who Shaped the Presidents*. New York: Morrow, 2000.

Asbell, Bernard. *The FDR Memoirs: A Speculation on History*. New York: Doubleday, 1973.

Ashburn, Frank Davis. *Peabody of Groton: A Portrait*. New York: Coward-McCann, 1944.

Banner, Stuart. *The Death Penalty*. Cambridge: Harvard University Press, 2002.

Barber, Benjamin. *The Truth of Power*. New York: W. W. Norton & Co., 2002.

Barone, Michael. *Our Country: The Shaping of America from Roosevelt to Reagan*. New York: The Free Press, 1990.

Barry, John M., *Rising Tide*. New York: Simon & Schuster, 1997.

Beatty, Jack, ed., *Pols: Great Writing on American Politics from Bryan to Reagan*. New York: Public Affairs, 2004.

Bellush, Bernard. *Franklin D. Roosevelt as Governor of New York City*. New York: Columbia University Press, 1955.

Bergman, Andrew. *We're in the Money: Depression America and Its Films*. Chicago: Elephant Paperbacks, 1992.

Bernstein, Robert. *Walter Wanger: Hollywood Independent*. Berkeley: University of California Press, 1994.

Beschloss, Michael. *The Conquerors: Roosevelt, Truman, and the Destruction of Hitler's Germany, 1941–1945*. New York: Simon & Schuster, 2002.

———. *Kennedy and Roosevelt: The Uneasy Alliance*. New York: Harper & Row, 1980.

Black, Conrad. *Franklin Delano Roosevelt: Champion of Freedom*. New York: Public Affairs, 2003.

Brauer, Carl M. *Presidential Transitions: Eisenhower Through Reagan*. New York: Oxford University Press, 1986.

Brendom, Piers. *The Dark Valley: A Panorama of the 1930s*. New York: Alfred A. Knopf, 2000.

Brinkley, Alan. *Voices of Protest*. New York: Alfred A. Knopf, 1982.

———. *Liberalism and Its Discontents*. Cambridge: Harvard University Press, 1988.

———. *The End of Reform*. New York: Vintage, 1995.

Brinkley, David. *Washington Goes to War*. New York: Ballantine Books, 1988.

Buhite, Russell D. and David W. Levy, eds. *FDR's Fireside Chats*. New York: Penguin Books, 1992.

Burns, James McGregor. *Roosevelt: The Lion and the Fox*. New York: Harcourt, Brace, 1956.

———. *Leadership*. New York: Harper & Row, 1978.

Burrough, Bryan. *Public Enemies*. New York: Penguin, 2004.

Capra, Frank. *The Name Above the Title*. New York: Macmillan, 1971.

Caro, Robert. *The Power Broker: Robert Moses and the Fall of New York*. New York: Random House, 1975.

———. *The Years of Lyndon Johnson: The Path to Power*. New York: Alfred A. Knopf, 1982.

Carter, Richard. *Breakthrough: The Saga of Jonas Salk*. New York: Trident Press, 1966.

Conkin, Paul K. *The New Deal*. College Park, MD: University of Maryland, 1967.

Cook, Blanche Wiesen. *Eleanor Roosevelt. Vol. I: 1884–1933*. New York: Viking Press, 1992.

———. *Eleanor Roosevelt. Vol. II: 1933–1938*. New York: Penguin Books, 1999.

Cowley, Malcolm. *The Dream of the Golden Mountains: Remembering the 1930s*. New York: Penguin Books, 1964.

Cowley, Robert, ed. *What If?: Eminent Historians Imagine What Might Have Been*. New York: Berkley Books, 2002.

Crane, Katharine. *Mr. Carr of State*. New York: St. Martin's Press, 1960.

Crowther, Bosley. *Hollywood Rajah*. New York: Holt, 1960.

Culver, John C. and John Hyde. *American Dreamer: A Life of Henry A. Wallace*. New York: W. W. Norton & Co., 2000.

Curtis, Charles Grant, Jr. "Franklin D. Roosevelt and the Commonwealth of Broadcasting." Unpublished Thesis, Harvard University.

Dall, Curtis. *FDR: My Exploited Father-in-Law*. Torrance, CA: Institute for Historical Review, 1968.

Dallek, Robert. *Franklin D. Roosevelt and American Foreign Policy, 1932–1945*. New York: Oxford University Press, 1979.

Daniels, Jonathan. *The Time Between the Wars*. Garden City, NY: Doubleday & Co., 1966.

———. *Washington Quadrille*. Garden City, NY: Doubleday & Co., 1968.

Davis, Kenneth S. *FDR: The Beckoning of Destiny, 1882–1928*. New York: G. P. Putnam's Sons, 1971.

———. *FDR: The New Deal Years, 1933–1937*. New York: Random House, 1979.

———. *FDR: The New York Years, 1928–1933*. New York: Random House, 1985.

Dickson, Paul, and Thomas B. Allen. *The Bonus Army*. New York: Walker & Co., 2004.

Donovan, Hedley. *Roosevelt to Reagan*. New York: Harper & Row, 1982.

Donovan, Robert J. *The Assassins*. New York: Harper & Brothers, 1952.

Edwards, Russell Thomas. *Where Roosevelt Met the Forgotten Man*. Privately printed by National Press Club, 1946.

Eichengreen, Barry. *Golden Fetters: The Gold Standard and the Great Depression, 1919 to 1939*. New York: Oxford University Press, 1992.

Ellis, Joseph. *American Sphinx: The Character of Thomas Jefferson*. New York: Alfred A. Knopf, 1998.

Emerson, Ralph Waldo. *Great Essays: Representative Men*. New York: Houston Peterson, 1960.

Falasca-Zamponi, Simonetta. *Fascist Spectacle*. Berkeley: University of California Press, 1997

Farley, James A. *Behind the Ballots: The Personal History of a Politician*. New York: Harcourt, Brace & Co., 1938.

———. *Jim Farley's Story*. New York: McGraw-Hill, 1948.

Feis, Herbert. *1933: Characters in Crisis*. Boston: Little, Brown, 1966.

Fiskin, James S. *The Voice of the People*. New Haven: Yale University Press, 1995.

Flynn, Edward J. *You're the Boss*. New York: Viking, 1947.

Frank, Jerome. *Persuasion and Healing*. Baltimore: Johns Hopkins University Press, 1961.

Freidel, Frank. *FDR: Launching the New Deal*. Boston: Little, Brown, 1973.

———. *Franklin D. Roosevelt: A Rendezvous with Destiny*. Boston: Little, Brown, 1990.

Freud, Anna, and Dorothy T. Burlingham. *War and Children*. New York: Ernst Willard, 1943.

Fried, Albert. *FDR and His Enemies*. New York: St. Martin's Press, 1999.

Friedman, Benjamin. *The Moral Consequences of Economic Growth*. New York: Alfred A. Knopf, 2005.

Friedman, Milton, and Anna Schwartz. *A Monetary History of the United States, 1857–1960*. Princeton: Princeton University Press, 1963.

Galbraith, John Kenneth. *A Life in Our Times*. Boston: Houghton Mifflin, 1981.

Gallagher, Hugh Gregory. *FDR's Splendid Deception*. New York: Dodd, Mead & Co., 1985.

Gay, Peter. *Freud: A Life for Our Time*. New York: W. W. Norton & Co., 1988.

Gelderman, Carol. *All the President's Words*. New York: Walker & Co., 1997.

Gill, Brendan. *Here at The New Yorker*. New York: Random House, 1975.

Glynn, Carroll J., et al., ed. *Public Opinion*. Boulder, Co: Westview Press, 1998.

Goldberg, Richard Thayer. *The Making of Franklin D. Roosevelt*. Cambridge: Abt Books, 1981.

Goleman, Daniel. *Emotional Intelligence*. New York: Bantam, 1995.

Goodwin, Doris Kearns. *No Ordinary Time*. New York: Simon & Schuster, 1994.

Gould, Lewis L. *The Most Exclusive Club*. New York: Basic Books, 2005.

Grunwald, Lisa, and Stephen J. Adler, eds. *Letters of the Century*. New York: Random House, 1999.

Gunther, John. *Roosevelt in Retrospect*. New York: Harper & Brothers, 1950.

Handlin, Oscar. *Al Smith and His America*. Boston: Little, Brown, 1958.

Harrity, Richard, and Ralph G. Martin, *The Human Side of FDR: A Pictorial Biography*. New York: Duell, Sloan & Pearce, 1960.

Hartz, Louis. *The Liberal Tradition in America*. New York: Harcourt, 1963.

Herring, Pendleton. *Presidential Leadership*. New York: Rinehart & Co., 1940.

Hickok, Lorena. *Reluctant First Lady*. New York: Dodd, Mead, 1962.

Hiltzik, Michael A. *The Plot Against Social Security*. New York: HarperCollins, 2005.

Hobson, Fred. *Mencken: A Life*. New York: Random House, 1994.

Hofstadter, Richard. *The American Political Tradition and the Men Who Made It*. New York: Alfred A. Knopf, 1948.

Hoopes, Roy. *Ralph Ingersoll*. New York: Atheneum, 1985.

Hoover, Irwin Hood. *Forty Two Years in the White House*. Boston: Houghton Mifflin, 1934.

Hoover, Herbert. *Memoirs: The Great Depression, 1929–1941*. New York: Macmillan, 1952.

Houck, Davis W. *FDR and Fear Itself: The First Inaugural Address*. College Station, TX: Texas A & M University Press, 2002.

Hoyt, Edwin P. *Jumbos and Jackasses*. Garden City, NY: Doubleday, 1960.

Hurd, Charles. *When the New Deal Was Young and Gay*. New York: Hawthorn Books, 1965.

Ickes, Harold. *The Secret Diaries of Harold Ickes: The First Thousand Days*. New York: Simon & Schuster, 1953.

Jackson, Robert T. *That Man*. New York: Oxford University Press, 2003.

James, Marquis. *Mr. Garner of Texas*. Indianapolis: Bobbs-Merrill, 1939.

Johnson, Paul. *Intellectuals*. New York: Harper & Row, 1988.

Johnson, Walter. *1600 Pennsylvania Avenue*. Boston: Little, Brown, 1963.

Joslin, Theodore G. *Hoover Off the Record*. New York: Doubleday, 1934.

Jung, C. G. *Memories, Dreams, Reflections*. New York: Alfred A Knopf, 1961.

Katznelson, Ira. *When Affirmative Action Was White*. New York: W. W. Norton & Co., 2005.

Kennan, George F. *Memoirs: 1925–1950*. New York: Bantam Books, 1969.

Kennedy, David M. *FDR: Freedom from Fear*. New York: Oxford University Press, 1999.

Kennedy, Susan Estabrook. *The Banking Crisis of 1933*. Lexington: University of Kentucky Press, 1974.

Kleeman, Rita Hall. *Gracious Lady*. New York: D. Appleton-Century, 1935.

Klein, Jonas. *Beloved Island: Franklin and Eleanor and the Legacy of Campobello*. Forest Dale, VT: Paul S. Eriksson, 2000.

Kobler, John. *Ardent Spirits: The Rise and Fall of Prohibition*. New York: Da Capo Press, 1993.

Krock, Arthur. *Memoirs*. New York: Popular Library, 1968.

Lacey, Robert. *Ford: The Men and the Machine*. Boston: Little, Brown, 1986.

Larrabee, Eric. *Commander in Chief: Franklin D. Roosevelt, His Lieutenants and Their War*. New York: Harper & Row, 1987.

Lash, Joseph P. *Eleanor and Franklin*. New York: W. W. Norton & Co., 1971.

———. *Dealers and Dreamers*. New York: Doubleday, 1988.

Leonard, Jonathan Norton. *Three Years Down*. New York: Carrick & Evans, 1939.

Lerner, Max. *Wounded Titans*. New York: Arcade Publishing, 1996.

Leuchtenburg, William E. *Franklin D. Roosevelt and the New Deal*. New York: Harper & Row, 1963.

———. *In the Shadow of FDR*. Ithaca: Cornell University Press, 1983.

———. *The FDR Years*. New York: Columbia University Press, 1995.

Levine, Lawrence W., and Cornelia R. Levine. *The People and the President: America's Conversation with FDR*. Boston: Beacon Press, 2002.

Lind, Michael. *The Next American Nation*. New York: The Free Press, 1995.

Lindley, Ernest K. *The Roosevelt Revolution*. New York: Viking, 1933.

Lippmann, Walter. *Interpretations, 1933–1935*. New York: The Macmillan Company, 1936.

Looker, Earle. *The American Way: Franklin Roosevelt in Action*. New York: John Day Company, 1933.

Louchheim, Katie, ed. *The Making of the New Deal*. Cambridge: Harvard University Press, 1983.

Lowenthal, Leo, and Norbert Guterman. *Prophet of Deceit: A Study of the Techniques of the American Agitator*. New York: Harper & Bros., 1949

Lynd, Robert S. and Helen. *Middletown in Transition*. New York: Harcourt, Brace & Co., 1937.

Lyons, Eugene. *Herbert Hoover: A Biography*. Garden City, NY: Doubleday & Co., 1964.

Manchester, William. *Death of a President*. New York: Harper & Row, 1967.

———. *The Glory and the Dream*. Boston: Little, Brown, 1974.

———. "The Great Bank Holiday," *Holiday* magazine, February 1960.

Maney, Patrick J. *The Roosevelt Presence*. New York: Twayne Publishers, 1992.

McEntee, J. J. *Final Report of the Director at the Civilian Conservation Corps*. Washington, DC: Government Printing Office, 1942.

Mcfarlane, Malcolm. *Bing Crosby: Day by Day*. Lanham, MD: Scarecrow Press, 2001.

McKean, David. *Tommy the Cork*. South Royalton, VT: Steerforth Press, 2004.

Meacham, Jon. *Franklin and Winston*. New York: Random House, 2003.

Mencken, H. L. *The Vintage Mencken*. New York: Alfred A. Knopf, 1955.

Merry, Robert W. *Taking on the World: Joseph and Stewart Alsop—Guardians of the American Century*. New York: Viking, 1996.

Metcalfe, Philip. *1933*. New York: Harper & Row, 1988.

Meyers, William Starr, and Walter H. Newton, eds. *The Hoover Administration: A Documented Narrative*. New York: Charles Scribner's Sons, 1936.

Meyrowitz, Joshua. *No Sense of Place: The Impact of Electronic Media on Social Behavior*. New York: Oxford University Press, 1985.

Michelson, Charles. *The Ghost Talks*. New York: G. P. Putnam's Sons, 1944.

Miller, Nathan. *FDR: An Intimate History*. New York: Doubleday, 1983.

Mitchell, Broadus. *The Depression Decade*. New York: Rinehart, 1947.

Mitgang, Herbert. *Once Upon a Time in New York*. New York: The Free Press, 2000.

Moley, Raymond. *After Seven Years*. New York: Harper & Bros., 1939.

———. *The First New Deal*. New York: Harcourt, Brace & World, 1966.

———. *27 Masters of Politics*. New York: Funk & Wagnalls, 1949.

Mosley, Leonard. *Marshall: Hero for Our Times*. New York: Hearst Books, 1982.

Murphy, Bruce Allen. *The Brandeis Frankfurter Connection*. New York: Oxford University Press, 1982.

Nasaw, David. *The Chief: The Life of William Randolph Hearst*. Boston: Houghton Mifflin, 2000.

Neal, Steve. *Happy Days Are Here Again*. New York: William Morrow, 2004.

Nesbitt, Henrietta. *White House Diary: FDR's Housekeeper*. New York: Doubleday & Co., 1948.

Neustadt, Richard E. *Presidential Power*. New York: John Wiley & Sons, 1960.

———, and Ernest R. May. *Thinking in Time*. New York: The Free Press, 1986.

Norris, George. *Fighting Liberal: The Autobiography of George Norris*. New York: Macmillan, 1945.

O'Connor, Len. *Clout: Mayor Daley and His City*. Chicago: Henry Regnery, 1975.

Page, Benjamin, and Robert I. Shapiro. *The Rational Public: Fifty Years of Trends in Americans' Policy Preferences*. Chicago: University of Chicago Press, 1992.

Paper, Lewis. *Brandeis*. Englewood Cliffs, NJ: Prentice-Hall, 1983.

Parks, Lillian Rogers with Frances Spatz Leighton. *The Roosevelts: A Family in Turmoil*. Englewood Cliffs, NJ: Prentice-Hall, 1981.

Peek, George N. *Why Quit Our Own?* New York: D. Van Nostrand Co., 1936.

Perkins, Frances. *The Roosevelt I Knew*. New York: Viking Press, 1946.

Peters, Charles. *Five Days in Philadelphia*. New York: Public Affairs, 2005.

Phillips, Cabell. *From the Crash to the Blitz*. New York: Macmillan, 1969.

Picchi, Blaise. *The Five Weeks of Giuseppe Zangara*. Chicago: Academy Chicago Publishers, 1998.

Pinkerton, James P. *What Comes Next*. New York: Hyperion, 1995.

Potter, Jeffrey. *Men, Money and Magic: The Story of Dorothy Schiff*. New York: Coward-McCann, 1976.

Pottker, Jan. *Sara and Eleanor*. New York: St. Martin's Press, 2004.

Powell, Jim. *FDR's Folly: How Franklin D. Roosevelt and His New Deal Prolonged the Depression*. New York: Crown Forum, 2003.

Pusey, Merlo J. *Eugene Meyer*. New York: Alfred A. Knopf, 1974.

Reilly, Michael F. *Reilly of the White House*. New York: Simon & Schuster, 1947.

Reinsch, J. Leonard. *Getting Elected: From Radio and Roosevelt to Television and Reagan*. New York: Hippocrene Books, 1988.

Robertson, David. *Sly and Able: A Political Biography of James F. Byrnes*. New York: W. W. Norton & Co., 1994.

Robinson, Edgar Eugene. *The Roosevelt Leadership, 1933–45*. Philadelphia: J. B. Lippincott, 1955.

Rodgers, Elizabeth Marion. *The Impossible H. L. Mencken*. New York: Doubleday, 1991.

Rollins, Alfred B., Jr. *Roosevelt and Howe*. New York: Alfred A. Knopf, 1962.

Roosevelt, David B. *Grandmere: A Personal History of Eleanor Roosevelt*. New York: Warner Books, 2003.

Roosevelt, Elliott. *FDR: His Personal Letters*. New York: Duell, Sloan & Pearce, 1950.

———. *An Untold Story: The Roosevelts of Hyde Park*. New York: Dell Publishing Co., 1974.

———, and James Brough. *A Rendezvous with Destiny*. New York: G. P. Putnam's Sons, 1975.

Roosevelt, Eleanor. *This I Remember*. New York: Harper & Bros., 1949.

———. *This Is My Story*. New York: Harper & Bros., 1937.

Roosevelt, James, and Bill Libby. *My Parents: A Different View*. Chicago: Playboy Press, 1976.

———, and Sidney Shalett. *Affectionately, F.D.R.* New York: Harcourt, Brace, 1959.

Roosevelt, Mrs. James. *My Boy Franklin*. New York: Ray Long & Richard R. Smith, 1933.

Rosen, Eliot A. *Hoover, Roosevelt and the Brains Trust*. New York: Columbia University Press, 1977.

Rosenman, Samuel. *Working with Roosevelt*. New York: Harper & Bros., 1952.

———, ed. *The Public Papers and Addresses of Franklin D. Roosevelt (PPA)*. Vols. 1–5. New York: Random House, 1938–50.

Safire, William. *Safire's New Political Dictionary*. New York: Random House, 1993.

Salmond, John A. *The Civilian Conservation Corps, 1933–1942: A New Deal Case Study*. Durham, NC: Duke University Press, 1967.

Sargent, James E. *Roosevelt and the Hundred Days*. New York: Garland Publishing, 1981.

Schlesinger, Arthur M., Jr. *The Coming of the New Deal*. Boston: Houghton Mifflin, 1958.

———. *The Crisis of Confidence*. Boston: Houghton Mifflin, 1969.

———. *The Crisis of the Old Order*. Boston: Houghton Mifflin, 1956.

———. *The Cycles of American History*. Boston: Houghton Mifflin, 1986.

———. *The Politics of Upheaval*. Boston: Houghton Mifflin, 1960.

———. *A Thousand Days*. Boston: Houghton Mifflin, 1965.

Schwarz, Jordan. *The Interregnum of Despair*. Urbana: University of Illinois Press, 1970.

Seldes, George. *Witness to a Century*. New York: Ballantine Books, 1987.

Sherwood, Robert E. *Roosevelt and Hopkins*. New York: Harper & Bros., 1948.

Simon, James F. *Independent Journey: The Life of William O. Douglas*. New York: Harper & Row, 1980.

Slayton, Robert A. *Empire Statesman: The Rise and Redemption of Al Smith*. New York: The Free Press, 2001.

Smith, Gene. *The Shattered Dream*. New York: William Morrow, 1970.

Smith, Richard Norton. *An Uncommon Man: The Triumph of Herbert Hoover*. New York: Simon & Schuster, 1984.

———. *The Colonel: The Life and Legend of Robert R. McCormick*. Boston: Houghton Mifflin, 1997.

Smith, Timothy G., ed. *Merriman Smith's Book of Presidents*. New York: W. W. Norton & Co., 1972.

Stacks, John F. *Scotty: James B. Reston and the Rise and Fall of American Journalism*. New York: Little, Brown, 2002.

Starling, Edmund W. *Starling of the White House*. Chicago: People's Book Club, 1946.

Steel, Ronald. *Walter Lippmann and the American Century*. New York: Random House, 1980.

Stiles, Lela. *The Man Behind Roosevelt*. New York: World Publishing Co., 1954.

Stimson, Henry L., and McGeorge Bundy. *On Active Service in Peace and War*. New York: Harper & Row, 1947.

Streitmatter, Rodger, ed. *Empty Without You: The Intimate Letters of Eleanor Roosevelt and Lorena Hickok*. New York: Da Capo Press, 1998.

Sullivan, Lawrence. *Prelude to Panic: The Story of the Bank Holiday*. Washington, DC: Statesman Press, 1936.

Swanberg, W. A. *Citizen Hearst*. New York: Scribner's, 1961.

Timmons, Bascom N. *Jesse H. Jones: The Man and the Statesman*. New York: Rinehart & Co., 1956.

Tugwell, Rexford. *The Brains Trust*. New York: Viking Press, 1968.

———. *The Democratic Roosevelt*. Garden City, NY: Doubleday & Co., 1957.

———. *In Search of Roosevelt*. Cambridge: Harvard University Press, 1972.

———. *Roosevelt's Revolution*. New York: Macmillan, 1977.

Tully, Grace. *FDR: My Boss*. New York: Charles Scribner's Sons, 1949.

Unofficial Observer [John Franklin Carter]. *The New Dealers*. New York: Simon & Schuster, 1933.

Vaughan, Susan C. *Half Full, Half Empty: Understanding the Psychological Roots of Optimism*. New York: Harcourt, 2000.

Walch, Timothy, and Dwight M. Miller, eds. *Herbert Hoover and Franklin D. Roosevelt: A Documentary History*. Westport: Greenwood Press, 1998.

Waldman, Michael., ed. *My Fellow Americans: The Most Important Speeches of American Presidents*. Naperville, IL: Sourcebooks, 2003.

Wallace, Chris. *Character: Profiles in Presidential Power*. New York: Rugged Land, 2004.

Ward, Geoffrey C. *Before the Trumpet*. New York: Harper & Row, 1985.

———. *A First-Class Temperament*. New York: Harper & Row, 1989.

———, ed. *Closest Companion*. New York: Houghton Mifflin, 1995.

Warner, Emily Smith. *The Happy Warrior: The Story of My Father, Alfred E. Smith*. Garden City, NY: Doubleday & Co., 1956.

Warren, Harris Gaylord. *Herbert Hoover and the Great Depression*. New York: Oxford University Press, 1959.

Wead, Doug. *The Raising of a President*. New York: Atria Books, 2005.

Wecter, Dixon. *The Age of the Great Depression*. New York: The Macmillan Co., 1948.

Wehle, Louis B. *Hidden Threads of History: Wilson Through Roosevelt*. New York: The Macmillan Co., 1953.

Weisman, Steven R. *The Great Tax Wars*. New York: Simon & Schuster, 2002.

Weld, John. *September Song*. Lanham, MD: Scarecrow Press, 1998.

Wharton, Don., ed. *The Roosevelt Omnibus*. New York: Alfred A. Knopf, 1934.

White, William Allen. *The Autobiography of William Allen White*. New York: The Macmillan Co., 1946.

Wickenden, Dorothy, ed. *The New Republic Reader*. New York: Basic Books, 1994.

Williams, T. Harry. *Huey Long*. New York: Alfred A. Knopf, 1969.

Wills, Garry. *Certain Trumpets: The Call of Leaders*. New York: Simon & Schuster, 1994.

Wilson, Edmund. *American Earthquake*. Garden City, NY: Doubleday & Co., 1958.

———. *The Thirties*. New York: Farrar, Straus & Giroux, 1980.

Wilson, Robert. A., ed. *Character Above All: Ten Presidents from FDR to George Bush*. New York: Simon & Schuster, 1995.

Winfield, Betty Houchin. *FDR and the News Media*. Chicago: University of Illinois Press, 1990.

Wolfe, Alan. *Return to Greatness*. Princeton: Princeton University Press, 2005.

Zinn, Howard. *A People's History of the United States*. New York: Harper & Row, 1980.

NEWSPAPERS

Chicago Tribune
Detroit Free Press
Detroit News
New York Daily News
New York Herald-Tribune
New York Times (NYT)
Washington Post

MAGAZINES

The Atlantic
Esquire
Harpers
Holiday

Ladies' Home Journal
The Literary Digest
The Nation
The New Republic (TNR)
Newsweek
The New York Review of Books
The New Yorker
Saturday Evening Post
Time

DOCUMENTARIES

David Grubin Productions, *FDR*. Boston: WGBH, *The American Experience*, 1994
CCNY TV, Roundtable on 30th anniversary of FDR's Inaugural, 1963

INTERVIEWS

Susan Thomas Armour, August 5, 2002
Mary Bain, September 12, 2002
Jimmy Breslin, May 7, 2003
James McGregor Burns, April 17, 2003
Bill Clinton, August 9, 2001
Leon Despres, September 13, 2002
George Elsey, May 3, 2003
Richard Flynn, November 8, 2005
Timothy Flynn, November 11, 2005
Gerald Ford, July 19, 2001
Robert Morgenthau, November 2, 2002
Richard E. Neustadt, September 25, 2002
Robert Rosenman, October 7, 2002
Martin Siegel, September 5, 2002
Walter Sondheim, October 2, 2002
Studs Terkel, August 15, 2001

PAPERS

Adolf Berle Papers
Basil O'Connor Papers
Columbia University Oral History Project (COHP), Columbia University, New York: Charles Bledsoe, Marquis Childs, Arthur Krock, Eugene Meyer, Raymond Moley, Basil O'Connor, Frances Perkins, Rexford Tugwell, James Warburg.
Democratic National Committee Papers
Edward Flynn Papers
Eleanor Roosevelt Papers
Family, Business Personal (FBP)

Franklin D. Roosevelt Presidential Library and Museum (FDRL), Hyde Park, New
    York
Herbert Hoover Presidential Library, West Branch, Iowa
    Walch-Miller Documents (WM)
    Meyers-Newton Documents (MN)
Lorena Hickok Papers
Louis Howe Papers
President's Personal File (PPF)
Raymond Moley Papers, Hoover Institution on War, Revolution and Peace,
    Palo Alto: Stanford University, California
Rexford Tugwell Papers
Roosevelt Family Papers (RFP)
Sam Rosenman Papers
Speech Files

~ ACKNOWLEDGMENTS ~

I recently discovered some old papers of mine. "FDR was an amazing man and a great president because he knew what he was doing," I wrote in a school report when I was eleven years old. "[He] was not physically strong but his spirit was." For anyone who doesn't have time to read this book, that's all you need to know. Even when he didn't consciously know what he was doing, the instinctive part of him did. The year I wrote that, 1968, was closer to 1933 than to 2006. The people who gave me the consciousness to think that way are my parents, Jim and Joanne Alter. Along with several gifted teachers, they bestowed the love of American history and politics that made this book possible.

In examining the voluminous collection of published and unpublished work about Roosevelt, I tried to rely on primary sources. This approach helped me unearth some intriguing and overlooked documents and oral histories and to peruse obscure books that have been out of print for more than sixty years. But I've also come to a fresh appreciation of those legendary historians who have brilliantly brought FDR and his times to life, including Michael Beschloss, Alan Brinkley, James MacGregor Burns, Blanche Cook, Kenneth S. Davis, Frank Freidel, Doris Kearns Goodwin, David M. Kennedy, William E. Leuchtenberg, Arthur M. Schlesinger, Jr., and Geoffrey C. Ward. I owe a special debt to Beschloss, Brinkley, and Ward (whose work on the young Roosevelt is definitive) for reviewing the manuscript. They have all deepened my appreciation for the idea, attributed to the Dutch historian Peter Geyl, that "history is an argument without end."

During my visits to the Franklin D. Roosevelt Library in Hyde Park, New York, archivist Bob Clark was especially useful in filling the black hole in the records between January 1, 1933, when FDR left the governorship, and March 4, 1933, when he became president. Thanks also to Karen Anson, Virginia Lewick, Mark Renovitch, and Alisha Vivona at FDRL. (Note to scholars: They suggested I not cite the box numbers from which FDRL documents came, because the entire classification system is being overhauled.) Diane Lobb-Boyce of the National Park Service gave me a private tour of FDR's Hyde Park study and bedroom, and a great tip about an attic find that revealed how much Ogden Mills despised Roosevelt. William vanden Heuvel of the Franklin and Eleanor Roosevelt Institute and the Lincoln scholars David Herbert Donald and Harold Holzer were important early sources of encouragement.

At the Herbert Hoover Presidential Library in West Branch, Iowa, I'm indebted to Timothy Walch and Dwight M. Miller for pulling together the fascinating documents that shed light on the HH-FDR relationship, and to Brad Bowers, Matthew Schaefer, and Craig Wright for their suggestions. At the Hoover Institution at Stanford, the staff helped me navigate the Raymond Moley Papers, which have been consulted by surprisingly few historians of the period. I'm also grateful to the Library of Congress and to the Columbia University library for their invaluable oral history collections.

Special thanks to Mary Bain, Leon Despres, George Elsey, Patrick and Richard Flynn, Robert Morgenthau, the late Richard Neustadt, Robert Rosenman (who gave me access to some papers of his father not available at FDRL), Martin Siegel, Walter Sondheim, the late Michael Straight, and Studs Terkel for their personal memories of FDR and the period, and to Susan Thomas Armour for recalling her late husband's story of witnessing the Zangara assassination attempt as a child. Former Presidents Gerald Ford and Bill Clinton were generous enough to explain to me how Roosevelt's Fireside Chats influenced them.

I was fortunate to find energetic and talented research assistants at various points, including Sarah Childress, Geoff Gagnon, Barney Gimbel, David Greenhouse, Seth Stevenson, Dan Stolz, and Alan Wirzbicki. Dan Blumenthal helped me find a couple of gems in the Hyde Park archives and introduced me to his mother, Dr. Ellen Blumenthal, who along with another psychiatrist, Dr. James P. Frosch, gave me a better understanding of the origins of FDR's self-confidence.

Several friends came through magnificently in reading drafts, including the awful early ones, and in providing other support. Thanks to Barbara Azzoli, Ian Frazier, Peter Kaplan, Jonas Klein, Judy McGhee, David McKean, Newt Minnow, Cliff Sloan, Keith Ulrich, and Jacob Weisberg for saving me from myself. Michael Waldman deserves special mention for talking me through this from start to finish. Fellow alumni of *The Washington Monthly*, including Jason DeParle, Jim Fallows, Phil Keisling, Joe Nocera, Walter Shapiro, and our FDR-loving leader, Charlie Peters, all offered terrific suggestions. Walter Issacson, an early source of book-writing inspiration, and Evan Thomas, were wise men in helping me find structure. My agent, Amanda Urban, and her husband, Ken Auletta, have always been there for me.

Thanks to Rick Smith, Mark Whitaker, and Tom Watson of *Newsweek* for putting up with the work interruptions this book required, and to Andy Nagorski and Ellis Cose for logistical advice. And I'm especially grateful to historian and Managing Editor Jon Meacham, who read the manuscript twice. I get other good karma at work because *Newsweek* is located in the old General Motors Building at 251 W. 57th Street, where FDR kept an office at DNC headquarters during 1928. Over at Rockefeller Center, Jeff Zucker of NBC News assigned me to report a 1999 *Today Show* story on great turning points of the twentieth century that first sparked my interest in the Zangara assassination attempt. At Simon & Schuster, Roger Labrie, Elizabeth Hayes, Victoria Meyer, Ann Adelman, Lisa Healy, and Serena Jones smoothed the way. Of course the book owes its existence to the legendary Alice Mayhew, who patiently had lunch with me every year or so for more than a decade to discuss book ideas. When I finally got going on FDR in 2001, she offered encouragement, tough love, meticulous line editing, a title, and the peerless editorial instincts that made this happen.

In the middle of writing, I was diagnosed with lymphoma and underwent surgery, chemotherapy, and a stem cell transplant. Studying FDR's example—both the cheerful spirit in which he fought his own disease and the hope he conveyed to a despairing nation—turns out to have been more personally inspiring than I could have imagined. I'm thankful to Dr. Andrew Zelenetz, Dr. Lawrence Werther, Dr. Barry Salky, Dr. Stephen Nimer, Dr. Tarun Kewelramani, Dr. Audrey Hamilton, and the staff of Memorial Sloan-Kettering Cancer Center for keeping me healthy enough to complete this book, and to Dr. Jerome

Groopman for being my great friend and tireless advocate through a difficult time. The same goes for literally hundreds of other friends who have reached out to me in the last couple of years. I wish I could list you all.

Most important, my family backed me all the way. My brother, Harrison Alter, and my sisters, Jennifer Alter Warden and Jamie Alter Lynton, offered both moral and editorial support, as did their spouses and other Lazars, Greenhouses, and Lyntons. My father read the manuscript, clued me in to "When Thousands Cheer," and otherwise offered wise counsel, and my mother, who spent three days shepherding Eleanor Roosevelt around campus when she was a student at Mount Holyoke in the 1940s, was the catalyst for the project. Mom was characteristically frank while keeping her long-held faith that this day would come.

Finally, our terrific children, Charlotte, Tommy, and Molly, were understanding when I was holed up night after night on the third floor, and my wonderful wife, Emily, my rock, showed her usual good sense and good humor while anchoring everything in the rest of our life so I could get this done. To them, all of my love.

— INDEX —

⏤ ABOUT THE AUTHOR ⏤

Jonathan Alter is a senior editor at *Newsweek*, where since 1991 he has written an acclaimed column on politics, history, media, and society at large. He is also an analyst and contributing correspondent for NBC News. He lives in Montclair, New Jersey, with his wife and three children.